THE SECRET TO
GETTING RICH
TRILOGY

THE SECRET TO GETTING RICH TRILOGY

THE ULTIMATE LAW OF ATTRACTION CLASSICS

THINK AND GROW RICH
NAPOLEON HILL

THE SCIENCE OF GETTING RICH
W. D. WATTLES

THE MASTER KEY
CHARLES F. HAANEL

Ulysses Press

Published by:
ULYSSES PRESS
P.O. Box 3440
Berkeley, CA 94703
www.ulyssespress.com

ISBN10: 1-56975-662-7
ISBN13: 978-1-56975-662-1
Library of Congress Control Number: 2007907741

Printed in Canada by Transcontinental Printing

10 9 8 7 6 5 4 3 2 1

Acquisitions Editor: Nick Denton-Brown
Editorial and production: Kate Allen, Lauren Harrison, Lisa Kester,
    Tamara Kowalski, Judith Metzener, Abby Reser, Emma Silvers
Cover design: DiAnna VanEycke

Distributed by Publishers Group West

TABLE OF CONTENTS

BOOK ONE:

THINK AND GROW RICH

NAPOLEON HILL

CONTENTS

PREFACE

This book conveys the experience of more than 500 men of great wealth, who began at scratch, with nothing to give in return for riches except THOUGHTS, IDEAS and ORGANIZED PLANS.

Here you have the entire philosophy of money-making, just as it was organized from the actual achievements of the most successful men known to the American people during the past fifty years. It describes WHAT TO DO, also, HOW TO DO IT!

It presents complete instructions on HOW TO SELL YOUR PERSONAL SERVICES.

It provides you with a perfect system of self-analysis that will readily disclose what has been standing between you and "the big money" in the past.

It describes the famous Andrew Carnegie formula of personal achievement by which he accumulated hundreds of millions of dollars for himself and made no fewer than a score of millionaires of men to whom he taught his secret.

Perhaps you do not need all that is to be found in the book—no one of the 500 men from whose experiences it was written did—but you may need ONE IDEA, PLAN OR SUGGESTION to start you toward your goal. Somewhere in the book you will find this needed stimulus.

The book was inspired by Andrew Carnegie, after he had made his millions and retired. It was written by the man to whom Carnegie disclosed the astounding secret of his riches—the same man to whom the 500 wealthy men revealed the source of their riches.

In this volume will be found the thirteen principles of money-making essential to every person who accumulates sufficient money to guarantee financial independence. It is estimated that the research which went into the preparation, before the book was written or could be written—research covering more than twenty-five years of continuous effort—could not be duplicated at a cost of less than $100,000.00.

Moreover, the knowledge contained in the book never can be duplicated, at any cost, for the reason that more than half of the 500 men who supplied the information it brings have passed on.

Riches cannot always be measured in money!

Money and material things are essential for freedom of body and mind, but there are some who will feel that the greatest of all riches can be evaluated only in terms of lasting friendships, harmonious family relationships, sympathy and understanding between business associates, and introspective harmony which brings one peace of mind measurable only in spiritual values!

All who read, understand and apply this philosophy will be better prepared to attract and enjoy these higher estates which always have been and always will be denied to all except *those who are ready for them.*

Be prepared, therefore, when you expose yourself to the influence of this philosophy, to experience a CHANGED LIFE which may help you not only to negotiate your way through life with harmony and understanding, but also to prepare you for the accumulation of material riches in abundance.

AUTHOR'S INTRODUCTION

IN EVERY chapter of this book, mention has been made of the money-making secret which has made fortunes for more than five hundred exceedingly wealthy men whom I have carefully analyzed over a long period of years.

The secret was brought to my attention by Andrew Carnegie, more than a quarter of a century ago. The canny, lovable old Scotsman carelessly tossed it into my mind, when I was but a boy. Then he sat back in his chair, with a merry twinkle in his eyes, and watched carefully to see if I had brains enough to understand the full significance of what he had said to me.

When he saw that I had grasped the idea, he asked if I would be willing to spend twenty years or more, preparing myself to take it to the world, to men and women who, without the secret, might go through life as failures. I said I would, and with Mr. Carnegie's cooperation, I have kept my promise.

This book contains the secret, after having been put to a practical test by thousands of people, in almost every walk of life. It was Mr. Carnegie's idea that the magic formula, which gave him a stupendous fortune, ought to be placed within reach of people who do not have time to investigate how men make money, and it was his hope that I might test and demonstrate the soundness of the formula through the experience of men and women in every calling. He believed the formula should be taught in all public schools and colleges, and expressed the opinion that if it were properly taught it would so revolutionize the entire educational system that the time spent in school could be reduced to less than half.

His experience with Charles M. Schwab, and other young men of Mr. Schwab's type, convinced Mr. Carnegie that much of that which is taught in the schools is of no value whatsoever in connection with the business of earning a living or accumulating riches. He had arrived at this decision, because he had taken into his business one young man after another, many of them with but little schooling, and by coaching them in the use of this formula, developed in them rare leadership. Moreover, *his coaching made fortunes for everyone of them who followed his instructions.*

In the chapter on Faith, you will read the astounding story of the organization of the giant United States Steel Corporation, as it was conceived and carried out by one of the young men through whom Mr. Carnegie proved that his formula will work *for all who are ready for it.* This single application of the secret, by that young man—Charles M. Schwab—made him a huge fortune in both money and OPPOR-TUNITY. Roughly speaking, this particular application of the formula was worth *six hundred million dollars.*

These facts—and they are facts well known to almost everyone who knew Mr. Carnegie—give you a fair idea of what the reading of this book may bring to you, provided you *KNOW WHAT IT IS THAT YOU WANT.*

Even before it had undergone twenty years of practical testing, the secret was passed on to more than one hundred thousand men and women who have used it for their personal benefit, as Mr. Carnegie planned that they should. Some have made fortunes with it. Others have used it successfully in creating harmony in their homes. A clergyman used it so effectively that it brought him an income of up-wards of $75,000.00 a year.

Arthur Nash, a Cincinnati tailor, used his near-bankrupt business as a "guinea pig" on which to test the formula. The business came to life and made a fortune for its owners. It is still thriving, although Mr. Nash has gone. The experiment was so unique that newspapers and magazines, gave it more than a million dollars' worth of laudatory publicity.

The secret was passed on to Stuart Austin Wier, of Dallas, Texas. He was ready for it—so ready that he gave up his profession and studied law. Did he succeed? That story is told too.

I gave the secret to Jennings Randolph, the day he graduated from College, and he has used it so successfully that he is now serving his third term as a Member of Congress, with an excellent opportunity to keep on using it until it carries him to the White House.

While serving as Advertising Manager of the LaSalle Extension University, when it was little more than a name, I had the privilege of seeing J. G. Chapline, President of the University, use the formula so effectively that he has since made the LaSalle one of the great extension schools of the country.

The secret to which I refer has been mentioned no fewer than a hundred times, throughout this book. It has not been directly named, for it seems to work more successfully when it is merely uncovered and left in sight, where THOSE WHO ARE READY, and SEARCHING FOR IT, may pick it up. That is why Mr. Carnegie tossed it to me so quietly, without giving me its specific name.

If you are READY to put it to use, you will recognize this secret at least once in every chapter. I wish I might feel privileged to tell you how you will know if you are ready, but that would deprive you of much of the benefit you will receive when you make the discovery in your own way.

While this book was being written, my own son, who was then finishing the last year of his college work, picked up the manuscript of chapter two, read it, and discovered the secret for himself. He used the information so effectively that he went directly into a responsible position at a beginning salary greater than the aver-age man ever earns. His story has been briefly described in chapter two. When you read it, perhaps you will dismiss any feeling you may have had, at the beginning of the book, that it promised too much. And, too, if you have ever been discouraged, if you have had difficulties to surmount which took the very soul out of you, if you have tried and failed, if you were ever handicapped by illness or physical affliction, this story of my son's discovery and use of the Carnegie formula may prove to be the oasis in the Desert of Lost Hope, for which you have been searching.

This secret was extensively used by President Woodrow Wilson, during the World War. It was passed on to every soldier who fought in the war, carefully wrapped in the training received before going to the front. President Wilson told me it was a strong factor in raising the funds needed for the war.

More than twenty years ago, Hon. Manuel L. Quezon (then Resident Commissioner of the Philippine Islands), was inspired by the secret to gain freedom for his people. He has gained freedom for the Philippines, and is the first President of the free state.

A peculiar thing about this secret is that those who once acquire it and use it, find themselves literally swept on to success, with but little effort, and they never again submit to failure! If you doubt this, study the names of those who have used it, wherever they have been mentioned, check their records for yourself, and be convinced.

There is no such thing as SOMETHING FOR NOTHING!

The secret to which I refer cannot be had without a price, although the price is far less than its value. It cannot be had at any price by those who are not intentionally searching for it. It cannot be given away, it cannot be purchased for money, for the reason that it comes in two parts. One part is already in possession of those who are ready for it.

The secret serves equally well, all who are ready for it. Education has nothing to do with it. Long before I was born, the secret had found its way into the possession of Thomas A. Edison, and he used it so intelligently that he became the world's leading inventor, although he had but three months of schooling.

The secret was passed on to a business associate of Mr. Edison. He used it so effectively that, although he was then making only $12,000 a year, he accumulated a great fortune, and retired from active business while still a young man. You will find his story at the beginning of the first chapter. It should convince you that riches are not beyond your reach, that you can still be what you wish to be, that money, fame, recognition and happiness can be had by all who are ready and determined to have these blessings.

How do I know these things? You should have the answer before you finish this book. You may find it in the very first chapter, or on the last page.

While I was performing the twenty year task of research, which I had undertaken at Mr. Carnegie's request, I analyzed hundreds of well known men, many of whom admitted that they had accumulated their vast fortunes through the aid of the Carnegie secret; among these men were:—

HENRY FORD
WILLIAM WRIGLEY JR.
JOHN WANAMAKER
JAMES J. HILL
GEORGE S. PARKER
E.M.STATLER
HENRY L. DOHERTY
CYRUS H. K. CURTIS
CHARLES M. SCHWAB
WOODROW WILSON
WM. HOWARD TAFT
DR. FRANK GUNSAULUS
FRANK A. MUNSEY
ELBERT H. GARY
DR. ALEXANDER GRAHAM BELL
JUDGE DANIEL T. WRIGHT
JOHN D. ROCKEFELLER
STUART AUSTIN WIER
FRANK A. VANDERLIP
F. W. WOOLWORTH
COL. ROBERT A. DOLLAR
HON. JENNINGS RANDOLPH
EDWIN C. BARNES

THEODORE ROOSEVELT
JOHN W. DAVIS
ELBERT HUBBARD
WILBUR WRIGHT
WILLIAM JENNINGS BRYAN
DR. DAVID STARR JORDAN
J. ODGEN ARMOUR
GEORGE EASTMAN
ARTHUR BRISBANE
HARRIS F. WILLIAMS
LUTHER BURBANK
EDWARD W. BOK
DANIEL WILLARD
KING GILLETTE
RALPH A. WEEKS
JOHN H. PATTERSON
JULIUS ROSENWALD
THOMAS A. EDISON
DR. FRANK CRANE
GEORGE M. ALEXANDER
J. G. CHAPLINE
EDWARD A. FILENE
ARTHUR NASH

CLARENCE DARROW

These names represent but a small fraction of the hundreds of well known Americans whose achievements, financially and otherwise, prove that those who understand and apply the Carnegie secret, reach high stations in life. I have never known anyone who was inspired to use the secret, who did not achieve noteworthy success in his chosen calling. I have never known any person to distinguish himself, or to accumulate riches of any consequence, without possession of the secret. From these two facts I draw the conclusion that the secret is more important, as a part of the knowledge essential for self-determination, than any which one receives through what is popularly known as "education."

What is EDUCATION, anyway? This has been answered in full detail.

As far as schooling is concerned, many of these men had very little. John Wanamaker once told me that what little schooling he had, he acquired in very much the same manner as a modern locomotive takes on water, by "scooping it up as it runs." Henry Ford never reached high school, let alone college. I am not attempting to minimize the value of schooling, but I am trying to express my earnest belief that those who master and apply the secret will reach high stations, accumulate riches, and bargain with life on their own terms, even if their schooling has been meager.

Somewhere, as you read, the secret to which I refer will jump from the page and stand boldly before you, IF YOU ARE READY FOR IT! When it appears, you will recognize it. Whether you receive the sign in the first or the last chapter, stop for a moment when it presents itself, and turn down a glass, for that occasion will mark the most important turning-point of your life.

We pass now, to Chapter One, and to the story of my very dear friend, who has generously acknowledged having seen the mystic sign, and whose business achievements are evidence enough that he turned down a glass. As you read his story, and the others, remember that they deal with the important problems of life, such as all men experience. The problems arising from one's endeavor to earn a living, to find hope, courage, contentment and peace of mind; to accumulate riches and to enjoy freedom of body and spirit.

Remember, too, as you go through the book, that it deals with facts and not with fiction, its purpose being to convey a great universal truth through which all who are READY may learn, not only *WHAT* TO DO, BUT ALSO *HOW* TO DO IT! and receive, as well, THE NEEDED STIMULUS TO MAKE A START.

As a final word of preparation, before you begin the first chapter, may I offer one brief suggestion which may provide a clue by which the Carnegie secret may be recognized? It is this—*ALL ACHIEVEMENT, ALL EARNED RICHES, HAVE THEIR BEGINNING IN AN IDEA!* If you are ready for the secret, you already possess one half of it, therefore, you will readily recognize the other half the moment it reaches your mind.

THE AUTHOR

INTRODUCTION:
The Man Who "Thought" His Way into Partnership
with Thomas A. Edison

TRULY, "thoughts are things," and powerful things at that, when they are mixed with definiteness of purpose, persistence, and a BURNING DESIRE for their translation into riches, or other material objects.

A little more than thirty years ago, Edwin C. Barnes discovered how true it is that men really do THINK AND GROW RICH. His discovery did not come about at one sitting. It came little by little, beginning with a BURNING DESIRE to become a business associate of the great Edison.

One of the chief characteristics of Barnes' Desire was that it was *definite*. He wanted to work *with* Edison, not *for* him. Observe, carefully, the description of how he went about translating his DESIRE into reality, and you will have a better understanding of the thirteen principles which lead to riches.

When this DESIRE, or impulse of thought, first flashed into his mind he was in no position to act upon it. Two difficulties stood in his way. He did not know Mr. Edison, and he did not have enough money to pay his railroad fare to Orange, New Jersey.

These difficulties were sufficient to have discouraged the majority of men from making any attempt to carry out the desire. But his was no ordinary desire! He was so determined to find a way to carry out his desire that he finally decided to travel by "blind baggage," rather than be defeated. (To the uninitiated, this means that he went to East Orange on a freight train).

He presented himself at Mr. Edison's laboratory, and announced he had come to go into business with the inventor. In speaking of the first meeting between Barnes and Edison, years later, Mr. Edison said, "He stood there before me, looking like an ordinary tramp, *but there was something in the expression of his face which conveyed the impression that he was determined to get what he had come after.* I had learned, from years of experience with men, that when a man really DESIRES a thing so deeply that he is willing to stake his entire future on a single turn of the wheel in order to get it, he is sure to win. I gave him the opportunity he asked for, *because I saw he had made up his mind to stand by until he succeeded.* Subsequent events proved that no mistake was made."

Just what young Barnes said to Mr. Edison on that occasion was far less important than *that which he thought*. Edison, himself, said so! It could not have been the young man's appearance which got him his start in the Edison office, for that was definitely against him. It was what he THOUGHT that counted.

If the significance of this statement could be conveyed to every person who reads it, there would be no need for the remainder of this book.

Barnes did not get his partnership with Edison on his first interview. He did get a chance to work in the Edison offices, at a very nominal wage, doing work that was unimportant to Edison, but most important to Barnes, because it gave him an opportunity to display his "merchandise" where his intended "partner" could see it.

Months went by. Apparently nothing happened to bring the coveted goal which Barnes had set up in his mind as his DEFINITE MAJOR PURPOSE. But something important was happening in Barnes' mind. He was constantly intensifying his DESIRE to become the business associate of Edison.

Psychologists have correctly said that "when one is truly ready for a thing, it puts in its appearance." Barnes was ready for a business association with Edison, moreover, he was DETERMINED TO REMAIN READY UNTIL HE GOT THAT WHICH HE WAS SEEKING.

He did not say to himself, "Ah well, what's the use? I guess I'll change my mind and try for a salesman's job." But, he did say, "I came here to go into business with Edison, and I'll accomplish this end if it takes the remainder of my life." *He meant it!* What a different story men would have to tell if only they would adopt a DEFINITE PURPOSE, and stand by that purpose until it had time to become an all-consuming obsession!

Maybe young Barnes did not know it at the time, but his bulldog determination, his persistence in standing back of a single DESIRE, was destined to mow down all opposition, and bring him the opportunity he was seeking.

When the opportunity came, it appeared in a different form, and from a different direction than Barnes had expected. That is one of the tricks of opportunity. It has a sly habit of slipping in by the back door, and often it comes disguised in the form of misfortune, or temporary defeat. Perhaps this is why so many fail to recognize opportunity.

Mr. Edison had just perfected a new office device, known at that time, as the Edison Dictating Machine (now the Ediphone). His salesmen were not enthusiastic over the machine. They did not believe it could be sold without great effort. Barnes saw his opportunity. It had crawled in quietly, hidden in a queer looking machine which interested no one but Barnes and the inventor.

Barnes knew he could sell the Edison Dictating Machine. He suggested this to Edison, and promptly got his chance. He did sell the machine. In fact, he sold it so successfully that Edison gave him a contract to distribute and market it all over the nation. Out of that business association grew the slogan, "Made by Edison and installed by Barnes."

The business alliance has been in operation for more than thirty years. Out of it Barnes has made himself rich in money, but he has done something infinitely greater, he has proved that one really may "Think and Grow Rich."

How much actual cash that original DESIRE of Barnes' has been worth to him, I have no way of knowing. Perhaps it has brought him two or three million dollars, but the amount, whatever it is, becomes insignificant when compared with the greater asset he acquired in the form of definite knowledge that *an intangible impulse of thought can be transmuted into its physical counterpart* by the application of known principles.

Barnes literally *thought* himself into a partnership with the great Edison! He thought himself into a fortune. He had nothing to start with, except the capacity to KNOW WHAT HE WANTED, AND THE DETERMINATION TO STAND BY THAT DESIRE UNTIL HE REALIZED IT.

He had no money to begin with. He had but little education. He had no influence. But he did have initiative, faith, and the will to win. With these intangible forces he *made himself* number one man with the greatest inventor who ever lived.

Now, let us look at a different situation, and study a man who had plenty of tangible evidence of riches, but lost it, *because he stopped* three feet short of the goal he was seeking.

THREE FEET FROM GOLD

One of the most common causes of failure is the habit of quitting when one is overtaken by *temporary defeat*. Every person is guilty of this mistake at one time or another.

An uncle of R. U. Darby was caught by the "gold fever" in the gold-rush days, and went west to DIG AND GROW RICH. He had never heard that *more gold has been mined from the brains of men than has ever been taken from the earth*. He staked a claim and went to work with pick and shovel. The going was hard, but his lust for gold was definite.

After weeks of labor, he was rewarded by the discovery of the shining ore. He needed machinery to bring the ore to the surface. Quietly, he covered up the mine, retraced his footsteps to his home in Williamsburg, Maryland, told his relatives and a few neighbors of the "strike." They got together money for the needed machinery, had it shipped. The uncle and Darby went back to work the mine.

The first car of ore was mined, and shipped to a smelter. The returns proved they had one of the richest mines in Colorado! A few more cars of that ore would clear the debts. Then would come the big killing in profits.

Down went the drills! Up went the hopes of Darby and Uncle! Then something happened! The vein of gold ore disappeared! They had come to the end of the rainbow, and the pot of gold was no longer there! They drilled on, desperately trying to pick up the vein again—all to no avail.

Finally, they decided to QUIT.

They sold the machinery to a junk man for a few hundred dollars, and took the train back home. Some "junk" men are dumb, but not this one! He called in a mining engineer to look at the mine and do a little calculating. The engineer advised that the project had failed, because the owners were not familiar with "fault lines." His calculations showed that the vein would be found JUST THREE FEET FROM WHERE THE DARBYS HAD STOPPED DRILLING! That is exactly where it was found!

The "Junk" man took millions of dollars in ore from the mine, because he knew enough to seek expert counsel before giving up.

Most of the money which went into the machinery was procured through the efforts of R. U. Darby, who was then a very young man. The money came from his relatives and neighbors, because of their faith in him. He paid back every dollar of it, although he was years in doing so.

Long afterward, Mr. Darby recouped his loss many times over, *when he made the discovery* that DESIRE can be transmuted into gold. The discovery came after he went into the business of selling life insurance.

Remembering that he lost a huge fortune, because he STOPPED three feet from gold, Darby profited by the experience in his chosen work, by the simple method of saying to himself, "I stopped three feet from gold, but I will never stop *because men say 'no'* when I ask them to buy insurance."

Darby is one of a small group of fewer than fifty men who sell more than a million dollars in life insurance annually. He owes his "stickability" to the lesson he learned from his "quitability" in the gold mining business.

Before success comes in any man's life, he is sure to meet with much temporary defeat, and, perhaps, some failure. When defeat overtakes a man, the easiest and most logical thing to do is to QUIT. That is exactly what the majority of men do.

More than five hundred of the most successful men this country has ever known, told the author their greatest success came just one step *beyond* the point at which defeat had overtaken them. Failure is a trickster with a keen sense of irony and cunning. It takes great delight in tripping one when success is almost within reach.

A FIFTY CENT LESSON IN PERSISTENCE

Shortly after Mr. Darby received his degree from the "University of Hard Knocks," and had decided to profit by his experience in the gold mining business, he had the good fortune to be present on an occasion that proved to him that "No" does not necessarily mean no.

One afternoon he was helping his uncle grind wheat in an old fashioned mill. The uncle operated a large farm on which a number of colored sharecrop farmers lived. Quietly, the door was opened, and a small colored child, the daughter of a tenant, walked in and took her place near the door.

The uncle looked up, saw the child, and barked at her roughly, "what do you want?"

Meekly, the child replied, "My mammy say send her fifty cents."

"I'll not do it," the uncle retorted, "Now you run on home."

"Yas sah," the child replied. *But she did not move.*

The uncle went ahead with his work, so busily engaged that he did not pay enough attention to the child to observe that she did not leave. When he looked up and saw her still standing there, he yelled at her, "I told you to go on home! Now go, or I'll take a switch to you."

The little girl said "yas sah," *but she did not budge an inch.*

The uncle dropped a sack of grain he was about to pour into the mill hopper, picked up a barrel stave, and started toward the child with an expression on his face that indicated trouble.

Darby held his breath. He was certain he was about to witness a murder. He knew his uncle had a fierce temper. He knew that colored children were not supposed to defy white people in that part of the country.

When the uncle reached the spot where the child was standing, she quickly stepped forward one step, looked up into his eyes, and screamed at the top of her shrill voice, *"MY MAMMY'S GOTTA HAVE THAT FIFTY CENTS!"*

The uncle stopped, looked at her for a minute, then slowly laid the barrel stave on the floor, put his hand in his pocket, took out half a dollar, and gave it to her.

The child took the money and slowly backed toward the door, never taking her eyes off the man *whom she had just conquered.* After she had gone, the uncle sat down on a box and looked out the window into space for more than ten minutes. He was pondering, with awe, over the whipping he had just taken.

Mr. Darby, too, was doing some thinking. That was the first time in all his experience that he had seen a colored child deliberately *master* an adult white person. How did she do it. What happened to his uncle that caused him to lose his fierceness and become as docile as a lamb? What strange power did this child use that made her master over her superior? These and other similar questions flashed into Darby's mind, but he did not find the answer until years later, when he told me the story.

Strangely, the story of this unusual experience was told to the author in the old mill, on the very spot where the uncle took his whipping. Strangely, too, I had devoted nearly a quarter of a century to the study of the power which enabled an ignorant, illiterate colored child to conquer an intelligent man.

As we stood there, in that musty old mill, Mr. Darby repeated the story of the unusual conquest, and finished by asking, "What can you make of it? What strange power did that child use, that so completely whipped my uncle?"

The answer to his question will be found in the principles described in this book. The answer is full and complete. It contains details and instructions sufficient to enable anyone to understand, and apply the same force which the little child accidentally stumbled upon.

Keep your mind alert, and you will observe exactly what strange power came to the rescue of the child, you will catch a glimpse of this power in the next chapter. Somewhere in the book you will find an idea that will quicken your receptive powers, and place at your command, for your own benefit, this same irresistible power. The awareness of this power may come to you in the first chapter, or it may flash into your mind in some subsequent chapter. It may come in the form of a single idea. Or, it may come in the nature of a plan, or a purpose. Again, it may cause you to go back into your past experiences of failure or defeat, and bring to the surface some lesson by which you can regain all that you lost through defeat.

After I had described to Mr. Darby the power unwittingly used by the little colored child, he quickly retraced his thirty years of experience as a life insurance salesman, and frankly acknowledged that his success in that field was due, in no small degree, to the lesson be had learned from the child.

Mr. Darby pointed out: "every time a prospect tried to bow me out, without buying, I saw that child standing there in the old mill, her big eyes glaring in defiance, and I said to myself, 'I've gotta make this sale.' The better portion of all sales I have made, were made after people had said 'NO'."

He recalled, too, his mistake in having stopped only three feet from gold, "but," he said, "that experience was a blessing in disguise. It taught me to *keep on keeping on,* no matter how hard the going may be, a lesson I needed to learn before I could succeed in anything."

This story of Mr. Darby and his uncle, the colored child and the gold mine, doubtless will be read by hundreds of men who make their living by selling life insurance, and to all of these, the author wishes to offer the suggestion that Darby owes to these two experiences his ability to sell more than a million dollars of life insurance every year.

Life is strange, and often imponderable! Both the successes and the failures have their roots in simple experiences. Mr. Darby's experiences were commonplace and simple enough, yet they held the answer to his destiny in life, therefore they were as important (to him) as life itself. He profited by these two dramatic experiences, because *he analyzed them,* and found the lesson they taught. But what of the man who has neither the time, nor the inclination to study failure in search of knowledge that may lead to success? Where, and how is he to learn the art of converting defeat into stepping stones to opportunity?

In answer to these questions, this book was written.

The answer called for a description of thirteen principles, but remember, as you read, the answer *you* may be seeking, to the questions which have caused you to ponder over the strangeness of life, may be found *in your own mind,* through some idea, plan, or purpose which may spring into your mind as you read.

One sound idea is all that one needs to achieve success. The principles described in this book, contain the best, and the most practical of all that is known, concerning ways and means of creating useful ideas.

Before we go any further in our approach to the description of these principles, we believe you are entitled to receive this important suggestion...WHEN RICHES BEGIN TO COME THEY COME SO QUICKLY, IN SUCH GREAT ABUNDANCE, THAT ONE WONDERS WHERE THEY HAVE BEEN HIDING DURING ALL THOSE LEAN YEARS. This is an astounding statement, and all the more so, when we take into consideration the popular belief, that riches come only to those who work hard and long.

When you begin to THINK AND GROW RICH, you will observe that riches begin with a state of mind, with definiteness of purpose, with little or no hard work. You, and every other person, ought to be interested in knowing how to acquire that state of mind which will attract riches. I spent twenty-five years in research, analyzing more than 25,000 people, because I, too, wanted to know "how wealthy men become that way."

Without that research, this book could not have been written.

Here take notice of a very significant truth, viz: The business depression started in 1929, and continued on to an all time record of destruction, until some-time after President Roosevelt entered office. Then the depression began to fade into nothingness. Just as an electrician in a theatre raises the lights so gradually that darkness is transmuted into light before you realize it, so did the spell of fear in the minds of the people gradually fade away and become faith.

Observe very closely, as soon as you master the principles of this philosophy, and begin to follow the instructions for applying those principles, your financial status will begin to improve, and everything you touch will begin to transmute itself into an asset for your benefit. Impossible? Not at all!

One of the main weaknesses of mankind is the average man's familiarity with the word "impossible." He knows all the rules which will NOT work. He knows all the things which CANNOT be done. This book was written for those who seek the rules which have made others successful, and are willing to *stake everything* on those rules.

A great many years ago I purchased a fine dictionary. The first thing I did with it was to turn to the word "impossible," and neatly clip it out of the book. That would not be an unwise thing for you to do.

Success comes to those who become SUCCESS CONSCIOUS.

Failure comes to those who indifferently allow themselves to become FAILURE CONSCIOUS.

The object of this book is to help all who seek it, to learn the art of changing their minds from FAILURE CONSCIOUSNESS to SUCCESS CONSCIOUSNESS.

Another weakness found in altogether too many people, is the habit of measuring everything, and everyone, by *their own* impressions and beliefs. Some who will read this, will believe that no one can THINK AND GROW RICH. They cannot think in terms of riches, because their thought habits have been steeped in poverty, want, misery, failure, and defeat.

These unfortunate people remind me of a prominent Chinese, who came to America to be educated in American ways. He attended the University of Chicago.

One day President Harper met this young Oriental on the campus, stopped to chat with him for a few minutes, and asked what had impressed him as being the most noticeable characteristic of the American people.

"Why," the Chinaman exclaimed, "the queer slant of your eyes. Your eyes are off slant!"

What do we say about the Chinese?

We refuse to believe that which we do not understand. We foolishly believe that our own limitations are the proper measure of limitations. Sure, the other fellow's eyes are "off slant," BECAUSE THEY ARE NOT THE SAME AS OUR OWN.

Millions of people look at the achievements of Henry Ford, after he has arrived, and envy him, because of his good fortune, or luck, or genius, or whatever it is that they credit for Ford's fortune. Perhaps one person in every hundred thousand knows the secret of Ford's success, and those who do know are too modest, or too reluctant, to speak of it, *because of its simplicity.* A single transaction will illustrate the "secret" perfectly.

A few years back, Ford decided to produce his now famous V-8 motor. He chose to build an engine with the entire eight cylinders cast in one block, and instructed his engineers to produce a design for the engine. The design was placed on paper, but the engineers agreed, to a man, that it was simply *impossible* to cast an eight cylinder gas engine block in one piece.

Ford said, "Produce it anyway."

"But," they replied, "it's impossible!"

"Go ahead," Ford commanded, "and stay on the job until you succeed no matter how much time is required."

The engineers went ahead. There was nothing else for them to do, if they were to remain on the Ford staff. Six months went by, nothing happened. Another six months passed, and still nothing happened. The engineers tried every conceivable plan to carry out the orders, but the thing seemed out of the question; *"impossible!"*

At the end of the year Ford checked with his engineers, and again they informed him they had found no way to carry out his orders.

"Go right ahead," said Ford, "I want it, and I'll have it."

They went ahead, and then, as if by a stroke of magic, the secret was discovered.

The Ford DETERMINATION had won once more!

This story may not be described with minute accuracy, but the sum and substance of it is correct. Deduce from it, you who wish to THINK AND GROW RICH, the secret of the Ford millions, if you can. You'll not have to look very far.

Henry Ford is a success, because he understands, and *applies* the principles of success. One of these is DESIRE: knowing what one wants. Remember this Ford story as you read, and pick out the lines in which the secret of his stupendous achievement have been described. If you can do this, if you can lay your finger on the particular group of principles which made Henry Ford rich, you can equal his achievements in almost any calling for which you are suited.

YOU ARE "THE MASTER OF YOUR FATE, THE CAPTAIN OF YOUR SOUL," BECAUSE . . .

When Henley wrote the prophetic lines, "I am the Master of my Fate, I am the Captain of my Soul," he should have informed us that we are the Masters of our Fate, the Captains of our Souls, *because* we have the power to control our thoughts.

He should have told us that the ether in which this little earth floats, in which we move and have our being, is a form of energy moving at an inconceivably high rate of vibration, and that the ether is filled with a form of universal power which ADAPTS itself to the nature of the thoughts we hold in our minds; and INFLUENCES us, in natural ways, to transmute our thoughts into their physical equivalent.

If the poet had told us of this great truth, we would know WHY IT IS that we are the Masters of our Fate, the Captains of our Souls. He should have told us, with great emphasis, that this power makes no attempt to discriminate between destructive thoughts and constructive thoughts, that it will urge us to translate into physical reality thoughts of poverty, just as quickly as it will influence us to act upon thoughts of riches.

He should have told us, too, that our brains become magnetized with the dominating thoughts which we hold in our minds, and, by means with which no man is familiar, these "magnets" attract to us the forces, the people, the circumstances of life which harmonize with the nature of our *dominating* thoughts.

He should have told us, that before we can accumulate riches in great abundance, we must magnetize our minds with intense DESIRE for riches, that we must become "money conscious" until the DESIRE for money drives us to create definite plans for acquiring it.

But, being a poet, and not a philosopher, Henley contented himself by stating a great truth in poetic form, leaving those who followed him to interpret the Philosophical meaning of his lines.

Little by little, the truth has unfolded itself, until it now appears certain that the principles described in this book, hold the secret of mastery over our economic fate.

We are now ready to examine the first of these principles. Maintain a spirit of open-mindedness, and remember as you read, they are the invention of no one man. The principles were gathered from the life experiences of more than 500 men who actually accumulated riches in huge amounts; men who began in poverty, with but little education, without influence. The principles worked for these men. You can put them to work for your own enduring benefit.

You will find it easy, not hard, to do.

Before you read the next chapter, I want you to know that it conveys factual information which might easily change your entire financial destiny, as it has so definitely brought changes of stupendous proportions to two people described.

I want you to know, also, that the relationship between these two men and myself, is such that I could have taken no liberties with the facts, even if I had wished to do so. One of them has been my closest personal friend for almost twenty-five years, the other is my own son. The unusual success of these two men, success which they generously accredit to the principle described in the next chapter, more than justifies this personal reference as a means of emphasizing the far-flung power of this principle.

Almost fifteen years ago, I delivered the Commencement Address at Salem College, Salem, West Virginia. I emphasized the principle described in the next chapter, with so much intensity that one of the members of the graduating class definitely appropriated it, and made it a part of his own philosophy. The young man is now a Member of Congress, and an important factor in the present administration. Just before this book went to the publisher, he wrote me a letter in which he so clearly stated his opinion of the principle outlined in the next chapter, that I have chosen to publish his letter as an introduction to that chapter.

It gives you an idea of the rewards to come.

> "My dear Napoleon:
>
> "My service as a Member of Congress having given me an insight into the problems of men and women, I am writing to offer a suggestion which may become helpful to thousands of worthy people.
>
> "With apologies, I must state that the suggestion, if acted upon, will mean several years of labor and responsibility for you, but I am enheartened to make the suggestion, because I know your great love for rendering useful service.
>
> "In 1922, you delivered the Commencement address at Salem College, when I was a member of the graduating class. In that address, you planted in my mind an idea which has been responsible for the opportunity I now have to serve the people of my State, and will be responsible, in a very large measure, for whatever success I may have in the future.
>
> "The suggestion I have in mind is, that you put into a book the sum and substance of the address you delivered at Salem College, and in that way give the people of America an opportunity to profit by your many years of experience and association with the men who, by their greatness, have made America the richest nation on earth.
>
> "I recall, as though it were yesterday, the marvelous description you gave of the method by which Henry Ford, with but little schooling, without a dollar, with no influential friends, rose to great heights. I made up my mind then, even before you had finished your speech, that I would make a place for myself, no matter how many difficulties I had to surmount.
>
> "Thousands of young people will finish their schooling this year, and within the next few years. Every one of them will be seeking just such a message of practical encouragement as the one I received from you. They will want to know where to turn,

what to do, to get started in life. You can tell them, because you have helped to solve the problems of so many, many people.

"If there is any possible way that you can afford to render so great a service, may I offer the suggestion that you include with every book, one of your Personal Analysis Charts, in order that the purchaser of the book may have the benefit of a complete self-inventory, indicating, as you indicated to me years ago, exactly what is standing in the way of success.

"Such a service as this, providing the readers of your book with a complete, unbiased picture of their faults and their virtues, would mean to them the difference between success and failure. The service would be priceless.

"Millions of people are now facing the problem of staging a come-back, because of the depression, and I speak from personal experience when I say, I know these earnest people would welcome the opportunity to tell you their problems, and to receive your suggestions for the solution.

"You know the problems of those who face the necessity of beginning all over again. There are thousands of people in America today who would like to know how they can convert ideas into money, people who must start at scratch, without finances, and recoup their losses. If anyone can help them, you can.

"If you publish the book, I would like to own the first copy that comes from the press, personally autographed by you.

"With best wishes, believe me,

"Cordially yours,

"JENNINGS RANDOLPH"

CHAPTER TWO

DESIRE:

THE STARTING POINT OF ALL ACHIEVEMENT:
The First Step toward Riches

WHEN Edwin C. Barnes climbed down from the freight train in Orange, N.J., more than thirty years ago, he may have resembled a tramp, but his *thoughts* were those of a king!

As he made his way from the railroad tracks to Thomas A. Edison's office, his mind was at work. He saw himself *standing in Edison's presence*. He heard himself asking Mr. Edison for an opportunity to carry out the one CONSUMING OBSESSION OF HIS LIFE, a BURNING DESIRE to become the business associate of the great inventor.

Barnes' desire was not a *hope!* It was not a *wish!* It was a keen, pulsating DESIRE, which transcended everything else. It was DEFINITE.

The desire was not new when he approached Edison. It had been Barnes' *dominating desire* for a long time. In the beginning, when the desire first appeared in his mind, it may have been, probably was, only a wish, but it was no mere wish when he appeared before Edison with it.

A few years later, Edwin C. Barnes again stood before Edison, in the same office where he first met the inventor. This time his DESIRE had been translated into reality. *He was in business with Edison.* The dominating DREAM OF HIS LIFE had become a reality. Today, people who know Barnes envy him, because of the "break" life yielded him. They see him in the days of his triumph, without taking the trouble to investigate the *cause* of his success.

Barnes succeeded because he chose a definite goal, placed all his energy, all his will power, all his effort, everything back of that goal. He did not become the partner of Edison the day he arrived. He was content to start in the most menial work, as long as it provided an opportunity to take even one step toward his cherished goal.

Five years passed before the chance he had been seeking made its appearance. During all those years not one ray of hope, not one promise of attainment of his DESIRE had been held out to him. To everyone, except himself, he appeared only another cog in the Edison business wheel, but in his own mind, HE WAS THE PARTNER OF EDISON EVERY MINUTE OF THE TIME, from the very day that he first went to work there.

It is a remarkable illustration of the power of a DEFINITE DESIRE. Barnes won his goal, because he wanted to be a business associate of Mr. Edison, more than he wanted anything else. He created a plan by which to attain that purpose. But he BURNED ALL BRIDGES BEHIND HIM. He stood by his DESIRE until it became the dominating obsession of his life—and—finally a fact.

When he went to Orange, he did not say to himself, "I will try to induce Edison to give me a job of some sort." He said, "I will see Edison, and put him on notice that I have come to go into business with him."

He did not say, "I will work there for a few months, and if I get no encouragement, I will quit and get a job somewhere else." He did say, "I will start anywhere. I will do anything Edison tells me to do, but *before I am through,* I will be his associate."

He did not say, "I will keep my eyes open for another opportunity, in case I fail to get what I want in the Edison organization." He said, "There is but ONE thing in this world that I am determined to have, and that is a business association with Thomas A. Edison. I will burn all bridges behind me, and stake my ENTIRE FUTURE on my ability to get what I want."

He left himself no possible way of retreat. He had to win or perish!

That is all there is to the Barnes story of success!

A long while ago, a great warrior faced a situation which made it necessary for him to make a decision which insured his success on the battlefield. He was about to send his armies against a powerful foe, whose men outnumbered his own. He loaded his soldiers into boats, sailed to the enemy's country, unloaded soldiers and equipment, then gave the order to burn the ships that had carried them. Addressing his men before the first battle, he said, "You see the boats going up in smoke. That means that we cannot leave these shores alive unless we win! We now have no choice—*we win—or we perish!*" They won.

Every person who wins in any undertaking must be willing to burn his ships and cut all sources of retreat. Only by so doing can one be sure of maintaining that state of mind known as a BURNING DESIRE TO WIN, essential to success.

The morning after the great Chicago fire, a group of merchants stood on State Street, looking at the smoking remains of what had been their stores. They went into a conference to decide if they would try to rebuild, or leave Chicago and start over in a more promising section of the country. They reached a decision—all except one—to leave Chicago.

The merchant who decided to stay and rebuild pointed a finger at the remains of his store, and said, "Gentlemen, on that very spot I will build the world's greatest store, no matter how many times it may burn down."

That was more than fifty years ago. The store was built. It stands there today, a towering monument to the power of that state of mind known as a BURNING DESIRE. The easy thing for Marshal Field to have done, would have been exactly what his fellow merchants did. When the going was hard, and the future looked dismal, they pulled up and went where the going seemed easier.

Mark well this difference between Marshal Field and the other merchants, because it is the same difference which distinguishes Edwin C. Barnes from thousands of other young men who have worked in the Edison organization. It is the same difference which distinguishes practically all who succeed from those who fail.

Every human being who reaches the age of understanding of the purpose of money, wishes for it. *Wishing* will not bring riches. But *desiring* riches with a state of mind that becomes an obsession, then planning definite ways and means to acquire riches, and backing those plans with persistence which *does not recognize failure*, will bring riches.

The method by which DESIRE for riches can be transmuted into its financial equivalent, consists of six definite, practical steps, viz:

First. Fix in your mind the *exact* amount of money you desire. It is not sufficient merely to say "I want plenty of money." Be definite as to the amount. (There is a psychological reason for definiteness which will be described in a subsequent chapter).

Second. Determine exactly what you intend to give in return for the money you desire. (There is no such reality as "something for nothing.")

Third. Establish a definite date when you intend to *possess* the money you desire.

Fourth. Create a definite plan for carrying out your desire, and begin *at once*, whether you are ready or not, to put this plan into *action*.

Fifth. Write out a clear, concise statement of the amount of money you intend to acquire, name the time limit for its acquisition, state what you intend to give in return for the money, and describe clearly the plan through which you intend to accumulate it.

Sixth. Read your written statement aloud, twice daily, once just before retiring at night, and once after arising in the morning. AS YOU READ—SEE AND FEEL AND BELIEVE YOURSELF ALREADY IN POSSESSION OF THE MONEY.

It is important that you follow the instructions described in these six steps. It is especially important that you observe, and follow the instructions in the sixth paragraph. You may complain that it is impossible for you to "see yourself in possession of money" before you actually have it. Here is where a BURNING DESIRE will come to your aid. If you truly DESIRE money so keenly that your desire is an obsession, you will have no difficulty in convincing yourself that you will acquire it. The object is to want money, and to become so determined to have it that you CONVINCE yourself you will have it.

Only those who become "money conscious" ever accumulate great riches. "Money consciousness" means that the mind has become so thoroughly saturated with the DESIRE for money, that one can see one's self already in possession of it.

To the uninitiated, who has not been schooled in the working principles of the human mind, these instructions may appear impractical. It may be helpful, to all who fail to recognize the soundness of the six steps, to know that the information they convey, was received from Andrew Carnegie, who began as an ordinary laborer in the steel mills, but managed, despite his humble beginning, to make these principles yield him a fortune of considerably more than one hundred million dollars.

It may be of further help to know that the six steps here recommended were carefully scrutinized by the late Thomas A. Edison, who placed his stamp of approval upon them as being, not only the steps essential for the accumulation of money, but necessary for the attainment of *any definite goal.*

The steps call for no "hard labor." They call for no sacrifice. They do not require one to become ridiculous, or credulous. To apply them calls for no great amount of education. But the successful application of these six steps does call for sufficient *imagination* to enable one to see, and to understand, that accumulation of money cannot be left to chance, good fortune, and luck. One must realize that all who have accumulated great fortunes, first did a certain amount of dreaming, hoping, wishing, DESIRING, and PLANNING *before* they acquired money.

You may as well know, right here, that you can never have riches in great quantities, UNLESS you can work yourself into a white heat of DESIRE for money, and actually BELIEVE you will possess it.

You may as well know, also that every great leader, from the dawn of civilization down to the present, was a dreamer. Christianity is the greatest potential power in the world today, because its founder was an intense dreamer who had the vision and the imagination to see realities in their mental and spiritual form before they had been transmuted into physical form.

If you do not see great riches in your imagination, you will never see them in your bank balance.

Never, in the history of America has there been so great an opportunity for practical dreamers as now exists. The six year economic collapse has reduced all men, substantially, to the same level. A new race is about to be run. The stakes represent huge fortunes which will be accumulated within the next ten years. The rules of the race have changed, because we now live in a CHANGED WORLD that definitely favors the masses, those who had but little or no opportunity to win under the conditions existing during the depression, when fear paralyzed growth and development.

We who are in this race for riches, should be encouraged to know that this changed world in which we live is demanding new ideas, new ways of doing things, new leaders, new inventions, new methods of teaching, new methods of marketing, new books, new literature, new features for the radio, new ideas for moving pictures. Back of all this demand for new and better things, there is one quality which one must possess to win, and that is DEFINITENESS OF PURPOSE, the knowledge of what one wants, and a burning DESIRE to possess it.

The business depression marked the death of one age, and the birth of another.

This changed world requires practical dreamers who can, *and will* put their dreams into action. The practical dreamers have always been, and always will be the patternmakers of civilization.

We who desire to accumulate riches, should remember the real leaders of the world always have been men who harnessed, and put into practical use, the intangible, unseen forces of unborn opportunity, and have converted those forces, (or impulses of thought), into sky-scrapers, cities, factories, airplanes, automobiles, and every form of convenience that makes life more pleasant.

Tolerance, and an open mind are practical necessities of the dreamer of today. Those who are afraid of new ideas are doomed before they start. Never has there been a time more favorable to pioneers than the present. True, there is no wild and woolly west to be conquered, as in the days of the Covered Wagon; but there is a vast business, financial, and industrial world to be remoulded and redirected along new and better lines.

In planning to acquire your share of the riches, let no one influence you to scorn the dreamer. To win the big stakes in this changed world, you must catch the spirit of the great pioneers of the past, whose dreams have given to civilization all that it has of value, the spirit which serves as the life-blood of our own country— your opportunity and mine, to develop and market our talents.

Let us not forget, Columbus dreamed of an Unknown world, staked his life on the existence of such a world, and discovered it!

Copernicus, the great astronomer, dreamed of a multiplicity of worlds, and revealed them! No one denounced him as "impractical" *after* he had triumphed. Instead, the world worshipped at his shrine, thus proving once more that "SUCCESS REQUIRES NO APOLOGIES, FAILURE PERMITS NO ALIBIS."

If the thing you wish to do is right, and *you believe in it,* go ahead and do it! Put your dream across, and never mind what "they" say if you meet with temporary defeat, for "they," perhaps, do not know that EVERY FAILURE BRINGS WITH IT THE SEED OF AN EQUIVALENT SUCCESS.

Henry Ford, poor and uneducated, dreamed of a horseless carriage, went to work with what tools he possessed, without waiting for opportunity to favor him, and now evidence of his dream belts the entire earth. He has put more wheels into operation than any man who ever lived, because he was not afraid to back his dreams.

Thomas Edison dreamed of a lamp that could be operated by electricity, began where he stood to put his dream into action, and despite more than *ten thousand failures,* he stood by that dream until he made it a physical reality. Practical dreamers DO NOT QUIT!

Whelan dreamed of a chain of cigar stores, transformed his dream into action, and now the United Cigar Stores occupy the best corners in America.

Lincoln dreamed of freedom for the black slaves, put his dream into action, and barely missed living to see a united North and South translate his dream into reality.

The Wright brothers dreamed of a machine that would fly through the air.

Now one may see evidence all over the world, that they dreamed soundly.

Marconi dreamed of a system for harnessing the intangible forces of the ether. Evidence that he did not dream in vain, may be found in every wireless and radio in the world. Moreover, Marconi's dream brought the humblest cabin, and the most stately manor house side by side. It made the people of every nation on earth back-door neighbors. It gave the President of the United States a medium by which he may talk to all the people of America at one time, and on short notice. It may interest you to know that Marconi's "friends" had him taken into custody, and examined in a psychopathic hospital, when he announced he had discovered a principle through which he could send messages through the air, without the aid of wires, or other direct physical means of communication. The dreamers of today fare better.

The world has become accustomed to new discoveries. Nay, it has shown a willingness to reward the dreamer who gives the world a new idea.

"The greatest achievement was, at first, and for a time, but a dream."

"The oak sleeps in the acorn. The bird waits in the egg, and in the highest vision of the soul, a waking angel stirs. DREAMS ARE THE SEEDLINGS OF REALITY."

Awake, arise, and assert yourself, you dreamers of the world. Your star is now in the ascendency. The world depression brought the opportunity you have been waiting for. It taught people humility, tolerance, and open-mindedness.

The world is filled with an abundance of OPPORTUNITY which the dreamers of the past never knew.

A BURNING DESIRE TO BE, AND TO DO is the starting point from which the dreamer must take off. Dreams are not born of indifference, laziness, or lack of ambition.

The world no longer scoffs at the dreamer, nor calls him impractical. If you think it does, take a trip to Tennessee, and witness what a dreamer President has done in the way of harnessing, and using the great water power of America. A score of years ago, such a dream would have seemed like madness.

You have been disappointed, you have undergone defeat during the depression, you have felt the great heart within you crushed until it bled. Take courage, for these experiences have tempered the spiritual metal of which you are made—they are assets of incomparable value.

Remember, too, that all who succeed in life get off to a bad start, and pass through many heartbreaking struggles before they "arrive." The turning point in the lives of those who succeed, usually comes at the moment of some crisis, through which they are introduced to their "other selves."

John Bunyan wrote the Pilgrim's Progress, which is among the finest of all English literature, after he had been confined in prison and sorely punished, because of his views on the subject of religion.

O. Henry discovered the genius which slept within his brain, after he had met with great misfortune, and was confined in a prison cell, in Columbus, Ohio. Being FORCED, through misfortune, to become acquainted with his "other self," and to use his IMAGINATION, he discovered himself to be a great author instead of a miserable criminal and outcast. Strange and varied are the ways of life, and stranger still are the ways of Infinite Intelligence, through which men are sometimes forced to undergo all sorts of punishment before discovering their own brains, and their own capacity to create useful ideas through imagination.

Edison, the world's greatest inventor and scientist, was a "tramp" telegraph operator, he failed innumerable times before he was driven, finally, to the discovery of the genius which slept within his brain.

Charles Dickens began by pasting labels on blacking pots. The tragedy of his first love penetrated the depths of his soul, and converted him into one of the world's truly great authors. That tragedy produced, first, David Copperfield, then a succession of other works that made this a richer and better world for all who read his books. Disappointment over love affairs, generally has the effect of driving men to drink, and women to ruin; and this, because most people never learn the art of transmuting their strongest emotions into dreams of a constructive nature.

Helen Keller became deaf, dumb, and blind shortly after birth. Despite her greatest misfortune, she has written her name indelibly in the pages of the history of the great. Her entire life has served as evidence that *no one ever is defeated until defeat has been accepted as a reality*.

Robert Burns was an illiterate country lad, he was cursed by poverty, and grew up to be a drunkard in the bargain. The world was made better for his having lived, because he clothed beautiful thoughts in poetry, and thereby plucked a thorn and planted a rose in its place.

Booker T. Washington was born in slavery, handicapped by race and color. Because he was tolerant, had an open mind at all times, on all subjects, and was a DREAMER, he left his impress for good on an entire race.

Beethoven was deaf, Milton was blind, but their names will last as long as time endures, because they dreamed and translated their dreams into organized thought.

Before passing to the next chapter, kindle anew in your mind the fire of hope, faith, courage, and tolerance. If you have these states of mind, and a working knowledge of the principles described, all else that you need will come to you, when you are READY for it. Let Emerson state the thought in these words, "Every proverb, every book, every byword that belongs to thee for aid and comfort shall surely come home through open or winding passages. Every friend whom not thy fantastic will, but the great and tender soul in thee craveth, shall lock thee in his embrace."

There is a difference between WISHING for a thing and being READY to receive it. No one is *ready* for a thing, until he *believes* he can acquire it. The state of mind must be BELIEF, not mere hope or wish. Open-mindedness is essential for belief. Closed minds do not inspire faith, courage, and belief.

Remember, no more effort is required to aim high in life, to demand abundance and prosperity, than is required to accept misery and poverty. A great poet has correctly stated this universal truth through these lines:

"I bargained with Life for a penny,
And Life would pay no more,
However I begged at evening
When I counted my scanty store.

"For Life is a just employer,
He gives you what you ask,
But once you have set the wages,
Why, you must bear the task.

"I worked for a menial's hire,
Only to learn, dismayed,
That any wage I had asked of Life,
Life would have willingly paid."

DESIRE OUTWITS MOTHER NATURE

As a fitting climax to this chapter, I wish to introduce one of the most unusual persons I have ever known. I first saw him twenty-four years ago, a few minutes after he was born. He came into the world without any physical sign of ears, and the doctor admitted, when pressed for an opinion, that the child might be deaf, and mute for life.

I challenged the doctor's opinion. I had the right to do so, I was the child's father. I, too, reached a decision, and rendered an opinion, but I expressed the opinion silently, in the secrecy of my own heart. I decided that my son would hear and speak. Nature could send me a child without ears, but Nature *could not induce me to accept* the reality of the affliction.

In my own mind I knew that my son would hear and speak. How? I was sure there must be a way, and I knew I would find it. I thought of the words of the immortal Emerson, "The whole course of things goes to teach us faith. We need only obey. There is guidance for each of us, and by lowly listening, we shall hear *the right word.*"

The right word? DESIRE! More than anything else, I DESIRED that my son should not be a deaf mute. From that desire I never receded, not for a second.

Many years previously, I had written, "Our only limitations are those we set up in our own minds." For the first time, I wondered if that statement were true. Lying on the bed in front of me was a newly born child, without the natural equipment of hearing. Even though he might hear and speak, he was obviously disfigured for life. Surely, this was a limitation which that child had not set up in his own mind.

What could I do about it? Somehow I would find a way to transplant into that child's mind my own BURNING DESIRE for ways and means of conveying sound to his brain without the aid of ears.

As soon as the child was old enough to cooperate, I would fill his mind so completely with a BURNING DESIRE to hear, that Nature would, by methods of her own, translate it into physical reality.

All this thinking took place in my own mind, but I spoke of it to no one. Everyday I renewed the pledge I had made to myself, not to accept a deaf mute for a son.

As he grew older, and began to take notice of things around him, we observed that he had a slight degree of hearing. When he reached the age when children usually begin talking, he made no attempt to speak, but we could tell by his actions that he could hear certain sounds slightly. That was all I wanted to know! I was convinced that if he could hear, even slightly, he might develop still greater hearing capacity. Then something happened which gave me hope. It came from an entirely unexpected source.

We bought a victrola. When the child heard the music for the first time, he went into ecstasies, and promptly appropriated the machine. He soon showed a preference for certain records, among them, "It's a Long Way to Tipperary." On one occasion, he played that piece over and over, for almost two hours, standing in front of the victrola, *with his teeth clamped on the edge of the case.* The significance of this self-formed habit of his did not become clear to us until years afterward, for we had never heard of the principle of "bone conduction" of sound at that time.

Shortly after he appropriated the victrola, I discovered that he could hear me quite clearly when I spoke with my lips touching his mastoid bone, or at the base of the brain. These discoveries placed in my possession the necessary media by which I began to translate into reality my *Burning Desire* to help my son develop hearing and speech. By that time he was making stabs at speaking certain words. The outlook was far from encouraging, but DESIRE BACKED BY FAITH knows no such word as impossible.

Having determined that he could hear the sound of my voice plainly, I began, immediately, to transfer to his mind the desire to hear and speak. I soon discovered that the child enjoyed bedtime stories, so I went to work, creating stories designed to develop in him self-reliance, imagination, and a *keen desire to hear and to be normal.*

There was one story in particular, which I emphasized by giving it some new and dramatic coloring each time it was told. It was designed to plant in his mind the thought that his affliction was not a liability, but an asset of great value. Despite the fact that all the philosophy I had examined clearly indicated that EVERY ADVERSITY BRINGS WITH IT THE SEED OF AN EQUIVALENT ADVANTAGE, I must confess that I had not the slightest idea *how* this affliction could ever become an asset. However, I continued my practice of wrapping that philosophy in bedtime stories, hoping the time would come when he would find some plan by which his handicap could be made to serve some useful purpose.

Reason told me plainly, that there was no adequate compensation for the lack of ears and natural hearing equipment. DESIRE backed by FAITH, pushed reason aside, and inspired me to carry on.

As I analyze the experience in retrospect, I can see now, that my son's *faith in me* had much to do with the astounding results. He did not question anything I told him. I sold him the idea that he had a distinct *advantage* over his older brother, and that this advantage would reflect itself in many ways. For example, the teachers in school would observe that he had no ears, and, because of this, they would show him special attention and treat him with extraordinary kindness. They always did. His mother saw to that, by visiting the teachers and arranging with them to give the child the extra attention necessary. I sold him the idea, too, that when he became old enough to sell newspapers, (his older brother had already become a newspaper merchant), he would have a big advantage over his brother, for the reason that people would pay him extra money for his wares, because they could see that he was a bright, industrious boy, despite the fact he had no ears.

We could notice that, gradually, the child's hearing was improving. Moreover, he had not the slightest tendency to be self-conscious, because of his affliction. When he was about seven, he showed the first evidence that our method of servicing his mind was bearing fruit. For several months he begged for the privilege of selling newspapers, but his mother would not give her consent. She was afraid that his deafness made it unsafe for him to go on the street alone.

Finally, he took matters in his own hands. One afternoon, when he was left at home with the servants, he climbed through the kitchen window, shinnied to the ground, and set out on his own. He borrowed six cents in capital from the neighborhood shoemaker, invested it in papers, sold out, reinvested, and kept repeating until late in the evening. After balancing his accounts, and paying back the six cents he had borrowed from his banker, he had a net profit of forty-two cents. When we got home that night, we found him in bed asleep, with the money tightly clenched in his hand.

His mother opened his hand, removed the coins, and cried. Of all things! Crying over her son's first victory seemed so inappropriate. My reaction was the reverse. I laughed heartily, for I knew that my endeavor to plant in the child's mind an attitude of faith in himself had been successful.

His mother saw, in his first business venture, a little deaf boy who had gone out in the streets and risked his life to earn money. I saw a brave, ambitious, self-reliant little business man whose stock in himself had been increased a hundred percent, because he had gone into business on his own initiative, and had won. The transaction pleased me, because I knew that he had given evidence of a trait of resourcefulness that would go with him all through life. Later events proved this to be true. When his older brother wanted something, he would lie down on the floor, kick his feet in the air, cry for it—and get it. When the "little deaf boy" wanted something, he would plan a way to earn the money, then buy it for himself. He still follows that plan!

Truly, my own son has taught me that handicaps can be converted into stepping stones on which one may climb toward some worthy goal, unless they are accepted as obstacles, and used as alibis.

The little deaf boy went through the grades, high school, and college without being able to hear his teachers, excepting when they shouted loudly, at close range. He did not go to a school for the deaf. WE WOULD NOT PERMIT HIM TO LEARN THE SIGN LANGUAGE. We were determined that he should live a normal life, and associate with normal children, and we stood by that decision, although it cost us many heated debates with school officials.

While he was in high school, he tried an electrical hearing aid, but it was of no value to him; due, we believed, to a condition that was disclosed when the child was six, by Dr. J. Gordon Wilson, of Chicago, when he operated on one side of the boy's head, and discovered that there was no sign of natural hearing equipment.

During his last week in college, (eighteen years after the operation), something happened which marked the most important turning-point of his life. Through what seemed to be mere chance, he came into possession of another electrical hearing device, which was sent to him on trial. He was slow about testing it, due to his disappointment with a similar device. Finally he picked the instrument up, and more or less carelessly, placed it on his head, hooked up the battery, and lo! as if by a stroke of magic, his lifelong DESIRE FOR NORMAL HEARING BECAME A REALITY! For the first time in his life he heard practically as well as any person with normal hearing. "God moves in mysterious ways, His wonders to perform."

Overjoyed because of the Changed World which had been brought to him through his hearing device, he rushed to the telephone, called his mother, and heard her voice perfectly. The next day he plainly heard the voices of his professors in class, for the first time in his life! Previously he could hear them only when they shouted, at short range. He heard the radio. He *heard* the talking pictures. For the first time in his life, he could converse freely with other people, without the necessity of their having to speak loudly. Truly, he had come into possession of a Changed World. We had refused to accept Nature's error, and, by PERSISTENT DESIRE, we had induced Nature to correct that error, through the only practical means available.

DESIRE had commenced to pay dividends, but the victory was not yet complete. The boy still had to find a definite and practical way to convert his handicap into an *equivalent asset*.

Hardly realizing the significance of what had already been accomplished, but intoxicated with the joy of his newly discovered world of sound, he wrote a letter to the manufacturer of the hearing-aid, enthusiastically describing his experience. Something in his letter; something, perhaps which was not written on the lines, but back of them; caused the company to invite him to New York. When he arrived, he was escorted through the factory, and while talking with the Chief Engineer, telling him about his changed world, a hunch, an idea, or an inspiration—call it what you wish—flashed into his mind. It was *this impulse of thought* which converted his affliction into an asset, destined to pay dividends in both money and happiness to thousands for all time to come.

The sum and substance of that impulse of thought was this: It occurred to him that he might be of help to the millions of deafened people who go through life without the benefit of hearing devices, if he could find a way to tell them the story of his Changed World. Then and there, he reached a decision to devote the remainder of his life to rendering useful service to the hard of hearing.

For an entire month, he carried on an intensive research, during which he analyzed the entire marketing system of the manufacturer of the hearing device, and created ways and means of communicating with the hard of hearing all over the world for the purpose of sharing with them his newly discovered "Changed World." When this was done, he put in writing a two-year plan, based upon his findings. When he presented the plan to the company, he was instantly given a position, for the purpose of carrying out his ambition.

Little did he dream, when he went to work, that he was destined to bring hope and practical relief to thousands of deafened people who, without his help, would have been doomed forever to deaf mutism.

Shortly after he became associated with the manufacturer of his hearing aid, he invited me to attend a class conducted by his company, for the purpose of teaching deaf mutes to hear, and to speak. I had never heard of such a form of education, therefore I visited the class, skeptical but hopeful that my time would not be entirely wasted. Here I saw a demonstration which gave me a greatly enlarged vision of what I had done to arouse and keep alive in my son's mind the DESIRE for normal hearing. I saw deaf mutes actually being taught to hear and to speak, through application of the self-same principle I had used, more than twenty years previously, in saving my son from deaf mutism.

Thus, through some strange turn of the Wheel of Fate, my son, Blair, and I have been destined to aid in correcting deaf mutism for those as yet unborn, because we are the only living human beings, as far as I know, who have established definitely the fact that deaf mutism can be corrected to the extent of restoring to normal life those who suffer with this affliction. It has been done for one; it will be done for others.

There is no doubt in my mind that Blair would have been a deaf mute all his life, if his mother and I had not managed to shape his mind as we did. The doctor who attended at his birth told us, confidentially, the child might never hear or speak. A few weeks ago, Dr. Irving Voorhees, a noted specialist on such cases, examined Blair very thoroughly. He was astounded when he learned how well my son now hears, and speaks, and said his examination indicated that "theoretically, the boy should not be able to hear at all." But the lad does hear, despite the fact that X-ray pictures show there is no opening in the skull, whatsoever, from where his ears should be to the brain.

When I planted in his mind the DESIRE to hear and talk, and live as a normal person, there went with that impulse some strange influence which caused Nature to become bridge-builder, and span the gulf of silence between his brain and the outer world, by some means which the keenest medical specialists have not been able to interpret. It would be sacrilege for me to even conjecture as to how Nature performed this miracle. It would be unforgivable if I neglected to tell the world as much as I know of the humble part I assumed in the strange experience. It is my duty, and a privilege to say I believe, and not without reason, that nothing is impossible to the person who backs DESIRE with enduring FAITH.

Verily, a BURNING DESIRE has devious ways of transmuting itself into its physical equivalent. Blair DESIRED normal hearing; now he has it! He was born with a handicap which might easily have sent one with a less defined DESIRE to the street with a bundle of pencils and a tin cup. That handicap now promises to serve as the medium by which he will render useful service to many millions of hard of hearing, also, to give him useful employment at adequate financial compensation the remainder of his life.

The little "white lies" I planted in his mind when he was a child, by leading him to BELIEVE his affliction would become a great asset, which he could capitalize, has justified itself. Verily, there is nothing, right or wrong, which BELIEF, plus BURNING DESIRE, cannot make real. These qualities are free to everyone.

In all my experience in dealing with men and women who had personal problems, I never handled a single case which more definitely demonstrates the power of DESIRE. Authors sometimes make the mistake of writing of subjects of which they have but superficial, or very elementary knowledge. It has been my good fortune to have had the privilege of testing the soundness of the POWER OF DESIRE, through the affliction of my own son. Perhaps it was providential that the experience came as it did, for surely no one is better prepared than he, to serve as an example of what happens when DESIRE is put to the test. *If Mother Nature bends to the will of desire, is it logical that mere men can defeat a burning desire?*

Strange and imponderable is the power of the human mind! We do not understand the method by which it uses every circumstance, every individual, every physical thing within its reach, as a means of transmuting DESIRE into its physical counterpart. Perhaps science will uncover this secret.

I planted in my son's mind the DESIRE to hear and to speak as any normal person hears and speaks. That DESIRE has now become a reality. I planted in his mind the DESIRE to convert his greatest handicap into his greatest asset. That DESIRE has been realized. The modus operandi by which this astounding result was achieved is not hard to describe. It consisted of three very definite facts; first, I MIXED FAITH with the DESIRE for normal hearing, which I passed on to my son. Second, I communicated my desire to him in every conceivable way available, through persistent, continuous effort, over a period of years. Third, HE BELIEVED ME!

As this chapter was being completed, news came of the death of Mme. Schuman-Heink. One short paragraph in the news dispatch gives the clue to this unusual woman's stupendous success as a singer. I quote the paragraph, because the clue it contains is none other than DESIRE.

Early in her career, Mme. Schuman-Heink visited the director of the Vienna

Court Opera, to have him test her voice. But, he did not test it. After taking one look at the awkward and poorly dressed girl, he exclaimed, none too gently, "With such a face, and with no personality at all, how can you ever expect to succeed in opera? My good child, give up the idea. Buy a sewing machine and go to work. YOU CAN NEVER BE A SINGER."

Never is a long time! The director of the Vienna Court Opera knew much about the technique of singing. He knew little about the power of desire, when it assumes the proportion of an obsession. If he had known more of that power, he would not have made the mistake of condemning genius without giving it an opportunity.

Several years ago, one of my business associates became ill. He became worse as time went on, and finally was taken to the hospital for an operation. Just before he was wheeled into the operating room, I took a look at him, and wondered how anyone as thin and emaciated as he, could possibly go through a major operation successfully. The doctor warned me that there was little if any chance of my ever seeing him alive again. But that was the DOCTOR'S OPINION. It was not the opinion of the patient. Just before he was wheeled away, he whispered feebly, "Do not be disturbed, Chief, I will be out of here in a few days." The attending nurse looked at me with pity. But the patient did come through safely. After it was all over, his physician said, "Nothing but his own desire to live saved him. He never would have pulled through if he had not refused to accept the possibility of death."

I believe in the power of DESIRE backed by FAITH, because I have seen this power lift men from lowly beginnings to places of power and wealth; I have seen it rob the grave of its victims; I have seen it serve as the medium by which men staged a comeback after having been defeated in a hundred different ways; I have seen it provide my own son with a normal, happy, successful life, despite Nature's having sent him into the world without ears.

How can one harness and use the power of DESIRE? This has been answered through this, and the subsequent chapters of this book. This message is going out to the world at the end of the longest, and perhaps, the most devastating depression America has ever known. It is reasonable to presume that the message may come to the attention of many who have been wounded by the depression, those who have lost their fortunes, others who have lost their positions, and great numbers who must reorganize their plans and stage a comeback. To all these I wish to convey the thought that all achievement, no matter what may be its nature, or its purpose, must begin with an intense, BURNING DESIRE for something definite.

Through some strange and powerful principle of " mental chemistry" which she has never divulged, Nature wraps up in the impulse of STRONG DESIRE "that something" which recognizes no such word as impossible, and accepts no such reality as failure.

CHAPTER THREE

FAITH:

VISUALIZATION OF, AND BELIEF
IN ATTAINMENT OF DESIRE:
The Second Step toward Riches

FAITH is the head chemist of the mind. When FAITH is blended with the vibration of thought, the subconscious mind instantly picks up the vibration, translates it into its spiritual equivalent, and transmits it to Infinite Intelligence, as in the case of prayer.

The emotions of FAITH, LOVE, and SEX are the most powerful of all the major positive emotions. When the three are blended, they have the effect of "coloring" the vibration of thought in such a way that it instantly reaches the subconscious mind, where it is changed into its spiritual equivalent, the only form that induces a response from Infinite Intelligence.

Love and faith are psychic; related to the spiritual side of man. Sex is purely biological, and related only to the physical. The mixing, or blending, of these three emotions has the effect of opening a direct line of communication between the finite, thinking mind of man, and Infinite Intelligence.

HOW TO DEVELOP FAITH

There comes, now, a statement which will give a better understanding of the importance the principle of auto-suggestion assumes in the transmutation of desire into its physical, or monetary equivalent; namely: FAITH is a state of mind which may be induced, or created, by affirmation or repeated instructions to the subconscious mind, through the principle of auto-suggestion.

As an illustration, consider the purpose for which you are, presumably, reading this book. The object is, naturally, to acquire the ability to transmute the intangible thought impulse of DESIRE into its physical counterpart, money. By following the instructions laid down in the chapters on auto-suggestion, and the subconscious mind, as summarized in the chapter on auto-suggestion, you may CONVINCE the subconscious mind that you *believe* you will receive that for which you ask, and it will act upon that belief, which your subconscious mind passes back to you in the form of "FAITH," followed by definite plans for procuring that which you desire.

The method by which one develops FAITH, where it does not already exist, is extremely difficult to describe, almost as difficult, in fact, as it would be to describe the color of red to a blind man who has never seen color, and has nothing with which to compare what you describe to him. Faith is a state of mind which you may develop at will, after you have mastered the thirteen principles, because it is a state of mind which develops voluntarily, through application and use of these principles.

Repetition of affirmation of orders to your subconscious mind is the only known method of voluntary development of the emotion of faith.

Perhaps the meaning may be made clearer through the following explanation as to the way men sometimes become criminals. Stated in the words of a famous criminologist, "When men first come into contact with crime, they abhor it. If they remain in contact with crime for a time, they become accustomed to it, and endure it. If they remain in contact with it long enough, they finally embrace it, and become influenced by it."

This is the equivalent of saying that any impulse of thought which is repeatedly passed on to the subconscious mind is, finally, accepted and acted upon by the subconscious mind, which proceeds to translate that impulse into its physical equivalent, by the most practical procedure available.

In connection with this, consider again the statement, ALL THOUGHTS WHICH HAVE BEEN EMOTIONALIZED, (given feeling) AND MIXED WITH FAITH, begin immediately to translate themselves into their physical equivalent or counterpart.

The emotions, or the "feeling" portion of thoughts, are the factors which give thoughts vitality, life, and action. The emotions of Faith, Love, and Sex, when mixed with any thought impulse, give it greater action than any of these emotions can do singly.

Not only thought impulses which have been mixed with FAITH, but those which have been mixed with any of the positive emotions, or any of the negative emotions, may reach, and influence the subconscious mind.

From this statement, you will understand that the subconscious mind will translate into its physical equivalent, a thought impulse of a negative or destructive nature, just as readily as it will act upon thought impulses of a positive or constructive nature. This accounts for the strange phenomenon which so many millions of people experience, referred to as "misfortune," or "bad luck."

There are millions of people who BELIEVE themselves "doomed" to poverty and failure, because of some strange force over which they BELIEVE they have no control. They are the creators of their own "misfortunes," because of this negative BELIEF, which is picked up by the subconscious mind, and translated into its physical equivalent.

This is an appropriate place at which to suggest again that you may benefit, by passing on to your subconscious mind, any DESIRE which you wish translated into its physical, or monetary equivalent, in a state of expectancy or BELIEF that the transmutation will actually take place. Your BELIEF, or FAITH, is the element which determines the action of your subconscious mind. There is nothing to hinder you from "deceiving" your subconscious mind when giving it instructions through auto-suggestion, as I deceived my son's subconscious mind.

To make this "deceit" more realistic, conduct yourself just as you would, if you were ALREADY IN POSSESSION OF THE MATERIAL THING WHICH YOU ARE DEMANDING, when you call upon your subconscious mind.

The subconscious mind will transmute into its physical equivalent, by the most direct and practical media available, any order which is given to it in a state of BELIEF, or FAITH that the order will be carried out.

Surely, enough has been stated to give a starting point from which one may, through experiment and practice, acquire the ability to mix FAITH with any order given to the subconscious mind. Perfection will come through practice. It *cannot* come by merely *reading* instructions.

If it be true that one may become a criminal by association with crime, (and this is a known fact), it is equally true that one may develop faith by voluntarily suggesting to the subconscious mind that one has faith. The mind comes, finally, to take on the nature of the influences which dominate it. Understand this truth, and you will know why it is essential for you to encourage the *positive emotions* as dominating forces of your mind, and discourage—and *eliminate* negative emotions.

A mind dominated by positive emotions, becomes a favorable abode for the state of mind known as faith. A mind so dominated may, at will, give the subconscious mind instructions, which it will accept and act upon immediately.

FAITH IS A STATE OF MIND WHICH MAY BE INDUCED BY AUTO-SUGGESTION

All down the ages, the religionists have admonished struggling humanity to "have faith" in this, that, and the other dogma or creed, but they have failed to tell people HOW to have faith. They have not stated that "faith is a state of mind, and that it may be induced by self-suggestion."

In language which any normal human being can understand, we will describe all that is known about the principle through which FAITH may be developed, where it does not already exist.

Have Faith in yourself; Faith in the Infinite.

Before we begin, you should be reminded again that:

FAITH is the "eternal elixir" which gives life, power, and action to the impulse of thought!

The foregoing sentence is worth reading a second time, and a third, and a fourth. It is worth reading aloud!

FAITH is the starting point of all accumulation of riches!

FAITH is the basis of all "miracles," and all mysteries which cannot be analyzed by the rules of science!

FAITH is the only known antidote for FAILURE!

FAITH is the element, the "chemical" which, when mixed with prayer, gives one direct communication with Infinite Intelligence.

FAITH is the element which transforms the ordinary vibration of thought, created by the finite mind of man, into the spiritual equivalent.

FAITH is the only agency through which the cosmic force of Infinite Intelligence can be harnessed and used by man.

EVERY ONE OF THE FOREGOING STATEMENTS IS CAPABLE OF PROOF!

The proof is simple and easily demonstrated. It is wrapped up in the principle of auto-suggestion. Let us center our attention, therefore, upon the subject of self-suggestion, and find out what it is, and what it is capable of achieving.

It is a well known fact that one comes, finally, to BELIEVE whatever one repeats to one's self, *whether the statement be true or false.* If a man repeats a lie over and over, he will eventually accept the lie as truth. Moreover, he will BELIEVE it to be the truth. Every man is what he is, because of the DOMINATING THOUGHTS which he permits to occupy his mind. Thoughts which a man deliberately places in his own mind, and encourages with sympathy, and with which he mixes any one or more of the emotions, constitute the motivating forces, which direct and control his every movement, act, and deed!

Comes, now, a very significant statement of truth:

THOUGHTS WHICH ARE MIXED WITH ANY OF THE FEELINGS OF EMOTIONS, CONSTITUTE A "MAGNETIC" FORCE WHICH ATTRACTS, FROM THE VIBRATIONS OF THE ETHER, OTHER SIMILAR, OR RELATED THOUGHTS. A thought thus "magnetized" with emotion may be compared to a seed which, when planted in fertile soil, germinates, grows, and multiplies itself over and over again, until that which was originally one small seed, becomes countless millions of seeds of the SAME BRAND!

The ether is a great cosmic mass of eternal forces of vibration. It is made up of both destructive vibrations and constructive vibrations. It carries, at all times, vibrations of fear, poverty, disease, failure, misery; and vibrations of prosperity, health, success, and happiness, just as surely as it carries the sound of hundreds of orchestrations of music, and hundreds of human voices, all of which maintain their own individuality, and means of identification, through the medium of radio.

From the great storehouse of the ether, the human mind is constantly attracting vibrations which harmonize with that which DOMINATES the human mind. Any thought, idea, plan, or purpose which one *holds* in one's mind attracts, from the vibrations of the ether, a host of its relatives, adds these "relatives" to its own force, and grows until it becomes the dominating, MOTIVATING MASTER of the individual in whose mind it has been housed.

Now, let us go back to the starting point, and become informed as to how the original seed of an idea, plan, or purpose may be planted in the mind. The information is easily conveyed: any idea, plan, or purpose may be placed in the mind *through repetition of thought.* This is why you are asked to write out a statement of your major purpose, or Definite Chief Aim, commit it to memory, and repeat it, in audible words, day after day, until these vibrations of sound have reached your subconscious mind.

We are what we are, because of the vibrations of thought which we pick up and register, through the stimuli of our daily environment.

Resolve to throw off the influences of any unfortunate environment, and to build your own life to ORDER. Taking inventory of mental assets and liabilities you will discover that your greatest weakness is lack of self-confidence. This handicap can be surmounted, and timidity translated into courage, through the aid of the principle of auto-suggestion. The application of this principle may be made through a simple arrangement of positive thought impulses stated in writing, memorized, and repeated, until they become a part of the working equipment of the subconscious faculty of your mind.

SELF-CONFIDENCE FORMULA

First. I know that I have the ability to achieve the object of my Definite Purpose in life, therefore, I DEMAND of myself persistent, continuous action toward its attainment, and I here and now promise to render such action.

Second. I realize the dominating thoughts of my mind will eventually reproduce themselves in outward, physical action, and gradually transform themselves into physical reality, therefore, I will concentrate my thoughts for thirty minutes daily, upon the task of thinking of the person I intend to become, thereby creating in my mind a clear mental picture of that person.

Third. I know through the principle of auto-suggestion, any desire that I persistently hold in my mind will eventually seek expression through some practical means of attaining the object back of it, therefore, I will devote ten minutes daily to demanding of myself the development of SELF-CONFIDENCE.

Fourth. I have clearly written down a description of my DEFINITE CHIEF AIM in life, and I will never stop trying, until I shall have developed sufficient self-confidence for its attainment.

Fifth. I fully realize that no wealth or position can long endure, unless built upon truth and justice, therefore, I will engage in no transaction which does not benefit all whom it affects. I will succeed by attracting to myself the forces I wish to use, and the cooperation of other people. I will induce others to serve me, because of my willingness to serve others. I will eliminate hatred, envy, jealousy, selfishness, and cynicism, by developing love for all humanity, because I know that a negative attitude toward others can never bring me success. I will cause others to believe in me, because I will believe in them, and in myself.

I will sign my name to this formula, commit it to memory, and repeat it aloud once a day, with full FAITH that it will gradually influence my THOUGHTS and ACTIONS so that I will become a self-reliant, and successful person.

Back of this formula is a law of Nature which no man has yet been able to explain. It has baffled the scientists of all ages. The psychologists have named this law "auto-suggestion," and let it go at that.

The name by which one calls this law is of little importance. The important fact about it is—it WORKS for the glory and success of mankind, IF it is used constructively. On the other hand, if used destructively, it will destroy just as readily. In this statement may be found a very significant truth, namely; that those who go down in defeat, and end their lives in poverty, misery, and distress, do so because of negative application of the principle of auto-suggestion. The cause may be found in the fact that ALL IMPULSES OF THOUGHT HAVE A TENDENCY TO CLOTHE THEMSELVES IN THEIR PHYSICAL EQUIVALENT.

The subconscious mind, (the chemical laboratory in which all thought impulses are combined, and made ready for translation into physical reality), makes no distinction between constructive and destructive thought impulses. It works with the material we feed it, through our thought impulses. The subconscious mind will translate into reality a thought driven by FEAR just as readily as it will translate into reality a thought driven by COURAGE, or FAITH.

The pages of medical history are rich with illustrations of cases of "suggestive suicide." A man may commit suicide through negative suggestion, just as effectively as by any other means. In a midwestern city, a man by the name of Joseph Grant, a bank official, "borrowed" a large sum of the bank's money, without the consent of the directors. He lost the money through gambling. One afternoon, the Bank Examiner came and began to check the accounts. Grant left the bank, took a room in a local hotel, and when they found him, three days later, he was lying in bed, wailing and moaning, repeating over and over these words, "My God, this will kill me! I cannot stand the disgrace." In a short time he was dead. The doctors pronounced the case one of "mental suicide."

Just as electricity will turn the wheels of industry, and render useful service if used constructively; or snuff out life if wrongly used, so will the law of auto-suggestion lead you to peace and prosperity, or down into the valley of misery, failure, and death, according to your degree of understanding and application of it.

If you fill your mind with FEAR, doubt and unbelief in your ability to connect with, and use the forces of Infinite Intelligence, the law of auto-suggestion will take this spirit of unbelief and use it as a pattern by which your subconscious mind will translate it into its physical equivalent.

THIS STATEMENT IS AS TRUE AS THE STATEMENT THAT TWO AND TWO ARE FOUR!

Like the wind which carries one ship East, and another West, the law of auto-suggestion will lift you up or pull you down, according to the way you set your sails of THOUGHT.

The law of auto-suggestion, through which any person may rise to altitudes of achievement which stagger the imagination, is well described in the following verse:

> "If you *think you* are beaten, you are,
> If you *think you* dare not, you don't
> If you like to win, but you *think you* can't,
> It is almost certain you won't.

> "If you *think* you'll lose, you're lost
> For out of the world we find,
> Success begins with a fellow's will—
> It's all in the *state of mind.*

> "If you *think* you are outclassed, you are,
> You've got to *think* high to rise,
> You've got to *be sure of yourself* before
> You can ever win a prize.

> "Life's battles don't always go
> To the stronger or faster man,
> But soon or late the man who wins
> Is the man WHO THINKS HE CAN!"

Observe the words which have been emphasized, and you will catch the deep meaning which the poet had in mind.

Somewhere in your make-up (perhaps in the cells of your brain) there lies *sleeping,* the seed of achievement which, if aroused and put into action, would carry you to heights, such as you may never have hoped to attain.

Just as a master musician may cause the most beautiful strains of music to pour forth from the strings of a violin, so may you arouse the genius which lies asleep in your brain, and cause it to drive you upward to whatever goal you may wish to achieve.

Abraham Lincoln was a failure at everything he tried, until he was well past the age of forty. He was a Mr. Nobody from Nowhere, until a great experience came into his life, aroused the sleeping genius within his heart and brain, and gave world one of its really great men. That "experience" was mixed with the emotions of sorrow and LOVE. It came to him through Anne Rutledge, the only woman whom he ever truly loved.

It is a known fact that the emotion of LOVE is closely akin to the state of mind known as FAITH, and this for the reason that Love comes very near to translating one's thought impulses into their spiritual equivalent. During his work of research, the author discovered, from the analysis of the lifework and achievements of hundreds of men of outstanding accomplishment, that there was the influence of a woman's love back of nearly EVERY ONE OF THEM. The emotion of love, in the human heart and brain, creates a favorable field of magnetic attraction, which causes an influx of the higher and finer vibrations which are afloat in the ether.

If you wish evidence of the power of FAITH, study the achievements of men and women who have employed it. At the head of the list comes the Nazarene. Christianity is the greatest single force which influences the minds of men. The basis of Christianity is FAITH, no matter how many people may have perverted, or misinterpreted the meaning of this great force, and no matter how many dogmas and creeds have been created in its name, which do not reflect its tenets.

The sum and substance of the teachings and the achievements of Christ, which may have been interpreted as "miracles," were nothing more nor less than FAITH. If there are any such phenomena as "miracles" they are produced only through the state of mind known as FAITH! Some teachers of religion, and many who call themselves Christians, neither understand nor practice FAITH.

Let us consider the power of FAITH, as it is now being demonstrated, by a man who is well known to all of civilization, Mahatma Gandhi, of India. In this man the world has one of the most astounding examples known to civilization, of the possibilities of FAITH. Gandhi wields more potential power than any man living at this time, and this despite the fact that he has none of the orthodox tools of power, such as money, battle ships, soldiers, and materials of warfare. Gandhi has no money, he has no home, he does not own a suit of clothes, but HE DOES HAVE POWER. How does he come by that power?

HE CREATED IT OUT OF HIS UNDERSTANDING OF THE PRINCIPLE OF FAITH, AND THROUGH HIS ABILITY TO TRANSPLANT THAT FAITH INTO THE MINDS OF TWO HUNDRED MILLION PEOPLE.

Gandhi has accomplished, through the influence of FAITH, that which the strongest military power on earth could not, and never will accomplish through soldiers and military equipment. He has accomplished the astounding feat of INFLUENCING two hundred million minds to COALESCE AND MOVE IN UNISON, AS A SINGLE MIND.

What other force on earth, except FAITH could do as much?

There will come a day when employees as well as employers will discover the possibilities of FAITH. That day is dawning. The whole world has had ample opportunity, during the recent business depression, to witness what the LACK OF FAITH will do to business.

Surely, civilization has produced a sufficient number of intelligent human beings to make use of this great lesson which the depression has taught the world. During this depression, the world had evidence in abundance that widespread FEAR will paralyze the wheels of industry and business. Out of this experience will arise leaders in business and industry who will profit by the example which Gandhi has set for the world, and they will apply to business the same tactics which he has used in building the greatest following known in the history of the world. These leaders will come from the rank and file of the unknown men, who now labor in the steel plants, the coal mines, the automobile factories, and in the small towns and cities of America.

Business is due for a reform, make no mistake about this! The methods of the past, based upon economic combinations of FORCE and FEAR, will be supplanted by the better principles of FAITH and cooperation. Men who labor will receive more than daily wages; they will receive dividends from the business, the same as those who supply the capital for business; but, first they must GIVE MORE TO THEIR EMPLOYERS, and stop this bickering and bargaining by force, at the expense of the Public. *They must earn the right to dividends!*

Moreover and this is the most important thing of all—THEY WILL BE LED BY LEADERS WHO WILL UNDERSTAND AND APPLY THE PRINCIPLES EMPLOYED BY MAHATMA GANDHI. Only in this way may leaders get from their followers the spirit of FULL cooperation which constitutes power in its highest and most enduring form.

This stupendous machine age in which we live, and from which we are just emerging, has taken the soul out of men. Its leaders have driven men as though they were pieces of cold machinery; they were forced to do so by the employees who have bargained, at the expense of all concerned, to *get* and not to *give*. The watchword of the future will be HUMAN HAPPINESS AND CONTENTMENT, and when this state of mind shall have been attained, the production will take care of itself, more effectively than anything that has ever been accomplished where men did not, and could not mix FAITH and individual interest with their labor.

Because of the need for faith and cooperation in operating business and industry, it will be both interesting and profitable to analyze an event which provides an excellent understanding of the method by which industrialists and business men accumulate great fortunes, by *giving* before they try to *get*.

The event chosen for this illustration dates back to 1900, when the United States Steel Corporation was being formed. As you read the story, keep in mind these fundamental facts and you will understand how IDEAS have been converted into huge fortunes.

First, the huge United States Steel Corporation was born in the mind of Charles M. Schwab, in the form of an IDEA he created through his IMAGINATION! Second, he mixed FAITH with his IDEA. Third, he formulated a PLAN for the transformation of his IDEA into physical and financial reality. Fourth, he put his plan into action with his famous speech at the University Club. Fifth, he applied, and followed-through on his PLAN with PERSISTENCE, and backed it with firm DECISION until it had been fully carried out. Sixth, he prepared the way for success by a BURNING DESIRE for success.

If you are one of those who have often wondered how great fortunes are accumulated, this story of the creation of the United States Steel Corporation will be enlightening. If you have any doubt that men can THINK AND GROW RICH, this story should dispel that doubt, because you can plainly see in the story of the

United States Steel, the application of a major portion of the thirteen principles described in this book.

This astounding description of the power of an IDEA was dramatically told by John Lowell, in the New York World-Telegram, with whose courtesy it is here reprinted.

A PRETTY AFTER-DINNER SPEECH
FOR A BILLION DOLLARS

"When, on the evening of December 12, 1900, some eighty of the nation's financial nobility gathered in the banquet hall of the University Club on Fifth Avenue to do honor to a young man from out of the West, not half a dozen of the guests realized they were to witness the most significant episode in American industrial history.

"J. Edward Simmons and Charles Stewart Smith, their hearts full of gratitude for the lavish hospitality bestowed on them by Charles M. Schwab during a recent visit to Pittsburgh, had arranged the dinner to introduce the thirty-eight-year-old steel man to eastern banking society. But they didn't expect him to stampede the convention. They warned him, in fact, that the bosoms within New York's stuffed shirts would not be responsive to oratory, and that, if he didn't want to bore the Stillmans and Harrimans and Vanderbilts, he had better limit himself to fifteen or twenty minutes of polite vaporings and let it go at that.

"Even John Pierpont Morgan, sitting on the right hand of Schwab as became his imperial dignity, intended to grace the banquet table with his presence only briefly. And so far as the press and public were concerned, the whole affair was of so little moment that no mention of it found its way into print the next day.

"So the two hosts and their distinguished guests ate their way through the usual seven or eight courses. There was little conversation and what there was of it was restrained. Few of the bankers and brokers had met Schwab, whose career had flowered along the banks of the Monongahela, and none knew him well. But before the evening was over, they—and with them Money Master Morgan—were to be swept off their feet, and a billion-dollar baby, the United States Steel Corporation, was to be conceived.

"It is perhaps unfortunate, for the sake of history, that no record of Charlie Schwab's speech at the dinner ever was made. He repeated some parts of it at a later date during a similar meeting of Chicago bankers. And still later, when the Government brought suit to dissolve the Steel Trust, he gave his own version, from the witness stand, of the remarks that stimulated Morgan into a frenzy of financial activity.

"It is probable, however, that it was a 'homely' speech, somewhat ungrammatical (for the niceties of language never bothered Schwab), full of epigram and threaded with wit. But aside from that it had a galvanic force and effect upon the five billions of estimated capital that was represented by the diners. After it was over and the gathering was still under its spell, although Schwab had talked for ninety minutes, Morgan led the orator to a recessed window where, dangling their legs from the high, uncomfortable seat, they talked for an hour more.

"The magic of the Schwab personality had been turned on, full force, but what was more important and lasting was the full-fledged, clear-cut program he laid down for the aggrandizement of Steel. Many other men had tried to interest Morgan in slapping together a steel trust after the pattern of the biscuit, wire and hoop, sugar, rubber, whisky, oil or chewing gum combinations. John W. Gates, the gambler, had urged it, but Morgan distrusted him. The Moore boys, Bill and Jim, Chicago stock jobbers who had glued together a match trust and a cracker corporation, had urged it and failed. Elbert H. Gary, the sanctimonious country lawyer, wanted to foster it, but he wasn't big enough to be impressive. Until Schwab's eloquence took J. P. Morgan to the heights from which he could visualize the solid results of the most daring financial undertaking ever conceived, the project was regarded as a delirious dream of easy-money crackpots.

"The financial magnetism that began, a generation ago, to attract thousands of small and sometimes inefficiently managed companies into large and competition-crushing combinations, had become operative in the steel world through the devices of that jovial business pirate, John W. Gates. Gates already had formed the American Steel and Wire Company out of a chain of small concerns, and together with Morgan had created the Federal Steel Company. The National Tube and American Bridge companies were two more Morgan concerns, and the Moore Brothers had forsaken the match and cookie business to form the 'American' group—Tin Plate, Steel Hoop, Sheet Steel—and the National Steel Company.

"But by the side of Andrew Carnegie's gigantic vertical trust, a trust owned and operated by fifty-three partners, those other combinations were picayune. They might combine to their heart's content but the whole lot of them couldn't make a dent in the Carnegie organization, and Morgan knew it.

"The eccentric old Scot knew it, too. From the magnificent heights of Skibo Castle he had viewed, first with amusement and then with resentment, the attempts of Morgan's smaller companies to cut into his business. When the attempts became too bold, Carnegie's temper was translated into anger and retaliation. He decided to duplicate every mill owned by his rivals. Hitherto, he hadn't been interested in wire, pipe, hoops, or sheet. Instead, he was content to sell such companies the raw steel and let them work it into whatever shape they wanted. Now, with Schwab as his chief and able lieutenant, he planned to drive his enemies to the wall.

"So it was that in the speech of Charles M. Schwab, Morgan saw the answer to his problem of combination. A trust without Carnegie—giant of them all—would be no trust at all, a plum pudding, as one writer said, without the plums.

"Schwab's speech on the night of December 12, 1900, undoubtedly carried the inference, though not the pledge, that the vast Carnegie enterprise could be brought under the Morgan tent. He talked of the world future for steel, of reorganization for efficiency, of specialization, of the scrapping of unsuccessful mills and concentration of effort on the flourishing properties, of economies in the ore traffic, of economies in overhead and administrative departments, of capturing foreign markets.

"More than that, he told the buccaneers among them wherein lay the errors of their customary piracy. Their purposes, he inferred, had been to create monopolies, raise prices, and pay themselves fat dividends out of privilege. Schwab condemned the system in his heartiest manner. The shortsightedness of such a policy, he told his hearers, lay in the fact that it restricted the market in an era when everything cried for expansion. By cheapening the cost of steel, he argued, an ever-expanding market would be created; more uses for steel would be devised, and a goodly portion of the world trade could be captured. Actually, though he did not know it, Schwab was an apostle of modern mass production.

"So the dinner at the University Club came to an end. Morgan went home, to think about Schwab's rosy predictions. Schwab went back to Pittsburgh to run the steel business for 'Wee Andra Carnegie,' while Gary and the rest went back to their stock tickers, to fiddle around in anticipation of the next move.

"It was not long coming. It took Morgan about one week to digest the feast of reason Schwab had placed before him. When he had assured himself that no financial indigestion was to result, he sent for Schwab—and found that young man rather coy. Mr. Carnegie, Schwab indicated, might not like it if he found his trusted company president had been flirting with the Emperor of Wall Street, the Street upon which Carnegie was resolved never to tread. Then it was suggested by John W. Gates the go-between, that if Schwab 'happened' to be in the Bellevue Hotel in Philadelphia, J. P. Morgan might also 'happen' to be there. When Schwab arrived, however, Morgan was inconveniently ill at his New York home, and so, on the elder man's pressing invitation, Schwab went to New York and presented himself at the door of the financier's library.

"Now certain economic historians have professed the belief that from the beginning to the end of the drama, the stage was set by Andrew Carnegie—that the dinner to Schwab, the famous speech, the Sunday night conference between Schwab and the Money King, were events arranged by the canny Scot. The truth is exactly the opposite. When Schwab was called in to consummate the deal, he didn't even know whether 'the little boss,' as Andrew was called, would so much as listen to an offer to sell, particularly to a group of men whom Andrew regarded as being endowed with something less than holiness. But Schwab did take into the conference with him, in his own handwriting, six sheets of copper-plate figures, representing to his mind the physical worth and the potential earning capacity of every steel company he regarded as an essential star in the new metal firmament.

"Four men pondered over these figures all night. The chief, of course, was Morgan, steadfast in his belief in the Divine Right of Money. With him was his aristocratic partner, Robert Bacon, a scholar and a gentleman. The third was John W. Gates whom Morgan scorned as a gambler and used as a tool. The fourth was Schwab, who knew more about the processes of making and selling steel than any whole group of men then living. Throughout that conference, the Pittsburgher's figures were never questioned. If he said a company was worth so much, then it was worth that much and no more. He was insistent, too, upon including in the combination only those concerns he nominated. He had conceived a corporation in which there would be no duplication, not even to satisfy the greed of friends who wanted to unload their companies upon the broad Morgan shoulders. Thus he left out, by design, a number of the larger concerns upon which the Walruses and Carpenters of Wall Street had cast hungry eyes.

"When dawn came, Morgan rose and straightened his back. Only one question remained.

"'Do you think you can persuade Andrew Carnegie to sell?' he asked.

"'I can try,' said Schwab.

"'If you can get him to sell, I will undertake the matter,' said Morgan.

"So far so good. But would Carnegie sell? How much would he demand? (Schwab thought about $320,000,000). What would he take payment in? Common or preferred stocks? Bonds? Cash? Nobody could raise a third of a billion dollars in cash.

"There was a golf game in January on the frostcracking heath of the St. Andrews links in Westchester, with Andrew bundled up in sweaters against the cold, and Charlie talking volubly, as usual, to keep his spirits up. But no word of business was mentioned until the pair sat down in the cozy warmth of the Carnegie cottage hard by. Then, with the same persuasiveness that had hypnotized eighty millionaires at the University Club, Schwab poured out the glittering promises of retirement in comfort, of untold millions to satisfy the old man's social caprices. Carnegie capitulated, wrote a figure on a slip of paper, handed it to Schwab and said, 'all right, that's what we'll sell for.'

"The figure was approximately $400,000,000, and was reached by taking the $320,000,000 mentioned by Schwab as a basic figure, and adding to it $80,000,000 to represent the increased capital value over the previous two years.

"Later, on the deck of a trans-Atlantic liner, the Scotsman said ruefully to Morgan, 'I wish I had asked you for $100,000,000 more.'

'If you had asked for it, you'd have gotten it,' Morgan told him cheerfully.

●

"There was an uproar, of course. A British correspondent cabled that the foreign steel world was 'appalled' by the gigantic combination. President Hadley, of Yale, declared that unless trusts were regulated the country might expect 'an emperor in Washington within the next twenty-five years.' But that able stock manipulator, Keene, went at his work of shoving the new stock at the public so vigorously that all the excess water—estimated by some at nearly $600,000,000—was absorbed in a twinkling. So Carnegie had his millions, and the Morgan syndicate had $62,000,000 for all its 'trouble,' and all the 'boys,' from Gates to Gary, had their millions.

●

"The thirty-eight-year-old Schwab had his reward. He was made president of the new corporation and remained in control until 1930."

The dramatic story of "Big Business" which you have just finished, was included in this book, because it is a perfect illustration of the method by which

DESIRE CAN BE TRANSMUTED INTO ITS PHYSICAL EQUIVALENT!

I imagine some readers will question the statement that a mere, intangible DESIRE can be converted into its physical equivalent. Doubtless some say, "You cannot convert NOTHING into SOMETHING!" The answer is in the story of United States Steel.

That giant organization was created in the mind of one man. The plan by which the organization was provided with the steel mills that gave it financial stability was created in the mind of the same man. His FAITH, his DESIRE, his IMAGINATION, his PERSISTENCE were the real ingredients that went into United States Steel. The steel mills and mechanical equipment acquired by the corporation, AFTER IT HAD BEEN BROUGHT INTO LEGAL EXISTENCE, were incidental, but careful analysis will disclose the fact that the appraised value of the properties acquired by the corporation increased in value by an estimated SIX HUNDRED MILLION DOLLARS, by the mere transaction which consolidated them under one management.

In other words, Charles M. Schwab's IDEA, plus the FAITH with which he conveyed it to the minds of J. P. Morgan and the others, was marketed for a profit of approximately $600,000,000. Not an insignificant sum for a single IDEA!

What happened to some of the men who took their share of the millions of dollars of profit made by this transaction, is a matter with which we are not now concerned. The important feature of the astounding achievement is that it serves as unquestionable evidence of the soundness of the philosophy described in this book, because this philosophy was the warp and the woof of the entire transaction. Moreover, the practicability of the philosophy has been established by the fact that the United States Steel Corporation prospered, and became one of the richest and most powerful corporations in America, employing thousands of people, developing new uses for steel, and opening new markets; thus proving that the $600,000,000 in profit which the Schwab IDEA produced was earned.

RICHES begin in the form of THOUGHT!

The amount is limited only by the person in whose mind the THOUGHT is put into motion. FAITH removes limitations! Remember this when you are ready to bargain with Life for whatever it is that you ask as your price for having passed this way.

Remember, also, that the man who created the United States Steel Corporation was practically unknown at the time. He was merely Andrew Carnegie's "Man Friday" until he gave birth to his famous IDEA. After that he quickly rose to a position of power, fame, and riches.

THERE ARE NO LIMITATIONS TO THE MIND
EXCEPT THOSE WE *ACKNOWLEDGE*

* * *

BOTH *POVERTY* AND *RICHES* ARE
THE OFFSPRING OF THOUGHT

CHAPTER FOUR

AUTO-SUGGESTION:

THE MEDIUM FOR INFLUENCING THE SUBCONSCIOUS MIND:
The Third Step toward Riches

AUTO-SUGGESTION is a term which applies to all suggestions and all self-administered stimuli which reach one's mind through the five senses. Stated in another way, auto-suggestion is self-suggestion. It is the agency of communication between that part of the mind where conscious thought takes place, and that which serves as the seat of action for the subconscious mind.

Through the dominating thoughts which one permits to remain in the conscious mind, (whether these thoughts be negative or positive, is immaterial) the principle of auto-suggestion voluntarily reaches the subconscious mind and influences it with these thoughts.

NO THOUGHT, whether it be negative or positive, CAN ENTER THE SUBCONSCIOUS MIND WITHOUT THE AID OF THE PRINCIPLE OF AUTO-SUGGESTION, with the exception of thoughts picked up from the ether. Stated differently, all sense impressions which are perceived through the five senses, are stopped by the CONSCIOUS thinking mind, and may be either passed on to the subconscious mind, or rejected, at will. The conscious faculty serves, therefore, as an outerguard to the approach of the subconscious.

Nature has so built man that he has ABSOLUTE CONTROL over the material which reaches his subconscious mind, through his five senses, although this is not meant to be construed as a statement that man always EXERCISES this control. In the great majority of instances, he does NOT exercise it, which explains why so many people go through life in poverty.

Recall what has been said about the subconscious mind resembling a fertile garden spot, in which weeds will grow in abundance, if the seeds of more desirable crops are not sown therein. AUTO-SUGGESTION is the agency of control through which an individual may voluntarily feed his subconscious mind on thoughts of a creative nature, or, by neglect, permit thoughts of a destructive nature to find their way into this rich garden of the mind.

You were instructed, in the last of the six steps described in the chapter on Desire, to read ALOUD twice daily the WRITTEN statement of your DESIRE FOR MONEY, and to SEE AND FEEL yourself ALREADY in possession of the money!

By following these instructions, you communicate the object of your DESIRE directly to your SUBCONSCIOUS mind in a spirit of absolute FAITH. Through repetition of this procedure, you voluntarily create thought habits which are favorable to your efforts to transmute desire into its monetary equivalent.

Go back to these six steps described in chapter two, and read them again, very carefully, before you proceed further. Then (when you come to it), read very carefully the four instructions for the organization of your "Master Mind" group, described in the chapter on Organized Planning. By comparing these two sets of instructions with that which has been stated on auto-suggestion, you, of course, will see that the instructions involve the application of the principle of auto-suggestion.

Remember, therefore, when reading aloud the statement of your desire (through which you are endeavoring to develop a "money consciousness"), that the mere reading of the words is of NO CONSEQUENCE—UNLESS you mix emotion, or feeling with your words. If you repeat a million times the famous Emil Coué formula, "Day by day, in every way, I am getting better and better," without mixing emotion and FAITH with your words, you will experience no desirable results. Your subconscious mind recognizes and acts upon ONLY thoughts which have been well-mixed with emotion or feeling.

This is a fact of such importance as to warrant repetition in practically every chapter, because the lack of understanding of this is the main reason the majority of people who try to apply the principle of auto-suggestion get no desirable results.

Plain, unemotional words do not influence the subconscious mind. You will get no appreciable results until you learn to reach your subconscious mind with thoughts, or spoken words which have been well emotionalized with BELIEF.

Do not become discouraged, if you cannot control and direct your emotions the first time you try to do so. Remember, there is no such possibility as SOMETHING FOR NOTHING. Ability to reach, and influence your subconscious mind has its price, and you MUST PAY THAT PRICE. You cannot cheat, even if you desire to do so. The price of ability to influence your subconscious mind is everlasting PERSISTENCE in applying the principles described here. You cannot develop the desired ability for a lower price. You, and YOU ALONE, must decide whether or not the reward for which you are striving (the "money consciousness"), is worth the price you must pay for it in effort.

Wisdom and "cleverness" alone, will not attract and retain money except in a few very rare instances, where the law of averages favors the attraction of money through these sources. The method of attracting money described here, does not depend upon the law of averages. Moreover, the method plays no favorites. It will work for one person as effectively as it will for another. Where failure is experienced, it is the individual, *not the method*, which has failed. If you try and fail, make another effort, and still another, until you succeed.

Your ability to use the principle of auto-suggestion will depend, very largely, upon your capacity to CONCENTRATE upon a given DESIRE until that desire becomes a BURNING OBSESSION.

When you begin to carry out the instructions in connection with the six steps described in the second chapter, it will be necessary for you to make use of the principle of CONCENTRATION.

Let us here offer suggestions for the effective use of concentration. When you begin to carry out the first of the six steps, which instructs you to "fix in your own mind the EXACT amount of money you desire," hold your thoughts on that amount of money by CONCENTRATION, or fixation of attention, with your eyes closed, until you can ACTUALLY SEE the physical appearance of the money. Do this at least once each day. As you go through these exercises, follow the instructions given in the chapter on FAITH, and see yourself actually IN POSSESSION OF THE MONEY!

Here is a most significant fact—the subconscious mind takes any orders given it in a spirit of absolute FAITH, and acts upon those orders, although the orders often have to be presented *over and over again*, through repetition, before they are interpreted by the subconscious mind. Following the preceding statement, consider the possibility of playing a perfectly legitimate "trick" on your subconscious mind, by making it believe, *because you believe it*, that you must have the amount of money you are visualizing, that this money is already awaiting your claim, that the subconscious mind MUST hand over to you practical plans for acquiring the money which is yours.

Hand over the thought suggested in the preceding paragraph to your IMAGINATION, and see what your imagination can, or will do, to create practical plans for the accumulation of money through transmutation of your desire.

DO NOT WAIT for a definite, plan, through which you intend to exchange services or merchandise in return for the money you are visualizing, but begin at once to see yourself in possession of the money, DEMANDING and EXPECTING meanwhile, that your subconscious mind will hand over the plan, or plans you need. Be on the alert for these plans, and when they appear, put them into ACTION IMMEDIATELY. When the plans appear, they will probably "flash" into your mind through the sixth sense, in the form of an "inspiration." This inspiration may be considered a direct "telegram," or message from Infinite Intelligence. Treat it with respect, and act upon it as soon as you receive it. Failure to do this will be FATAL to your success.

In the fourth of the six steps, you were instructed to "Create a definite plan for carrying out your desire, and begin at once to put this plan into action." You should follow this instruction in the manner described in the preceding paragraph. Do not trust to your "reason" when creating your plan for accumulating money through the transmutation of desire. Your reason is faulty. Moreover, your reasoning faculty may be lazy, and, if you depend entirely upon it to serve you, it may disappoint you.

When visualizing the money you intend to accumulate, (with closed eyes), *see yourself rendering the service, or delivering the merchandise you intend to give in return for this money. This is important!*

SUMMARY OF INSTRUCTIONS

The fact that you are reading this book is an indication that you earnestly seek knowledge. It is also an indication that you are a student of this subject. If you are only a student, there is a chance that you may learn much that you did not know, but you will learn only by assuming an attitude of humility. If you choose to follow some of the instructions but neglect, or refuse to follow others—*you will fail!* To get satisfactory results, you must follow ALL instructions in a spirit of FAITH.

The instructions given in connection with the six steps in the second chapter will now be summarized, and blended with the principles covered by this chapter, as follows:

First. Go into some quiet spot (preferably in bed at night) where you will not be disturbed or interrupted, close your eyes, and repeat aloud, (so you may hear your own words) the written statement of the amount of money you intend to accumulate, the time limit for its accumulation, and a description of the service or merchandise you intend to give in return for the money. As you carry out these instructions, SEE YOURSELF ALREADY IN POSSESSION OF THE MONEY.

For example: —Suppose that you intend to accumulate $50,000 by the first of January, five years hence, that you intend to give personal services in return for the money, in the capacity of a salesman. Your written statement of your purpose should be similar to the following:

"By the first day of January, 19.., I will have in my possession $50,000, which will come to me in various amounts from time to time during the interim.

"In return for this money I will give the most efficient service of which I am capable, rendering the fullest possible quantity, and the best possible quality of service in the capacity of salesman of .... (describe the service or merchandise you intend to sell).

"I believe that I will have this money in my possession. My faith is so strong that I can now see this money before my eyes. I can touch it with my hands. It is now awaiting transfer to me at the time, and in the proportion that I deliver the service I intend to render in return for it. I am awaiting a plan by which to accumulate this money, and I will follow that plan, when it is received."

Second. Repeat this program night and morning until you can see, (in your imagination) the money you intend to accumulate.

Third. Place a written copy of your statement where you can see it night and morning, and read it just before retiring, and upon arising until it has been memorized.

Remember, as you carry out these instructions, that you are applying the principle of auto-suggestion, for the purpose of giving orders to your subconscious mind. Remember, also, that your subconscious mind will act ONLY upon instructions which are emotionalized, and handed over to it with "feeling." FAITH is the strongest, and most productive of the emotions. Follow the instructions given in the chapter on FAITH.

These instructions may, at first, seem abstract. Do not let this disturb you. Follow the instructions, no matter how abstract or impractical they may, at first, appear to be. The time will soon come, if you do as you have been instructed, *in spirit as well as in act,* when a whole new universe of power will unfold to you.

Scepticism, in connection with ALL new ideas, is characteristic of all human beings. But if you follow the instructions outlined, your scepticism will soon be replaced by belief, and this, in turn, will soon become crystallized into ABSOLUTE FAITH. Then you will have arrived at the point where you may truly say, "I am the master of my fate, I am the captain of my soul!"

Many philosophers have made the statement, that man is the master of his own *earthly* destiny, but most of them have failed to say *why* he is the master. The reason that man may be the master of his own earthly status, and especially his financial status, is thoroughly explained in this chapter. Man may become the master of himself, and of his environment, because he has the POWER TO INFLUENCE HIS OWN SUBCONSCIOUS MIND, and through it, gain the cooperation of Infinite Intelligence.

You are now reading the chapter which represents the keystone to the arch of this philosophy. The instructions contained in this chapter must be understood and APPLIED WITH PERSISTENCE, if you succeed in transmuting desire into money.

The actual performance of transmuting DESIRE into money, involves the use of auto-suggestion as an agency by which one may reach, and influence, the subconscious mind. The other principles are simply tools with which to apply auto-suggestion. Keep this thought in mind, and you will, at all times, be conscious of the important part the principle of auto-suggestion is to play in your efforts to accumulate money through the methods described in this book.

Carry out these instructions as though you were a small child. Inject into your efforts something of the FAITH of a child. The author has been most careful, to see that no impractical instructions were included, because of his sincere desire to be helpful.

After you have read the entire book, come back to this chapter, and follow in spirit, and in action, this instruction:

READ THE ENTIRE CHAPTER ALOUD ONCE EVERY NIGHT, UNTIL YOU BECOME THOROUGHLY CONVINCED THAT THE PRINCIPLE OF AUTO-SUGGESTION IS SOUND, THAT IT WILL ACCOMPLISH FOR YOU ALL THAT HAS BEEN CLAIMED FOR IT. AS YOU READ, *UNDERSCORE WITH A PENCIL* EVERY SENTENCE WHICH IMPRESSES YOU FAVORABLY.

Follow the foregoing instruction to the letter, and it will open the way for a complete understanding, and mastery of the principles of success.

CHAPTER FIVE

SPECIALIZED KNOWLEDGE:
PERSONAL EXPERIENCES OR OBSERVATIONS
The Fourth Step toward Riches

THERE are two kinds of knowledge. One is general, the other is specialized. General knowledge, no matter how great in quantity or variety it may be, is of but little use in the accumulation of money. The faculties of the great universities possess, in the aggregate, practically every form of general knowledge known to civilization. *Most of the professors have but little or no money.* They specialize on *teaching* knowledge, but they do not specialize on the organization, or the *use* of knowledge.

KNOWLEDGE will not attract money, unless it is organized, and intelligently directed, through practical PLANS OF ACTION, to the DEFINITE END of accumulation of money. Lack of understanding of this fact has been the source of confusion to millions of people who falsely believe that "knowledge is power." It is nothing of the sort! Knowledge is only *potential* power. It becomes power only when, and if, it is organized into definite plans of action, and directed to a definite end.

This "missing link" in all systems of education known to civilization today, may be found in the failure of educational institutions to teach their students HOW TO ORGANIZE AND USE KNOWLEDGE AFTER THEY ACQUIRE IT.

Many people make the mistake of assuming that, because Henry Ford had but little "schooling," he is not a man of "education." Those who make this mistake do not know Henry Ford, nor do they understand the real meaning of the word "educate." That word is derived from the Latin word "educo," meaning to educe, to draw out, to DEVELOP FROM WITHIN.

An educated man is not, necessarily, one who has an abundance of general or specialized knowledge. An educated man is one who has so developed the faculties of his mind that he may acquire anything he wants, or its equivalent, without violating the rights of others. Henry Ford comes well within the meaning of this definition.

During the world war, a Chicago newspaper published certain editorials in which, among other statements, Henry Ford was called "an ignorant pacifist." Mr. Ford objected to the statements, and brought suit against the paper for libeling him. When the suit was tried in the Courts, the attorneys for the paper pleaded justification, and placed Mr. Ford, himself, on the witness stand, for the purpose of proving to the jury that he was ignorant. The attorneys asked Mr. Ford a great variety of questions, all of them intended to prove, by his own evidence, that, while he might possess considerable specialized knowledge pertaining to the manufacture of automobiles, he was, in the main, ignorant.

Mr. Ford was plied with such questions as the following:

"Who was Benedict Arnold?" and "How many soldiers did the British send over to America to put down the Rebellion of 1776?" In answer to the last question, Mr. Ford replied, "I do not know the exact number of soldiers the British sent over, but I have heard that it was a considerably larger number than ever went back."

Finally, Mr. Ford became tired of this line of questioning, and in reply to a particularly offensive question, he leaned over, pointed his finger at the lawyer who had asked the question, and said, "If I should really WANT to answer the foolish question you have just asked, or any of the other questions you have been asking me, let me remind you that I have a row of electric push-buttons on my desk, and by pushing the right button, I can summon to my aid men who can answer ANY question I desire to ask concerning the business to which I am devoting most of my efforts. Now, will you kindly tell me, WHY I should clutter up my mind with general knowledge, for the purpose of being able to answer questions, when I have men around me who can supply any knowledge I require?"

There certainly was good logic to that reply.

That answer floored the lawyer. Every person in the courtroom realized it was the answer, not of an ignorant man, but of a man of EDUCATION. Any man is educated who knows where to get knowledge when he needs it, and how to organize that knowledge into definite plans of action. Through the assistance of his "Master Mind" group, Henry Ford had at his command all the specialized knowledge he needed to enable him to become one of the wealthiest men in America. *It was not essential that he have this knowledge in his own mind.* Surely no person who has sufficient inclination and intelligence to read a book of this nature can possibly miss the significance of this illustration.

Before you can be sure of your ability to transmute DESIRE into its monetary equivalent, you will require SPECIALIZED KNOWLEDGE of the service, merchandise, or profession which you intend to offer in return for fortune. Perhaps you may need much more specialized knowledge than you have the ability or the inclination to acquire, and if this should be true, you may bridge your weakness through the aid of your "Master Mind" group.

Andrew Carnegie stated that he, personally, knew nothing about the technical end of the steel business; moreover, he did not particularly care to know anything about it. The specialized knowledge which he required for the manufacture and marketing of steel, he found available through the individual units of his MASTER MIND GROUP.

The accumulation of great fortunes calls for POWER, and power is acquired through highly organized and intelligently directed specialized knowledge, but that knowledge does not, necessarily, have to be in the possession of the man who accumulates the fortune.

The preceding paragraph should give hope and encouragement to the man with ambition to accumulate a fortune, who has not possessed himself of the necessary "education" to supply such specialized knowledge as he may require. Men sometimes go through life suffering from "inferiority complexes," because they are not men of "education." The man who can organize and direct a "Master Mind" group of men who possess knowledge useful in the accumulation of money, is just as much a man of education as any man in the group. REMEMBER THIS, if you suffer from a feeling of inferiority, because your schooling has been limited.

Thomas A. Edison had only three months of "schooling" during his entire life. He did not lack education, neither did he die poor.

Henry Ford had less than a sixth grade "schooling" but he has managed to do pretty well by himself, financially.

SPECIALIZED KNOWLEDGE is among the most plentiful, and the cheapest forms of service which may be had! If you doubt this, consult the payroll of any university.

IT PAYS TO KNOW HOW TO PURCHASE KNOWLEDGE

First of all, decide the sort of specialized knowledge you require, and the purpose for which it is needed. To a large extent your major purpose in life, the goal toward which you are working, will help determine what knowledge you need. With this question settled, your next move requires that you have accurate information concerning dependable sources of knowledge. The more important of these are:

(a) One's own experience and education
(b) Experience and education available through cooperation of others (Master Mind Alliance)
(c) Colleges and Universities
(d) Public Libraries (Through books and periodicals in which may be found all the knowledge organized by civilization)
(e) Special Training Courses (Through night schools and home study schools in particular.)

As knowledge is acquired it must be organized and put into use, for a definite purpose, through practical plans. Knowledge has no value except that which can be gained from its application toward some worthy end. This is one reason why college degrees are not valued more highly. They represent nothing but miscellaneous knowledge.

If you contemplate taking additional schooling, first determine the purpose for which you want the knowledge you are seeking, then learn where this particular sort of knowledge can be obtained, from reliable sources.

Successful men, in all callings, never stop acquiring specialized knowledge related to their major purpose, business, or profession. Those who are not successful usually make the mistake of believing that the knowledge acquiring period ends when one finishes school. The truth is that schooling does but little more than to put one in the way of learning how to acquire practical knowledge.

With this Changed World which began at the end of the economic collapse, came also astounding changes in educational requirements. The order of the day is SPECIALIZATION! This truth was emphasized by Robert P. Moore, secretary of appointments of Columbia University.

"SPECIALISTS MOST SOUGHT

"Particularly sought after by employing companies are candidates who have specialized in some field—business-school graduates with training in accounting and statistics, engineers of all varieties, journalists, architects, chemists, and also outstanding leaders and activity men of the senior class.

"The man who has been active on the campus, whose personality is such that he gets along with all kinds of people and who has done an adequate job with his studies has a most decided edge over the strictly academic student. Some of these, because of their all-around qualifications, have received several offers of positions, a few of them as many as six.

"In departing from the conception that the 'straight A' student was invariably the one to get the choice of the better jobs, Mr. Moore said that most companies look not only to academic records but to activity records and personalities of the students.

"One of the largest industrial companies, the leader in its field, in writing to Mr. Moore concerning prospective seniors at the college, said:

"We are interested primarily in finding men who can make exceptional progress in management work. For this reason we emphasize qualities of character, intelligence and personality far more than specific educational background."

"APPRENTICESHIP' PROPOSED

"Proposing a system of 'apprenticing' students in offices, stores and industrial occupations during the summer vacation, Mr. Moore asserts that after the first two or three years of college, every student should be asked 'to choose a definite future course and to call a halt if he has been merely pleasantly drifting without purpose through an unspecialized academic curriculum.'

"Colleges and universities must face the practical consideration that all professions and occupations now demand specialists," he said, urging that educational institutions accept more direct responsibility for vocational guidance.

One of the most reliable and practical sources of knowledge available to those who need specialized schooling, is the night schools operated in most large cities. The correspondence schools give specialized training anywhere the U.S. mails go, on all subjects that can be taught by the extension method. One advantage of home study training is the flexibility of the study program which permits one to study during spare time. Another stupendous advantage of home study training (if the school is carefully chosen), is the fact that most courses offered by home study schools carry with them generous privileges of consultation which can be of priceless value to those needing specialized knowledge. No matter where you live, you can share the benefits.

Anything acquired without effort, and without cost is generally unappreciated, often discredited; perhaps this is why we get so little from our marvelous opportunity in public schools. The SELF-DISCIPLINE one receives from a definite program of specialized study makes up to some extent, for the wasted opportunity when knowledge was available without cost. Correspondence schools are highly organized business institutions. Their tuition fees are so low that they are forced to insist upon prompt payments. Being asked to pay, whether the student makes good grades or poor, has the effect of causing one to follow through with the course when he would otherwise drop it. The correspondence schools have not stressed this point sufficiently, for the truth is that their collection departments constitute the very finest sort of training on DECISION, PROMPTNESS, ACTION and THE HABIT OF FINISHING THAT WHICH ONE BEGINS.

I learned this from experience, more than twenty-five years ago. I enrolled for a home study course in Advertising. After completing eight or ten lessons I stopped studying, but the school did not stop sending me bills. Moreover, it insisted upon payment, whether I kept up my studies or not. I decided that if I had to pay for the course (which I had legally obligated myself to do), I should complete the lessons and get my money's worth. I felt, at the time, that the collection system of the school was somewhat too well organized, but I learned later in life that it was a valuable part of my training for which no charge had been made. Being forced to pay, I went ahead and completed the course. Later in life I discovered that the efficient collection system of that school had been worth much in the form of money earned, because of the training in advertising I had so reluctantly taken.

We have in this country what is said to be the greatest public school system in the world. We have invested fabulous sums for fine buildings, we have provided convenient transportation for children living in the rural districts, so they may attend the best schools, but there is one astounding weakness to this marvelous system—IT IS FREE! One of the strange things about human beings is that they value only that which has a price. The free schools of America, and the free public libraries, do not impress people *because they are free*. This is the major reason why so many people find it necessary to acquire additional training after they quit school and go to work. It is also one of the major reasons why EMPLOYERS GIVE GREATER CONSIDERATION TO EMPLOYEES WHO TAKE HOME STUDY COURSES. They have learned, from experience, that any person who has the ambition to give up a part of his spare time to studying at home has in him those qualities which make for leadership. This recognition is not a charitable gesture, it is sound business judgment upon the part of the employers.

There is one weakness in people for which there is no remedy. It is the universal weakness of LACK OF AMBITION! Persons, especially salaried people, who schedule their spare time, to provide for home study, seldom remain at the bottom very long. Their action opens the way for the upward climb, removes many obstacles from their path, and gains the friendly interest of those who have the power to put them in the way of OPPORTUNITY.

The home study method of training is especially suited to the needs of employed people who find, after leaving school, that they must acquire additional specialized knowledge, but cannot spare the time to go back to school.

The changed economic conditions prevailing since the depression have made it necessary for thousands of people to find additional, or new sources of income. For the majority of these, the solution to their problem may be found only by acquiring specialized knowledge. Many will be forced to change their occupations entirely. When a merchant finds that a certain line of merchandise is not selling, he usually supplants it with another that is in demand. The person whose business is that of marketing personal services must also be an efficient merchant. If his services do not bring adequate returns in one occupation, he must change to another, where broader opportunities are available.

Stuart Austin Wier prepared himself as a Construction Engineer and followed this line of work until the depression limited his market to where it did not give him the income he required. He took inventory of himself, decided to change his profession to law, went back to school and took special courses by which he prepared himself as a corporation lawyer. Despite the fact the depression had not ended, he completed his training, passed the Bar Examination, and quickly built a lucrative law practice, in Dallas, Texas; in fact he is turning away clients.

Just to keep the record straight, and to anticipate the alibis of those who will say, "I couldn't go to school because I have a family to support," or "I'm too old," I will add the information that Mr. Wier was past forty, and married when he went back to school. Moreover, by carefully selecting highly specialized courses, in colleges best prepared to teach the subjects chosen, Mr. Wier completed in two years the work for which the majority of law students require four years. IT PAYS TO KNOW HOW TO PURCHASE KNOWLEDGE!

The person who stops studying merely because he has finished school is forever hopelessly doomed to mediocrity, no matter what may be his calling. The way of success is the way of continuous pursuit of knowledge.

Let us consider a specific instance.

During the depression a salesman in a grocery store found himself without a position. Having had some bookkeeping experience, he took a special course in accounting, familiarized himself with all the latest bookkeeping and office equipment, and went into business for himself. Starting with the grocer for whom he had formerly worked, he made contracts with more than 100 small merchants to keep their books, at a very nominal monthly fee. His idea was so practical that he soon found it necessary to set up a portable office in a light delivery truck, which he equipped with modern bookkeeping machinery. He now has a fleet of these book-keeping offices "on wheels" and employs a large staff of assistants, thus providing small merchants with accounting service equal to the best that money can buy, at very nominal cost.

Specialized knowledge, plus imagination, were the ingredients that went into this unique and successful business. Last year the owner of that business paid an income tax of almost ten times as much as was paid by the merchant for whom he worked when the depression forced upon him a temporary adversity which proved to be a blessing in disguise.

The beginning of this successful business was an IDEA!

Inasmuch as I had the privilege of supplying the unemployed salesman with that idea, I now assume the further privilege of suggesting another idea which has within it the possibility of even greater income. Also the possibility of rendering useful service to thousands of people who badly need that service.

The idea was suggested by the salesman who gave up selling and went into the business of keeping books on a wholesale basis. When the plan was suggested as a solution of his unemployment problem, he quickly exclaimed, "I like the idea, but I would not know how to turn it into cash." In other words, he complained he would not know how to market his bookkeeping knowledge *after he acquired it.*

So, that brought up another problem which had to be solved. With the aid of a young woman typist, clever at hand lettering, and who could put the story together, a very attractive book was prepared, describing the advantages of the new system of bookkeeping. The pages were neatly typed and pasted in an ordinary scrapbook, which was used as a silent salesman with which the story of this new business was so effectively told that its owner soon had more accounts than he could handle.

There are thousands of people, all over the country, who need the services of a merchandising specialist capable of preparing an attractive brief for use in marketing personal services. The aggregate annual income from such a service might easily exceed that received by the largest employment agency, and the benefits of the service might be made far greater to the purchaser than any to be obtained from an employment agency.

The IDEA here described was born of necessity, to bridge an emergency which had to be covered, but it did not stop by merely serving one person. The woman who created the idea has a keen IMAGINATION. She saw in her newly born brain-child the making of a new profession, one that is destined to render valuable service to thousands of people who need practical guidance in marketing personal services.

Spurred to action by the instantaneous success of her first "PREPARED PLAN TO MARKET PERSONAL SERVICES," this energetic woman turned next to the solution of a similar problem for her son who had just finished college, but had been totally unable to find a market for his services. The plan she originated for his use was the finest specimen of merchandising of personal services I have ever seen.

When the plan book had been completed, it contained nearly fifty pages of beautifully typed, properly organized information, telling the story of her son's native ability, schooling, personal experiences, and a great variety of other information too extensive for description. The plan book also contained a complete description of the position her son desired, together with a marvelous word picture of the exact plan he would use in filling the position.

The preparation of the plan book required several week's labor, during which time its creator sent her son to the public library almost daily, to procure data needed in selling his services to best advantage. She sent him, also to all the competitors of his prospective employer, and gathered from them vital information concerning their business methods which was of great value in the formation of the plan he intended to use in filling the position he sought. When the plan had been finished, it contained more than half a dozen very fine suggestions for the use and benefit of the prospective employer. (The suggestions were put into use by the company).

One may be inclined to ask, "Why go to all this trouble to secure a job?" The answer is straight to the point, also it is dramatic, because it deals with a subject which assumes the proportion of a tragedy with millions of men and women whose sole source of income is personal services.

The answer is, "DOING A THING WELL NEVER IS TROUBLE! THE PLAN PREPARED BY THIS WOMAN FOR THE BENEFIT OF HER SON, HELPED HIM GET THE JOB FOR WHICH HE APPLIED, AT THE FIRST INTERVIEW, AT A SALARY FIXED BY HIMSELF."

Moreover—and this, too, is important—THE POSITION DID NOT REQUIRE THE YOUNG MAN TO START AT THE BOTTOM. HE BEGAN AS A JUNIOR EXECUTIVE, AT AN EXECUTIVE'S SALARY.

"Why go to all this trouble?" do you ask?

Well, for one thing, the PLANNED PRESENTATION of this young man's application for a position clipped off no less than ten years of time he would have required to get to where he began, had he "started at the bottom and worked his way up."

This idea of starting at the bottom and working one's way up may appear to be sound, but the major objection to it is this—too many of those who begin at the bottom never manage to lift their heads high enough to be seen by OPPORTUNITY, so they remain at the bottom. It should be remembered, also, that the outlook from the bottom is not so very bright or encouraging. It has a tendency to kill off ambition. We call it "getting into a rut," which means that we accept our fate because we form the HABIT of daily routine, a habit that finally becomes so strong we cease to try to throw it off. And that is another reason why it pays to start one or two steps above the bottom. By so doing one forms the HABIT of looking around, of observing how others get ahead, of seeing OPPORTUNITY, and of embracing it without hesitation.

Dan Halpin is a splendid example of what I mean. During his college days, he was manager of the famous 1930 National Championship Notre Dame football team, when it was under the direction of the late Knute Rockne.

Perhaps he was inspired by the great football coach to aim high, and NOT MISTAKE TEMPORARY DEFEAT FOR FAILURE, just as Andrew Carnegie, the great industrial leader, inspired his young business lieutenants to set high goals for themselves. At any rate, young Halpin finished college at a mighty unfavorable time, when the depression had made jobs scarce, so, after a fling at investment banking and motion pictures, he took the first opening with a potential future he could find—selling electrical hearing aids on a commission basis. ANYONE COULD START IN THAT SORT OF JOB, AND HALPIN KNEW IT, but it was enough to open the door of opportunity to him.

For almost two years, he continued in a job not to his liking, and he would never have risen above that job if he had not done something about his dissatisfaction. He aimed, first, at the job of Assistant Sales Manager of his company, and got the job. That one step upward placed him high enough above the crowd to enable him to see still greater opportunity, also, it placed him where OPPORTUNITY COULD SEE HIM.

He made such a fine record selling hearing aids, that A. M. Andrews, Chairman of the Board of the Dictograph Products Company, a business competitor of the company for which Halpin worked, wanted to know something about that man Dan Halpin who was taking big sales away from the long established Dictograph Company. He sent for Halpin. When the interview was over, Halpin was the new Sales Manager, in charge of the Acousticon Division. Then, to test young Halpin's metal, Mr. Andrews went away to Florida for three months, leaving him to sink or swim in his new job. He did not sink! Knute Rockne's spirit of "All the world loves a winner, and has no time for a loser," inspired him to put so much into his job that he was recently elected Vice-President of the company, and General Manager of the Acousticon and Silent Radio Division, a job which most men would be proud to earn through ten years of loyal effort. Halpin turned the trick in little more than six months.

It is difficult to say whether Mr. Andrews or Mr. Halpin is more deserving of eulogy, for the reason that both showed evidence of having an abundance of that very rare quality known as IMAGINATION. Mr. Andrews deserves credit for seeing, in young Halpin, a "go-getter" of the highest order. Halpin deserves credit for REFUSING TO COMPROMISE WITH LIFE BY ACCEPTING AND KEEPING A JOB HE DID NOT WANT, and that is one of the major points I am trying to emphasize through this entire philosophy—that we rise to high positions or remain at the bottom BECAUSE OF CONDITIONS WE CAN CONTROL IF WE DESIRE TO CONTROL THEM.

I am also trying to emphasize another point, namely, that both success and failure are largely the results of HABIT! I have not the slightest doubt that Dan

Halpin's close association with the greatest football coach America ever knew, planted in his mind the same brand of DESIRE to excel which made the Notre Dame football team world famous. Truly, there is something to the idea that hero-worship is helpful, provided one worships a WINNER. Halpin tells me that Rockne was one of the world's greatest leaders of men in all history.

My belief in the theory that business associations are vital factors, both in failure and in success, was recently demonstrated, when my son Blair was negotiating with Dan Halpin for a position. Mr. Halpin offered him a beginning salary of about one half what he could have gotten from a rival company. I brought parental pressure to bear, and induced him to accept the place with Mr. Halpin, because I BELIEVE THAT CLOSE ASSOCIATION WITH ONE WHO REFUSES TO COMPROMISE WITH CIRCUMSTANCES HE DOES NOT LIKE, IS AN ASSET THAT CAN NEVER BE MEASURED IN TERMS OF MONEY.

The bottom is a monotonous, dreary, unprofitable place for any person. That is why I have taken the time to describe how lowly beginnings may be circumvented by proper planning. Also, that is why so much space has been devoted to a description of this new profession, created by a woman who was inspired to do a fine job of PLANNING because she wanted her son to have a favorable "break."

With the changed conditions ushered in by the world economic collapse, came also the need for newer and better ways of marketing PERSONAL SERVICES. It is hard to determine why someone had not previously discovered this stupendous need, in view of the fact that more money changes hands in return for personal services than for any other purpose. The sum paid out monthly, to people who work for wages and salaries, is so huge that it runs into hundreds of millions, and the annual distribution amounts to billions.

Perhaps some will find, in the IDEA here briefly described, the nucleus of the riches they DESIRE! Ideas with much less merit have been the seedlings from which great fortunes have grown. Woolworth's Five and Ten Cent Store idea, for example, had far less merit, but it piled up a fortune for its creator.

Those seeing OPPORTUNITY lurking in this suggestion will find valuable aid in the chapter on Organized Planning. Incidentally, an efficient merchandiser of personal services would find a growing demand for his services wherever there are men and women who seek better markets for their services. By applying the Master Mind principle, a few people with suitable talent, could form an alliance, and have a paying business very quickly. One would need to be a fair writer, with a flair for advertising and selling, one handy at typing and hand lettering, and one should be a first class business getter who would let the world know about the service. If one person possessed all these abilities, he might carry on the business alone, until it outgrew him.

The woman who prepared the "Personal Service Sales Plan" for her son now receives requests from all parts of the country for her cooperation in preparing similar plans for others who desire to market their personal services for more money.

She has a staff of expert typists, artists, and writers who have the ability to drama-tize the case history so effectively that one's personal services can be marketed for much more money than the prevailing wages for similar services. She is so confi-dent of her ability that she accepts, as the major portion of her fee, a percentage of the *increased* pay she helps her clients to earn.

It must not be supposed that her plan merely consists of clever salesmanship by which she helps men and women to demand and receive more money for the same services they formerly sold for less pay. She looks after the interests of the purchaser as well as the seller of personal services, and so prepares her plans that the employer receives full value for the additional money he pays. The method by which she accomplishes this astonishing result is a professional secret which she discloses to no one excepting her own clients.

If you have the IMAGINATION, and seek a more profitable outlet for your per-sonal services, this suggestion may be the stimulus for which you have been searching. The IDEA is capable of yielding an income far greater than that of the "average" doctor, lawyer, or engineer whose education required several years in college. The idea is saleable to those seeking new positions, in practically all posi-tions calling for managerial or executive ability, and those desiring re-arrangement of incomes in their present positions.

There is no fixed price for sound IDEAS!

Back of all IDEAS is specialized knowledge. Unfortunately, for those who do not find riches in abundance, specialized knowledge is more abundant and more easily acquired than IDEAS. Because of this very truth, there is a universal demand and an ever-increasing opportunity for the person capable of helping men and women to sell their personal services advantageously. Capability means IMAGINA-TION, the one quality needed to combine specialized knowledge with IDEAS, in the form of ORGANIZED PLANS designed to yield riches.

If you have IMAGINATION this chapter may present you with an idea sufficient to serve as the beginning of the riches you desire. Remember, the IDEA is the main thing. Specialized knowledge may be found just around the corner—any corner!

CHAPTER SIX

IMAGINATION:
THE WORKSHOP OF THE MIND
The Fifth Step toward Riches

THE imagination is literally the workshop wherein are fashioned all plans created by man. The impulse, the DESIRE, is given shape, form, and ACTION through the aid of the imaginative faculty of the mind.

It has been said that man can create anything which he can imagine.

Of all the ages of civilization, this is the most favorable for the development of the imagination, because it is an age of rapid change. On every hand one may contact stimuli which develop the imagination.

Through the aid of his imaginative faculty, man has discovered, and harnessed, more of Nature's forces during the past fifty years than during the entire history of the human race, previous to that time. He has conquered the air so completely, that the birds are a poor match for him in flying. He has harnessed the ether, and made it serve as a means of instantaneous communication with any part of the world. He has analyzed, and weighed the sun at a distance of millions of miles, and has determined, through the aid of IMAGINATION, the elements of which it consists. He has discovered that his own brain is both a broadcasting, and a receiving station for the vibration of thought, and he is beginning now to learn how to make practical use of this discovery. He has increased the speed of locomotion, until he may now travel at a speed of more than three hundred miles an hour. The time will soon come when a man may breakfast in New York, and lunch in San Francisco.

MAN'S ONLY LIMITATION, within reason, LIES IN HIS DEVELOPMENT AND USE OF HIS IMAGINATION. He has not yet reached the apex of development in the use of his imaginative faculty. He has merely discovered that he has an imagination, and has commenced to use it in a very elementary way.

TWO FORMS OF IMAGINATION

The imaginative faculty functions in two forms. One is known as "synthetic imagination," and the other as "creative imagination."

SYNTHETIC IMAGINATION:—Through this faculty, one may arrange old concepts, ideas, or plans into new combinations. This faculty *creates* nothing. It merely works with the material of experience, education, and observation with which it is fed. It is the faculty used most by the inventor, with the exception of the "genius" who draws upon the creative imagination, when he cannot solve his problem through synthetic imagination.

CREATIVE IMAGINATION: —Through the faculty of creative imagination, the finite mind of man has direct communication with Infinite Intelligence. It is the faculty through which "hunches" and "inspirations" are received. It is by this faculty that all basic, or new ideas axe handed over to man. It is through this faculty that thought vibrations from the minds of others are received. It is through this faculty that one individual may "tune in," or communicate with the subconscious minds of other men.

The creative imagination works automatically, in the manner described in subsequent pages. This faculty functions ONLY when the conscious mind is vibrating at an exceedingly rapid rate, as for example, when the conscious mind is stimulated through the emotion of a *strong desire*.

The creative faculty becomes more alert, more receptive to vibrations from the sources mentioned, in proportion to its development through USE. This statement is significant! Ponder over it before passing on.

Keep in mind as you follow these principles, that the entire story of how one may convert DESIRE into money cannot be told in one statement. The story will be complete, only when one has MASTERED, ASSIMILATED, and BEGUN TO MAKE USE of all the principles.

The great leaders of business, industry, finance, and the great artists, musicians, poets, and writers became great, because they developed the faculty of creative imagination.

Both the synthetic and creative faculties of imagination become more alert with use, just as any muscle or organ of the body develops through use.

Desire is only a thought, an impulse. It is nebulous and ephemeral. It is abstract, and of no value, until it has been transformed into its physical counterpart. While the synthetic imagination is the one which will be used most frequently, in the process of transforming the impulse of DESIRE into money, you must keep in mind the fact, that you may face circumstances and situations which demand use of the creative imagination as well.

Your imaginative faculty may have become weak through inaction. It can be revived and made alert through USE. This faculty does not die, though it may become quiescent through lack of use.

Center your attention, for the time being, on the development of the synthetic imagination, because this is the faculty which you will use more often in the process of converting desire into money.

Transformation of the intangible impulse, of DESIRE, into the tangible reality, of MONEY, calls for the use of a plan, or plans. These plans must be formed with the aid of the imagination, and mainly, with the synthetic faculty.

Read the entire book through, then come back to this chapter, and begin at once to put your imagination to work on the building of a plan, or plans, for the transformation of your DESIRE into money. Detailed instructions for the building of plans have been given in almost every chapter. Carry out the instructions best suited to your needs, reduce your plan to writing, if you have not already done so. The moment you complete this, you will have DEFINITELY given concrete form to the intangible DESIRE. Read the preceding sentence once more. Read it aloud, very slowly, and as you do so, remember that the moment you reduce the statement of your desire, and a plan for its realization, to writing, you have actually TAKEN THE FIRST of a series of steps, which will enable you to convert the thought into its physical counterpart.

The earth on which you live, you, yourself, and every other material thing are the result of evolutionary change, through which microscopic bits of matter have been organized and arranged in an orderly fashion.

Moreover—and this statement is of stupendous importance—this earth, every one of the billions of individual cells of your body, and every atom of matter, *began as an intangible form of energy.*

DESIRE is thought impulse! Thought impulses are forms of energy. When you begin with the thought impulse, DESIRE, to accumulate money, you are drafting into your service the same "stuff" that Nature used in creating this earth, and every material form in the universe, including the body and brain in which the thought impulses function.

As far as science has been able to determine, the entire universe consists of but two elements—matter and energy.

Through the combination of energy and matter, has been created everything perceptible to man, from the largest star which floats in the heavens, down to, and including man, himself.

You are now engaged in the task of trying to profit by Nature's method. You are (sincerely and earnestly, we hope), trying to adapt yourself to Nature's laws, by endeavoring to convert DESIRE into its physical or monetary equivalent. YOU CAN DO IT! IT HAS BEEN DONE BEFORE!

You can build a fortune through the aid of laws which are immutable. But, first, you must become familiar with these laws, and learn to USE them. Through repetition, and by approaching the description of these principles from every conceivable angle, the author hopes to reveal to you the secret through which every great fortune has been accumulated. Strange and paradoxical as it may seem, the "secret" is NOT A SECRET. Nature, herself, advertises it in the earth on which we live, the stars, the planets suspended within our view, in the elements above and around us, in every blade of grass, and every form of life within our vision.

Nature advertises this "secret" in the terms of biology, in the conversion of a tiny cell, so small that it may be lost on the point of a pin, into the HUMAN BEING now reading this line. The conversion of desire into its physical equivalent is, certainly, no more miraculous!

Do not become discouraged if you do not fully comprehend all that has been stated. Unless you have long been a student of the mind, it is not to be expected that you will assimilate all that is in this chapter upon a first reading.

But you will, in time, make good progress.

The principles which follow will open the way for understanding of imagination. Assimilate that which you understand, as you read this philosophy for the first time, then, when you reread and study it, you will discover that something has happened to clarify it, and give you a broader understanding of the whole. Above all, DO NOT STOP, nor hesitate in your study of these principles until you have read the book at least THREE times, for then, you will not want to stop.

HOW TO MAKE PRACTICAL USE OF IMAGINATION

Ideas are the beginning points of all fortunes. Ideas are products of the imagination. Let us examine a few well known ideas which have yielded huge fortunes, with the hope that these illustrations will convey definite information concerning the method by which imagination may be used in accumulating riches.

THE ENCHANTED KETTLE

Fifty years ago, an old country doctor drove to town, hitched his horse, quietly slipped into a drug store by the back door, and began "dickering" with the young drug clerk.

His mission was destined to yield great wealth to many people. It was destined to bring to the South the most far-flung benefit since the Civil War.

For more than an hour, behind the prescription counter, the old doctor and the clerk talked in low tones. Then the doctor left. He went out to the buggy and brought back a large, old fashioned kettle, a big wooden paddle (used for stirring the contents of the kettle), and deposited them in the back of the store.

The clerk inspected the kettle, reached into his inside pocket, took out a roll of bills, and handed it over to the doctor. The roll contained exactly $500.00—the clerk's entire savings!

The doctor handed over a small slip of paper on which was written a secret formula. The words on that small slip of paper were worth a King's ransom! *But not to the doctor!* Those magic words were needed to start the kettle to boiling, but neither the doctor nor the young clerk knew what fabulous fortunes were destined to flow from that kettle.

The old doctor was glad to sell the outfit for five hundred dollars. The money would pay off his debts, and give him freedom of mind. The clerk was taking a big chance by staking his entire life's savings on a mere scrap of paper and an old kettle! He never dreamed his investment would start a kettle to overflowing with gold that would surpass the miraculous performance of Aladdin's lamp.

What the clerk *really purchased* was an IDEA!

The old kettle and the wooden paddle, and the secret message on a slip of paper were incidental. The strange performance of that kettle began to take place after the new owner mixed with the secret instructions an ingredient of which the doctor knew nothing.

Read this story carefully, give your imagination a test! See if you can discover what it was that the young man added to the secret message, which caused the kettle to overflow with gold. Remember, as you read, that this is not a story from Arabian Nights. Here you have a story of facts, stranger than fiction, facts which began in the form of an IDEA.

Let us take a look at the vast fortunes of gold this idea has produced. It has paid, and still pays huge fortunes to men and women all over the world, who distribute the contents of the kettle to millions of people.

The Old Kettle is now one of the world's largest consumers of sugar, thus providing jobs of a permanent nature to thousands of men and women engaged in growing sugar cane, and in refining and marketing sugar.

The Old Kettle consumes, annually, millions of glass bottles, providing jobs to huge numbers of glass workers.

The Old Kettle gives employment to an army of clerks, stenographers, copy writers, and advertising experts throughout the nation. It has brought fame and fortune to scores of artists who have created magnificent pictures describing the product.

The Old Kettle has converted a small Southern city into the business capital of the South, where it now benefits, directly, or indirectly, every business and practically every resident of the city.

The influence of this idea now benefits every civilized country in the world, pouring out a continuous stream of gold to all who touch it.

Gold from the kettle built and maintains one of the most prominent colleges of the South, where thousands of young people receive the training essential for success.

The Old Kettle has done other marvelous things.

All through the world depression, when factories, banks and business houses were folding up and quitting by the thousands, the owner of this Enchanted Kettle went marching on, *giving continuous employment* to an army of men and women all over the world, and paying out extra portions of gold to those who, long ago, *had faith in the idea.*

If the product of that old brass kettle could talk, it would tell thrilling tales of romance in every language. Romances of love, romances of business, romances of professional men and women who are daily being stimulated by it.

The author is sure of at least one such romance, for he was a part of it, and it all began not far from the very spot on which the drug clerk purchased the old kettle. It was here that the author met his wife, and it was she who first told him of the Enchanted Kettle. It was the product of that Kettle they were drinking when he asked her to accept him "for better or worse."

Now that you know the content of the Enchanted Kettle is a world famous drink, it is fitting that the author confess that the home city of the drink supplied him with a wife, also that the drink itself provides him with *stimulation of thought without intoxication,* and thereby it serves to give the refreshment of mind which an author must have to do his best work.

Whoever you are, wherever you may live, whatever occupation you may be engaged in, just remember in the future, every time you see the words "Coca-Cola," that its vast empire of wealth and influence grew out of a single IDEA, and that the mysterious ingredient the drug clerk—Asa Candler—mixed with the secret formula was . . . IMAGINATION!

Stop and think of that, for a moment.

Remember, also, that the thirteen steps to riches, described in this book, were the media through which the influence of Coca-Cola has been extended to every city, town, village, and cross-roads of the world, and that ANY IDEA you may create, as *sound and meritorious* as Coca-Cola, has the possibility of duplicating the stupendous record of this world-wide thirst-killer.

Truly, thoughts are things, and their scope of operation is the world, itself.

WHAT I WOULD DO IF I HAD A MILLION DOLLARS

This story proves the truth of that old saying, "where there's a will, there's a way." It was told to me by that beloved educator and clergyman, the late Frank W. Gunsaulus, who began his preaching career in the stockyards region of South Chicago.

While Dr. Gunsaulus was going through college, he observed many defects in our educational system, defects which he believed he could correct, if he were the head of a college. His *deepest desire* was to become the directing head of an educational institution in which young men and women would be taught to "learn by doing."

He made up his mind to organize a new college in which he could carry out his ideas, without being handicapped by orthodox methods of education.

He needed a million dollars to put the project across! Where was he to lay his hands on so large a sum of money? That was the question that absorbed most of this ambitious young preacher's thought.

But he couldn't seem to make any progress.

Every night he took that thought to bed with him. He got up with it in the morning. He took it with him everywhere he went. He turned it over and over in his mind until it became a consuming *obsession* with him. A million dollars is a lot of money. He recognized that fact, but he also recognized the truth that *the only limitation is that which one sets up in one's own mind.*

Being a philosopher as well as a preacher, Dr. Gunsaulus recognized, as do all who succeed in life, that DEFINITENESS OF PURPOSE is the starting point from which one must begin. He recognized, too, that definiteness of purpose takes on animation, life, and power when backed by a BURNING DESIRE to translate that purpose into its material equivalent.

He knew all these great truths, yet he did not know where, or how to lay his hands on a million dollars. The natural procedure would have been to give up and quit, by saying, "Ah well, my idea is a good one, but I cannot do anything with it, because I never can procure the necessary million dollars." That is exactly what the majority of people would have said, but it is not what Dr. Gunsaulus said. What he said, and what he did are so important that I now introduce him, and let him speak for himself.

"One Saturday afternoon I sat in my room thinking of ways and means of raising the money to carry out my plans. For nearly two years, I had been thinking, but I *had done nothing but think!*

"The time had come for ACTION!

"I made up my mind, then and there, that I would get the necessary million dollars within a week. How? I was not concerned about that. The main thing of importance was the *decision* to get the money within a specified time, and I want to tell you that the moment I reached a definite decision to get the money within a specified time, a strange feeling of assurance came over me, such as I had never before experienced. Something inside me seemed to say, 'Why didn't you reach that decision a long time ago? The money was waiting for you all the time!'

"Things began to happen in a hurry. I called the newspapers and announced I would preach a sermon the following morning, entitled, 'What I would do if I had a Million Dollars.'

"I went to work on the sermon immediately, but I must tell you, frankly, the task was not difficult, because I had been preparing that sermon for almost two years. The spirit back of it was a part of me!

"Long before midnight I had finished writing the sermon. I went to bed and slept with a feeling of confidence, for *I could see myself already in possession of the million dollars.*

"Next morning I arose early, went into the bathroom, read the sermon, then knelt on my knees and asked that my sermon might come to the attention of someone who would supply the needed money.

"While I was praying I again had that feeling of assurance that the money would be forthcoming. In my excitement, I walked out without my sermon, and did not discover the oversight until I was in my pulpit and about ready to begin delivering it.

"It was too late to go back for my notes, and what a blessing that I couldn't go back! Instead, my own subconscious mind yielded the material I needed. When I arose to begin my sermon, I closed my eyes, and spoke with all my heart and soul of my dreams. I not only talked to my audience, but I fancy I talked also to God. I told what I would do with a million dollars if that amount were placed in my hands. I described the plan I had in mind for organizing a great educational institution, where young people would learn to do practical things, and at the same time develop their minds.

"When I had finished and sat down, a man slowly arose from his seat, about three rows from the rear, and made his way toward the pulpit. I wondered what he was going to do. He came into the pulpit, extended his hand, and said, 'Reverend, I liked your sermon. I believe you can do everything you said you would, if you had a million dollars. To prove that I believe in you and your sermon, if you will come to my office tomorrow morning, I will give you the million dollars. My name is Phillip D. Armour.'"

Young Gunsaulus went to Mr. Armour's office and the million dollars was presented to him. With the money, he founded the Armour Institute of Technology.

That is more money than the majority of preachers ever see in an entire lifetime, yet the thought impulse back of the money was created in the young preacher's mind in a fraction of a minute. The necessary million dollars came as a result of an idea. Back of the idea was a DESIRE which young Gunsaulus had been nursing in his mind for almost two years.

Observe this important fact . . . HE GOT THE MONEY WITHIN THIRTY-SIX HOURS AFTER HE REACHED A DEFINITE DECISION IN HIS OWN MIND TO GET IT, AND DECIDED UPON A DEFINITE PLAN FOR GETTING IT!

There was nothing new or unique about young Gunsaulus' vague thinking about a million dollars, and weakly hoping for it. Others before him, and many since his time, have had similar thoughts. But there was something very unique and different about the decision he reached on that memorable Saturday, when he put vagueness into the background, and definitely said, "I WILL get that money within a week!"

God seems to throw Himself on the side of the man who knows *exactly* what he wants, *if he is determined* to get JUST THAT!

Moreover, the principle through which Dr. Gunsaulus got his million dollars is still alive! It is available to you! This universal law is as workable today as it was when the young preacher made use of it so successfully. This book describes, step by step, the thirteen elements of this great law, and suggests how they may be put to use.

Observe that Asa Candler and Dr. Frank Gunsaulus had one characteristic in common. Both knew the astounding truth that IDEAS CAN BE TRANSMUTED INTO CASH THROUGH THE POWER OF DEFINITE PURPOSE, PLUS DEFINITE PLANS.

If you are one of those who believe that hard work and honesty, alone, will bring riches, perish the thought! It is not true! Riches, when they come in huge quantities, are never the result of HARD work! Riches come, if they come at all, in response to definite demands, based upon the application of definite principles, and not by chance or luck.

Generally speaking, an idea is an impulse of thought that impels action, by an appeal to the imagination. All master salesmen know that ideas can be sold where merchandise cannot. Ordinary salesmen do not know this—that is why they are "ordinary."

A publisher of books, which sell for a nickel, made a discovery that should be worth much to publishers generally. He learned that many people buy titles, and not contents of books. By merely changing the name of one book that was not moving, his sales on that book jumped upward more than a million copies. The inside of the book was not changed in any way. He merely ripped off the cover bearing the title that did not sell, and put on a new cover with a title that had "box-office" value.

That, as simple as it may seem, was an IDEA! It was IMAGINATION.

There is no standard price on ideas. The creator of ideas makes his own price, and, if he is smart, gets it.

The moving picture industry created a whole flock of millionaires. Most of them were men who couldn't create ideas—BUT—they had the imagination to recognize ideas when they saw them.

The next flock of millionaires will grow out of the radio business, which is new and not overburdened with men of keen imagination. The money will be made by those who discover or create new and more meritorious radio programs and have the imagination to recognize merit, and to give the radio listeners a chance to profit by it.

The sponsor! That unfortunate victim who now pays the cost of all radio "entertainment," soon will become idea conscious, and demand something for his money. The man who beats the sponsor to the draw, and supplies programs that render useful service, is the man who will become rich in this new industry.

Crooners and light chatter artists who now pollute the air with wisecracks and silly giggles, will go the way of all light timbers, and their places will be taken by real artists who interpret carefully planned programs which have been designed to service the minds of men, as well as provide entertainment.

Here is a wide open field of opportunity screaming its protest at the way it is being butchered, because of lack of imagination, and begging for rescue at any price. Above all, the thing that radio needs is new IDEAS!

If this new field of opportunity intrigues you, perhaps you might profit by the suggestion that the successful radio programs of the future will give more attention to creating "buyer" audiences, and less attention to "listener" audiences. Stated more plainly, the builder of radio programs who succeeds in the future, must find practical ways to convert "listeners" into "buyers." Moreover, the successful producer of radio programs in the future must key his features so that he can definitely show its effect upon the audience.

Sponsors are becoming a bit weary of buying glib selling talks, based upon statements grabbed out of thin air. They want, and in the future will demand, indisputable proof that the Whoosit program not only gives millions of people the silliest giggle ever, but that the silly giggler can sell merchandise!

Another thing that might as well be understood by those who contemplate entering this new field of opportunity, radio advertising is going to be handled by an entirely new group of advertising experts, separate and distinct from the old time newspaper and magazine advertising agency men. The old timers in the advertising game *cannot read* the modern radio scripts, because they have been schooled to SEE ideas. The new radio technique demands men who can interpret ideas from a *written* manuscript in terms of *SOUND!* It cost the author a year of hard labor, and many thousands of dollars to learn this.

Radio, right now, is about where the moving pictures were, when Mary Pickford and her curls first appeared on the screen. There is plenty of room in radio for those who can *produce or recognize* IDEAS.

If the foregoing comment on the opportunities of radio has not started your idea factory to work, you had better forget it. Your opportunity is in some other field. If the comment intrigued you in the slightest degree, then go further into it, and you may find the one IDEA you need to round out your career.

Never let it discourage you if you have no experience in radio. Andrew Carnegie knew very little about making steel—I have Carnegie's own word for this—but he made practical use of two of the principles described in this book, and made the steel business yield him a fortune.

The story of practically every great fortune starts with the day when a creator of ideas and a seller of ideas got together and worked in harmony. Carnegie surrounded himself with men who could do all that he could not do. Men who created ideas, and men who put ideas into operation, and made himself and the others fabulously rich.

Millions of people go through life hoping for favorable "breaks." Perhaps a favorable break can get one an opportunity, but the safest plan is not to depend upon luck. It was a favorable "break" that gave me the biggest opportunity of my life—*but*—twenty-five years of *determined effort* had to be devoted to that opportunity before it became an asset.

The "break" consisted of my good fortune in meeting and gaining the cooperation of Andrew Carnegie. On that occasion Carnegie planted in my mind the *idea* of organizing the principles of achievement into a philosophy of success. Thousands of people have profited by the discoveries made in the twenty-five years of research, and several fortunes have been accumulated through the application of the philosophy. The beginning was simple. It was an IDEA which anyone might have developed.

The favorable break came through Carnegie, but what about the DETERMINATION, DEFINITENESS OF PURPOSE, and the DESIRE TO ATTAIN THE GOAL, and the PERSISTENT EFFORT OF TWENTY-FIVE YEARS? It was no ordinary DESIRE that survived disappointment, discouragement, temporary defeat, criticism, and constant reminding of "waste of time." It was a BURNING DESIRE! an OBSESSION!

When the idea was first planted in my mind by Mr. Carnegie, it was coaxed, nursed, and enticed to *remain alive.* Gradually, the idea became a giant under its own power, and it coaxed, nursed, and drove me. Ideas are like that. First you give life and action and guidance to ideas, then they take on power of their own and sweep aside all opposition.

Ideas are intangible forces, but they have more power than the physical brains that give birth to them. They have the power to live on, after the brain that creates them has returned to dust. For example, take the power of Christianity. That began with a simple idea, born in the brain of Christ. Its chief tenet was, "do unto others as you would have others do unto you." Christ has gone back to the source from whence He came, but His IDEA goes marching on. Some day, it may grow up, and come into its own, then it will have fulfilled Christ's deepest DESIRE. The IDEA has been developing only two thousand years. Give it time!

SUCCESS REQUIRES NO EXPLANATIONS

* * *

FAILURE PERMITS NO ALIBIS

CHAPTER SEVEN

ORGANIZED PLANNING
THE CRYSTALLIZATION OF DESIRE INTO ACTION
The Sixth Step toward Riches

You have learned that everything man creates or acquires, begins in the form of DESIRE, that desire is taken on the first lap of its journey, from the abstract to the concrete, into the workshop of the IMAGINATION, where PLANS for its transition are created and organized.

In Chapter two, you were instructed to take six definite, practical steps, as your first move in translating the desire for money into its monetary equivalent. One of these steps is the formation of a DEFINITE, practical plan, or plans, through which this transformation may be made.

You will now be instructed how to build plans which will be practical, viz:—

(a) Ally yourself with a group of as many people as you may need for the creation, and carrying out of your plan, or plans for the accumulation of money—making use of the "Master Mind" principle described in a later chapter. (Compliance with this instruction is *absolutely essential*. Do not neglect it.)

(b) Before forming your "Master Mind" alliance, decide what advantages, and benefits, *you* may offer the individual members of your group, in return for their cooperation. No one will work indefinitely without some form of compensation. No intelligent person will either request or expect another to work without adequate compensation, although this may not always be in the form of money.

(c) Arrange to meet with the members of your "Master Mind" group at least twice a week, and more often if possible, until you have jointly perfected the necessary plan, or plans for the accumulation of money.

(d) Maintain PERFECT HARMONY between yourself and every member of your "Master Mind" group. If you fail to carry out this instruction to the letter, you may expect to meet with failure. The "Master Mind" principle *cannot* obtain where PERFECT HARMONY does not prevail.

Keep in mind these facts:—

FIRST. You are engaged in an undertaking of major importance to you. To be sure of success, you must have plans which are faultless.

SECOND. You must have the advantage of the experience, education, native ability and imagination of other minds. This is in harmony with the methods followed by every person who has accumulated a great fortune.

No individual has sufficient experience, education, native ability, and knowledge to insure the accumulation of a great fortune, without the cooperation of other people. Every plan you adopt, in your endeavor to accumulate wealth, should be the joint creation of yourself and every other member of your "Master Mind" group. You may originate your own plans, either in whole or in part, but SEE THAT THOSE PLANS ARE CHECKED, AND APPROVED BY THE MEMBERS OF YOUR "MASTER MIND" ALLIANCE.

If the first plan which you adopt does not work successfully, replace it with a new plan, if this new plan fails to work, replace it, in turn with still another, and so on, until you find a plan which DOES WORK. Right here is the point at which the majority of men meet with failure, because of their lack of PERSISTENCE in creating new plans to take the place of those which fail.

The most intelligent man living cannot succeed in accumulating money—nor in any other undertaking—without plans which are practical and workable. Just keep this fact in mind, and remember when your plans fail, that temporary defeat is not permanent failure. It may only mean that your plans have not been sound. Build other plans. Start all over again.

Thomas A. Edison "failed" ten thousand times before he perfected the incandescent electric light bulb. That is—he met with *temporary defeat* ten thousand times, before his efforts were crowned with success.

Temporary defeat should mean only one thing, the certain knowledge that there is something wrong with your plan. Millions of men go through life in misery and poverty, because they lack a sound plan through which to accumulate a fortune.

Henry Ford accumulated a fortune, not because of his superior mind, but because he adopted and followed a PLAN which proved to be sound. A thousand men could be pointed out, each with a better education than Ford's, yet each of whom lives in poverty, because he does not possess the RIGHT plan for the accumulation of money.

Your achievement can be no greater than your PLANS are sound. That may seem to be an axiomatic statement, but it is true. Samuel Insull lost his fortune of over one hundred million dollars. The Insull fortune was built on plans which were sound. The business depression forced Mr. Insull to CHANGE HIS PLANS; and the CHANGE brought "temporary defeat," because his new plans were NOT SOUND. Mr. Insull is now an old man, he may, consequently, accept "failure" instead of "temporary defeat," but if his experience turns out to be FAILURE, it will be for the reason that he lacks the fire of PERSISTENCE to rebuild his plans.

No man is ever whipped, until he QUITS—*in his own mind.*

This fact will be repeated many times, because it is so easy to "take the count" at the first sign of defeat.

James J. Hill met with temporary defeat when he first endeavored to raise the necessary capital to build a railroad from the East to the West, but he, too turned defeat into victory *through new plans*.

Henry Ford met with temporary defeat, not only at the beginning of his automobile career, but after he had gone far toward the top. He created new plans, and went marching on to financial victory.

We see men who have accumulated great fortunes, but we often recognize only their triumph, overlooking the temporary defeats which they had to surmount before "arriving."

NO FOLLOWER OF THIS PHILOSOPHY CAN REASONABLY EXPECT TO ACCUMULATE A FORTUNE WITHOUT EXPERIENCING "TEMPORARY DEFEAT." When defeat comes, accept it as a signal that your plans are not sound, rebuild those plans, and set sail once more toward your coveted goal. If you give up before your goal has been reached, you are a "quitter." A QUITTER NEVER WINS—AND—A WINNER NEVER QUITS. Lift this sentence out, write it on a piece of paper in letters an inch high, and place it where you will see it every night before you go to sleep, and every morning before you go to work.

When you begin to select members for your "Master Mind" group, endeavor to select those who do not take defeat seriously.

Some people foolishly believe that only MONEY can make money. This is not true! DESIRE, transmuted into its monetary equivalent, through the principles laid down here, is the agency through which money is "made." Money, of itself, is nothing but inert matter. It cannot move, think, or talk, but it can "hear" when a man who DESIRES it, calls it to come!

PLANNING THE SALE OF SERVICES

The remainder of this chapter has been given over to a description of ways and means of marketing personal services. The information here conveyed will be of practical help to any person having any form of personal services to market, but it will be of priceless benefit to those who aspire to leadership in their chosen occupations.

Intelligent planning is essential for success in any undertaking designed to accumulate riches. Here will be found detailed instructions to those who must begin the accumulation of riches by selling personal services.

It should be encouraging to know that practically all the great fortunes began in the form of compensation for personal services, or from the sale of IDEAS. What else, except ideas and personal services, would one not possessed of property have to give in return for riches?

Broadly speaking, there are two types of people in the world. One type is known as LEADERS, and the other as FOLLOWERS. Decide at the outset whether you intend to become a leader in your chosen calling, or remain a follower. The difference in compensation is vast. The follower cannot reasonably expect the compensation to which a leader is entitled, although many followers make the mistake of expecting such pay.

It is no disgrace to be a follower. On the other hand, it is no credit to remain a follower. Most great leaders began in the capacity of followers. They became great leaders because they were INTELLIGENT FOLLOWERS. With few exceptions, the man who cannot follow a leader intelligently, cannot become an efficient leader. The man who can follow a leader most efficiently, is usually the man who develops into leadership most rapidly. An intelligent follower has many advantages, among them the OPPORTUNITY TO ACQUIRE KNOWLEDGE FROM HIS LEADER.

THE MAJOR ATTRIBUTES OF LEADERSHIP

The following are important factors of leadership:—

1. UNWAVERING COURAGE based upon knowledge of self, and of one's occupation. No follower wishes to be dominated by a leader who lacks self-confidence and courage. No intelligent follower will be dominated by such a leader very long.

2. SELF-CONTROL. The man who cannot control himself, can never control others. Self-control sets a mighty example for one's followers, which the more intelligent will emulate.

3. A KEEN SENSE OF JUSTICE. Without a sense of fairness and justice, no leader can command and retain the respect of his followers.

4. DEFINITENESS OF DECISION. The man who wavers in his decisions, shows that he is not sure of himself. He cannot lead others successfully.

5. DEFINITENESS OF PLANS. The successful leader must plan his work, and work his plan. A leader who moves by guesswork, without practical, definite plans, is comparable to a ship without a rudder. Sooner or later he will land on the rocks.

6. THE HABIT OF DOING MORE THAN PAID FOR. One of the penalties of leadership is the necessity of willingness, upon the part of the leader, to do more than he requires of his followers.

7. A PLEASING PERSONALITY. No slovenly, careless person can become a successful leader. Leadership calls for respect. Followers will not respect a leader who does not grade high on all of the factors of a Pleasing Personality.

8. SYMPATHY AND UNDERSTANDING. The successful leader must be in sympathy with his followers. Moreover, he must understand them and their problems.

9. MASTERY OF DETAIL. Successful leadership calls for mastery of details of the leader's position.

10. WILLINGNESS TO ASSUME FULL RESPONSIBILITY. The successful leader must be willing to assume responsibility for the mistakes and the shortcomings of his followers. If he tries to shift this responsibility, he will not remain the leader. If one of his followers makes a mistake, and shows himself incompetent, the leader must consider that it is *he* who failed.

11. COOPERATION. The successful leader must understand, and *apply* the

principle of cooperative effort and be able to induce his followers to do the same. Leadership calls for POWER, and power calls for COOPERATION.

There are two forms of Leadership. The first, and by far the most effective, is LEADERSHIP BY CONSENT of, and with the sympathy of the followers. The second is LEADERSHIP BY FORCE, without the consent and sympathy of the followers.

History is filled with evidences that Leadership by Force cannot endure. The downfall and disappearance of "Dictators" and kings is significant. It means that people will not follow forced leadership indefinitely.

The world has just entered a new era of relationship between leaders and followers, which very clearly calls for new leaders, and a new brand of leadership in business and industry. Those who belong to the old school of leadership-by-force, must acquire an understanding of the new brand of leadership (cooperation) or be relegated to the rank and file of the followers. There is no other way out for them.

The relationship of employer and employee, or of leader and follower, in the future, will be one of mutual cooperation, based upon an equitable division of the profits of business. In the future, the relationship of employer and employee will be more like a partnership than it has been in the past.

Napoleon, Kaiser Wilhelm of Germany, the Czar of Russia, and the King of Spain were examples of leadership by force. Their leadership passed. Without much difficulty, one might point to the prototypes of these ex-leaders, among the business, financial, and labor leaders of America who have been dethroned or slated to go. *Leadership-by-consent* of the followers is the only brand which can endure!

Men may follow the forced leadership temporarily, but they will not do so willingly.

The new brand of LEADERSHIP will embrace the eleven factors of leadership, described in this chapter, as well as some other factors. The man who makes these the basis of his leadership, will find abundant opportunity to lead in any walk of life. The depression was prolonged, largely, because the world lacked LEADERSHIP of the new brand. At the end of the depression, the demand for leaders who are competent to apply the new methods of leadership has greatly exceeded the supply. Some of the old type of leaders will reform and adapt themselves to the new brand of leadership, but generally speaking, the world will have to look for new timber for its leadership.

This necessity may be your OPPORTUNITY!

THE 10 MAJOR CAUSES OF FAILURE IN LEADERSHIP

We come now to the major faults of leaders who fail, because it is just as essential to know WHAT NOT TO DO as it is to know what to do.

1.   INABILITY TO ORGANIZE DETAILS. Efficient leadership calls for ability to organize and to master details. No genuine leader is ever "too busy" to do anything which may be required of him in his capacity as leader. When a man, whether he is a leader or follower, admits that he is "too busy" to

change his plans, or to give attention to any emergency, he admits his inefficiency. The successful leader must be the master of all details connected with his position. That means, of course, that he must acquire the habit of relegating details to capable lieutenants.

2. UNWILLINGNESS TO RENDER HUMBLE SERVICE. Truly great leaders are willing, when occasion demands, to perform any sort of labor which they would ask another to perform. "The greatest among ye shall be the servant of all" is a truth which all able leaders observe and respect.

3. EXPECTATION OF PAY FOR WHAT THEY "KNOW" INSTEAD OF WHAT THEY DO WITH THAT WHICH THEY KNOW. The world does not pay men for that which they "know." It pays them for what they DO, or induce others to do.

4. FEAR OF COMPETITION FROM FOLLOWERS. The leader who fears that one of his followers may take his position is practically sure to realize that fear sooner or later. The able leader trains understudies to whom he may delegate, at will, any of the details of his position. Only in this way may a leader multiply himself and prepare himself to be at many places, and give attention to many things at one time. It is an eternal truth that men receive more pay for their ABILITY TO GET OTHERS TO PERFORM, than they could possibly earn by their own efforts. An efficient leader may, through his knowledge of his job and the magnetism of his personality, greatly increase the efficiency of others, and induce them to render more service and better service than they could render without his aid.

5. LACK OF IMAGINATION. Without imagination, the leader is incapable of meeting emergencies, and of creating plans by which to guide his followers efficiently.

6. SELFISHNESS. The leader who claims all the honor for the work of his followers, is sure to be met by resentment. The really great leader CLAIMS NONE OF THE HONORS. He is contented to see the honors, when there are any, go to his followers, because he knows that most men will work harder for commendation and recognition than they will for money alone.

7. INTEMPERANCE. Followers do not respect an intemperate leader. Moreover, intemperance in any of its various forms, destroys the endurance and the vitality of all who indulge in it.

8. DISLOYALTY. Perhaps this should have come at the head of the list. The leader who is not loyal to his trust, and to his associates, those above him, and those below him, cannot long maintain his leadership. Disloyalty marks one as being less than the dust of the earth, and brings down on one's head the contempt he deserves. Lack of loyalty is one of the major causes of failure in every walk of life.

9. EMPHASIS OF THE "AUTHORITY" OF LEADERSHIP. The efficient leader leads by encouraging, and not by trying to instill fear in the hearts of his followers. The leader who tries to impress his followers with his

"authority" comes within the category of leadership through FORCE. If a leader is a REAL LEADER, he will have no need to advertise that fact except by his conduct—his sympathy, understanding, fairness, and a demonstration that he knows his job.

10. EMPHASIS OF TITLE. The competent leader requires no "title" to give him the respect of his followers. The man who makes too much over his title generally has little else to emphasize. The doors to the office of the real leader are open to all who wish to enter, and his working quarters are free from formality or ostentation.

These are among the more common of the causes of failure in leadership. Any one of these faults is sufficient to induce failure. Study the list carefully if you aspire to leadership, and make sure that you are free of these faults.

SOME FERTILE FIELDS IN WHICH "NEW LEADERSHIP" WILL BE REQUIRED

Before leaving this chapter, your attention is called to a few of the fertile fields in which there has been a decline of leadership, and in which the new type of leader may find an abundance of OPPORTUNITY.

First. In the field of politics there is a most insistent demand for new leaders; a demand which indicates nothing less than an emergency. The majority of politicians have, seemingly, become high-grade, legalized racketeers. They have increased taxes and debauched the machinery of industry and business until the people can no longer stand the burden.

Second. The banking business is undergoing a reform. The leaders in this field have almost entirely lost the confidence of the public. Already the bankers have sensed the need of reform, and they have begun it.

Third. Industry calls for new leaders. The old type of leaders thought and moved in terms of dividends instead of thinking and moving in terms of human equations! The future leader in industry, to endure, must regard himself as a quasi-public official whose duty it is to manage his trust in such a way that it will work hardship on no individual, or group of individuals. Exploitation of working men is a thing of the past. Let the man who aspires to leadership in the field of business, industry, and labor remember this.

Fourth. The religious leader of the future will be forced to give more attention to the temporal needs of his followers, in the solution of their economic and personal problems of the present, and less attention to the dead past, and the yet unborn future.

Fifth. In the professions of law, medicine, and education, a new brand of leadership, and to some extent, new leaders will become a necessity. This is especially true in the field of education. The leader in that field must, in the future, find ways and means of teaching people HOW TO APPLY the knowledge they receive in school. He must deal more with PRACTICE and less with THEORY.

Sixth. New leaders will be required in the field of Journalism. Newspapers of the future, to be conducted successfully, must be divorced from "special privilege" and relieved from the subsidy of advertising. They must cease to be organs of propaganda for the interests which patronize their advertising columns. The type of newspaper which publishes scandal and lewd pictures will eventually go the way of all forces which debauch the human mind.

These are but a few of the fields in which opportunities for new leaders and a new brand of leadership are now available. The world is undergoing a rapid change. This means that the media through which the changes in human habits are promoted, must be adapted to the changes. The media here described, are the ones which, more than any others, determine the trend of civilization.

WHEN AND HOW TO APPLY FOR A POSITION

The information described here is the net result of many years of experience during which thousands of men and women were helped to market their services effectively. It can, therefore, be relied upon as sound and practical.

Media through Which Services May be Marketed

Experience has proved that the following media offer the most direct and effective methods of bringing the buyer and seller of personal services together.

1. EMPLOYMENT BUREAUS. Care must be taken to select only reputable bureaus, the management of which can show adequate records of achievement of satisfactory results. There are comparatively few such bureaus.

2. ADVERTISING in newspapers, trade journals, magazines, and radio. Classified advertising may usually be relied upon to produce satisfactory results in the case of those who apply for clerical or ordinary salaried positions. Display advertising is more desirable in the case of those who seek executive connections, the copy to appear in the section of the paper which is most apt to come to the attention of the class of employer being sought. The copy should be prepared by an expert, who understands how to inject sufficient selling qualities to produce replies.

3. PERSONAL LETTERS OF APPLICATION, directed to particular firms or individuals most apt to need such services as are being offered. Letters should be *neatly typed*, ALWAYS, and signed by hand. With the letter, should be sent a complete "brief" or outline of the applicant's qualifications. Both the letter of application and the brief of experience or qualifications should be prepared by an expert. (See instructions as to information to be supplied).

4. APPLICATION THROUGH PERSONAL ACQUAINTANCES. When possible, the applicant should endeavor to approach prospective employers

through some mutual acquaintance. This method of approach is particularly advantageous in the case of those who seek executive connections and do not wish to appear to be "peddling" themselves.

5. APPLICATION IN PERSON. In some instances, it may be more effective if the applicant offers personally, his services to prospective employers, in which event a complete written statement of qualifications for the position should be presented, for the reason that prospective employers often wish to discuss with associates, one's record.

Information to Be Supplied in a Written "Brief"

This brief should be prepared as carefully as a lawyer would prepare the brief of a case to be tried in court. Unless the applicant is experienced in the preparation of such briefs, an expert should be consulted, and his services enlisted for this purpose. Successful merchants employ men and women who understand the art and the psychology of advertising to present the merits of their merchandise. One who has personal services for sale should do the same. The following information should appear in the brief:

1. *Education.* State briefly, but definitely, what schooling you have had, and in what subjects you specialized in school, giving the reasons for that specialization.

2. *Experience.* If you have had experience in connection with positions similar to the one you seek, describe it fully, state names and addresses of former employers. Be sure to bring out clearly any *special* experience you may have had which would equip you to fill the position you seek.

3. *References.* Practically every business firm desires to know all about the previous records, antecedents, etc., of prospective employees who seek positions of responsibility. Attach to your brief photostatic copies of letters from:
   a. Former employers
   b. Teachers under whom you studied
   c. Prominent people whose judgment may be relied upon.

4. *Photograph of self.* Attach to your brief a recent, unmounted photograph of yourself.

5. *Apply for a specific position.* Avoid application for a position without describing EXACTLY what particular position you seek. Never apply for "just a position." That indicates you lack specialized qualifications.

6. *State your qualifications* for the particular position for which you apply. Give full details as to the reason you believe you are qualified for the particular position you seek. This is THE MOST IMPORTANT DETAIL OF YOUR APPLICATION. It will determine, more than anything else, what consideration you receive.

7. *Offer to go to work on probation.* In the majority of instances if you are determined to have the position for which you apply, it will be most effective if you offer to work for a week, or a month, or for a sufficient length

of time to enable your prospective employer to judge your value WITH-OUT PAY. This may appear to be a radical suggestion, but experience has proved that it seldom fails to win at least a trial. If you are SURE OF YOUR QUALIFICATIONS, a trial is all you need. Incidentally, such an offer indicates that you have confidence in your ability to fill the position you seek. It is most convincing. If your offer is accepted, and you make good, more than likely you will be paid for your "probation" period. Make clear the fact that your offer is based upon:

    a. Your confidence in your ability to fill the position.

    b. Your confidence in your prospective employer's decision to employ you after trial.

    c. Your DETERMINATION to have the position you seek.

8. *Knowledge of your prospective employer's business.* Before applying for a position, do sufficient research in connection with the business to familiarize yourself thoroughly with that business, and indicate in your brief the knowledge you have acquired in this field. This will be impressive, as it will indicate that you have imagination, and a real interest in the position you seek.

Remember that it is not the lawyer who knows the most law, but the one who best prepares his case, who wins. If your "case" is properly prepared and presented, your victory will have been more than half won at the outset.

Do not be afraid of making your brief too long. Employers are just as much interested in purchasing the services of well-qualified applicants as you are in securing employment. In fact, the success of most successful employers is due, in the main, to their ability to select well-qualified lieutenants. They want all the information available.

Remember another thing; neatness in the preparation of your brief will indicate that you are a painstaking person. I have helped to prepare briefs for clients which were so striking and out of the ordinary that they resulted in the employment of the applicant without a personal interview.

When your brief has been completed, have it neatly bound by an experienced binder, and lettered by an artist, or printer similar to the following:

BRIEF OF THE QUALIFICATIONS OF

Robert K. Smith

APPLYING FOR THE POSITION OF

Private Secretary to

The President of

THE BLANK COMPANY, Inc.

Change names each time brief is shown.

This personal touch is sure to command attention. Have your brief neatly typed or mimeographed on the finest paper you can obtain, and bound with a heavy paper of the book-cover variety, the binder to be changed, and the proper firm name to be inserted if it is to be shown to more than one company. Your photograph should be pasted on one of the pages of your brief. Follow these instructions to the letter, improving upon them wherever your imagination suggests.

Successful salesmen groom themselves with care. They understand that first impressions are lasting. Your brief is your salesman. Give it a good suit of clothes, so it will stand out in bold contrast to anything your prospective employer ever saw, in the way of an application for a position. If the position you seek is worth having, it is worth going after with care. Moreover, if you sell yourself to an employer in a manner that impresses him with your individuality, you probably will receive more money for your services from the very start, than you would if you applied for employment in the usual conventional way.

If you seek employment through an advertising agency, or an employment agency, have the agent use copies of your brief in marketing your services. This will help to gain preference for you, both with the agent, and the prospective employers.

HOW TO GET THE EXACT POSITION YOU DESIRE

Everyone enjoys doing the kind of work for which he is best suited. An artist loves to work with paints, a craftsman with his hands, a writer loves to write. Those with less definite talents have their preferences for certain fields of business and industry. If America does anything well, it offers a full range of occupations, tilling the soil, manufacturing, marketing, and the professions.

First. Decide EXACTLY what kind of a job you want. If the job doesn't already exist, perhaps you can create it.

Second. Choose the company, or individual for whom you wish to work.

Third. Study your prospective employer, as to policies, personnel, and chances of advancement.

Fourth. By analysis of yourself, your talents and capabilities, figure WHAT YOU CAN OFFER, and plan ways and means of giving advantages, services, developments, ideas that *you believe* you can successfully deliver.

Fifth. Forget about "a job." Forget whether or not there is an opening. Forget the usual routine of "have you got a job for me?" Concentrate on what *you can give.*

Sixth. Once you have your plan in mind, arrange with an experienced writer to put it on paper in neat form, and in full detail.

Seventh. Present it to the *proper person with authority* and he will do the rest. Every company is looking for men who can give something of value, whether it be ideas, services, or "connections." Every company has room for the man who has a definite plan of action which is to the advantage of that company.

This line of procedure may take a few days or weeks of extra time, but the difference in income, in advancement, and in gaining recognition will save years of hard work at small pay. It has many advantages, from one to five years of time in reaching a chosen goal.

Every person who starts, or "gets in" half way up the ladder, does so by deliberate and careful planning, (excepting, of course, the Boss' son).

THE NEW WAY OF MARKETING SERVICES
"Jobs" are now "Partnerships"

Men and women who market their services to best advantage in the future, must recognize the stupendous change which has taken place in connection with the relationship between employer and employee.

In the future, the "Golden Rule," and not the "Rule of Gold" will be the dominating factor in the marketing of merchandise as well as personal services. The future relationship between employers and their employees will be more in the nature of a partnership consisting of:

     a. The employer
     b. The employee
     c. The public they serve

This new way of marketing personal services is called new for many reasons, first, both the employer and the employee of the future will be considered as fellow-employees whose business it will be to SERVE THE PUBLIC EFFICIENTLY. In times past, employers, and employees have bartered among themselves, driving the best bargains they could with one another, not considering that in the final analysis they were, in reality, BARGAINING AT THE EXPENSE OF THE THIRD PARTY, THE PUBLIC THEY SERVED.

The depression served as a mighty protest from an injured public, whose rights had been trampled upon in every direction by those who were clamoring for individual advantages and profits. When the debris of the depression shall have been cleared away, and business shall have been once again restored to balance, both employers and employees will recognize that they are NO LONGER PRIVILEGED TO DRIVE BARGAINS AT THE EXPENSE OF THOSE WHOM THEY SERVE. The real employer of the future will be the public. This should be kept uppermost in mind by every person seeking to market personal services effectively.

Nearly every railroad in America is in financial difficulty. Who does not remember the day when, if a citizen enquired at the ticket office, the time of departure of a train, he was abruptly referred to the bulletin board instead of being politely given the information?

The street car companies have experienced a "change of times" also. There was a time not so very long ago when street car conductors took pride in giving argument to passengers. Many of the street car tracks have been removed and passengers ride on a bus, whose driver is "the last word in politeness."

All over the country street car tracks are rusting from abandonment, or have been taken up. Wherever street cars are still in operation, passengers may now ride without argument, and one may even hail the car in the middle of the block, and the motorman will OBLIGINGLY pick him up.

HOW TIMES HAVE CHANGED! That is just the point I am trying to emphasize. TIMES HAVE CHANGED! Moreover, the change is reflected not merely in railroad offices and on street cars, but in other walks of life as well. The "public-be-damned" policy is now passé. It has been supplanted by the "we-are-obligingly-at-your-service, sir," policy.

The bankers have learned a thing or two during this rapid change which has taken place during the past few years. Impoliteness on the part of a bank official, or bank employee today is as rare as it was conspicuous a dozen years ago. In the years past, some bankers (not all of them, of course), carried an atmosphere of austerity which gave every would-be borrower a chill when he even thought of approaching his banker for a loan.

The thousands of bank failures during the depression had the effect of removing the mahogany doors behind which bankers formerly barricaded themselves. They now sit at desks in the open, where they may be seen and approached at will by any depositor, or by anyone who wishes to see them, and the whole atmosphere of the bank is one of courtesy and understanding.

It used to be customary for customers to have to stand and wait at the corner grocery until the clerks were through passing the time of day with friends, and the proprietor had finished making up his bank deposit, before being waited upon. Chain stores, managed by COURTEOUS MEN who do everything in the way of service, short of shining the customer's shoes, have PUSHED THE OLD-TIME MERCHANTS INTO THE BACKGROUND. TIME MARCHES ON!

"Courtesy" and "Service" are the watch-words of merchandising today, and apply to the person who is marketing personal services even more directly than to the employer whom he serves, because, in the final analysis, both the employer and his employee are EMPLOYED BY THE PUBLIC THEY SERVE. If they fail to serve well, they pay by the loss of their privilege of serving.

We can all remember the time when the gasmeter reader pounded on the door hard enough to break the panels. When the door was opened, he pushed his way in, uninvited, with a scowl on his face which plainly said, "what-the-hell-did-you-keep-me-waiting-for?" All that has undergone a change. The meter-man now conducts himself as a gentleman who is "delighted-to-be-at-your-service-sir." Before the gas companies learned that their scowling meter-men were accumulating liabilities never to be cleared away, the polite salesmen of oil burners came along and did a land office business.

During the depression, I spent several months in the anthracite coal region of Pennsylvania, studying conditions which all but destroyed the coal industry. Among several very significant discoveries, was the fact that greed on the part of operators and their employees was the chief cause of the loss of business for the operators, and loss of jobs for the miners.

Through the pressure of a group of overzealous labor leaders, representing the employees, and the greed for profits on the part of the operators, the anthracite business suddenly dwindled. The coal operators and their employees drove sharp bargains with one another, adding the cost of the "bargaining" to the price of the coal, until, finally, they discovered they had BUILT UP A WONDERFUL BUSINESS FOR THE MANUFACTURERS OF OIL BURNING OUTFITS AND THE PRODUCERS OF CRUDE OIL.

"The wages of sin is death!" Many have read this in the Bible, but few have discovered its meaning. Now, and for several years, the entire world has been listening BY FORCE, to a sermon which might well be called "WHATSOEVER A MAN SOWETH, THAT SHALL HE ALSO REAP."

Nothing as widespread and effective as the depression could possibly be "just a coincidence." Behind the depression was a CAUSE. Nothing ever happens without a CAUSE. In the main, the cause of the depression is traceable directly to the worldwide habit of trying to REAP without SOWING.

This should not be mistaken to mean that the depression represents a crop which the world is being FORCED to reap without having SOWN. The trouble is that the world *sowed the wrong sort of seed.* Any farmer knows he cannot sow the seed of thistles, and reap a harvest of grain. Beginning at the outbreak of the world war, the people of the world began to sow the seed of service inadequate in both quality and quantity. Nearly everyone was engaged in the pastime of trying to GET WITHOUT GIVING.

These illustrations are brought to the attention of those who have personal services to market, to show that we are where we are, and what we are, because of *our own conduct!* If there is a principle of cause and effect, which controls business, finance, and transportation, this same principle controls individuals and determines their economic status.

WHAT IS YOUR "QQS" RATING?

The causes of success in marketing services EFFECTIVELY and permanently, have been clearly described. Unless those causes are studied, analyzed, understood and APPLIED, no man can market his services effectively and permanently. Every person must be his own salesman of personal services. The QUALITY and the QUANTITY of service rendered, and the SPIRIT in which it is rendered, determine to a large extent, the price, and the duration of employment. To market Personal services effectively, (which means a permanent market, at a satisfactory price, under pleasant conditions), one must adopt and follow the "QQS" formula which means that QUALITY, plus QUANTITY, plus the proper SPIRIT of cooperation, equals perfect salesmanship of service. Remember the "QQS" formula, but do more—APPLY IT AS A HABIT!

Let us analyze the formula to make sure we understand exactly what it means.

1. *QUALITY* of service shall be construed to mean the performance of every
   detail, in connection with your position, in the most efficient manner

possible, with the object of greater efficiency always in mind.

2. *QUANTITY* of service shall be understood to mean the HABIT of rendering all the service of which you are capable, at all times, with the purpose of increasing the amount of service rendered as greater skill is developed through practice and experience. Emphasis is again placed on the word HABIT.

3. *SPIRIT* of service shall be construed to mean the HABIT of agreeable, harmonious conduct which will induce cooperation from associates and fellow employees.

Adequacy of QUALITY and QUANTITY of service is not sufficient to maintain a permanent market for your services. The conduct, or the SPIRIT in which you deliver service, is a strong determining factor in connection with both the price you receive, and the duration of employment.

Andrew Carnegie stressed this point more than others in connection with his description of the factors which lead to success in the marketing of personal services. He emphasized again, and again, the necessity for HARMONIOUS CONDUCT. He stressed the fact that he would not retain any man, no matter how great a QUANTITY, or how efficient the QUALITY of his work, *unless* he worked in a spirit of HARMONY. Mr. Carnegie insisted upon men being AGREEABLE. To prove that he placed a high value upon this quality, he permitted many men *who conformed to his standards* to become very wealthy. Those who did not conform, had to make room for others.

The importance of a pleasing personality has been stressed, because it is a factor which enables one to render service in the proper SPIRIT. If one has a personality which PLEASES, and renders service in a spirit of HARMONY, these assets often make up for deficiencies in both the QUALITY, and the QUANTITY of service one renders. Nothing, however, can be SUCCESSFULLY SUBSTITUTED FOR PLEASING CONDUCT.

THE CAPITAL VALUE OF YOUR SERVICES

The person whose income is derived entirely from the sale of personal services is no less a merchant than the man who sells commodities, and it might well be added, such a person is subject to EXACTLY THE SAME RULES of conduct as the merchant who sells merchandise.

This has been emphasized, because the majority of people who live by the sale of personal services make the mistake of considering themselves free from the rules of conduct, and the responsibilities attached to those who are engaged in marketing commodities.

The new way of marketing services has practically forced both employer and, employee into partnership alliances, through which both take into consideration the rights of the third party, THE PUBLIC THEY SERVE.

The day of the "go-getter" has passed. He has been supplanted by the "go-giver." High-pressure methods in business finally blew the lid off. There will never be the need to put the lid back on, because, in the future, business will be conducted by methods that will require no pressure.

The actual capital value of your brains may be determined by the amount of income you can produce (by marketing your services). A fair estimate of the capital value of your services may be made by multiplying your annual income by sixteen and two-thirds, as it is reasonable to estimate that your annual income represents six percent of your capital value. Money rents for 6% per annum. Money is worth no more than brains. It is often worth much less.

Competent "brains," if effectively marketed, represent a much more desirable form of capital than that which is required to conduct a business dealing in commodities, because "brains" are a form of capital which cannot be permanently depreciated through depressions, nor can this form of capital be stolen or spent. Moreover, the money which is essential for the conduct of business is as worthless as a sand dune, until it has been mixed with efficient "brains."

THE THIRTY MAJOR CAUSES OF FAILURE

How Many of These Are Holding You Back?

Life's greatest tragedy consists of men and women who earnestly try, and fail! The tragedy lies in the overwhelmingly large majority of people who fail, as compared to the few who succeed.

I have had the privilege of analyzing several thousand men and women, 98% of who were classified as "failures." There is something radically wrong with a civilization and a system of education, which permit 98% of the people to go through their life as failures. But I did not write this book for the purpose of moralizing on the rights and wrongs of the world; that would require a book a hundred times the size of this one.

My analysis work proved that there are thirty major reasons for failure, and thirteen major principles through which people accumulate fortunes. In this chapter, a description of the thirty major causes of failure will be given. As you go over the list, check yourself by it, point by point, for the purpose of discovering how many of these causes-of-failure stand between you and success.

1. UNFAVORABLE HEREDITARY BACKGROUND. There is little, if anything, which can be done for people who are born with a deficiency in brain power. This philosophy offers but one method of bridging this weakness—through the aid of the Master Mind. Observe with profit, however, that this is the ONLY one of the thirty causes of failure which may not be *easily corrected* by any individual.

2. LACK OF A WELL-DEFINED PURPOSE IN LIFE. There is no hope of success for the person who does not have a central purpose, or *definite goal* at which to aim. Ninety-eight out of every hundred of those whom I

have analyzed, had no such aim. Perhaps this was the MAJOR CAUSE OF THEIR FAILURE.

3. LACK OF AMBITION TO AIM ABOVE MEDIOCRITY. We offer no hope for the person who is so indifferent as to not to want to get ahead in life, and who is not willing to pay the price.

4. INSUFFICIENT EDUCATION. This is a handicap which may be overcome with comparative ease. Experience has proven that the best-educated people are often those who are known as "self-made," or self-educated. It takes more than a college degree to make one a person of education. Any person who is educated is one who has learned to get whatever he wants in life without violating the rights of others. Education consists, not so much of knowledge effectively and persistently APPLIED. Men are paid, not merely for what they know, but more particularly for WHAT THEY DO WITH THAT WHICH THEY KNOW.

5. LACK OF SELF-DISCIPLINE. Discipline comes through self-control. This means that one must control all negative qualities. Before you can control conditions, you must first control yourself. Self-mastery is the hardest job you will ever tackle. If you do not conquer self, you will be conquered by self. You may see at one and the same time both your best friend and your greatest enemy, by stepping in front of a mirror.

6. ILL HEALTH. No person may enjoy outstanding success without good health. Many of the causes of ill health are subject to mastery and control. These, in the main are:
    a. Overeating of foods not conducive to health
    b. Wrong habits of thought; giving expression to negatives
    c. Wrong use of, and over indulgence in sex
    d. Lack of proper physical exercise
    e. An inadequate supply of fresh air, due to improper breathing

7. UNFAVORABLE ENVIRONMENTAL INFLUENCES DURING CHILDHOOD. "As the twig is bent, so shall the tree grow." Most people who have criminal tendencies acquire them as the result of bad environment, and improper associates during childhood.

8. PROCRASTINATION. This is one of the most common causes of failure. "Old Man Procrastination" stands within the shadow of every human being, waiting his opportunity to spoil one's chances of success. Most of us go through life as failures, because we are waiting for the "time to be right" to start doing something worthwhile. Do not wait. The time will never be "just right." Start where you stand, and work with whatever tools you may have at your command, and better tools will be found as you go along.

9. LACK OF PERSISTENCE. Most of us are good "starters" but poor "finishers" of everything we begin. Moreover, people are prone to give up at the first signs of defeat. There is no substitute for PERSISTENCE. The person

who makes PERSISTENCE his watch-word, discovers that "Old Man Failure" finally becomes tired, and makes his departure. Failure cannot cope with PERSISTENCE.

10. NEGATIVE PERSONALITY. There is no hope of success for the person who repels people through a negative personality. Success comes through the application of POWER, and power is attained through the cooperative efforts of other people. A negative personality will not induce cooperation.

11. LACK OF CONTROLLED SEXUAL URGE. Sex energy is the most powerful of all the stimuli which move people into ACTION. Because it is the most powerful of the emotions, it must be controlled, through transmutation, and converted into other channels.

12. UNCONTROLLED DESIRE FOR "SOMETHING FOR NOTHING." The gambling instinct drives millions of people to failure. Evidence of this may be found in a study of the Wall Street crash of '29, during which millions of people tried to make money by gambling on stock margins.

13. LACK OF A WELL DEFINED POWER OF DECISION. Men who succeed reach decisions Promptly, and change them, if at all, very slowly. Men who fail, reach decisions, if at all, very slowly, and change them frequently, and quickly. Indecision and procrastination are twin brothers. Where one is found, the other may usually be found also. Kill off this pair before they completely "hog-tie" you to the treadmill of FAILURE.

14. ONE OR MORE OF THE SIX BASIC FEARS. These fears have been analyzed for you in a later chapter. They must be mastered before you can market your services effectively.

15. WRONG SELECTION OF A MATE IN MARRIAGE. This a most common cause of failure. The relationship of marriage brings people intimately into contact. Unless this relationship is harmonious, failure is likely to follow. Moreover, it will be a form of failure that is marked by misery and unhappiness, destroying all signs of AMBITION.

16. OVER-CAUTION. The person who takes no chances, generally has to take whatever is left when others are through choosing. Overcaution is as bad as under-caution. Both are extremes to be guarded against. Life itself is filled with the element of chance.

17. WRONG SELECTION OF ASSOCIATES IN BUSINESS. This is one of the most common causes of failure in business. In marketing personal services, one should use great care to select an employer who will be an inspiration, and who is, himself, intelligent and successful. We emulate those with whom we associate most closely. Pick an employer who is worth emulating.

18. SUPERSTITION AND PREJUDICE. Superstition is a form of fear. It is also a sign of ignorance. Men who succeed keep open minds and are afraid of nothing.

19. WRONG SELECTION OF A VOCATION. No man can succeed in a line

of endeavor which he does not like. The most essential step in the marketing of personal services is that of selecting an occupation into which you can throw yourself wholeheartedly.

20. LACK OF CONCENTRATION OF EFFORT. The "jack-of-all-trades" seldom is good at any. Concentrate all of your efforts on one DEFINITE CHIEF AIM.

21. THE HABIT OF INDISCRIMINATE SPENDING. The spend-thrift cannot succeed, mainly because he stands eternally in FEAR OF POVERTY. Form the habit of systematic saving by putting aside a definite percentage of your income. Money in the bank gives one a very safe foundation of COURAGE when bargaining for the sale of personal services. Without money, one must take what one is offered, and be glad to get it.

22. LACK OF ENTHUSIASM. Without enthusiasm one cannot be convincing. Moreover, enthusiasm is contagious, and the person who has it, under control, is generally welcome in any group of people.

23. INTOLERANCE. The person with a "closed" mind on any subject seldom gets ahead. Intolerance means that one has stopped acquiring knowledge. The most damaging forms of intolerance are those connected with religious, racial, and political differences of opinion.

24. INTEMPERANCE. The most damaging forms of intemperance are connected with eating, strong drink, and sexual activities. Overindulgence in any of these is fatal to success.

25. INABILITY TO COOPERATE WITH OTHERS. More people lose their positions and their big opportunities in life, because of this fault, than for all other reasons combined. It is a fault which no well-informed business man, or leader will tolerate.

26. POSSESSION OF POWER THAT WAS NOT ACQUIRED THROUGH SELF EFFORT. (Sons and daughters of wealthy men, and others who inherit money which they did not earn). Power in the hands of one who did not acquire it gradually, is often fatal to success. QUICK RICHES are more dangerous than poverty.

27. INTENTIONAL DISHONESTY. There is no substitute for honesty. One may be temporarily dishonest by force of circumstances over which one has no control, without permanent damage. But, there is NO HOPE for the person who is dishonest by choice. Sooner or later, his deeds will catch up with him, and he will pay by loss of reputation, and perhaps even loss of liberty.

28. EGOTISM AND VANITY. These qualities serve as red lights which warn others to keep away. THEY ARE FATAL TO SUCCESS.

29. GUESSING INSTEAD OF THINKING. Most people are too indifferent or lazy to acquire FACTS with which to THINK ACCURATELY. They prefer to act on "opinions" created by guesswork or snap-judgments.

30. LACK OF CAPITAL. This is a common cause of failure among those who

start out in business for the first time, without sufficient reserve of capital to absorb the shock of their mistakes, and to carry them over until they have established a REPUTATION.

31. Under this, name any particular cause of failure from which you have suffered that has not been included in the foregoing list.

In these thirty major causes of failure is found a description of the tragedy of life, which obtains for practically every person who tries and fails. It will be helpful if you can induce someone who knows you well to go over this list with you, and help to analyze you by the thirty causes of failure. It may be beneficial if you try this alone. Most people cannot see themselves as others see them. You may be one who cannot.

The oldest of admonitions is "Man, know thyself!" If you market merchandise successfully, you must know the merchandise. The same is true in marketing personal services. You should know all of your weaknesses in order that you may either bridge them or eliminate them entirely. You should know your strength in order that you may call attention to it when selling your services. You can know yourself only through *accurate* analysis.

The folly of ignorance in connection with self was displayed by a young man who applied to the manager of a well known business for a position. He made a very good impression until the manager asked him what salary he expected. He replied that he had no fixed sum in mind (*lack of a definite aim*). The manager then said, "We will pay you all you are worth, after we try you out for a week."

"I will not accept it," the applicant replied, "because I AM GETTING MORE THAN THAT WHERE I AM NOW EMPLOYED."

Before you even start to negotiate for a readjustment of your salary in your present position, or to seek employment elsewhere, BE SURE THAT YOU ARE WORTH MORE THAN YOU NOW RECEIVE.

It is one thing to WANT money—everyone wants more—but it is something entirely different to be WORTH MORE! Many people mistake their WANTS for their JUST DUES. Your financial requirements or wants have nothing whatever to do with your WORTH. Your value is established entirely by your ability to render useful service or your capacity to induce others to render such service.

TAKE INVENTORY OF YOURSELF
28 Questions You Should Answer
Annual self-analysis is an essential in the effective marketing of personal services, as is annual inventory in merchandising. Moreover, the yearly analysis should disclose a DECREASE IN FAULTS, and an increase in VIRTUES. One goes ahead, stands still, or goes backward in life. One's object should be, of course, to go ahead. Annual self-analysis will disclose whether advancement has been made, and if so, how much. It will also disclose any backward steps one may have made. The effective marketing of personal services requires one to move forward even if the

progress is slow.

Your annual self-analysis should be made at the end of each year, so you can include in your New Year's Resolutions any improvements which the analysis indicates should be made. Take this inventory by asking yourself the following questions, and by checking your answers with the aid of someone who will not permit you to deceive yourself as to their accuracy.

Self-Analysis Questionnaire for Personal Inventory

1. Have I attained the goal which I established as my objective for this year? (You should work with a definite yearly objective to be attained as a part of your major life objective).

2. Have I delivered service of the best possible QUALITY of which I was capable, or could I have improved any part of this service?

3. Have I delivered service in the greatest possible QUANTITY of which I was capable?

4. Has the spirit of my conduct been harmonious, and cooperative at all times?

5. Have I permitted the habit of PROCRASTINATION to decrease my efficiency, and if so, to what extent?

6. Have I improved my PERSONALITY, and if so, in what ways?

7. Have I been PERSISTENT in following my plans through to completion?

8. Have I reached DECISIONS PROMPTLY AND DEFINITELY on all occasions?

9. Have I permitted any one or more of the six basic fears to decrease my efficiency?

10. Have I been either "over-cautious," or "undercautious?"

11. Has my relationship with my associates in work been pleasant, or unpleasant? If it has been unpleasant, has the fault been partly, or wholly mine?

12. Have I dissipated any of my energy through lack of CONCENTRATION of effort?

13. Have I been open minded and tolerant in connection with all subjects?

14. In what way have I improved my ability to render service?

15. Have I been intemperate in any of my habits?

16 Have I expressed, either openly or secretly, any form of EGOTISM?

17 Has my conduct toward my associates been such that it has induced them to RESPECT me?

18 Have my opinions and DECISIONS been based upon guesswork, or accuracy of analysis and THOUGHT?

19. Have I followed the habit of budgeting my time, my expenses, and my income, and have I been conservative in these budgets?

20. How much time have I devoted to UNPROFITABLE effort which I might have used to better advantage?

21. How may I RE-BUDGET my time, and change my habits so I will be more efficient during the coming year?

22. Have I been guilty of any conduct which was not approved by my conscience?

23. In what ways have I rendered MORE SERVICE AND BETTER SERVICE than I was paid to render?

24. Have I been unfair to anyone, and if so, in what way?

25. If I had been the purchaser of my own services for the year, would I be satisfied with my purchase?

26. Am I in the right vocation, and if not, why not?

27. Has the purchaser of my services been satisfied with the service I have rendered, and if not, why not?

28. What is my present rating on the fundamental principles of success? (Make this rating fairly, and frankly, and have it checked by someone who is courageous enough to do it accurately).

Having read and assimilated the information conveyed through this chapter, you are now ready to create a practical plan for marketing your personal services. In this chapter will be found an adequate description of every principle essential in planning the sale of personal services, including the major attributes of leadership; the most common causes of failure in leadership; a description of the fields of opportunity for leadership; the main causes of failure in all walks of life, and the important questions which should be used in self-analysis.

This extensive and detailed presentation of accurate information has been included, because it will be needed by all who must begin the accumulation of riches by marketing personal services. Those who have lost their fortunes, and those who are just beginning to earn money, have nothing but personal services to offer in return for riches, therefore it is essential that they have available the practical information needed to market services to best advantage.

The information contained in this chapter will be of great value to all who aspire to attain leadership in any calling. It will be particularly helpful to those aiming to market their services as business or industrial executives.

Complete assimilation and understanding of the information here conveyed will be helpful in marketing one's own services, and it will also help one to become more analytical and capable of judging people. The information will be priceless to personnel directors, employment managers, and other executives charged with the selection of employees, and the maintenance of efficient organizations. If you doubt this statement, test its soundness by answering in writing the twenty-eight self-analysis questions. That might be both interesting and profitable, even though you do not doubt the soundness of the statement.

WHERE AND HOW ONE MAY FIND OPPORTUNITIES TO ACCUMULATE RICHES

Now that we have analyzed the principles by which riches may be accumulated, we naturally ask, "where may one find favorable opportunities to apply these principles?" Very well, let us take inventory and see what the United States of America offer the person seeking riches, great or small.

To begin with, let us remember, *all of us,* that we live in a country where *every law-abiding citizen enjoys freedom of thought and freedom of deed unequaled anywhere in the world.* Most of us have never taken inventory of the advantages of this freedom. We have never compared our unlimited freedom with the curtailed freedom in other countries.

Here we have freedom of thought, freedom in the choice and enjoyment of education, freedom in religion, freedom in politics, freedom in the choice of a business, profession or occupation, freedom to accumulate and own without molestation, *ALL THE PROPERTY WE CAN ACCUMULATE,* freedom to choose our place of residence, freedom in marriage, freedom through equal opportunity to all races, freedom of travel from one state to another, freedom in our choice of foods, and freedom to *AIM FOR ANY STATION IN LIFE FOR WHICH WE HAVE PREPARED OURSELVES,* even for the presidency of the United States.

We have other forms of freedom, but this list will give a bird's eye view of the most important, which constitute OPPORTUNITY of the highest order. This advantage of freedom is all the more conspicuous because the United States is the only country guaranteeing to every citizen, whether native born or naturalized, so broad and varied a list of freedom.

Next, let us recount some of the blessings which our widespread freedom has placed within our hands. Take the average American family for example (meaning, the family of average income) and sum up the benefits available to every member of the family, in this land of OPPORTUNITY and plenty!

   a. **FOOD.** Next to freedom of thought and deed comes FOOD, CLOTHING, and
      SHELTER, the three basic necessities of life.

      Because of our universal freedom the average American family has
      available, at its very door, the choicest selection of food to be found anywhere in the world, and at prices within its financial range.

      A family of two, living in the heart of Times Square district of New
      York City, far removed from the source of production of foods, took careful inventory of the cost of a simple breakfast, with this astonishing result:

Articles of food;	Cost at the breakfast table:
Grape Fruit Juice, (From Florida)	.02
Rippled Wheat Breakfast food (Kansas Farm)	.02
Tea (From China)	.02
Bananas (From South America)	.02½
Toasted Bread (From Kansas Farm)	.01
Fresh Country Eggs (From Utah)	.07
Sugar (From Cuba, or Utah)	.00½
Butter and Cream (From New England)	.03
Grand total	.20

It is not very difficult to obtain FOOD in a country where two people can have breakfast consisting of all they want or need for a dime apiece! Observe that this simple breakfast was gathered, by some strange form of magic (?) from China, South America, Utah, Kansas and the New England States, and delivered on the breakfast table, ready for consumption, in the very heart of the most crowded city in America, at a cost well within the means of the most humble laborer.

The cost included all federal, state and city taxes! (Here is a fact the politicians did not mention when they were crying out to the voters to throw their opponents out of office because the people were being taxed to death).

b. **SHELTER**. This family lives in a comfortable apartment, heated by steam, lighted with electricity, with gas for cooking, all for $65.00 a month. In a smaller city, or a more sparsely settled part of New York city, the same apartment could be had for as low as $20.00 a month.

The toast they had for breakfast in the food estimate was toasted on an electric toaster, which cost but a few dollars, the apartment is cleaned with a vacuum sweeper that is run by electricity. Hot and cold water is available, at all times, in the kitchen and the bathroom. The food is kept cool in a refrigerator that is run by electricity. The wife curls her hair, washes her clothes and irons them with easily operated electrical equipment, on power obtained by sticking a plug in the wall. The husband shaves with an electric shaver, and they receive entertainment from all over the world, twenty four hours a day, if they want it, without cost, by merely turning the dial of their radio.

There are other conveniences in this apartment, but the foregoing list will give a fair idea of some of the concrete evidences of the freedom we, of America, enjoy. *(And this is neither political nor economic propaganda)*.

c. **CLOTHING**. Anywhere in the United States, the woman of average clothing requirements can dress very comfortably and neatly for less than $200.00 a year, and the average man can dress for the same, or less.

Only the three basic necessities of food, clothing, and shelter have been mentioned. The average American citizen has other privileges and advantages available in return for modest effort, not exceeding eight hours per day of labor. Among these is the privilege of automobile transportation, with which one can go and come at will, at very small cost.

The average American has security of property rights not found in any other country in the world. He can place his surplus money in a bank with the assurance that his government will protect it, and make good to him if the bank fails. If an American citizen wants to travel from one state to another he needs no passport, no one's permission. He may go when he pleases, and return at will. Moreover, he may travel by train, private automobile, bus, airplane, or ship, as his pocketbook permits. In Germany, Russia, Italy, and most of the other European and Oriental countries, the people cannot travel with so much freedom, and at so little cost.

THE "MIRACLE" THAT HAS
PROVIDED THESE BLESSINGS

We often bear politicians proclaiming the freedom of America, when they solicit votes, but seldom do they take the time or devote sufficient effort to the analysis of the source or nature of this "freedom." Having no axe to grind, no grudge to express, no ulterior motives to be carried out, I have the privilege of going into a frank analysis of that mysterious, abstract, greatly misunderstood "SOMETHING" which gives to every citizen of America more blessings, more opportunities to accumulate wealth, more freedom of every nature, than may be found in any other country.

I have the right to analyze the source and nature of this UNSEEN POWER, because I know, and have known for more than a quarter of a century, many of the men who organized that power, and many who are now responsible for its maintenance.

The name of this mysterious benefactor of mankind is CAPITAL!

CAPITAL consists not alone of money particularly of highly organized, intelligent groups of men who plan ways and means of using money efficiently for the good of the public, and profitably to themselves.

These groups consist of scientists, educators, chemists, inventors, business analysts, publicity men, transportation experts, accountants, lawyers, doctors, and both men and women who have highly specialized knowledge in all fields of industry and business. They pioneer, experiment, and blaze trails in new fields of endeavor. They support colleges, hospitals, public schools, build good roads, publish newspapers, pay most of the cost of government, and take care of the multitudinous detail essential to human progress. Stated briefly, the capitalists are the brains of civilization, because they supply the entire fabric of which all education, enlightenment and human progress consists.

Money, without brains, always is dangerous. Properly used, it is the most important essential of civilization. The simple breakfast here described could not have been delivered to the New York family at a dime each, *or at any other price,* if organized capital had not provided the machinery, the ships, the railroads, and the huge armies of trained men to operate them.

Some slight idea of the importance of ORGANIZED CAPITAL may be had by trying to imagine yourself burdened with the responsibility of collecting, without the aid of capital, and delivering to the New York City family, the simple breakfast described.

To supply the tea, you would have to make a trip to China or India, both a very long way from America. Unless you are an excellent swimmer, you would become rather tired before making the round trip. Then, too, another problem would confront you. What would you use for money, even if you had the physical endurance to swim the ocean?

To supply the sugar, you would have to take another long swim to Cuba, or a long walk to the sugar beet section of Utah. But even then, you might come back without the sugar, because organized effort and money are necessary to produce sugar, to say nothing of what is required to refine, transport, and deliver it to the breakfast table anywhere in the United States.

The eggs, you could deliver easily enough from the barn yards near New York City, but you would have a very long walk to Florida and return, before you could serve the two glasses of grapefruit juice.

You would have another long walk, to Kansas, or one of the other wheat growing states, when you went after the four slices of wheat bread.

The Rippled Wheat Biscuits would have to be omitted from the menu, because they would not be available except through the labor of a trained organization of men and suitable machinery, ALL OF WHICH CALL FOR CAPITAL.

While resting, you could take off for another little swim down to South America, where you would pick up a couple of bananas, and on your return, you could take a short walk to the nearest farm having a dairy and pick up some butter and cream. Then your New York City family would be ready to sit down and enjoy breakfast, and *you could collect your two dimes for your labor!*

Seems absurd, doesn't it? Well, the procedure described would be the only possible way these simple items of food could be delivered to the heart of New York City, if we had no capitalistic system.

The sum of money required for the building and maintenance of the railroads and steam ships used in the delivery of that simple breakfast is so huge that it staggers one's imagination. It runs into hundreds of millions of dollars, not to mention the armies of trained employees required to man the ships and trains. But, transportation is only a part of the requirements of modern civilization in capitalistic America. Before there can be anything to haul, something must be grown from the ground, or manufactured and prepared for market. This calls for more millions of dollars for equipment, machinery, boxing, marketing, and for the wages of millions of men and women.

Steam ships and railroads do not spring up from the earth and function automatically. They come in response to the call of civilization, through the labor and ingenuity and organizing ability of men who have IMAGINATION, FAITH, ENTHUSIASM, DECISION, PERSISTENCE! These men are known as capitalists. They are motivated by the desire to build, construct, achieve, render useful service, earn profits and accumulate riches. And, because they RENDER SERVICE WITHOUT WHICH THERE WOULD BE NO CIVILIZATION, they put themselves in the way of great riches.

Just to keep the record simple and understandable, I will add that these capitalists are the self-same men of whom most of us have heard soap-box orators speak. They are the same men to whom radicals, racketeers, dishonest politicians and grafting labor leaders refer as "the predatory interests," or "Wall Street."

I am not attempting to present a brief for or against any group of men or any system of economics. I am not attempting to condemn collective bargaining when

I refer to "grafting labor leaders," nor do I aim to give a clean bill of health to all individuals known as capitalists.

The purpose of this book—A *purpose to which I have faithfully devoted over a quarter of a century*—is to present to all who want the knowledge, the most dependable philosophy through which individuals may accumulate riches in whatever amounts they desire.

I have here analyzed the economic advantages of the capitalistic system for the two-fold purpose of showing:

1. that all who seek riches must recognize and adapt themselves to the system that controls all approaches to fortunes, large or small, and

2. to present the side of the picture opposite to that being shown by politicians and demagogues who deliberately becloud the issues they bring up, by referring to organized capital as if it were something poisonous.

This is a capitalistic country, it was developed through the use of capital, and we who claim the right to partake of the blessings of freedom and opportunity, we who seek to accumulate riches here, may as well know that neither riches nor opportunity would be available to us if ORGANIZED CAPITAL had not provided these benefits.

For more than twenty years it has been a somewhat popular and growing pastime for radicals, self-seeking politicians, racketeers, crooked labor leaders, and on occasion religious leaders, to take pot-shots at "WALL STREET, THE MONEY CHANGERS, and BIG BUSINESS."

The practice became so general that we witnessed during the business depression, the unbelievable sight of high government officials lining up with the cheap politicians, and labor leaders, with the openly avowed purpose of throttling the system which has made Industrial America the richest country on earth. The line-up was so general and so well organized that it prolonged the worst depression America has ever known. It cost millions of men their jobs, because those jobs were inseparably a part of the industrial and capitalistic system which form the very backbone of the nation.

During this unusual alliance of government officials and self-seeking individuals who were endeavoring to profit by declaring "open season" on the American system of industry, a certain type of labor leader joined forces with the politicians and offered to deliver voters in return for legislation designed to permit men to TAKE RICHES AWAY FROM INDUSTRY BY ORGANIZED FORCE OF NUMBERS, INSTEAD OF THE BETTER METHOD OF GIVING A FAIR DAY'S WORK FOR A FAIR DAY'S PAY.

Millions of men and women throughout the nation are still engaged in this popular pastime of trying to GET without GIVING. Some of them are lined up with labor unions, where they demand SHORTER HOURS AND MORE PAY! Others do not take the trouble to work at all. THEY DEMAND GOVERNMENT RELIEF AND

ARE GETTING IT. Their idea of their rights of freedom was demonstrated in New York City, where violent complaint was registered with the Postmaster, by a group of "relief beneficiaries," because the Postmen awakened them at 7:30 A.M. to deliver Government relief checks. They DEMANDED that the time of delivery be set up to 10:00 o'clock.

If you are one of those who believe that riches can be accumulated by the mere act of men who organize themselves into groups and demand MORE PAY for LESS SERVICE, if you are one of those who DEMAND Government relief without early morning disturbance when the money is delivered to you, if you are one of those who believe in trading their votes to politicians in return for the passing of laws which permit the raiding of the public treasury, you may rest securely on your belief, with certain knowledge that no one will disturb you, because THIS IS A FREE COUNTRY WHERE EVERY MAN MAY THINK AS HE PLEASES, where nearly everybody can live with but little effort, where many may live well without doing any work whatsoever.

However, you should know the full truth concerning this FREEDOM of which so many people boast, and so few understand. As great as it is, as far as it reaches, as many privileges as it provides, IT DOES NOT, AND CANNOT BRING RICHES WITHOUT EFFORT.

There is but one dependable method of accumulating, and legally holding riches, and that is by rendering useful service. No system has ever been created by which men can legally acquire riches through mere force of numbers, or without giving in return an equivalent value of one form or another.

There is a principle known as the law of ECONOMICS! This is more than a theory. It is a law no man can beat.

Mark well the name of the principle, and remember it, because it is far more powerful than all the politicians and political machines. It is above and beyond the control of all the labor unions. It cannot be swayed, nor influenced nor bribed by racketeers or self-appointed leaders in any calling. Moreover, IT HAS AN ALL-SEEING EYE, AND A PERFECT SYSTEM OF BOOKKEEPING, in which it keeps an accurate account of the transactions of every human being engaged in the business of trying to get without giving. Sooner or later its auditors come around, look over the records of individuals both great and small, and demand an accounting.

"Wall Street, Big Business, Capital Predatory Interests," or whatever name you choose to give the system which has given us AMERICAN FREEDOM, represents a group of men who understand, respect, and adapt themselves to this powerful LAW OF ECONOMICS! Their financial continuation depends upon their respecting the law.

Most people living in America like this country, its capitalistic system and all. I must confess I know of no better country, where one may find greater opportunities to accumulate riches. Judging by their acts and deeds, there are some in this country who do not like it. That, of course is their privilege; if they do not like this country, its capitalistic system, its boundless opportunities, *THEY HAVE THE PRIV-ILEGE OF CLEARING OUT!* Always there are other countries, such as Germany, Russia, and Italy, where one may try one's hand at enjoying freedom, and accumulating riches providing one is not too particular.

America provides all the freedom and all the opportunity to accumulate riches that any honest person may require. When one goes hunting for game, one selects hunting grounds where game is plentiful. When seeking riches, the same rule would naturally obtain.

If it is riches you are seeking, do not overlook the possibilities of a country whose citizens are so rich that women, alone, spend over two hundred million dollars annually for lipsticks, rouge and cosmetics. Think twice, you who are seeking riches, before trying to destroy the Capitalistic System of a country whose citizens spend over fifty million dollars a year for GREETING CARDS, with which to express their appreciation of their FREEDOM!

If it is money you are seeking, consider carefully a country that spends hundreds of millions of dollars annually for cigarettes, the bulk of the income from which goes to only four major companies engaged in supplying this national builder of "nonchalance" and "quiet nerves."

By all means give plenty of consideration to a country whose people spend annually more than fifteen million dollars for the privilege of seeing moving pictures, and toss in a few additional millions for liquor, narcotics, and other less potent soft drinks and giggle-waters.

Do not be in too big a hurry to get away from a country whose people willingly, even eagerly, hand over millions of dollars annually for football, baseball, and prize fights.

And, by all means, STICK by a country whose inhabitants give up more than a million dollars a year for chewing gum, and another million for safety razor blades.

Remember, also, that this is but the beginning of the available sources for the accumulation of wealth. Only a few of the luxuries and non-essentials have been mentioned. But, remember that the business of producing, transporting, and marketing these few items of merchandise gives regular employment to MANY MILLIONS OF MEN AND WOMEN, who receive for their services MANY MILLIONS OF DOLLARS MONTHLY, and spend it freely for both the luxuries and the necessities.

Especially remember, that back of all this exchange of merchandise and personal services may be found an abundance of OPPORTUNITY to accumulate riches. Here our AMERICAN FREEDOM comes to one's aid. There is nothing to stop you, or anyone from engaging in any portion of the effort necessary to carry on these businesses. If one has superior talent, training, experience, one may accumulate riches in large amounts. Those not so fortunate may accumulate smaller amounts. Anyone may earn a living in return for a very nominal amount of labor.

So—there you are!

OPPORTUNITY has spread its wares before you. Step up to the front, select what you want, create your plan, put the plan into action, and follow through with

PERSISTENCE. "Capitalistic" America will do the rest. You can depend upon this much—CAPITALISTIC AMERICA INSURES EVERY PERSON THE OPPORTU-NITY TO RENDER USEFUL SERVICE, AND TO COLLECT RICHES IN PROPOR-TION TO THE VALUE OF THE SERVICE.

The "System" denies no one this right, but it does not, and cannot promise SOMETHING FOR NOTHING, because the system, itself, is irrevocably controlled by the LAW OF ECONOMICS which neither recognizes nor tolerates for long, GETTING WITHOUT GIVING.

The LAW OF ECONOMICS was passed by Nature! There is no Supreme Court to which violators of this law may appeal. The law hands out both penalties for its violation, and appropriate rewards for its observance, *without interference or the possibility of interference by any human being.* The law cannot be repealed. It is as fixed as the stars in the heavens, and subject to, and a part of the same system that controls the stars.

May one refuse to adapt one's self to the LAW OF ECONOMICS?

Certainly! This is a free country, where all men are born with equal rights, including the privilege of ignoring the LAW OF ECONOMICS.

What happens then?

Well, nothing happens until large numbers of men join forces for the avowed purpose of ignoring the law, and taking what they want by force. *THEN COMES THE DICTATOR, WITH WELL ORGANIZED FIRING SQUADS AND MACHINE GUNS!*

We have not yet reached that stage in America! But we have heard all we want to know about how the system works. Perhaps we shall be fortunate enough not to demand personal knowledge of so gruesome a reality. Doubtless we shall prefer to continue with our FREEDOM OF SPEECH, FREEDOM OF DEED, and FREEDOM TO RENDER USEFUL SERVICE IN RETURN FOR RICHES.

The practice, by Government officials of extending to men and women the privilege of raiding the public treasury in return for votes, sometimes results in election, but as night follows day, the, final payoff comes; when every penny wrongfully used, must be repaid with compound interest on compound interest. If those who make the grab are not forced to repay, the burden falls on their children, and their children's children, "even unto the third and fourth generations." There is no way to avoid the debt.

Men can, and sometimes do, form themselves into groups for the purpose of crowding wages up, and working hours down. There is a point beyond which they cannot go. It is the point at which the LAW OF ECONOMICS steps in, and the sheriff gets both the employer and the employees.

For six years, from 1929, to 1935, the people of America, both rich and poor, barely missed seeing the Old Man Economics hand over to the sheriff all the busi-nesses, and industries and banks. It was not a pretty sight! It did not increase our respect for mob psychology through which men cast reason to the winds and start trying to GET without GIVING.

We who went through those six discouraging years, when FEAR WAS IN THE SADDLE, AND FAITH WAS ON THE GROUND, cannot forget how ruthlessly the LAW OF ECONOMICS exacted its toll from both rich and poor, weak and strong, old and young. We shall not wish to go through another such experience.

These observations are not founded upon short-time experience. They are the result of twenty-five years of careful analysis of the methods of both the successful and the most unsuccessful men America has known.

CHAPTER EIGHT

DECISION:

THE MASTERY OF PROCRASTINATION
The Seventh Step toward Riches

Accurate analysis of over 25,000 men and women who had experienced failure, disclosed the fact that LACK OF DECISION was near the head of the list of the 30 major causes of FAILURE. This is no mere statement of a theory—*it is a fact.*

PROCRASTINATION, the opposite of DECISION, is a common enemy which practically every man must conquer.

You will have an opportunity to test your capacity to reach *quick* and *definite* DECISIONS when you finish reading this book, and are ready to begin putting into ACTION the principles which it describes.

Analysis of several hundred people who had accumulated fortunes well beyond the million dollar mark, disclosed the fact that *every one of them* had the habit of REACHING DECISIONS PROMPTLY, and of changing these decisions SLOWLY, if, and when they were changed. People who fail to accumulate money, *without exception,* have the habit of reaching decisions, IF AT ALL, very *slowly,* and of *changing these decisions quickly and often.*

One of Henry Ford's most outstanding qualities is his *habit* of reaching decisions quickly and definitely, and changing them slowly. This quality is so pronounced in Mr. Ford, that it has given him the reputation of being obstinate. It was this quality which prompted Mr. Ford to continue to manufacture his famous Model "T" (the world's ugliest car), when all of his advisors, and many of the purchasers of the car, were urging him to change it.

Perhaps, Mr. Ford delayed too long in making the change, but the other side of the story is, that Mr. Ford's firmness of decision yielded a huge fortune, before the change in model became *necessary.* There is but little doubt that Mr. Ford's habit of definiteness of decision assumes the proportion of obstinacy, but this quality is preferable to slowness in reaching decisions and quickness in changing them.

The majority of people who fail to accumulate money sufficient for their needs, are, generally, easily influenced by the "opinions" of others. They permit the newspapers and the "gossiping" neighbors to do their "thinking" for them. "Opinions" are the cheapest commodities on earth. Everyone has a flock of opinions ready to be wished upon anyone who will accept them. If you are influenced by "opinions" when you reach DECISIONS, you will not succeed in any undertaking, much less in that of transmuting YOUR OWN DESIRE into money.

If you are influenced by the opinions of others, you will have no DESIRE of your own.

Keep your own counsel, when you begin to put into practice the principles described here, by *reaching your own decisions* and following them. Take no one into your confidence, EXCEPT the members of your "Master Mind" group, and be very sure in your selection of this group, that you choose ONLY those who will be in COMPLETE SYMPATHY AND HARMONY WITH YOUR PURPOSE.

Close friends and relatives, while not meaning to do so, often handicap one through "opinions" and sometimes through ridicule, which is meant to be humorous. Thousands of men and women carry inferiority complexes with them all through life, because some well-meaning, but ignorant person destroyed their confidence through "opinions" or ridicule.

You have a brain and mind of your own. USE IT, and reach your own decisions. If you need facts or information from other people, to enable you to reach decisions, as you probably will in many instances; acquire these facts or secure the information you need quietly, without disclosing your purpose.

It is characteristic of people who have but a smattering or a veneer of knowledge to try to give the impression that they have much knowledge. Such people generally do TOO MUCH talking, and TOO LITTLE listening. Keep your eyes and ears wide open—and your mouth CLOSED, if you wish to acquire the habit of prompt DECISION. Those who talk too much do little else. If you talk more than you listen, you not only deprive yourself of many opportunities to accumulate useful knowledge, but you also disclose your PLANS and PURPOSES to people who will take great delight in defeating you, because they envy you.

Remember, also, that every time you open your mouth in the presence of a person who has an abundance of knowledge, you display to that person, your exact stock of knowledge, or your LACK of it! Genuine wisdom is usually conspicuous through *modesty and silence.*

Keep in mind the fact that every person with whom you associate is, like yourself, seeking the opportunity to accumulate money. If you talk about your plans too freely, you may be surprised when you learn that some other person has beaten you to your goal by PUTTING INTO ACTION AHEAD OF YOU, the plans of which you talked unwisely.

Let one of your first decisions be to KEEP A CLOSED MOUTH AND OPEN EARS AND EYES.

As a reminder to yourself to follow this advice, it will be helpful if you copy the following epigram in large letters and place it where you will see it daily.

"TELL THE WORLD WHAT YOU INTEND TO DO, BUT FIRST SHOW IT."

This is the equivalent of saying that "deeds, and not words, are what count most."

FREEDOM OR DEATH ON A DECISION

The value of decisions depends upon the courage required to render them. The great decisions, which served as the foundation of civilization, were reached by assuming great risks, which often meant the possibility of death.

Lincoln's decision to issue his famous Proclamation of Emancipation, which gave freedom to the colored people of America, was rendered with full understanding that his act would turn thousands of friends and political supporters against him. He knew, too, that the carrying out of that proclamation would mean death to thousands of men on the battlefield. In the end, it cost Lincoln his life. That required courage.

Socrates' decision to drink the cup of poison, rather than compromise in his personal belief, was a decision of courage. It turned Time ahead a thousand years, and gave to people then unborn, the right to freedom of thought and of speech.

The decision of Gen. Robert E. Lee, when he came to the parting of the way with the Union, and took up the cause of the South, was a decision of courage, for he well knew that it might cost him his own life, that it would surely cost the lives of others.

But, the greatest decision of all time, as far as any American citizen is concerned, was reached in Philadelphia, July 4, 1776, when fifty-six men signed their names to a document, which they well knew would bring freedom to all Americans, or *leave every one of the fifty-six hanging from a gallows!*

You have heard of this famous document, but you may not have drawn from it the great lesson in personal achievement it so plainly taught.

We all remember the date of this momentous decision, but few of us realize what courage that decision required. We remember our history, as it was taught; we remember dates, and the names of the men who fought; we remember Valley Forge, and Yorktown; we remember George Washington, and Lord Cornwallis. But we know little of the real forces back of these names, dates, and places. We know still less of that intangible POWER, which insured us freedom *long before Washington's armies reached Yorktown.*

We read the history of the Revolution, and falsely imagine that George Washington was the Father of our Country, that it was he who won our freedom, while the truth is—Washington was only an accessory after the fact, because victory for his armies had been insured long before Lord Cornwallis surrendered. This is not intended to rob Washington of any of the glory he so richly merited. Its purpose, rather, is to give greater attention to the astounding POWER that was the real cause of his victory.

It is nothing short of tragedy that the writers of history have missed, entirely, even the slightest reference to the irresistible POWER, which gave birth and freedom to the nation destined to set up new standards of independence for all the peoples of the earth. I say it is a tragedy, because it is the self-same POWER which must be used by every individual who surmounts the difficulties of Life, and forces Life to pay the price asked.

Let us briefly review the events which gave birth to this POWER. The story begins with an incident in Boston, March 5, 1770. British soldiers were patrolling the streets, by their presence, openly threatening the citizens. The colonists resented armed men marching in their midst. They began to express their resentment openly, hurling stones as well as epithets, at the marching soldiers, until the commanding officer gave orders, "Fix bayonets. . . . Charge!"

The battle was on. It resulted in the death and injury of many. The incident aroused such resentment that the Provincial Assembly, (made up of prominent colonists), called a meeting for the purpose of taking definite action. Two of the members of that Assembly were, John Hancock, and Samuel Adams—LONG LIVE THEIR NAMES! They spoke up courageously, and declared that a move must, be made to eject all British soldiers from Boston.

Remember this—a DECISION, in the minds of two men, might properly be called the beginning of the freedom which we, of the United States now enjoy. Remember, too, that the DECISION of these two men called for FAITH, and COURAGE, because it was dangerous.

Before the Assembly adjourned, Samuel Adams was appointed to call on the Governor of the Province, Hutchinson, and demand the withdrawal of the British troops.

The request was granted, the troops were removed from Boston, but the incident was not closed. It had caused a situation destined to change the entire trend of civilization. Strange, is it not, how the great changes, such as the American Revolution, and the World War, often have their beginnings in circumstances which seem unimportant? It is interesting, also, to observe that these important changes usually begin in the form of a DEFINITE DECISION in the minds of a relatively small number of people. Few of us know the history of our country well enough to realize that John Hancock, Samuel Adams, and Richard Henry Lee (of the Province of Virginia) were the real Fathers of our Country.

Richard Henry Lee became an important factor in this story by reason of the fact that he and Samuel Adams communicated frequently (by correspondence), sharing freely their fears and their hopes concerning the welfare of the people of their Provinces. From this practice, Adams conceived the idea that a mutual exchange of letters between the thirteen Colonies might help to bring about the coordination of effort so badly needed in connection with the solution of their problems. Two years after the clash with the soldiers in Boston (March '72), Adams presented this idea to the Assembly, in the form of a motion that a Correspondence Committee be established among the Colonies, with definitely appointed correspondents in each Colony, "for the purpose of friendly cooperation for the betterment of the Colonies of British America."

Mark well this incident! It was the beginning of the organization of the far-flung POWER destined to give freedom to you, and to me. The Master Mind had already been organized. It consisted of Adams, Lee, and Hancock. "I tell you further, that if two of you agree upon the earth concerning anything for which you ask, it will come to you from My Father, who is in Heaven."

The Committee of Correspondence was organized. Observe that this move provided the way for increasing the power of the Master Mind by adding to it men from all the Colonies. Take notice that this procedure constituted the first ORGANIZED PLANNING of the disgruntled Colonists.

In union there is strength! The citizens of the Colonies had been waging disorganized warfare against the British soldiers, through incidents similar to the Boston riot, but nothing of benefit had been accomplished. Their individual grievances had not been consolidated under one Master Mind. No group of individuals had put their hearts, minds, souls, and bodies together in one definite DECISION to settle their difficulty with the British once and for all, until Adams, Hancock, and Lee got together.

Meanwhile, the British were not idle. They, too, were doing some PLANNING and "Master-Minding" on their own account, with the advantage of having back of them money, and organized soldiery.

The Crown appointed Gage to supplant Hutchinson as the Governor of Massachusetts. One of the new Governor's first acts was to send a messenger to call on Samuel Adams, for the purpose of endeavoring to stop his opposition—by FEAR.

We can best understand the spirit of what happened by quoting the conversation between Col. Fenton, (the messenger sent by Gage), and Adams.

Col. Fenton: "I have been authorized by Governor Gage, to assure you, Mr. Adams, that the Governor has been empowered to confer upon you such benefits as would be satisfactory, [endeavor to win Adams by promise of bribes], upon the condition that you engage to cease in your opposition to the measures of the government. It is the Governor's advice to you, Sir, not to incur the further displeasure of his majesty. Your conduct has been such as makes you liable to penalties of an Act of Henry VIII, by which persons can be sent to England for trial for treason, or misprision of treason, at the discretion of a governor of a province. But, BY CHANGING YOUR POLITICAL COURSE, you will not only receive great personal advantages, but you will make your peace with the King."

Samuel Adams had the choice of two DECISIONS. He could cease his opposition, and receive personal bribes, or he could CONTINUE, AND RUN THE RISK OF BEING HANGED!

Clearly, the time had come when Adams was *forced* to reach *instantly,* a DECISION which could have cost his life. The majority of men would have found it difficult to reach such a decision. The majority would have sent back an evasive reply, but not Adams! He insisted upon Col. Fenton's word of honor, that the Colonel would deliver to the Governor the answer exactly as Adams would give it to him.

Adams' answer, "Then you may tell Governor Gage that I trust I have long since made my peace with the King of Kings. No personal consideration shall induce me to abandon the righteous cause of my Country. And, TELL GOVERNOR GAGE IT IS THE ADVICE OF SAMUEL ADAMS TO HIM, no longer to insult the feelings of an exasperated people."

Comment as to the character of this man seems unnecessary. It must be obvious to all who read this astounding message that its sender possessed loyalty of the highest order. *This is important.* (Racketeers and dishonest politicians have prostituted the honor for which such men as Adams died).

When Governor Gage received Adams' caustic reply, he flew into a rage, and issued a proclamation which read, "I do, hereby, in his majesty's name, offer and promise his most gracious pardon to all persons who shall forthwith lay down their arms, and return to the duties of peaceable subjects, excepting only from the benefit of such pardon, SAMUEL ADAMS AND JOHN HANCOCK, whose offences are of too flagitious a nature to admit of any other consideration but that of condign punishment."

As one might say, in modern slang, Adams and Hancock were "on the spot!" The threat of the irate Governor forced the two men to reach another DECISION, equally as dangerous. They hurriedly called a secret meeting of their staunchest followers. (Here the Master Mind began to take on momentum). After the meeting had been called to order, Adams locked the door, placed the key in his pocket, and informed all present that it was imperative that a Congress of the Colonists be organized, and that NO MAN SHOULD LEAVE THE ROOM UNTIL THE DECISION FOR SUCH A CONGRESS HAD BEEN REACHED.

Great excitement followed. Some weighed the possible consequences of such radicalism. (Old Man Fear). Some expressed grave doubt as to the wisdom of so *definite a decision* in defiance of the crown. Locked in that room were TWO MEN immune to Fear, blind to the possibility of Failure. Hancock and Adams. Through the influence of their minds, the others were induced to agree that, through the Correspondence Committee, arrangements should be made for a meeting of the First Continental Congress, to be held in Philadelphia, September 5, 1774.

Remember this date. It is more important than July 4, 1776. If there had been no DECISION to hold a Continental Congress, there could have been no signing of the Declaration of Independence.

Before the first meeting of the new Congress, another leader, in a different section of the country was deep in the throes of publishing a "Summary View of the Rights of British America." He was Thomas Jefferson, of the Province of Virginia, whose relationship to Lord Dunmore, (representative of the Crown in Virginia), was as strained as that of Hancock and Adams with their Governor.

Shortly after his famous Summary of Rights was published, Jefferson was informed that he was subject to prosecution for high treason against his majesty's government. Inspired by the threat, one of Jefferson's colleagues, Patrick Henry, boldly spoke his mind, concluding his remarks with a sentence which shall remain forever a classic, *"If this be treason, then make the most of it."*

It was such men as these who, without power, without authority, without military strength, without money, sat in solemn consideration of the destiny of the colonies, beginning at the opening of the First Continental Congress, and continuing at intervals for two years—until on June 7, 1776, Richard Henry Lee arose, addressed the Chair, and to the startled Assembly made this motion:

"Gentlemen, I make the motion that these United Colonies are, and of right ought to be free and independent states, that they be absolved from all allegiance to the British Crown, and that all political connection between them and the state of Great Britain is, and ought to be totally dissolved."

Lee's astounding motion was discussed fervently, and at such length that he began to lose patience. Finally, after days of argument, he again took the floor, and declared, in a clear, firm voice, "Mr. President, we have discussed this issue for days. It is the only course for us to follow. Why, then Sir, do we longer delay? Why still deliberate? Let this happy day give birth to an American Republic. Let her arise, not to devastate and to conquer, but to reestablish the reign of peace, and of law. The eyes of Europe are fixed upon us. She demands of us a living example of freedom, that may exhibit a contrast, in the felicity of the citizen, to the ever increasing tyranny."

Before his motion was finally voted upon, Lee was called back to Virginia, because of serious family illness, but before leaving, he placed his cause in the hands of his friend, Thomas Jefferson, who promised to fight until favorable action was taken. Shortly thereafter the President of the Congress (Hancock), appointed Jefferson as Chairman of a Committee to draw up a Declaration of Independence.

Long and hard the Committee labored, on a document which would mean, when accepted by the Congress that EVERY MAN WHO SIGNED IT, WOULD BE SIGNING HIS OWN DEATH WARRANT, should the Colonies lose in the fight with Great Britain, which was sure to follow.

The document was drawn, and on June 28, the original draft was read before the Congress. For several days it was discussed, altered, and made ready. On July 4, 1776, Thomas Jefferson stood before the Assembly, and fearlessly read the most momentous DECISION ever placed upon paper.

"When in the course of human events it is necessary for one people to dissolve the political bands which have connected them with another, and to assume, among the powers of the earth, the separate and equal station to which the laws of Nature, and of Nature's God entitle them, a decent respect to the opinions of mankind requires that they should declare the causes which impel them to the separation. . . . ."

When Jefferson finished, the document was voted upon, accepted, and signed by the fifty-six men, every one staking his own life upon his DECISION to write his name. By that DECISION came into existence a nation destined to bring to mankind forever, the privilege of making DECISIONS.

By decisions made in a similar spirit of Faith, and only by such decisions, can men solve their personal problems, and win for themselves high estates of material and spiritual wealth. Let us not forget this!

Analyze the events which led to the Declaration of Independence, and be convinced that this nation, which now holds a position of commanding respect and power among all nations of the world, was born of a DECISION created by a Master Mind, consisting of fifty-six men. Note well, the fact that it was their DECISION which insured the success of Washington's armies, because the *spirit* of that decision was in the heart of every soldier who fought with him, and served as a spiritual power which recognizes no such thing as FAILURE.

Note, also, (with great personal benefit), that the POWER which gave this nation its freedom, is the self-same power that must be used by every individual who becomes self-determining. This POWER is made up of the principles described in this book. It will not be difficult to detect, in the story of the Declaration of Independence, at least six of these principles; DESIRE, DECISION, FAITH, PERSISTENCE, THE MASTER MIND, and ORGANIZED PLANNING.

Throughout this philosophy will be found the suggestion that thought, backed by strong DESIRE, has a tendency to transmute itself into its physical equivalent. Before passing on, I wish to leave with you the suggestion that one may find in this story, and in the story of the organization of the United States Steel Corporation, a perfect description of the method by which thought makes this astounding transformation.

In your search for the secret of the method, do not look for a miracle, because you will not find it. You will find only the eternal laws of Nature. These laws are available to every person who has the FAITH and the COURAGE to use them. They may be used to bring freedom to a nation, or to accumulate riches. There is no charge save the time necessary to understand and appropriate them.

Those who reach DECISIONS promptly and definitely, know what they want, and generally get it. The leaders in every walk of life DECIDE quickly, and firmly. That is the major reason why they are leaders. The world has the habit of making room for the man whose words and actions show that he knows where he is going.

INDECISION is a habit which usually begins in youth. The habit takes on permanency as the youth goes through graded school, high school, and even through college, without DEFINITENESS OF PURPOSE. The major weakness of all educational systems is that they neither teach nor encourage the habit of DEFINITE DECISION.

It would be beneficial if no college would permit the enrollment of any student, unless and until the student declared his major purpose in matriculating. It would be of still greater benefit, if every student who enters the graded schools were compelled to accept training in the HABIT OF DECISION, and forced to pass a satisfactory examination on this subject before being permitted to advance in the grades.

The habit of INDECISION acquired because of the deficiencies of our school systems, goes with the student into the occupation he chooses . . . IF . . . in fact, he chooses his occupation. Generally, the youth just out of school seeks any job that can be found. He takes the first place he finds, because he has fallen into the habit of INDECISION. Ninety-eight out of every hundred people working for wages today, are in the positions they hold, because they lacked the DEFINITE-NESS OF DECISION to PLAN A DEFINITE POSITION, and the knowledge of how to choose an employer.

DEFINITENESS OF DECISION always requires courage, sometimes very great courage. The fifty-six men who signed the Declaration of Independence staked their lives on the DECISION to affix their signatures to that document. The person who reaches a DEFINITE DECISION to procure the particular job, and make life pay the price he asks, does not stake his life on that decision; he stakes his ECO-NOMIC FREEDOM. Financial independence, riches, desirable business and pro-fessional positions are not within reach of the person who neglects or refuses to EXPECT, PLAN, and DEMAND these things. The person who desires riches in the same spirit that Samuel Adams desired freedom for the Colonies, is sure to accu-mulate wealth.

In the chapter on Organized Planning, you will find complete instructions for marketing every type of personal services. You will find also detailed information on how to choose the employer you prefer, and the particular job you desire. These instructions will be of no value to you UNLESS YOU DEFINITELY DECIDE to organize them into a plan of action.

CHAPTER NINE

PERSISTENCE:

THE SUSTAINED EFFORT NECESSARY TO INDUCE FAITH
The Eighth Step toward Riches

PERSISTENCE is an essential factor in the procedure of transmuting DESIRE into its monetary equivalent. The basis of persistence is the POWER OF WILL.

Will-power and desire, when properly combined, make an irresistible pair. Men who accumulate great fortunes are generally known as cold-blooded, and sometimes ruthless. Often they are misunderstood. What they have is will-power, which they mix with persistence, and place back of their desires to *insure* the attainment of their objectives.

Henry Ford has been generally misunderstood to be ruthless and cold-blooded. This misconception grew out of Ford's habit of following through in all of his plans with PERSISTENCE.

The majority of people are ready to throw their aims and purposes overboard, and give up at the first sign of opposition or misfortune. A few carry on DESPITE all opposition, until they attain their goal. These few are the Fords, Carnegies, Rockefellers, and Edisons.

There may be no heroic connotation to the word "persistence," but the quality is to the character of man what carbon is to steel.

The building of a fortune, generally, involves the application of the entire thirteen factors of this philosophy. These principles must be understood, they must be applied with PERSISTENCE by all who accumulate money.

If you are following this book with the intention of applying the knowledge it conveys, your first test as to your PERSISTENCE will come when you begin to follow the six steps described in the second chapter. Unless you are one of the two out of every hundred who already have a DEFINITE GOAL at which you are aiming, and a DEFINITE PLAN for its attainment, you may read the instructions, and then pass on with your daily routine, and never comply with those instructions.

The author is checking you up at this point, because lack of persistence is one of the major causes of failure. Moreover, experience with thousands of people has proved that lack of persistence is a weakness common to the majority of men. It is a weakness which may be overcome by effort. The ease with which lack of persistence may be conquered will depend *entirely* upon the INTENSITY OF ONE'S DESIRE.

The starting point of all achievement is DESIRE. Keep this constantly in mind. Weak desires bring weak results, just as a small amount of fire makes a small amount of heat. If you find yourself lacking in persistence, this weakness may be remedied by building a stronger fire under your desires.

Continue to read through to the end, then go back to Chapter two, and start *immediately* to carry out the instructions given in connection with the six steps. The eagerness with which you follow these instructions will indicate clearly, how much, or how little you really DESIRE to accumulate money. If you find that you are indifferent, you may be sure that you have not yet acquired the "money consciousness" which you must possess, before you can be sure of accumulating a fortune.

Fortunes gravitate to men whose minds have been prepared to "attract" them, just as surely as water gravitates to the ocean. In this book may be found all the stimuli necessary to "attune" any normal mind to the vibrations which will attract the object of one's desires.

If you find you are weak in PERSISTENCE, center your attention upon the instructions contained in the chapter on "Power"; surround yourself with a "MASTER MIND" group, and through the cooperative efforts of the members of this group, you can develop persistence. You will find additional instructions for the development of persistence in the chapters on auto-suggestion, and the subconscious mind. Follow the instructions outlined in these chapters until your habit nature hands over to your subconscious mind, a clear picture of the object of your DESIRE. From that point on, you will not be handicapped by lack of persistence.

Your subconscious mind works continuously, while you are awake, and while you are asleep.

Spasmodic, or occasional effort to apply the rules will be of no value to you. To get RESULTS, you must apply all of the rules until their application becomes a fixed habit with you. In no other way can you develop the necessary "money consciousness."

POVERTY is attracted to the one whose mind is favorable to it, as money is attracted to him whose mind has been deliberately prepared to attract it, and through the same laws. POVERTY CONSCIOUSNESS WILL VOLUNTARILY SEIZE THE MIND WHICH IS NOT OCCUPIED WITH THE MONEY CONSCIOUSNESS. A poverty consciousness develops without *conscious* application of habits favorable to it. The money consciousness must be created to order, unless one is born with such a consciousness.

Catch the full significance of the statements in the preceding paragraph, and you will understand the importance of PERSISTENCE in the accumulation of a fortune. Without PERSISTENCE, you will be defeated, even before you start. With PERSISTENCE you will win.

If you have ever experienced a nightmare, you will realize the value of persistence. You are lying in bed, half awake, with a feeling that you are about to smother. You are unable to turn over, or to move a muscle. You realize that you

MUST BEGIN to regain control over your muscles. Through persistent effort of will-power, you finally manage to move the fingers of one hand. By continuing to move your fingers, you extend your control to the muscles of one arm, until you can lift it. Then you gain control of the other arm in the same manner. You finally gain control over the muscles of one leg, and then extend it to the other leg. THEN—WITH ONE SUPREME EFFORT OF WILL—you regain complete control over your muscular system, and "snap" out of your nightmare. The trick has been turned step by step.

You may find it necessary to "snap" out of your mental inertia, through a similar procedure, moving slowly at first, then increasing your speed, until you gain complete control over your will. Be PERSISTENT no matter how slowly you may, at first, have to move. WITH PERSISTENCE WILL COME SUCCESS.

If you select your "Master Mind" group with care, you will have in it, at least one person who will aid you in the development of PERSISTENCE. Some men who have accumulated great fortunes, did so because of NECESSITY. They developed the habit of PERSISTENCE, because they were so closely driven by circumstances, that they *had to become persistent.*

THERE IS NO SUBSTITUTE FOR PERSISTENCE! It cannot be supplanted by any other quality! Remember this, and it will hearten you, in the beginning, when the going may seem difficult and slow.

Those who have cultivated the HABIT of persistence seem to enjoy insurance against failure. No matter how many times they are defeated, they finally arrive up toward the top of the ladder. Sometimes it appears that there is a hidden Guide whose duty is to test men through all sorts of discouraging experiences. Those who pick themselves up after defeat and keep on trying, arrive; and the world cries "Bravo! I knew you could do it!" The hidden Guide lets no one enjoy great achievement without passing the PERSISTENCE TEST. Those who can't take it, simply do not make the grade.

Those who can "take it" are bountifully rewarded for their PERSISTENCE. They receive, as their compensation, whatever goal they are pursuing. That is not all! They receive something infinitely more important than material compensation—the knowledge that "EVERY FAILURE BRINGS WITH IT THE SEED OF AN EQUIVALENT ADVANTAGE."

There are exceptions to this rule; a few people know from experience the soundness of persistence. They are the ones who have not accepted defeat as being anything more than temporary. They are the ones whose DESIRES are so PERSISTENTLY APPLIED that defeat is finally changed into victory. We who stand on the side-lines of Life see the overwhelmingly large number who go down in defeat, never to rise again. We see the few who take the punishment of defeat *as an urge to greater effort.* These, fortunately, never learn to accept Life's reverse gear. But what we DO NOT SEE, what most of us never suspect of existing, is the silent but irresistible POWER which comes to the rescue of those who fight on in the face of discouragement. If we speak of this power at all we call it PERSISTENCE, and let it go at that. One thing we all know, if one does not possess PERSISTENCE, one does not achieve noteworthy success in any calling.

As these lines are being written, I look up from my work, and see before me, less than a block away, the great mysterious "Broadway," the "Graveyard of Dead Hopes," and the "Front Porch of Opportunity." From all over the world people have come to Broadway, seeking fame, fortune, power, love, or whatever it is that human beings call success. Once in a great while someone steps out from the long procession of seekers, and the world hears that another person has mastered Broadway. But Broadway is not easily nor quickly conquered. She acknowledges talent, recognizes genius, pays off in money, only *after* one has refused to QUIT.

Then we know he has discovered the secret of how to conquer Broadway. The secret is always inseparably attached to one word, PERSISTENCE!

The secret is told in the struggle of Fannie Hurst, whose PERSISTENCE conquered the Great White Way. She came to New York in 1915, to convert writing into riches. The conversion did not come quickly, BUT IT CAME. For four years Miss Hurst learned about "The Sidewalks of New York" from first hand experience. She spent her days laboring, and her nights HOPING. When hope grew dim, she did not say, "Alright Broadway, you win!" She said, "Very well, Broadway, you may whip some, but not me. I'm going to force you to give up."

One publisher (The Saturday Evening Post) sent her *thirty six* rejection slips, before she "broke the ice" and got a story across. The average writer, like the "average" in other walks of life, would have given up the job when the first rejection slip came. She pounded the pavements for four years to the tune of the publisher's "NO," because she was determined to win.

Then came the "payoff." The spell had been broken, the unseen Guide had tested Fannie Hurst, and she could take it. From that time on publishers made a beaten path to her door. Money came so fast she hardly had time to count it. Then the moving picture men discovered her, and money came not in small change, but in floods. The moving picture rights to her latest novel, "Great Laughter," brought $100,000.00, said to be the highest price ever paid for a story before publication. Her royalties from the sale of the book probably will run much more.

Briefly, you have a description of what PERSISTENCE is capable of achieving. Fannie Hurst is no exception. Wherever men and women accumulate great riches, you may be sure they first acquired PERSISTENCE. Broadway will give any beggar a cup of coffee and a sandwich, but it demands PERSISTENCE of those who go after the big stakes.

Kate Smith will say "amen" when she reads this. For years she sang, without money, and without price, before any microphone she could reach. Broadway said to her, "Come and get it, if you can take it." She did take it until one happy day Broadway got tired and said, "Aw, what's the use? You don't know when you're whipped, so name your price, and go to work in earnest." Miss Smith named her price! It was plenty. Away up in figures so high that one week's salary is far more than most people make in a whole year.

Verily it pays to be PERSISTENT!

And here is an encouraging statement which carries with it a suggestion of great significance—THOUSANDS OF SINGERS WHO EXCEL KATE SMITH ARE WALKING UP AND DOWN BROADWAY LOOKING FOR A "BREAK"—WITHOUT SUCCESS. Countless others have come and gone, many of them sang well enough, but they failed to make the grade because they lacked the courage to keep on keeping on, until Broadway became tired of turning them away.

Persistence is a state of mind, therefore it can be cultivated. Like all states of mind, persistence is based upon definite causes, among them these:—

a. DEFINITENESS OF PURPOSE. Knowing what one wants is the first and, perhaps, the most important step toward the development of persistence. A strong motive forces one to surmount many difficulties.

b. DESIRE. It is comparatively easy to acquire and to maintain persistence in pursuing the object of intense desire.

c. SELF-RELIANCE. Belief in one's ability to carry out a plan encourages one to follow the plan through with persistence. (Self-reliance can be developed through the principle described in the chapter on auto-suggestion).

d. DEFINITENESS OF PLANS. Organized plans, even though they may be weak and entirely impractical, encourage persistence.

e. ACCURATE KNOWLEDGE. Knowing that one's plans are sound, based upon experience or observation, encourages persistence; "guessing" instead of "knowing" destroys persistence.

f. CO-OPERATION. Sympathy, understanding, and harmonious cooperation with others tend to develop persistence.

g. WILL-POWER. The habit of concentrating one's thoughts upon the building of plans for the attainment of a definite purpose, leads to per sistence.

h. HABIT. Persistence is the direct result of habit. The mind absorbs and becomes a part of the daily experiences upon which it feeds. Fear, the worst of all enemies, can be effectively cured by *forced repetition of acts of courage.* Everyone who has seen active service in war knows this.

Before leaving the subject of PERSISTENCE, take inventory of yourself, and determine in what particular, if any, you are lacking in this essential quality. Measure yourself courageously, point by point, and see how many of the eight factors of persistence you lack. The analysis may lead to discoveries that will give you a new grip on yourself.

SYMPTOMS OF LACK OF PERSISTENCE

Here you will find the real enemies which stand between you and noteworthy achievement. Here you will find not only the "symptoms" indicating weakness of PERSISTENCE, but also the deeply seated subconscious causes of this weakness. Study the list carefully, and face yourself squarely IF YOU REALLY WISH TO KNOW WHO YOU ARE, AND WHAT YOU ARE CAPABLE OF DOING. These are the weaknesses which must be mastered by all who accumulate riches.

1. Failure to recognize and to clearly define exactly what one wants.
2. Procrastination, with or without cause. (Usually backed up with a formidable array of alibis and excuses).
3. Lack of interest in acquiring specialized knowledge.
4. Indecision, the habit of "passing the buck" on all occasions, instead of facing issues squarely. (Also backed by alibis).
5. The habit of relying upon alibis instead of creating definite plans for the solution of problems.
6. Self-satisfaction. There is but little remedy for this affliction, and no hope for those who suffer from it.
7. Indifference, usually reflected in one's readiness to compromise on all occasions, rather than meet opposition and fight it.
8. The habit of blaming others for one's mistakes, and accepting unfavorable circumstances as being unavoidable.
9. WEAKNESS OF DESIRE, due to neglect in the choice of MOTIVES that impel action.
10. Willingness, even eagerness, to quit at the first sign of defeat. (Based upon one or more of the 6 basic fears).
11. Lack of ORGANIZED PLANS, placed in writing where they may be analyzed.
12. The habit of neglecting to move on ideas, or to grasp opportunity when it presents itself.
13. WISHING instead of WILLING.
14. The habit of compromising with POVERTY instead of aiming at riches. General absence of ambition to *be*, to *do*, and to *own*.
15. Searching for all the short-cuts to riches, trying to GET without GIVING a fair equivalent, usually reflected in the habit of gambling, endeavoring to drive "sharp" bargains.
16. FEAR OF CRITICISM, failure to create plans and to put them into action, because of what other people will think, do, or say. This enemy belongs at the head of the list, because it generally exists in one's subconscious mind, where its presence is not recognized. (See the Six Basic Fears in a later chapter).

Let us examine some of the symptoms of the Fear of Criticism. The majority of people permit relatives, friends, and the public at large to so influence them that they cannot live their own lives, because they fear criticism.

Huge numbers of people make mistakes in marriage, stand by the bargain, and go through life miserable and unhappy, because they fear criticism which may follow if they correct the mistake. (Anyone who has submitted to this form of fear knows the irreparable damage it does, by destroying ambition, self-reliance, and the desire to achieve).

Millions of people neglect to acquire belated educations, after having left school, because they fear criticism.

Countless numbers of men and women, both young and old, permit relatives to wreck their lives in the name of DUTY, because they fear criticism. (Duty does not require any person to submit to the destruction of his personal ambitions and the right to live his own life in his own way).

People refuse to take chances in business, because they fear the criticism which may follow if they fail. *The fear of criticism, in such cases is stronger than the DESIRE for success.*

Too many people refuse to set high goals for themselves, or even neglect selecting a career, because they fear the criticism of relatives and "friends" who may say "Don't aim so high, people will think you are crazy."

When Andrew Carnegie suggested that I devote twenty years to the organization of a philosophy of individual achievement my first impulse of thought was fear of what people might say. The suggestion set up a goal for me, far out of proportion to any I had ever conceived. As quick as a flash, my mind began to create alibis and excuses, all of them traceable to the inherent FEAR OF CRITICISM. Something inside of me said, "You can't do it—the job is too big, and requires too much time—what will your relatives think of you?—how will you earn a living?—no one has ever organized a philosophy of success, what right have you to believe you can do it?—who are you, anyway, to aim so high?—remember your humble birth—what do you know about philosophy—people will think you are crazy—(and they did) —why hasn't some other person done this before now?"

These, and many other questions flashed into my mind, and demanded attention. It seemed as if the whole world had suddenly turned its attention to me with the purpose of ridiculing me into giving up all desire to carry out Mr. Carnegie's suggestion.

I had a fine opportunity, then and there, to kill off ambition before it gained control of me. Later in life, after having analyzed thousands of people, I discovered that MOST IDEAS ARE STILLBORN, AND NEED THE BREATH OF LIFE INJECTED INTO THEM THROUGH DEFINITE PLANS OF IMMEDIATE ACTION. The time to nurse an idea is at the time of its birth. Every minute it lives, gives it a better chance of surviving. The FEAR OF CRITICISM is at the bottom of the destruction of most ideas which never reach the PLANNING and ACTION stage.

Many people believe that material success is the result of favorable "breaks." There is an element of ground for the belief, but those depending entirely upon luck, are nearly always disappointed, because they overlook another important factor which must be present before one can be sure of success. It is the knowledge with which favorable "breaks" can be made to order.

During the depression, W. C. Fields, the comedian, lost all his money, and found himself without income, without a job, and his means of earning a living (vaudeville) no longer existed. Moreover, he was past sixty, when many men consider themselves "old." He was so eager to stage a comeback that he offered to work without pay, in a new field (movies). In addition to his other troubles, he fell and injured his neck. To many that would have been the place to give up and QUIT. But Fields was PERSISTENT. He knew that if he carried on he would get the "breaks" sooner or later, and he did get them, but not by chance.

Marie Dressler found herself down and out, with her money gone, with no job, when she was about sixty. She, too, went after the "breaks," and got them. Her PERSISTENCE brought an astounding triumph late in life, long beyond the age when most men and women are done with ambition to achieve.

Eddie Cantor lost his money in the 1929 stock crash, but he still had his PERSISTENCE and his courage. With these, plus two prominent eyes, he exploited himself back into an income of $10,000 a week! Verily, if one has PERSISTENCE, one can get along very well without many other qualities.

The only "break" anyone can afford to rely upon is a self-made "break." These come through the application of PERSISTENCE. The starting point is DEFINITENESS OF PURPOSE.

Examine the first hundred people you meet, ask them what they want most in life, and ninety eight of them will not be able to tell you. If you press them for an answer, some will say—SECURITY, many will say—MONEY, a few will say—HAPPINESS, others will say—FAME AND POWER, and still others will say—SOCIAL RECOGNITION, EASE IN LIVING, ABILITY TO SING, DANCE, or WRITE, but none of them will be able to define these terms, or give the slightest indication of a PLAN by which they hope to attain these vaguely expressed wishes. Riches do not respond to wishes. They respond only to definite plans, backed by definite desires, through constant PERSISTENCE.

HOW TO DEVELOP PERSISTENCE

There are four simple steps which lead to the habit of PERSISTENCE. They call for no great amount of intelligence, no particular amount of education, and but little time or effort. The necessary steps are:—

1.   A DEFINITE PURPOSE BACKED BY BURNING DESIRE FOR ITS FULFILLMENT.

2.   A DEFINITE PLAN, EXPRESSED IN CONTINUOUS ACTION.

3.   A MIND CLOSED TIGHTLY AGAINST ALL NEGATIVE AND DISCOURAGING INFLUENCES, including negative suggestions of relatives, friends and acquaintances.

4.   A FRIENDLY ALLIANCE WITH ONE OR MORE PERSONS WHO WILL
     ENCOURAGE ONE TO FOLLOW THROUGH WITH BOTH PLAN
     AND PURPOSE.

These four steps are essential for success in all walks of life. The entire purpose of the thirteen principles of this philosophy is to enable one to take these four steps as a matter of *habit*.

These are the steps by which one may control one's economic destiny.

They are the steps that lead to freedom and independence of thought.

They are the steps that lead to riches, in small or great quantities.

They lead the way to power, fame, and worldly recognition.

They are the four steps which guarantee favorable "breaks."

They are the steps that convert dreams into physical realities.

They lead, also, to the mastery of FEAR, DISCOURAGEMENT, INDIFFERENCE.

There is a magnificent reward for all who learn to take these four steps. It is the privilege of writing one's own ticket, and of making Life yield whatever price is asked.

I have no way of knowing the facts, but I venture to conjecture that Mrs. Wallis Simpson's great love for a man was not accidental, nor the result of favorable "breaks" alone. There was a burning desire, and careful searching at every step of the way. Her first duty was to love. What is the greatest thing on earth? The Master called it love—not man made rules, criticism, bitterness, slander, or political "marriages," but love.

She knew what she wanted, not after she met the Prince of Wales, but long before that. Twice when she had failed to find it, she had the courage to continue her search. "To thine own self be true, and it must follow, as the night the day, thou canst not then be false to any man."

Her rise from obscurity was of the slow, progressive, PERSISTENT order, but it was SURE! She triumphed over unbelievably long odds; and, no matter who you are, or what you may think of Wallis Simpson, or the king who gave up his Crown for her love, she is an astounding example of applied PERSISTENCE, an instructor on the rules of self-determination, from whom the entire world might profitably take lessons.

When you think of Wallis Simpson, think of one who knew what she wanted, and shook the greatest empire on earth to get it. Women who complain that this is a man's world, that women do not have an equal chance to win, owe it to themselves to study carefully the life of this unusual woman, who, at an age which most women consider "old," captured the affections of the most desirable bachelor in the entire world.

And what of King Edward? What lesson may we learn from his part in the world's greatest drama of recent times? Did he pay too high a price for the affections of the woman of his choice?

Surely no one but he can give the correct answer.

The rest of us can only conjecture. This much we know, the king came into the world without his own consent. He was born to great riches, without requesting them. He was persistently sought in marriage; politicians and statesmen throughout Europe tossed dowagers and princesses at his feet. Because he was the first born of his parents, he inherited a crown, which he did not seek, and perhaps did not desire. For more than forty years he was not a free agent, could not live his life in his own way, had but little privacy, and finally assumed duties inflicted upon him when he ascended the throne.

Some will say, "With all these blessings, King Edward should have found peace of mind, contentment, and joy of living."

The truth is that back of all the privileges of a crown, all the money, the fame, and the power inherited by King Edward, there was an emptiness which could be filled only by love.

His greatest DESIRE was for love. Long before he met Wallis Simpson, he doubtless felt this great universal emotion tugging at the strings of his heart, beating upon the door of his soul, and crying out for expression.

And when he met a kindred spirit, crying out for this same Holy privilege of expression, he recognized it, and without fear or apology, opened his heart and bade it enter. All the scandal-mongers in the world cannot destroy the beauty of this international drama, through which two people found love, and had the courage to face open criticism, renounce ALL ELSE to give it *holy* expression.

King Edward's DECISION to give up the crown of the world's most powerful empire, for the privilege of going the remainder of the way through life with the woman of his choice, was a decision that required courage. The decision also had a price, but who has the right to say the price was too great? Surely not He who said, "He among you who is without sin, let him cast the first stone."

As a suggestion to any evil-minded person who chooses to find fault with the Duke of Windsor, because his DESIRE was for LOVE, and for openly declaring his love for Wallis Simpson, and giving up his throne for her, let it be remembered that the OPEN DECLARATION was not essential. He could have followed the custom of clandestine liaison which has prevailed in Europe for centuries, without giving up either his throne, or the woman of his choice, and there would have been NO COMPLAINT FROM EITHER CHURCH OR LAITY. But this unusual man was built of sterner stuff. His love was clean. It was deep and sincere. It represented the one thing which, above ALL ELSE he truly DESIRED, therefore, he took what he wanted, and paid the price demanded.

If Europe had been blessed with more rulers with the human heart and the traits of honesty of ex-king Edward, for the past century, that unfortunate hemisphere now seething with greed, hate, lust, political connivance, and threats of war, would have a DIFFERENT AND A BETTER STORY TO TELL. A story in which Love and not Hate would rule.

In the words of Stuart Austin Wier we raise our cup and drink this toast to ex-king Edward and Wallis Simpson:

"Blessed is the man who has come to know that our muted thoughts are our sweetest thoughts.

"Blessed is the man who, from the blackest depths, can see the luminous figure of LOVE, and seeing, sing; and singing, say: 'Sweeter far than uttered lays are the thoughts I have of you.'"

In these words would we pay tribute to the two people who, more than all others of modern times, have been the victims of criticism and the recipients of abuse, because they found Life's greatest treasure, and claimed it.*

Most of the world will applaud the Duke of Windsor and Wallis Simpson, because of their PERSISTENCE in searching until they found life's greatest reward. ALL OF US CAN PROFIT by following their example in our own search for that which we demand of life.

What mystical power gives to men of PERSISTENCE the capacity to master difficulties? Does the quality of PERSISTENCE set up in one's mind some form of spiritual, mental or chemical activity which gives one access to supernatural forces? Does Infinite Intelligence throw itself on the side of the person who still fights on, after the battle has been lost, with the whole world on the opposing side?

These and many other similar questions have arisen in my mind as I have observed men like Henry Ford, who started at scratch, and built an Industrial Empire of huge proportions, with little else in the way of a beginning but PERSIST-ENCE. Or, Thomas A. Edison, who, with less than three months of schooling, became the world's leading inventor and converted PERSISTENCE into the talking machine, the moving picture machine, and the incandescent light, to say nothing of half a hundred other useful inventions.

I had the happy privilege of analyzing both Mr. Edison and Mr. Ford, year by year, over a long period of years, and therefore, the opportunity to study them at close range, so I speak from actual knowledge when I say that I found no quality save PERSISTENCE, in either of them, that even remotely suggested the major source of their stupendous achievements.

As one makes an impartial study of the prophets, philosophers, "miracle" men, and religious leaders of the past, one is drawn to the inevitable conclusion that PERSISTENCE, concentration of effort, and DEFINITENESS OF PURPOSE, were the major sources of their achievements.

Consider, for example, the strange and fascinating story of Mohammed; analyze his life, compare him with men of achievement in this modern age of industry and finance, and observe how they have one outstanding trait in common, PERSISTENCE!

If you are keenly interested in studying the strange power which gives potency to PERSISTENCE, read a biography of Mohammed, especially the one by Essad

*Mrs. Simpson read and approved this analysis.

Bey. This brief review of that book, by Thomas Sugrue, in the Herald-Tribune, will provide a preview of the rare treat in store for those who take the time to read the entire story of one of the most astounding examples of the power of PERSISTENCE known to civilization.

THE LAST GREAT PROPHET
Reviewed by Thomas Sugrue

"Mohammed was a prophet, but he never performed a miracle. He was not a mystic; he had no formal schooling; he did not begin his mission until he was forty. When he announced that he was the Messenger of God, bringing word of the true religion, he was ridiculed and labeled a lunatic. Children tripped him and women threw filth upon him. He was banished from his native city, Mecca, and his followers were stripped of their worldly goods and sent into the desert after him. When he had been preaching ten years he had nothing to show for it but banishment, poverty and ridicule. Yet before another ten years had passed, he was dictator of all Arabia, ruler of Mecca, and the head of a New World religion which was to sweep to the Danube and the Pyrenees before exhausting the impetus he gave it. That impetus was three-fold: the power of words, the efficacy of prayer and man's kinship with God.

"His career never made sense. Mohammed was born to impoverished members of a leading family of Mecca. Because Mecca, the crossroads of the world, home of the magic stone called the Caaba, great city of trade and the center of trade routes, was unsanitary, its children were sent to be raised in the desert by Bedouins. Mohammed was thus nurtured, drawing strength and health from the milk of nomad, vicarious mothers. He tended sheep and soon hired out to a rich widow as leader of her caravans. He traveled to all parts of the Eastern World, talked with many men of diverse beliefs and observed the decline of Christianity into warring sects. When he was twenty-eight, Khadija, the widow, looked upon him with favor, and married him. Her father would have objected to such a marriage, so she got him drunk and held him up while he gave the paternal blessing. For the next twelve years Mohammed lived as a rich and respected and very shrewd trader. Then he took to wandering in the desert, and one day he returned with the first verse of the Koran and told Khadija that the archangel Gabriel had appeared to him and said that he was to be the Messenger of God.

"The Koran, the revealed word of God, was the closest thing to a miracle in Mohammed's life. He had not been a poet; he had no gift of words. Yet the verses of the Koran, as he received them and recited them to the faithful, were better than any verses

which the professional poets of the tribes could produce. This, to
the Arabs, was a miracle. To them the gift of words was the greatest gift, the poet was all-powerful. In addition the Koran said that
all men were equal before God, that the world should be a democratic state—Islam. It was this political heresy, plus
Mohammed's desire to destroy all the 360 idols in the courtyard
of the Caaba, which brought about his banishment. The idols
brought the desert tribes to Mecca, and that meant trade. So the
business men of Mecca, the capitalists, of which he had been one,
set upon Mohammed. Then he retreated to the desert and
demanded sovereignty over the world.

"The rise of Islam began. Out of the desert came a flame
which would not be extinguished—a democratic army fighting as
a unit and prepared to die without wincing. Mohammed had
invited the Jews and Christians to join him; for he was not building a new religion. He was calling all who believed in one God to
join in a single faith. If the Jews and Christians had accepted his
invitation Islam would have conquered the world. They didn't.
They would not even accept Mohammed's innovation of humane
warfare. When the armies of the prophet entered Jerusalem not a
single person was killed because of his faith. When the crusaders
entered the city, centuries later, not a Moslem man, woman, or
child was spared. But the Christians did accept one Moslem
idea—the place of learning, the university."

CHAPTER TEN

POWER OF THE MASTER MIND:
THE DRIVING FORCE
The Ninth Step toward Riches

POWER is essential for success in the accumulation of money.

PLANS are inert and useless, without sufficient POWER to translate them into ACTION. This chapter will describe the method by which an individual may attain and apply POWER.

POWER may be defined as "organized and intelligently directed KNOWL-EDGE." Power, as the term is here used, refers to ORGANIZED effort, sufficient to enable an individual to transmute DESIRE into its monetary equivalent. ORGAN-IZED effort is produced through the coordination of effort of two or more people, who work toward a DEFINITE end, in a spirit of harmony.

POWER IS REQUIRED FOR THE ACCUMULATION OF MONEY! POWER IS NEC-ESSARY FOR THE RETENTION OF MONEY AFTER IT HAS BEEN ACCUMULATED!

Let us ascertain how power may be acquired. If power is "organized knowl-edge," let us examine the sources of knowledge:

a. **INFINITE INTELLIGENCE.** This source of knowledge may be contacted through the procedure described in another chapter, with the aid of Creative Imagination.

b. **ACCUMULATED EXPERIENCE.** The accumulated experience of man, (or that portion of it which has been organized and recorded), may be found in any well-equipped public library. An important part of this accumulated experience is taught in public schools and colleges, where it has been classified and organized.

c. **EXPERIMENT AND RESEARCH.** In the field of science, and in practically every other walk of life, men are gathering, classifying, and organizing new facts daily. This is the source to which one must turn when knowledge is not available through "accumulated experience." Here, too, the Creative Imagination must often be used.

Knowledge may be acquired from any of the foregoing sources. It may be con-verted into POWER by organizing it into definite PLANS and by expressing those plans in terms of ACTION.

Examination of the three major sources of knowledge will readily disclose the difficulty an individual would have, if he depended upon his efforts alone, in assembling knowledge and expressing it through definite plans in terms of ACTION. If his plans are comprehensive, and if they contemplate large proportions, he must, generally, induce others to cooperate with him, before he can inject into them the necessary element of POWER.

GAINING POWER THROUGH THE "MASTER MIND"

The "Master Mind" may be defined as: "Coordination of knowledge and effort, in a spirit of harmony, between two or more people, for the attainment of a definite purpose."

No individual may have great power without availing himself of the "Master Mind." In a preceding chapter, instructions were given for the creation of PLANS for the purpose of translating DESIRE into its monetary equivalent. If you carry out these instructions with PERSISTENCE and intelligence, and use discrimination in the selection of your "Master Mind" group, your objective will have been half-way reached, even before you begin to recognize it.

So you may better understand the "intangible" potentialities of power available to you, through a properly chosen "Master Mind" group, we will here explain the two characteristics of the Master Mind principle, one of which is economic in nature, and the other psychic. The economic feature is obvious. Economic advantages may be created by any person who surrounds himself with the advice, counsel, and personal cooperation of a group of men who are willing to lend him wholehearted aid, in a spirit of PERFECT HARMONY. This form of cooperative alliance has been the basis of nearly every great fortune. Your understanding of this great truth may definitely determine your financial status.

The psychic phase of the Master Mind principle is much more abstract, much more difficult to comprehend, because it has reference to the spiritual forces with which the human race, as a whole, is not well acquainted. You may catch a significant suggestion from this statement: "No two minds ever come together without, thereby, creating a third, invisible, intangible force which may be likened to a third mind."

Keep in mind the fact that there are only two known elements in the whole universe, energy and matter. It is a well known fact that matter may be broken down into units of molecules, atoms, and electrons. There are units of matter which may be isolated, separated, and analyzed.

Likewise, there are units of energy.

The human mind is a form of energy, a part of it being spiritual in nature. When the minds of two people are coordinated in a SPIRIT OF HARMONY, the spiritual units of energy of each mind form an affinity, which constitutes the "psychic" phase of the Master Mind.

The Master Mind principle, or rather the economic feature of it, was first called to my attention by Andrew Carnegie, over twenty-five years ago. Discovery of this principle was responsible for the choice of my life's work.

Mr. Carnegie's Master Mind group consisted of a staff of approximately fifty men, with whom he surrounded himself, for the DEFINITE PURPOSE of manufacturing and marketing steel. He attributed his entire fortune to the POWER he accumulated through this "Master Mind."

Analyze the record of any man who has accumulated a great fortune, and many of those who have accumulated modest fortunes, and you will find that they have either consciously, or unconsciously employed the "Master Mind" principle.

GREAT POWER CAN BE ACCUMULATED THROUGH NO OTHER PRINCIPLE!

ENERGY is Nature's universal set of building blocks, out of which she constructs every material thing in the universe, including man, and every form of animal and vegetable life. Through a process which only Nature completely understands, she translates energy into matter.

Nature's building blocks are available to man, in the energy involved in THINKING! Man's brain may be compared to an electric battery. It absorbs energy from the ether, which permeates every atom of matter, and fills the entire universe.

It is a well known fact that a group of electric batteries will provide more energy than a single battery. It is also a well known fact that an individual battery will provide energy in proportion to the number and capacity of the cells it contains.

The brain functions in a similar fashion. This accounts for the fact that some brains are more efficient than others, and leads to this significant statement—a group of brains coordinated (or connected) in a spirit of harmony, will provide more thought-energy than a single brain, just as a group of electric batteries will provide more energy than a single battery.

Through this metaphor it becomes immediately obvious that the Master Mind principle holds the secret of the POWER wielded by men who surround themselves with other men of brains.

There follows, now, another statement which will lead still nearer to an understanding of the psychic phase of the Master Mind principle: When a group of individual brains are coordinated and function in Harmony, the increased energy created through that alliance, becomes available to every individual brain in the group.

It is a well known fact that Henry Ford began his business career under the handicap of poverty, illiteracy, and ignorance. It is an equally well known fact that, within the inconceivably short period of ten years, Mr. Ford mastered these three handicaps, and that within twenty-five years he made himself one of the richest men in America. Connect with this fact, the additional knowledge that Mr. Ford's most rapid strides became noticeable, from the time he became a personal friend of Thomas A. Edison, and you will begin to understand what the influence of one mind upon another can accomplish. Go a step farther, and consider the fact that Mr. Ford's most outstanding achievements began from the time that he formed the acquaintances of Harvey Firestone, John Burroughs, and Luther Burbank, (each a man of great brain capacity), and you will have further evidence that POWER may be produced through friendly alliance of minds.

There is little if any doubt that Henry Ford is one of the best informed men in the business and industrial world. The question of his wealth needs no discussion. Analyze Mr. Ford's intimate personal friends, some of whom have already been mentioned, and you will be prepared to understand the following statement:—

"Men take on the nature and the habits and the POWER OF THOUGHT of those with whom they associate in a spirit of sympathy and harmony."

Henry Ford whipped poverty, illiteracy, and ignorance by allying himself with great minds, whose vibrations of thought he absorbed into his own mind. Through his association with Edison, Burbank, Burroughs, and Firestone, Mr. Ford added to his own brain power, the sum and substance of the intelligence, experience, knowledge, and spiritual forces of these four men. Moreover, he appropriated, and made use of the Master Mind principle through the methods of procedure described in this book.

This principle is available to you!

We have already mentioned Mahatma Gandhi. Perhaps the majority of those who have heard of Gandhi, look upon him as merely an eccentric little man, who goes around without formal wearing apparel, and makes trouble for the British Government.

In reality, Gandhi is not eccentric, but HE IS THE MOST POWERFUL MAN NOW LIVING. (Estimated by the number of his followers and their faith in their leader.) Moreover, he is probably the most powerful man who has ever lived. His power is passive, but it is real.

Let us study the method by which he attained his stupendous POWER. It may be explained in a few words. He came by POWER through inducing over two hundred million people to coordinate, with mind and body, in a spirit of HARMONY, for a DEFINITE PURPOSE.

In brief, Gandhi has accomplished a MIRACLE, for it is a miracle when two hundred million people can be induced—not forced—to cooperate in a spirit of HARMONY, for a limitless time. If you doubt that this is a miracle, try to induce ANY TWO PEOPLE to cooperate in a spirit of harmony for *any length of time.*

Every man who manages a business knows what a difficult matter it is to get employees to work together in a spirit even remotely resembling HARMONY.

The list of the chief sources from which POWER may be attained is, as you have seen, headed by INFINITE INTELLIGENCE. When two or more people coordinate in a spirit of HARMONY, and work toward a definite objective, they place themselves in position, through that alliance, to absorb power directly from the great universal storehouse of Infinite Intelligence. This is the greatest of all sources of POWER. It is the source to which the genius turns. It is the source to which every great leader turns, (whether he may be conscious of the fact or not).

The other two major sources from which the knowledge, necessary for the accumulation of POWER, may be obtained are no more reliable than the five senses of man. The senses are not always reliable. Infinite Intelligence DOES NOT ERR.

In subsequent chapters, the methods by which Infinite Intelligence may be most readily contacted will be adequately described.

This is not a course on religion. No fundamental principle described in this book should be interpreted as being intended to interfere either directly, or indirectly, with any man's religious habits. This book has been confined, exclusively, to instructing the reader how to transmute the DEFINITE PURPOSE OF DESIRE FOR MONEY, into its monetary equivalent.

Read, *THINK,* and meditate as you read. Soon, the entire subject will unfold, and you will see it in perspective. You are now seeing the detail of the individual chapters.

Money is as shy and elusive as the "old time" maiden. It must be wooed and won by methods not unlike those used by a determined lover, in pursuit of the girl of his choice. And, coincidental as it is, the POWER used in the "wooing" of money is not greatly different from that used in wooing a maiden. That power, when successfully used in the pursuit of money must be mixed with FAITH. It must be mixed with DESIRE. It must be mixed with PERSISTENCE. It must be applied through a plan, and that plan must be set into ACTION.

When money comes in quantities known as "the big money," it flows to the one who accumulates it, as easily as water flows down hill. There exists a great unseen stream of POWER, which may be compared to a river; except that one side flows in one direction, carrying all who get into that side of the stream, onward and upward to WEALTH—and the other side flows in the opposite direction, carrying all who are unfortunate enough to get into it (and not able to extricate themselves from it), downward to misery and POVERTY.

Every man who has accumulated a great fortune, has recognized the existence of this stream of life. It consists of one's THINKING PROCESS. The positive emotions of thought form the side of the stream which carries one to fortune. The negative emotions form the side which carries one down to poverty.

This carries a thought of stupendous importance to the person who is following this book with the object of accumulating a fortune.

If you are in the side of the stream of POWER which leads to poverty, this may serve as an oar, by which you may propel yourself over into the other side of the stream. It can serve you ONLY through application and use. Merely reading, and passing judgment on it, either one way or another, will in no way benefit you.

Some people undergo the experience of alternating between the positive and negative sides of the stream, being at times on the positive side, and at times on the negative side. The Wall Street crash of '29 swept millions of people from the positive to the negative side of the stream. These millions are struggling, some of them in desperation and fear, to get back to the positive side of the stream. This book was written especially for those millions.

Poverty and riches often change places. The Crash taught the world this truth, although the world will not long remember the lesson. Poverty may, and generally does, voluntarily take the place of riches. When riches take the place of poverty, the change is usually brought about through well-conceived and carefully executed PLANS. Poverty needs no plan. It needs no one to aid it, because it is bold and ruthless. Riches are shy and timid. They have to be "attracted."

> ANYBODY can WISH for riches, and most people do,
> but only a few know that a definite plan,
> plus a BURNING DESIRE for wealth,
> are the only dependable means of accumulating wealth.

CHAPTER ELEVEN

THE MYSTERY OF SEX TRANSMUTATION:
The Tenth Step toward Riches

The meaning of the word "transmute" is, in simple language, "the changing, or transferring of one element, or form of energy, into another."

The emotion of sex brings into being a state of mind.

Because of ignorance on the subject, this state of mind is generally associated with the physical, and because of improper influences, to which most people have been subjected, in acquiring knowledge of sex, things essentially physical have highly biased the mind.

The emotion of sex has back of it the possibility of three constructive potentialities, they are:—

1. The perpetuation of mankind.
2. The maintenance of health, (as a therapeutic agency, it has no equal).
3. The transformation of mediocrity into genius through transmutation.

Sex transmutation is simple and easily explained. It means the switching of the mind from thoughts of physical expression, to thoughts of some other nature.

Sex desire is the most powerful of human desires.

When driven by this desire, men develop keenness of imagination, courage, will-power, persistence, and creative ability unknown to them at other times. So strong and impelling is the desire for sexual contact that men freely run the risk of life and reputation to indulge it. When harnessed, and redirected along other lines, this motivating force maintains all of its attributes of keenness of imagination, courage, etc., which may be used as powerful creative forces in literature, art, or in any other profession or calling, including, of course, the accumulation of riches.

The transmutation of sex energy calls for the exercise of will-power, to be sure, but the reward is worth the effort. The desire for sexual expression is inborn and natural. The desire cannot, and should not be submerged or eliminated. But it should be given an outlet through forms of expression which enrich the body, mind, and spirit of man. If not given this form of outlet, through transmutation, it will seek outlets through purely physical channels.

A river may be dammed, and its water controlled for a time, but eventually, it will force an outlet. The same is true of the emotion of sex. It may be submerged and controlled for a time, but its very nature causes it to be ever seeking means of expression. If it is not transmuted into some creative effort it will find a less worthy outlet.

Fortunate, indeed, is the person who has discovered how to give sex emotion an outlet through some form of creative effort, for he has, by that discovery, lifted himself to the status of a genius.

Scientific research has disclosed these significant facts:

1. The men of greatest achievement are men with highly developed sex natures; men who have learned the art of sex transmutation.
2. The men who have accumulated great fortunes and achieved outstanding recognition in literature, art, industry, architecture, and the professions, were motivated by the influence of a woman.

The research from which these astounding discoveries were made, went back through the pages of biography and history for more than two thousand years. Wherever there was evidence available in connection with the lives of men and women of great achievement, it indicated most convincingly that they possessed highly developed sex natures.

The emotion of sex is an "irresistible force," against which there can be no such opposition as an "immovable body." When driven by this emotion, men become gifted with a super power for action. Understand this truth, and you will catch the significance of the statement that sex transmutation will lift one to the status of a genius.

The emotion of sex contains the secret of creative ability.

Destroy the sex glands, whether in man or beast, and you have removed the major source of action. For proof of this, observe what happens to any animal after it has been castrated. A bull becomes as docile as a cow after it has been altered sexually. Sex alteration takes out of the male, whether man or beast, all the FIGHT that was in him. Sex alteration of the female has the same effect.

THE TEN MIND STIMULI

The human mind responds to stimuli, through which it may be "keyed up" to high rates of vibration, known as enthusiasm, creative imagination, intense desire, etc. The stimuli to which the mind responds most freely are:—

1. The desire for sex expression
2. Love
3. A burning desire for fame, power, or financial gain, MONEY
4. Music
5. Friendship between either those of the same sex, or those of the opposite sex.
6. A Master Mind alliance based upon the harmony of two or more people who ally themselves for spiritual or temporal advancement.

7. Mutual suffering, such as that experienced by people who are persecuted.
8. Auto-suggestion
9. Fear
10. Narcotics and alcohol

The desire for sex expression comes at the head of the list of stimuli, which most effectively "step-up" the vibrations of the mind and start the "wheels" of physical action. Eight of these stimuli are natural and constructive. Two are destructive. The list is here presented for the purpose of enabling you to make a comparative study of the major sources of mind stimulation. From this study, it will be readily seen that the emotion of sex is, by great odds, the most intense and powerful of all mind stimuli.

This comparison is necessary as a foundation for proof of the statement that transmutation of sex energy may lift one to the status of a genius. Let us find out what constitutes a genius.

Some wiseacre has said that a genius is a man who "wears long hair, eats queer food, lives alone, and serves as a target for the joke makers." A better definition of a genius is, "a man who has discovered how to increase the vibrations of thought to the point where he can freely communicate with sources of knowledge not available through the ordinary rate of vibration of thought."

The person who thinks will want to ask some questions concerning this definition of genius. The first question will be, "How may one communicate with sources of knowledge which are not available through the ORDINARY rate of vibration of thought?"

The next question will be, "Are there known sources of knowledge which are available only to genii, and if so, WHAT ARE THESE SOURCES, and exactly how may they be reached?"

We shall offer proof of the soundness of some of the more important statements made in this book—or at least we shall offer evidence through which you may secure your own proof through experimentation, and in doing so, we shall answer both of these questions.

"GENIUS" IS DEVELOPED THROUGH THE SIXTH SENSE

The reality of a "sixth sense" has been fairly well established. This sixth sense is "Creative imagination." The faculty of creative imagination is one which the majority of people never use during an entire lifetime, and if used at all, it usually happens by mere accident. A relatively small number of people use, WITH DELIBERATION AND PURPOSE AFORETHOUGHT, the faculty of creative imagination. Those who use this faculty voluntarily, and with understanding of its functions, are GENII.

The faculty of creative imagination is the direct link between the finite mind of man and Infinite Intelligence. All so-called revelations, referred to in the realm of religion, and all discoveries of basic or new principles in the field of invention, take place through the faculty of creative imagination.

When ideas or concepts flash into one's mind, through what is popularly called a "hunch," they come from one or more of the following sources:—

1. Infinite Intelligence
2. One's subconscious mind, wherein is stored every sense impression and thought impulse which ever reached the brain through any of the five senses
3. From the mind of some other person who has just released the thought, or picture of the idea or concept, through conscious thought, or
4. From the other person's subconscious storehouse.

There are no other KNOWN sources from which "inspired" ideas or "hunches" may be received.

The creative imagination functions best when the mind is vibrating (due to some form of mind stimulation) at an exceedingly high rate. That is, when the mind is functioning at a rate of vibration higher than that of ordinary, normal thought.

When brain action has been stimulated, through one or more of the ten mind stimulants, it has the effect of lifting the individual far above the horizon of ordinary thought, and permits him to envision distance, scope, and quality of THOUGHTS not available on the lower plane, such as that occupied while one is engaged in the solution of the problems of business and professional routine.

When lifted to this higher level of thought, through any form of mind stimulation, an individual occupies, relatively, the same position as one who has ascended in an airplane to a height from which he may see over and beyond the horizon line which limits his vision, while on the ground. Moreover, while on this higher level of thought, the individual is not hampered or bound by any of the stimuli which circumscribe and limit his vision while wrestling with the problems of gaining the three basic necessities of food, clothing, and shelter. He is in a world of thought in which the ORDINARY, work-a-day thoughts have been as effectively removed as are the hills and valleys and other limitations of physical vision, when he rises in an airplane.

While on this exalted plane of THOUGHT, the creative faculty of the mind is given freedom for action. The way has been cleared for the sixth sense to function, it becomes receptive to ideas which could not reach the individual under any other circumstances. The "sixth sense" is the faculty which marks the difference between a genius and an ordinary individual.

The creative faculty becomes more alert and receptive to vibrations, originating outside the individual's subconscious mind, the more this faculty is used, and the more the individual relies upon it, and makes demands upon it for thought pulses. This faculty can developed only through use.

That which is known as one's "conscience" operates entirely through the faculty of the sixth sense.

The great artists, writers, musicians, and poets become great, because they acquire the habit of relying upon the "still small voice" which speaks from within, through the faculty of creative imagination. It is a fact well known to people who have "keen" imaginations that their best ideas come through so-called "hunches."

There is a great orator who does not attain to greatness, until he closes his eyes and begins to rely entirely upon the faculty of Creative Imagination. When asked why he closed his eyes just before the climaxes of his oratory, he replied, "I do it, because, then I speak through ideas which come to me from within."

One of America's most successful and best known financiers followed the habit of closing his eyes for two or three minutes before making a decision. When asked why he did this, he replied, "With my eyes closed, I am able to draw upon a source of superior intelligence."

The late Dr. Elmer R. Gates, of Chevy Chase, Maryland, created more than 200 useful patents, many of them basic, through the process of cultivating and using the creative faculty. His method is both significant and interesting to one interested in attaining to the status of genius, in which category Dr. Gates unquestionably belonged. Dr. Gates was one of the really great, though less publicized scientists of the world.

In his laboratory, he had what he called his "personal communication room." It was practically sound proof, and so arranged that all light could be shut out. It was equipped with a small table, on which he kept a pad of writing paper. In front of the table, on the wall, was an electric pushbutton, which controlled the lights. When Dr. Gates decided to draw upon the forces available to him through his Creative Imagination, he would go into his room, seat himself at the table, shut off the lights, and CONCENTRATE upon the KNOWN factors of the invention on which he was working, remaining in that position until ideas began to "flash" into his mind in connection with the UNKNOWN factors of the invention.

On one occasion, ideas came through so fast that he was forced to write for almost three hours. When his thoughts stopped flowing, and he examined his notes, he found they contained a minute description of principles which had not a parallel among the known data of the scientific world. Moreover, the answer to his problem was intelligently presented in these notes. In this manner Dr. Gates completed over 200 patents, which had been begun, but not completed, by "half-baked" brains. Evidence of the truth in this statement is in the United States Patent Office.

Dr. Gates earned his living by "sitting for ideas" for individuals and corporations. Some of the largest corporations in America paid him substantial fees, by the hour, for "sitting for ideas."

The reasoning faculty is often faulty, because it is largely guided by one's accumulated experience. Not all knowledge, which one accumulates through "experience," is accurate. Ideas received through the creative faculty are much more reliable, for the reason that they come from sources more reliable than any which are available to the reasoning faculty of the mind.

The main difference between the genius and the ordinary "crank" inventor, may be found in the fact that the genius works through his faculty of creative imagination, while the "crank" knows nothing of this faculty. The scientific inventor (such as Mr. Edison and Dr. Gates), makes use of both the synthetic and creative faculties of imagination.

For example, the scientific inventor, or "genius," begins an invention by organizing and combining the known ideas, or principles accumulated through experience, through the synthetic faculty (the reasoning faculty). If he finds this accumulated knowledge to be insufficient for the completion of his invention, he then draws upon the sources of knowledge available to him through his *creative* faculty. The method by which he does this varies with the individual, but this is the sum and substance of his procedure:

1.   HE STIMULATES HIS MIND SO THAT IT VIBRATES ON A HIGHER-THAN-AVERAGE PLANE, using one or more of the ten mind stimulants or some other stimulant of his choice.
2.   HE CONCENTRATES upon the known factors (the finished part) of his invention, and creates in his mind a perfect picture of unknown factors (the unfinished part), of his invention. He holds this picture in mind until it has been taken over by the subconscious mind, then relaxes by clearing his mind of ALL thought, and waits for his answer to "flash" into his mind.

Sometimes the results are both definite and immediate. At other times, the results are negative, depending upon the state of development of the "sixth sense," or creative faculty.

Mr. Edison tried out more than 10,000 different combinations of ideas through the synthetic faculty of his imagination before he "tuned in" through the creative faculty, and got the answer which perfected the incandescent light. His experience was similar when he produced the talking machine.

There is plenty of reliable evidence that the faculty of creative imagination exists. This evidence is available through accurate analysis of men who have become leaders in their respective callings, without having had extensive educations. Lincoln was a notable example of a great leader who achieved greatness, through the discovery, and use of his faculty of creative imagination. He discovered, and began to use this faculty as the result of the stimulation of love which he experienced after he met Anne Rutledge, a statement of the highest significance, in connection with the study of the source of genius.

The pages of history are filled with the records of great leaders whose achievements may be traced directly to the influence of women who aroused the creative faculties of their minds, through the stimulation of sex desire. Napoleon Bonaparte was one of these. When inspired by his first wife, Josephine, he was irresistible and invincible. When his "better judgment" or reasoning faculty prompted him to put Josephine aside, he began to decline. His defeat and St. Helena were not far distant.

If good taste would permit, we might easily mention scores of men, well known to the American people, who climbed to great heights of achievement under the stimulating influence of their wives, only to drop back to destruction AFTER money and power went to their heads, and they put aside the old wife for a new one. Napoleon was not the only man to discover that sex influence, *from the right source,* is more powerful than any substitute of expediency, which may be created by mere reason.

The human mind responds to stimulation!

Among the greatest, and most powerful of these stimuli is the urge of sex. When harnessed and transmuted, this driving force is capable of lifting men into that higher sphere of thought which enables them to master the sources of worry and petty annoyance which beset their pathway on the lower plane.

Unfortunately, only the genii have made the discovery. Others have accepted the experience of sex urge, without discovering one of its major potentialities—a fact which accounts for the great number of "others" as compared to the limited number of genii.

For the purpose of refreshing the memory, in connection with the facts available from the biographies of certain men, we here present the names of a few men of outstanding achievement, each of whom was known to have been of a highly sexed nature. The genius which was theirs undoubtedly found its source of power in transmuted sex energy:

GEORGE WASHINGTON	THOMAS JEFFERSON
NAPOLEON BONAPARTE	ELBERT HUBBARD
ELBERT H. GARY	WILLIAM SHAKESPEARE
OSCAR WILDE	WOODROW WILSON
ABRAHAM LINCOLN	JOHN H. PATTERSON
RALPH WALDO EMERSON	ANDREW JACKSON
ROBERT BURNS	ENRICO CARUSO

Your own knowledge of biography will enable you to add to this list. Find, if you can, a single man in all history of civilization, who achieved outstanding success in any calling, who was not driven by a well developed sex nature.

If you do not wish to rely upon biographies of men not now living, take inventory of those whom you know to be men of great achievement, and see if you can find one among them who is not highly sexed.

Sex energy is the creative energy of all genii. *There never has been, and never will be a great leader, builder, or artist lacking in this driving force of sex.*

Surely no one will misunderstand these statements to mean that ALL who are highly sexed are genii! Man attains to the status of a genius ONLY when, and IF, he stimulates his mind so that it draws upon the forces available, through the creative faculty of the imagination. Chief among the stimuli with which this "stepping up" of the vibrations may be produced is sex energy. The mere *possession* of this energy is not sufficient to produce a genius. The energy must be *transmuted* from desire for physical contact, into some *other* form of desire and action, before it will lift one to the status of a genius.

Far from becoming genii, because of great sex desires, the majority of men *lower* themselves, through misunderstanding and misuse of this great force, to the status of the lower animals.

WHY MEN SELDOM SUCCEED BEFORE FORTY

I discovered, from the analysis of over 25,000 people, that men who succeed in an outstanding way, seldom do so before the age of forty, and more often they do not strike their real pace until they are well beyond the age of fifty. This fact was so astounding that it prompted me to go into the study of its cause most carefully, carrying the investigation over a period of more than twelve years.

This study disclosed the fact that the major reason why the majority of men who succeed do not begin to do so before the age of forty to fifty, is their tendency to DISSIPATE their energies through over indulgence in physical expression of the emotion of sex. The majority of men *never* learn that the urge of sex has other possibilities, which far transcend in importance, that of mere physical expression. The majority of those who make this discovery, do so *after having wasted many years* at a period when the sex energy is at its height, prior to the age of forty-five to fifty. This usually is followed by noteworthy achievement.

The lives of many men up to, and sometimes well past the age of forty, reflect a continued dissipation of energies, which could have been more profitably turned into better channels. Their finer and more powerful emotions are sown wildly to the four winds. Out of this habit of the male, grew the term, "sowing his wild oats."

The desire for sexual expression is by far the strongest and most impelling of all the human emotions, and for this very reason this desire, when *harnessed and transmuted* into action, other than that of physical expression, may raise one to the status of a genius.

One of America's most able business men frankly admitted that his attractive secretary was responsible for most of the plans he created. He admitted that her presence lifted him to heights of creative imagination, such as he could experience under no other stimulus.

One of the most successful men in America owes most of his success to the influence of a very charming young woman, who has served as his source of inspiration for more than twelve years. Everyone knows the man to whom this reference is made, but not everyone knows the REAL SOURCE of his achievements.

History is not lacking in examples of men who attained to the status of genii, as the result of the use of artificial mind stimulants in the form of alcohol and narcotics. Edgar Allen Poe wrote the "Raven" while under the influence of liquor, "dreaming dreams that mortal never dared to dream before." James Whitcomb Riley did his best writing while under the influence of alcohol. Perhaps it was thus he saw "the ordered intermingling of the real and the dream, the mill above the river, and the mist above the stream." Robert Burns wrote best when intoxicated, "For Auld Lang Syne, my dear, we'll take a cup of kindness yet, for Auld Lang Syne."

But let it be remembered that many such men have destroyed themselves in the end. Nature has prepared her own potions with which men may safely stimulate their minds so they vibrate on a plane that enables them to tune in to fine and rare thoughts which come from—no man knows where! No satisfactory substitute for Nature's stimulants has ever been found.

It is a fact well known to psychologists that there is a very close relationship between sex desires and spiritual urges—a fact which accounts for the peculiar behavior of people who participate in the orgies known as religious "revivals," common among the primitive types.

The world is ruled, and the destiny of civilization is established, by the human emotions. People are influenced in their actions, not by reason so much as by "feelings." The creative faculty of the mind is set into action entirely by emotions, and *not by cold reason*. The most powerful of all human emotions is that of sex. There are other mind stimulants, some of which have been listed, but no one of them, nor all of them combined, can equal the driving power of sex.

A mind stimulant is any influence which will either temporarily, or permanently, increase the vibrations of thought. The ten major stimulants, described, are those most commonly resorted to. Through these sources one may commune with Infinite Intelligence, or enter, at will, the storehouse of the subconscious mind, either one's own, or that of another person, a procedure *which is all there is of genius*.

A teacher, who has trained and directed the efforts of more than 30,000 sales people, made the astounding discovery that highly sexed men are the most efficient salesmen. The explanation is, that the factor of personality known as "personal magnetism" is nothing more nor less than sex energy. Highly sexed people always have a plentiful supply of magnetism. Through cultivation and understanding, this vital force may be drawn upon and used to great advantage in the relationships between people. This energy may be communicated to others through the following media:

1. The hand-shake. The touch of the hand indicates, instantly, the presence of magnetism, or the lack of it.
2. The tone of voice. Magnetism, or sex energy, is the factor with which the voice may be colored, or made musical and charming.
3. Posture and carriage of the body. Highly sexed people move briskly, and with grace and ease.
4. The vibrations of thought. Highly sexed people mix the emotion of sex with their thoughts, or may do so at will, and in that way, may influence those around them.
5. Body adornment. People who are highly sexed are usually very careful about their personal appearance. They usually select clothing of a style becoming to their personality, physique, complexion, etc.

When employing salesmen, the more capable sales manager looks for the quality of personal magnetism as the *first requirement* of a salesman. People who lack sex energy will never become enthusiastic nor inspire others with enthusiasm, and enthusiasm is one of the most important requisites in salesmanship, no matter what one is selling.

The public speaker, orator, preacher, lawyer, or salesman who is lacking in sex energy is a "flop," as far as being able to influence others is concerned. Couple with this the fact, that most people can be influenced only through an appeal to their emotions, and you will understand the importance of sex energy as a part of the salesman's native ability. Master salesmen attain the status of mastery in selling, because they, either consciously, or unconsciously, *transmute* the energy of sex into SALES ENTHUSIASM! In this statement may be found a very practical suggestion as to the actual meaning of sex transmutation.

The salesman who knows how to take his mind off the subject of sex, and direct it in sales effort with as much enthusiasm and determination as he would apply to its original purpose, has acquired the art of sex transmutation, whether he knows it or not. The majority of salesmen who transmute their sex energy do so without being in the least aware of what they are doing, or how they are doing it.

Transmutation of sex energy calls for more will power than the average person cares to use for this purpose. Those who find it difficult to summon will-power sufficient for transmutation, may gradually acquire this ability. Though this requires will-power, the reward for the practice is more than worth the effort.

The entire subject of sex is one with which the majority of people appear to be unpardonably ignorant. The urge of sex has been grossly misunderstood, slandered, and burlesqued by the ignorant and the evil minded, for so long that the very word sex is seldom used in polite society. Men and women who are known to be blessed—yes, BLESSED—with highly sexed natures, are usually looked upon as being people who will bear watching. Instead of being called blessed, they are usually called cursed.

Millions of people, even in this age of enlightenment, have inferiority complexes which they developed because of this false belief that a highly sexed nature is a curse. These statements, of the virtue of sex energy, should not be construed as justification for the libertine. The emotion of sex is a virtue ONLY when used intelligently, and with discrimination. It may be misused, and often is, to such an extent that it debases, instead of enriches, both body and mind. The better use of this power is the burden of this chapter.

It seemed quite significant to the author, when he made the discovery that practically every great leader, whom he had the privilege of analyzing, was a man whose achievements were largely inspired by a woman. In many instances, the "woman in the case" was a modest, self-denying wife, of whom the public had heard but little or nothing. In a few instances, the source of inspiration has been traced to the "other woman." Perhaps such cases may not be entirely unknown to you.

Intemperance in sex habits is just as detrimental as intemperance in habits of drinking and eating. In this age in which we live, an age which began with the world war, intemperance in habits of sex is common. This orgy of indulgence may account for the shortage of great leaders. No man can avail himself of the forces of his creative imagination, while dissipating them. Man is the only creature on earth which violates Nature's purpose in this connection. Every other animal indulges its sex nature in moderation, and with purpose which harmonizes with the laws of nature. Every other animal responds to the call of sex only in "season." Man's inclination is to declare "open season."

Every intelligent person knows that stimulation in excess, through alcoholic drink and narcotics, is a form of intemperance which destroys the vital organs of the body, including the brain. Not every person knows, however, that over indulgence in sex expression may become a habit as destructive and detrimental to creative effort as narcotics or liquor.

A sex-mad man is not essentially different than a dope-mad man! Both have lost control over their faculties of reason and will-power. Sexual overindulgence may not only destroy reason and willpower, but it may also lead to either temporary, or permanent insanity. Many cases of hypochondria (imaginary illness) grow out of habits developed in ignorance of the true function of sex.

From these brief references to the subject, it may be readily seen that ignorance on the subject of sex transmutation, forces stupendous penalties upon the ignorant on the one hand, and withholds from them equally stupendous benefits, on the other.

Widespread ignorance on the subject of sex is due to the fact that the subject has been surrounded with mystery and beclouded by dark silence. The conspiracy of mystery and silence has had the same effect upon the minds of young people that the psychology of prohibition had. The result has been increased curiosity, and desire to acquire more knowledge on this "verboten" subject; and to the shame of all lawmakers, and most physicians—by training best qualified to educate youth on that subject—information has not been easily available.

Seldom does an individual enter upon highly creative effort in any field of endeavor before the age of forty. The average man reaches the period of his greatest capacity to create between forty and sixty. These statements are based upon analysis of thousands of men and women who have been carefully observed. They should be encouraging to those who fail to arrive before the age of forty, and to those who become frightened at the approach of "old age," around the forty-year mark. The years between forty and fifty are, as a rule, the most fruitful. Man should approach this age, not with fear and trembling, but with hope and eager anticipation.

If you want evidence that most men do not begin to do their best work before the age of forty, study the records of the most successful men known to the American people, and you will find it. Henry Ford had not "hit his pace" of achievement until he had passed the age of forty. Andrew Carnegie was well past forty before he began to reap the reward of his efforts. James J. Hill was still running a telegraph key at the age of forty. His stupendous achievements took place after that age. Biographies of American industrialists and financiers are filled with evidence that the period from forty to sixty is the most productive age of man.

Between the ages of thirty and forty, man begins to learn (if he ever learns), the art of sex transmutation. This discovery is generally accidental, and more often than otherwise, the man who makes it is totally unconscious of his discovery. He may observe that his powers of achievement have increased around the age of thirty-five to forty, but in most cases, he is not familiar with the cause of this change; that Nature begins to harmonize the emotions of love and sex in the individual, between the ages of thirty and forty, so that he may draw upon these great forces, and apply them jointly as stimuli to action.

Sex, alone, is a mighty urge to action, but its forces are like a cyclone—they are often uncontrollable. When the emotion of love begins to mix itself with the emotion of sex, the result is calmness of purpose, poise, accuracy of judgment, and balance. What person, who has attained to the age of forty, is so unfortunate as to be unable to analyze these statements, and to corroborate them by his own experience?

When driven by his desire to please a woman, based solely upon the emotion of sex, a man may be, and usually is, capable of great achievement, but his actions may be disorganized, distorted, and totally destructive. When driven by his desire to please a woman, based upon the motive of sex alone, a man may steal, cheat, and even commit murder. But when the emotion of LOVE is mixed with the emotion of sex, that same man will guide his actions with more sanity, balance, and reason.

Criminologists have discovered that the most hardened criminals can be reformed through the influence of a woman's *love.* There is no record of a criminal having been reformed solely through the sex influence. These facts are well known, but their cause is not. Reformation comes, if at all, through the *heart,* or the emotional side of man, *not* through his head, or reasoning side. Reformation means, "a change of heart." It does not mean a "change of head." A man may, because of reason, make certain changes in his personal conduct to avoid the consequences of undesirable effects, but GENUINE REFORMATION comes only through a change of heart—through a DESIRE to change.

Love, Romance, and Sex are all emotions capable of driving men to heights of super achievement. Love is the emotion which serves as a safety valve, and insures balance, poise, and constructive effort. When combined, these three emotions may lift one to an altitude of a genius. There are genii, however, who know but little of the emotion of love. Most of them may be found engaged in some form of action which is destructive, or at least, not based upon justice and fairness toward others. If good taste would permit, a dozen genii could be named in the field of industry and finance, who ride ruthlessly over the rights of their fellow men. They seem totally lacking in conscience. The reader can easily supply his own list of such men.

The emotions are states of mind. Nature has provided man with a "chemistry of the mind" which operates in a manner similar to the principles of chemistry of matter. It is a well known fact that, through the aid of chemistry of matter, a chemist may create a deadly poison by mixing certain elements, none of which are—in themselves—harmful in the right proportions. The emotions may, likewise, be combined so as to create a deadly poison. The emotions of sex and jealousy, when mixed, may turn a person into an insane beast.

The presence of any one or more of the destructive emotions in the human mind, through the chemistry of the mind, sets up a poison which may destroy one's sense of justice and fairness. In extreme cases, the presence of any combination of these emotions in the mind may destroy one's reason.

The road to genius consists of the development, control, and use of sex, love, and romance. Briefly, the process may be stated as follows:

Encourage the presence of these emotions as the dominating thoughts in one's mind, and discourage the presence of all the destructive emotions. The mind is a creature of habit. It thrives upon the *dominating* thoughts fed it. Through the faculty of will-power, one may discourage the presence of any emotion, and encourage the presence of any other. Control of the mind, through the power of will, is not difficult. Control comes from persistence, and habit. The secret of control lies in understanding the process of transmutation. When any negative emotion presents itself in one's mind, it can be transmuted into a positive, or constructive emotion, by the simple procedure of changing one's thoughts.

THERE IS NO OTHER ROAD TO GENIUS THAN THROUGH VOLUNTARY SELF EFFORT! A man may attain to great heights of financial or business achievement, solely by the driving force of sex energy, but history is filled with evidence that he may, and usually does, carry with him certain traits of character which rob him of the ability to either hold, or enjoy his fortune. This is worthy of analysis, thought, and meditation, for it states a truth, the knowledge of which may be helpful to women as well as men. Ignorance of this has cost thousands of people their privilege of HAPPINESS, even though they possessed riches.

The emotions of love and sex leave their unmistakable marks upon the features. Moreover, these signs are so visible, that all who wish may read them. The man who is driven by the storm of passion, based upon sex desires alone, plainly advertises that fact to the entire world, by the expression of his eyes, and the lines of his face. The emotion of love, when mixed with the emotion of sex, softens, modifies, and beautifies the facial expression. No character analyst is needed to tell you this—you may observe it for yourself.

The emotion of love brings out, and develops, the artistic and the aesthetic nature of man. It leaves its impress upon one's very soul, even after the fire has been subdued by time and circumstance.

Memories of love never pass. They linger, guide, and influence long after the source of stimulation has faded. There is nothing new in this. Every person, who has been moved by GENUINE LOVE, knows that it leaves enduring traces upon the human heart. The effect of love endures, because love is spiritual in nature. The man who cannot be stimulated to great heights of achievement by love, is hopeless—he is dead, though he may seem to live.

Even the memories of love are sufficient to lift one to a higher plane of creative effort. The major force of love may spend itself and pass away, like a fire which has burned itself out, but it leaves behind indelible marks as evidence that it passed that way. Its departure often prepares the human heart for a still greater love.

Go back into your yesterdays, at times, and bathe your mind in the beautiful memories of past love. It will soften the influence of the present worries and annoyances. It will give you a source of escape from the unpleasant realities of life, and maybe—who knows?—your mind will yield to you, during this temporary retreat into the world of fantasy, ideas, or plans which may change the entire financial or spiritual status of your life.

If you believe yourself unfortunate, because you have "loved and lost," perish the thought. One who has loved truly, can never lose entirely. Love is whimsical and temperamental. Its nature is ephemeral, and transitory. It comes when it pleases, and goes away without warning. Accept and enjoy it while it remains, but spend no time worrying about its departure. Worry will never bring it back.

Dismiss, also, the thought that love never comes but once. Love may come and go, times without number, but there are no two love experiences which affect one in just the same way. There may be, and there usually is, one love experience which leaves a deeper imprint on the heart than all the others, but all love experiences are beneficial, except to the person who becomes resentful and cynical when love makes its departure.

There should be no disappointment over love, and there would be none if people understood the difference between the emotions of love and sex. The major difference is that love is spiritual, while sex is biological. No experience, which touches the human heart with a spiritual force, can possibly be harmful, except through ignorance, or jealousy.

Love is, without question, life's greatest experience. It brings one into communion with Infinite Intelligence. When mixed with the emotions of romance and sex, it may lead one far up the ladder of creative effort. The emotions of love, sex, and romance, are sides of the eternal triangle of achievement-building genius. Nature creates genii through no other force.

Love is an emotion with many sides, shades, and colors. The love which one feels for parents, or children is quite different from that which one feels for one's sweetheart. The one is mixed with the emotion of sex, while the other is not.

The love which one feels in true friendship is not the same as that felt for one's sweetheart, parents, or children, but it, too, is a form of love.

Then, there is the emotion of love for things inanimate, such as the love of Nature's handiwork. But the most intense and burning of all these various kinds of love, is that experienced in the blending of the emotions of love and sex. Marriages, not blessed with the eternal affinity of love, properly balanced and proportioned, with sex, cannot be happy ones—and seldom endure. Love, alone, will not bring happiness in marriage, nor will sex alone. When these two beautiful emotions are blended, marriage may bring about a state of mind, closest to the spiritual that one may ever know on this earthly plane.

When the emotion of romance is added to those of love and sex, the obstructions between the finite mind of man and Infinite Intelligence are removed. Then a genius has been born!

What a different story is this, than those usually associated with the emotion of sex. Here is an interpretation of the emotion which lifts it out of the commonplace, and makes of it potter's clay in the hands of God, from which He fashions all that is beautiful and inspiring. It is an interpretation which would, when properly understood, bring harmony out of the chaos which exists in too many marriages. The disharmonies often expressed in the form of nagging, may usually be traced to *lack of knowledge* on the subject of sex. Where love, romance and the proper understanding of the emotion and function of sex abide, there is no disharmony between married people.

Fortunate is the husband whose wife understands the true relationship between the emotions of love, sex, and romance. When motivated by this holy triumvirate, no form of labor is burdensome, because even the most lowly form of effort takes on the nature of a labor of love.

It is a very old saying that "a man's wife may either make him or break him," but the reason is not always understood. The "making" and "breaking" is the result of the wife's understanding, or lack of understanding of the emotions of love, sex, and romance.

Despite the fact that men are polygamous, by the very nature of their biological inheritance, it is true that no woman has as great an influence on a man as his wife, unless he is married to a woman totally unsuited to his nature. If a woman permits her husband to lose interest in her, and become more interested in other women, it is usually because of her ignorance, or indifference toward the subjects of sex, love, and romance. This statement presupposes, of course, that genuine love once existed between a man and his wife. The facts are equally applicable to a man who permits his wife's interest in him to die.

Married people often bicker over a multitude of trivialities. If these are analyzed accurately, the real cause of the trouble will often be found to be indifference, or ignorance on these subjects.

Man's greatest motivating force is his desire to please woman! The hunter who excelled during prehistoric days, before the dawn of civilization, did so, because of his desire to appear great in the eyes of woman. Man's nature has not changed in this respect. The "hunter" of today brings home no skins of wild animals, but he indicates his desire for her favor by supplying fine clothes, motor cars, and wealth. Man has the same desire to please woman that he had before the dawn of civilization. The only thing that has changed, is his method of pleasing. Men who accumulate large fortunes, and attain to great heights of power and fame, do so, mainly, to satisfy their *desire to please women*. Take women out of their lives, and great wealth would be useless to most men. *It is this inherent desire of man to please woman, which gives woman the power to make or break a man.*

The woman who understands man's nature and tactfully caters to it, need have no fear of competition from other women. Men may be "giants" with indomitable will-power when dealing with other men, but they are easily managed by the women of their choice.

Most men will not admit that they are easily influenced by the women they prefer, because it is in the nature of the male to want to be recognized as the stronger of the species. Moreover, the intelligent woman recognizes this "manly trait" and very wisely makes no issue of it.

Some men know that they are being influenced by the women of their choice—their wives, sweethearts, mothers or sisters—but they tactfully refrain from rebelling against the influence because they are intelligent enough to know that NO MAN IS HAPPY OR COMPLETE WITHOUT THE MODIFYING INFLU-ENCE OF THE RIGHT WOMAN. The man who does not recognize this important truth deprives himself of the power which has done more to help men achieve success than all other forces combined.

CHAPTER TWELVE

THE SUBCONSCIOUS MIND:
THE CONNECTING LINK
The Eleventh Step toward Riches

THE SUBCONSCIOUS MIND consists of a field of consciousness, in which every impulse of thought that reaches the objective mind through any of the five senses, is classified and recorded, and from which thoughts may be recalled or withdrawn as letters may be taken from a filing cabinet.

It receives, and files, sense impressions or thoughts, regardless of their nature. You may VOLUNTARILY plant in your subconscious mind any plan, thought, or purpose which you desire to translate into its physical or monetary equivalent. The subconscious acts first on the dominating desires which have been mixed with emotional feeling, such as faith.

Consider this in connection with the instructions given in the chapter on DESIRE, for taking the six steps there outlined, and the instructions given in the chapter on the building and execution of plans, and you will understand the importance of the thought conveyed.

THE SUBCONSCIOUS MIND WORKS DAY AND NIGHT. Through a method of procedure, unknown to man, the subconscious mind draws upon the forces of Infinite Intelligence for the Power with which it voluntarily transmutes one's desires into their physical equivalent, making use always of the most practical media by which this end may be accomplished.

You cannot *entirely* control your subconscious mind, but you can voluntarily hand over to it any plan, desire, or purpose which you wish transformed into concrete form. Read, again, instructions for using the subconscious mind, in the chapter on autosuggestion.

There is plenty of evidence to support the belief that the subconscious mind is the connecting link between the finite mind of man and Infinite Intelligence. It is the intermediary through which one may draw upon the forces of Infinite Intelligence at will. It, alone, contains the secret process by which mental impulses are modified and changed into their spiritual equivalent. It, alone, is the medium through which prayer may be transmitted to the source capable of answering prayer.

The possibilities of creative effort connected with the subconscious mind are stupendous and imponderable. They inspire one with awe.

I never approach the discussion of the subconscious mind without a feeling of littleness and inferiority due, perhaps, to the fact that man's entire stock of knowledge on this subject is so pitifully limited. The very fact that the subconscious mind is the medium of communication between the thinking mind of man and Infinite Intelligence is, of itself, a thought which almost paralyzes one's reason.

After you have accepted, as a reality, the existence of the subconscious mind, and understand its possibilities, as a medium for transmuting your DESIRES into their physical or monetary equivalent, you will comprehend the full significance of the instructions given in the chapter on DESIRE. You will also understand why you have been repeatedly admonished to MAKE YOUR DESIRES CLEAR, AND TO REDUCE THEM TO WRITING. You will also understand the necessity of PERSISTENCE in carrying out instructions.

The thirteen principles are the stimuli with which you acquire the ability to reach, and to influence your subconscious mind. Do not become discouraged, if you cannot do this upon the first attempt. Remember that the subconscious mind may be voluntarily directed *only through habit,* under the directions given in the chapter on FAITH. You have not yet had time to master faith. Be patient. Be persistent.

A good many statements in the chapters on faith and auto-suggestion will be repeated here, for the benefit of YOUR subconscious mind. Remember, your subconscious mind functions voluntarily, *whether you make any effort to influence it or not.* This, naturally, suggests to you that thoughts of fear and poverty, and all negative thoughts serve as stimuli to your subconscious mind, *unless*, you master these impulses and give it more desirable food upon which it may feed.

The subconscious mind will not remain idle! If you fail to plant DESIRES in your subconscious mind, it will feed upon the thoughts which reach it as the *result of your neglect.* We have already explained that thought impulses, both negative and positive are reaching the subconscious mind continuously, from the four sources which were mentioned in the chapter on Sex Transmutation.

For the present, it is sufficient if you remember that you are living *daily*, in the midst of all manner of thought impulses which are reaching your subconscious mind, without your knowledge. Some of these impulses are negative, some are positive. You are now engaged in trying to help shut off the flow of negative impulses, and to aid in voluntarily influencing your subconscious mind, through positive impulses of DESIRE.

When you achieve this, you will possess the key which unlocks the door to your subconscious mind. Moreover, you will control that door so completely, that no undesirable thought may influence your subconscious mind.

Everything which man creates, BEGINS in the form of a thought impulse. Man can create nothing which he does not first conceive in THOUGHT. Through the aid of the imagination, thought impulses may be assembled into plans. The imagination, when under control, may be used for the creation of plans or purposes that lead to success in one's chosen occupation.

All thought impulses, intended for transmutation into their physical equivalent, voluntarily planted in the subconscious mind, must pass through the imagination, and be mixed with faith. The "mixing" of faith with a plan, or purpose, intended for submission to the subconscious mind, may be done ONLY through the imagination.

From these statements, you will readily observe that voluntary use of the subconscious mind calls for coordination and application of all the principles.

Ella Wheeler Wilcox gave evidence of her understanding of the power of the subconscious mind when she wrote:

"You never can tell what a thought will do
　　In bringing you hate or love—
For thoughts are things, and their airy wings
　　Are swifter than carrier doves.
They follow the law of the universe—
　　Each thing creates its kind,
And they speed O'er the track to bring you back
　　Whatever went out from your mind."

Mrs. Wilcox understood the truth, that thoughts which go out from one's mind, also imbed themselves deeply in one's subconscious mind, where they serve as a magnet, pattern, or blueprint by which the subconscious mind is influenced while translating them into their physical equivalent. Thoughts are truly things, for the reason that every material thing begins in the form of thought-energy.

The subconscious mind is more susceptible to influence by impulses of thought mixed with "feeling" or emotion, than by those originating solely in the reasoning portion of the mind. In fact, there is much evidence to support the theory, that ONLY emotionalized thoughts have any ACTION influence upon the subconscious mind. It is a well known fact that emotion or feeling, rules the majority of people. If it is true that the subconscious mind responds more quickly to, and is influenced more readily by thought impulses which are well mixed with emotion, it is essential to become familiar with the more important of the emotions. There are seven major positive emotions, and seven major negative emotions. The negatives *voluntarily* inject themselves into the thought impulses, which insure passage into the subconscious mind. The positives must be injected, through the principle of auto-suggestion, into the thought impulses which an individual wishes to pass on to his subconscious mind. (Instructions have been given in the chapter on auto-suggestion.)

These emotions, or feeling impulses, may be likened to yeast in a loaf of bread, because they constitute the ACTION element, which transforms thought impulses from the passive to the active state. Thus may one understand why thought impulses, which have been well mixed with emotion, are acted upon more readily than thought impulses originating in "cold reason."

You are preparing yourself to influence and control the "inner audience" of your subconscious mind, in order to hand over to it the DESIRE for money, which you wish transmuted into its monetary equivalent. It is essential, therefore, that you understand the method of approach to this "inner audience." You must speak its language, or it will not heed your call. It understands best the language of emotion or feeling. Let us, therefore describe here the seven major positive emotions, and the seven major negative emotions, so that you may draw upon the positives, and avoid the negatives, when giving instructions to your subconscious mind.

THE SEVEN MAJOR POSITIVE EMOTIONS

The emotion of DESIRE
The emotion of FAITH
The emotion of LOVE
The emotion of SEX
The emotion of ENTHUSIASM
The emotion of ROMANCE
The emotion of HOPE

There are other positive emotions, but these are the seven most powerful, and the ones most commonly used in creative effort. Master these seven emotions (they can be mastered only by USE), and the other positive emotions will be at your command when you need them. Remember, in this connection, that you are studying a book which is intended to help you develop a "money consciousness" by *filling your mind with positive emotions*. One does not become money conscious by filling one's mind with negative emotions.

THE SEVEN MAJOR NEGATIVE EMOTIONS
(To be avoided)

The emotion of FEAR
The emotion of JEALOUSY
The emotion of HATRED
The emotion of REVENGE
The emotion of GREED
The emotion of SUPERSTITION
The emotion of ANGER

Positive and negative emotions cannot occupy the Mind at the same time. One or the other must dominate. It is your responsibility to make sure that positive emotions constitute the dominating influence of your mind. Here the law of **HABIT** will come to your aid. *Form the habit* of applying and using the positive emotions! Eventually, they will dominate your mind so completely, that the negatives *cannot enter it*.

Only by following these instructions literally, and continuously, can you gain control over your subconscious mind. The presence of a single negative in your conscious mind is sufficient to *destroy* all chances of constructive aid from your subconscious mind.

If you are an observing person, you must have noticed that most people resort to prayer ONLY after everything else has FAILED! Or else they pray by a ritual of meaningless words. And, because it is a fact that most people who pray, do so ONLY AFTER EVERYTHING ELSE HAS FAILED, they go to prayer with their minds filled with FEAR and DOUBT, *which are the emotions the subconscious mind acts upon,* and passes on to Infinite Intelligence. Likewise, that is the emotion which Infinite Intelligence receives, and ACTS UPON.

If you pray for a thing, but have fear as you pray, that you may not receive it, or that your prayer will not be acted upon by Infinite Intelligence, your prayer *will have been in vain.*

Prayer does, sometimes, result in the realization of that for which one prays. If you have ever had the experience of receiving that for which you prayed, go back in your memory, and recall your actual STATE OF MIND, while you were praying, and you will know, for sure, that the theory here described is more than a theory.

The time will come when the schools and educational institutions of the country will teach the "science of prayer." Moreover, then prayer may be, and will be reduced to a science. When that time comes, (it will come as soon as mankind is ready for it, and demands it), no one will approach the Universal Mind in a state of fear, for the very good reason that there will be no such emotion as fear. Ignorance, superstition, and false teaching will have disappeared, and man will have attained his true status as a child of Infinite Intelligence. A few have already attained this blessing.

If you believe this prophesy is far-fetched, take a look at the human race in retrospect. Less than a hundred years ago, men believed the lightning to be evidence of the wrath of God, and feared it. Now, thanks to the power of FAITH, men have harnessed the lightning and made it turn the wheels of industry. Much less than a hundred years ago, men believed the space between the planets to be nothing but a great void, a stretch of dead nothingness. Now, thanks to this same power of FAITH, men know that far from being either dead or a void, the space between the planets is very much alive, that it is the highest form of vibration known, excepting, perhaps, the vibration of THOUGHT. Moreover, men know that this living, pulsating, vibratory energy which permeates every atom of matter, and fills every niche of space, connects every human brain with every other human brain.

What reason have men to believe that this same energy does not connect every human brain with Infinite Intelligence?

There are no toll-gates between the finite mind of man and Infinite Intelligence. The communication costs nothing except Patience, Faith, Persistence, Understanding, and a SINCERE DESIRE to communicate. Moreover, the approach can be made only by the individual himself. Paid prayers are worthless. Infinite Intelligence does no business by proxy. You either go direct, or you do not communicate.

You may buy prayer books and repeat them until the day of your doom, without avail. Thoughts which you wish to communicate to Infinite Intelligence, must undergo transformation, such as can be given only through your own subconscious mind.

The method by which you may communicate with Infinite Intelligence is very similar to that through which the vibration of sound is communicated by radio. If you understand the working principle of radio, you of course, know that sound cannot be communicated through the ether until it has been "stepped up," or changed into a rate of vibration which the human ear cannot detect. The radio sending station picks up the sound of the human voice, and "scrambles," or modifies it by stepping up the vibration millions of times. Only in this way, can the vibration of sound be communicated through the ether. After this transformation has taken place, the ether "picks up" the energy (which originally was in the form of vibrations of sound), carries that energy to radio receiving stations, and these receiving sets "step" that energy back down to its original rate of vibration so it is recognized as sound.

The subconscious mind is the intermediary, which translates one's prayers into terms which Infinite Intelligence can recognize, presents the message, and brings back the answer in the form of a definite plan or idea for procuring the object of the prayer. Understand this principle, and you will know why mere words read from a prayer book cannot, and will never serve as an agency of communication between the mind of man and Infinite Intelligence.

Before your prayer will reach Infinite Intelligence (a statement of the author's theory only), it probably is transformed from its original thought vibration into terms of spiritual vibration. Faith is the only known agency which will give your thoughts a spiritual nature. FAITH and FEAR make poor bedfellows. *Where one is found, the other cannot exist.*

CHAPTER THIRTEEN

THE BRAIN:

A BROADCASTING AND RECEIVING
STATION FOR THOUGHT
The Twelfth Step toward Riches

MORE than twenty years ago, the author, working in conjunction with the late Dr. Alexander Graham Bell, and Dr. Elmer R. Gates, observed that every human brain is both a broadcasting and receiving station for the vibration of thought.

Through the medium of the ether, in a fashion similar to that employed by the radio broadcasting principle, every human brain is capable of picking up vibrations of thought which are being released by other brains.

In connection with the statement in the preceding paragraph, compare, and consider the description of the Creative Imagination, as outlined in the chapter on Imagination. The Creative Imagination is the "receiving set" of the brain, which receives thoughts, released by the brains of others. It is the agency of communication between one's conscious, or reasoning mind, and the four sources from which one may receive thought stimuli.

When stimulated, or "stepped up" to a high rate of vibration, the mind becomes more receptive to the vibration of thought which reaches it through the ether from outside sources. This "stepping up" process takes place through the positive emotions, or the negative emotions. Through the emotions, the vibrations of thought may be increased.

Vibrations of an exceedingly high rate are the only vibrations picked up and carried, by the ether, from one brain to another. Thought is energy travelling at an exceedingly high rate of vibration. Thought, which has been modified or "stepped up" by any of the major emotions, vibrates at a much higher rate than ordinary thought, and it is this type of thought which passes from one brain to another, through the broadcasting machinery of the human brain.

The emotion of sex stands at the head of the list of human emotions, as far as intensity and driving force are concerned. The brain which has been stimulated by the emotion of sex, vibrates at a much more rapid rate than it does when that emotion is quiescent or absent.

The result of sex transmutation, is the increase of the rate of vibration of thoughts to such a pitch that the Creative Imagination becomes highly receptive to ideas, which it picks up from the ether. On the other hand, when the brain is vibrating at a rapid rate, it not only attracts thoughts and ideas released by other brains through the medium of the ether, but it gives to one's own thoughts that "feeling" which is essential before those thoughts will be picked up and acted upon by one's subconscious mind.

Thus, you will see that the broadcasting principle is the factor through which you mix feeling, or emotion with your thoughts and pass them on to your subconscious mind.

The subconscious mind is the "sending station" of the brain, through which vibrations of thought are broadcast. The Creative Imagination is the "receiving set," through which the vibrations of thought are picked up from the ether.

Along with the important factors of the subconscious mind, and the faculty of the Creative Imagination, which constitute the sending and receiving sets of your mental broadcasting machinery, consider now the principle of auto-suggestion, which is the medium by which you may put into operation your "broadcasting" station.

Through the instructions described in the chapter on auto-suggestion, you were definitely informed of the method by which DESIRE may be transmuted into its monetary equivalent.

Operation of your mental "broadcasting" station is a comparatively simple procedure. You have but three principles to bear in mind, and to apply, when you wish to use your broadcasting station—the SUBCONSCIOUS MIND, CREATIVE IMAGINATION and AUTO-SUGGESTION. The stimuli through which you put these three principles into action have been described—the procedure begins with DESIRE.

THE GREATEST FORCES ARE "INTANGIBLE"

The depression brought the world to the very border-line of understanding of the forces which are intangible and unseen. Through the ages which have passed, man has depended too much upon his physical senses, and has limited his knowledge to physical things, which he could see, touch, weigh, and measure.

We are now entering the most marvelous of all ages—an age which will teach us something of the intangible forces of the world about us. Perhaps we shall learn, as we pass through this age, that the "other self" is more powerful than the physical self we see when we look into a mirror.

Sometimes men speak lightly of the intangibles—the things which they cannot perceive through any of their five senses, and when we hear them, it should remind us that *all of us are controlled by forces which are unseen and intangible.*

The whole of mankind has not the power to cope with, nor to control the intangible force wrapped up in the rolling waves of the oceans. Man has not the capacity to understand the intangible force of gravity, which keeps this little earth suspended in mid-air, and keeps man from falling from it, much less the power to control that force. Man is entirely subservient to the intangible force which comes with a thunder storm, and he is just as helpless in the presence of the intangible force of electricity—nay, he does not even know what electricity is, where it comes from, or what is its purpose!

Nor is this by any means the end of man's ignorance in connection with things unseen and intangible. He does not understand the intangible force (and intelligence) wrapped up in the soil of the earth—*the force which provides him with every morsel of food he eats, every article of clothing he wears, every dollar he carries in his pockets.*

THE DRAMATIC STORY OF THE BRAIN

Last, but not least, man with all of his boasted culture and education, understands little or nothing of the intangible force (the greatest of all the intangibles) of *thought*. He knows but little concerning the physical brain, and its vast network of intricate machinery through which the power of thought is translated into its material equivalent, but he is now entering an age which shall yield enlightenment on the subject. Already men of science have begun to turn their attention to the study of this stupendous thing called a brain, and, while they are still in the kindergarten stage of their studies, they have uncovered enough knowledge to know that the central switchboard of the human brain, the number of lines which connect the brain cells one with another, equal the figure one, followed by fifteen million ciphers.

"The figure is so stupendous," said Dr. C. Judson Herrick, of the University of Chicago, "that astronomical figures dealing with hundreds of millions of light years, become insignificant by comparison. . . . It has been determined that there are from 10,000,000,000 to 14,000,000,000 nerve cells in the human cerebral cortex, and we know that these are arranged in definite patterns. These arrangements are not haphazard. They are orderly. Recently developed methods of electro-physiology draw off action currents from very precisely located cells, or fibers with micro-electrodes, amplify them with radio tubes, and record potential differences to a millionth of a volt."

It is inconceivable that such a network of intricate machinery should be in existence for the sole purpose of carrying on the physical functions incidental to growth and maintenance of the physical body. Is it not likely that the same system, which gives billions of brain cells the media for communication one with another, provides, also, the means of communication with other intangible forces?

After this book had been written, just before the manuscript went to the publisher, there appeared in the New York Times, an editorial showing that at least one great University, and one intelligent investigator in the field of mental phenomena, are carrying on an organized research through which conclusions have been reached that parallel many of those described in this and the following chapter. The editorial briefly analyzed the work carried on by Dr. Rhine, and his associates at Duke University, viz:—

"What is 'Telepathy'?

"A month ago we cited on this page some of the remarkable results achieved by Professor Rhine and his associates in Duke University from more than a hundred thousand tests to determine the existence of 'telepathy' and 'clairvoyance.' These results were summarized in the first two articles in Harpers Magazine. In the second which has now appeared, the author, E. H. Wright, attempts to summarize what has been learned, or what it seems reasonable to infer, regarding the exact nature of these 'extrasensory' modes of perception.

"The actual existence of telepathy and clairvoyance now seems to some scientists enormously probable as the result of Rhine's experiments. Various percipients were asked to name as many cards in a special pack as they could without looking at them and without other sensory access to them. About a score of men and women were discovered who could regularly name so many of the cards correctly that "there was not one chance in many a million of their having done their feats by luck or accident."

"But how did they do them? These powers, assuming that they exist, do not seem to be sensory. There is no known organ for them. The experiments worked just as well at distances of several hundred miles as they did in the same room. These facts also dispose, in Mr. Wright's opinion, of the attempt to explain telepathy or clairvoyance through any physical theory of radiation. All known forms of radiant energy decline inversely as the square of the distance traversed. Telepathy and clairvoyance do not. But they do vary through physical causes as our other mental powers do. Contrary to widespread opinion, they do not improve when the percipient is asleep or half-asleep, but, on the contrary, when he is most wide-awake and alert. Rhine discovered that a narcotic will invariably lower a percipient's score, while a stimulant will always send it higher. The most reliable performer apparently cannot make a good score unless he tries to do his best.

"One conclusion that Wright draws with some confidence is that telepathy and clairvoyance are really one and the same gift. That is, the faculty that 'sees' a card face down on a table seems to be exactly the same one that 'reads' a thought residing only in another mind. There are several grounds for believing this. So far, for example, the two gifts have been found in every person who enjoys either of them. In every one so far the two have been of equal vigor, almost exactly. Screens, walls, distances, have no effect at all on either. Wright advances from this conclusion to express what he puts forward as no more than the mere 'hunch' that other extra-sensory experiences, prophetic dreams, premonitions of disaster, and the like, may also prove to be part of the same faculty. The reader is not asked to accept any of these conclusions unless he finds it necessary, but the evidence that Rhine has piled up must remain impressive."

In view of Dr. Rhine's announcement in connection with the conditions under which the mind responds to what he terms "extra-sensory" modes of perception, I now feel privileged to add to, his testimony by stating that my associates and I have discovered what we believe to be the ideal conditions under which the mind can be stimulated so that the sixth sense described in the next chapter, can be made to function in a practical way.

The conditions to which I refer consist of a close working alliance between myself and two members of my staff. Through experimentation and practice, we have discovered how to stimulate our minds (by applying the principle used in connection with the "Invisible Counselors" described in the next chapter) so that we can, by a process of blending our three minds into one, find the solution to a great variety of personal problems which are submitted by my clients.

The procedure is very simple. We sit down at a conference table, clearly state the nature of the problem we have under consideration then begin discussing it. Each contributes whatever thoughts that may occur. The strange thing about this method of mind stimulation is that it places each participant in communication with unknown sources of knowledge definitely outside his own experience.

If you understand the principle described in the chapter on the Master Mind, you of course recognize the round-table procedure here described as being a practical application of the Master Mind.

This method of mind stimulation, through harmonious discussion of definite subjects, between three people, illustrates the simplest and most practical use of the Master Mind.

By adopting and following a similar plan any student of this philosophy may come into possession of the famous Carnegie formula briefly described in the introduction. If it means nothing to you at this time, mark this page and read it again after you have finished the last chapter.

THE "depression" was a blessing in disguise.

It reduced the whole world to a new starting point that gives every one a new opportunity.

CHAPTER FOURTEEN

THE SIXTH SENSE:
THE DOOR TO THE TEMPLE OF WISDOM
The Thirteenth Step toward Riches

THE "thirteenth" principle is known as the SIXTH SENSE, through which Infinite Intelligence may, and will communicate voluntarily, without any effort from, or demands by, the individual.

This principle is the apex of the philosophy. It can be assimilated, understood, and applied ONLY by first mastering the other twelve principles.

The SIXTH SENSE is that portion of the sub-conscious mind which has been referred to as the Creative Imagination. It has also been referred to as the "receiving set" through which ideas, plans, and thoughts flash into the mind. The "flashes" are sometimes called "hunches" or "inspirations."

The sixth sense defies description! It cannot be described to a person who has not mastered the other principles of this philosophy, because such a person has no knowledge, and no experience with which the sixth sense may be compared. Understanding of the sixth sense comes only by meditation through mind development *from within*. The sixth sense probably is the medium of contact between the finite mind of man and Infinite Intelligence, and for this reason, *it is a mixture of both the mental and the spiritual*. It is believed to be the point at which the mind of man contacts the Universal Mind.

After you have mastered the principles described in this book, you will be prepared to accept as truth a statement which may, otherwise, be incredible to you, namely:

Through the aid of the sixth sense, you will be warned of impending dangers in time to avoid them, and notified of opportunities in time to embrace them.

There comes to your aid, and to do your bidding, with the development of the sixth sense, a "guardian angel" who will open to you at all times the door to the Temple of Wisdom.

Whether or not this is a statement of truth, you will never know, except by following the instructions described in the pages of this book, or some similar method of procedure.

The author is not a believer in, nor an advocate of "miracles," for the reason that he has enough knowledge of Nature to understand that Nature *never deviates from her established laws.* Some of her laws are so incomprehensible that they produce what appear to be "miracles." The sixth sense comes as near to being a miracle as anything I have ever experienced, and it appears so, only because I do not understand the method by which this principle is operated.

This much the author does know—that there is a power, or a First Cause, or an Intelligence, which permeates every atom of matter, and embraces every unit of energy perceptible to man—that this Infinite Intelligence converts acorns into oak trees, causes water to flow down hill in response to the law of gravity, follows night with day, and winter with summer, each maintaining its proper place and relationship to the other. This Intelligence may, through the principles of this philosophy, be induced to aid in transmuting DESIRES into concrete, or material form. The author has this knowledge, because he has experimented with it and has EXPERIENCED IT.

Step by step, through the preceding chapters, you have been led to this, the last principle. If you have mastered each of the preceding principles, you are now prepared to accept, *without being skeptical,* the stupendous claims made here. If you have not mastered the other principles, you must do so before you may determine, definitely, whether or not the claims made in this chapter are fact or fiction.

While I was passing through the age of "hero-worship" I found myself trying to imitate those whom I most admired. Moreover, I discovered that the element of FAITH, with which I endeavored to imitate my idols, gave me great capacity to do so quite successfully.

I have never entirely divested myself of this habit of hero-worship, although I have passed the age commonly given over to such. My experience has taught me that the next best thing to being truly great, is to emulate the great, by feeling and action, as nearly possible.

Long before I had ever written a line for publication, or endeavored to deliver a speech in public, I followed the habit of reshaping my own character, by trying to imitate the nine men whose lives and life-works had been most impressive to me. These nine men were, Emerson, Paine, Edison, Darwin, Lincoln, Burbank, Napoleon, Ford, and Carnegie. Every night, over a long period of years, I held an imaginary Council meeting with this group whom I called my "Invisible Counselors."

The procedure was this. Just before going to sleep at night, I would shut my eyes, and see, in my imagination, this group of men seated with me around my Council Table. Here I had not only an opportunity to sit among those whom I considered to be great, but I actually dominated the group, by serving as the Chairman.

I had a very DEFINITE PURPOSE in indulging my imagination through these nightly meetings. My purpose was to rebuild my own character so it would represent a composite of the characters of my imaginary counselors. Realizing, as I did, early in life, that I had to overcome the handicap of birth in an environment of ignorance and superstition, I deliberately assigned myself the task of voluntary rebirth through the method here described.

BUILDING CHARACTER THROUGH AUTO-SUGGESTION

Being an earnest student of psychology, I knew, of course, that all men have become what they are, because of their DOMINATING THOUGHTS AND DESIRES. I knew that every deeply seated desire has the effect of causing one to seek outward expression through which that desire may be transmuted into reality. I knew that self-suggestion is a powerful factor in building character, that it is, in fact, the sole principle through which character is builded.

With this knowledge of the principles of mind operation, I was fairly well armed with the equipment needed in rebuilding my character. In these imaginary Council meetings I called on my Cabinet members for the knowledge I wished each to contribute, addressing myself to each member in audible words, as follows:—

"Mr. Emerson, I desire to acquire from you the marvelous understanding of Nature which distinguished your life. I ask that you make an impress upon my subconscious mind, of whatever qualities you possessed, which enabled you to understand and adapt yourself to the laws of Nature. I ask that you assist me in reaching and drawing upon whatever sources of knowledge are available to this end.

"Mr. Burbank, I request that you pass on to me the knowledge which enabled you to so harmonize the laws of Nature that you caused the cactus to shed its thorns, and become an edible food. Give me access to the knowledge which enabled you to make two blades of grass grow where but one grew before, and helped you to blend the coloring of the flowers with more splendor and harmony, for you, alone, have successfully gilded the lily.

"Napoleon, I desire to acquire from you, by emulation, the marvelous ability you possessed to inspire men, and to arouse them to greater and more determined spirit of action. Also to acquire the spirit of enduring FAITH, which enabled you to turn defeat into victory, and to surmount staggering obstacles. Emperor of Fate, King of Chance, Man of Destiny, I salute you!

"Mr Paine, I desire to acquire from you the freedom of thought and the courage and clarity with which to express convictions, which so distinguished you!

"Mr. Darwin, I wish to acquire from you the marvelous patience, and ability to study cause and effect, without bias or prejudice, so exemplified by you in the field of natural science.

"Mr. Lincoln, I desire to build into my own character the keen sense of justice, the untiring spirit of patience, the sense of humor, the human understanding, and the tolerance, which were your distinguishing characteristics.

"Mr. Carnegie, I am already indebted to you for my choice of a life-work, which has brought me great happiness and peace of mind. I wish to acquire a thorough understanding of the principles of *organized effort,* which you used so effectively in the building of a great industrial enterprise.

"Mr. Ford, you have been among the most helpful of the men who have supplied much of the material essential to my work. I wish to acquire your spirit of persistence, the determination, poise, and self-confidence which have enabled you to master poverty, organize, unify, and simplify human effort, so I may help others to follow in your footsteps.

"Mr. Edison, I have seated you nearest to me, at my right, because of the personal cooperation you have given me, during my research into the causes of success and failure. I wish to acquire from you the marvelous spirit of FAITH, with which you have uncovered so many of Nature's secrets, the spirit of unremitting toil with which you have so often wrested victory from defeat."

My method of addressing the members of the imaginary Cabinet would vary, according to the traits of character in which I was, for the moment, most interested in acquiring. I studied the records of their lives with painstaking are. After some months of this nightly procedure, I was astounded by the discovery that these imaginary figures became, apparently *real*.

Each of these nine men developed individual characteristics, which surprised me. For example, Lincoln developed the habit of always being late, then walking around in solemn parade. When he came, he walked very slowly, with his hands clasped behind him, and once in a while, he would stop as he passed, and rest his hand, momentarily, upon my shoulder. He always wore an expression of seriousness upon his face. Rarely did I see him smile. The cares of a sundered nation made him grave.

That was not true of the others. Burbank and Paine often indulged in witty repartee which seemed, at times, to shock the other members of the cabinet. One night Paine suggested that I prepare a lecture on "The Age of Reason," and deliver it from the pulpit of a church which I formerly attended. Many around the table laughed heartily at the suggestion. Not Napoleon! He drew his mouth down at the corners and groaned so loudly that all turned and looked at him with amazement. To him the church was but a pawn of the State, not to be reformed, but to be used, as a convenient inciter to mass activity by the people.

On one occasion Burbank was late. When he came, he was excited with enthusiasm, and explained that he had been late, because of an experiment he was making, through which he hoped to be able to grow apples on any sort of tree. Paine chided him by reminding him that it was an apple which started all the trouble between man and woman. Darwin chuckled heartily as he suggested that Paine should watch out for little serpents, when he went into the forest to gather apples, as they had the habit of growing into big snakes. Emerson observed—"No serpents, no apples," and Napoleon remarked, "No apples, no state!"

Lincoln developed the habit of always being the last one to leave the table after each meeting. On one occasion, he leaned across the end of the table, his arms folded, and remained in that position for many minutes. I made no attempt to disturb him. Finally, he lifted his head slowly, got up and walked to the door, then turned around, came back, and laid his hand on my shoulder and said, "My boy, you will need much courage if you remain steadfast in carrying out your purpose in life. But remember, when difficulties overtake you, the common people have common sense. Adversity will develop it."

One evening Edison arrived ahead of all the others. He walked over and seated himself at my left, where Emerson was accustomed to sit, and said, "You are destined to witness the discovery of the secret of life. When the time comes, you will observe that life consists of great swarms of energy, or entities, each as intelligent as human beings *think* themselves to be. These units of life group together like hives of bees, and remain together until they disintegrate, *through lack of harmony*. These units have differences of opinion, the same as human beings, and often fight among themselves. These meetings which you are conducting will be very helpful to YOU. They will bring to your rescue some of the same units of life which served the members of your Cabinet, during their lives. These units are eternal. THEY NEVER DIE! Your own thoughts and DESIRES serve as the magnet which attracts units of life, from the great ocean of life out there. Only the friendly units are attracted—the ones which harmonize with the nature of your DESIRES."

The other members of the Cabinet began to enter the room. Edison got up, and slowly walked around to his own seat. Edison was still living when this happened. It impressed me so greatly that I went to see him, and told him about the experience. He smiled broadly, and said, "Your dream was more a reality than you may imagine it to have been." He added no further explanation to his statement.

These meetings became so realistic that I became fearful of their consequences for several months. The uncanny I was afraid if I continued them I would lose sight of the fact that the meetings were purely *experiences of my imagination*.

Some six months after I had discontinued the practice I was awakened one night, or thought I was, when I saw Lincoln standing at my bedside. He said, "The world will soon need your services. It is about to undergo a period of chaos which will cause men and women to lose faith, and become panic stricken. Go ahead with your work and complete your philosophy. That is your mission in life. If you neglect it, for any cause whatsoever, you will be reduced to a primal state, and be compelled to retrace the cycles through which you have passed during thousands of years."

I was unable to tell, the following morning, whether I had dreamed this, or had actually been awake, and I have never since found out which it was, but I do know that the dream, if it were a dream, was so vivid in my mind the next day that I resumed my meetings the following night.

At our next meeting, the members of my Cabinet all filed into the room together, and stood at their accustomed places at the Council Table, while Lincoln raised a glass and said, "Gentlemen, let us drink a toast to a friend who has returned to the fold."

After that, I began to add new members to my Cabinet, until now it consists of more than fifty, among them Christ, St. Paul, Galileo, Copernicus, Aristotle, Plato, Socrates, Homer, Voltaire, Bruno, Spinoza, Drummond, Kant, Schopenhauer,

Newton, Confucius, Elbert Hubbard, Brann, Ingersoll, Wilson, and William James.

This is the first time that I have had the courage to mention this. Heretofore, I have remained quiet on the subject, because I knew, from my own attitude in connection with such matters, that I would be misunderstood if I described my unusual experience. I have been emboldened now to reduce my experience to the printed page, because I am now less concerned about what "they say" than I was in the years that have passed. One of the blessings of maturity is that it sometimes brings one greater courage to be truthful, regardless of what those who do not understand, may think or say.

Lest I be misunderstood, I wish here to state most emphatically, that I still regard my Cabinet meetings as being purely imaginary, but I feel entitled to suggest that, while the members of my Cabinet may be purely fictional, and the meetings existent only in my own imagination, they have led me into glorious paths of adventure, rekindled an appreciation of true greatness, encouraged creative endeavor, and emboldened the expression of honest thought.

Somewhere in the cell-structure of the brain, is located an organ which receives vibrations of thought ordinarily called "hunches." So far, science has not discovered where this organ of the sixth sense is located, but this is not important. The fact remains that human beings do receive accurate knowledge, through sources other than the physical senses. Such knowledge, generally, is received when the mind is under the influence of extraordinary stimulation. Any emergency which arouses the emotions, and causes the heart to beat more rapidly than normal may, and generally does, bring the sixth sense into action. Anyone who has experienced a near accident while driving, knows that on such occasions, the sixth sense often comes to one's rescue, and aids, by split seconds, in avoiding the accident.

These facts are mentioned preliminary to a statement of fact which I shall now make, namely, that during my meetings with the "Invisible Counselors," I find my mind most receptive to ideas, thoughts, and knowledge which reach me through the sixth sense. I can truthfully say that I owe entirely to my "Invisible Counselors" full credit for such ideas, facts, or knowledge as I received through "inspiration."

On scores of occasions, when I have faced emergencies, some of them so grave that my life was in jeopardy, I have been miraculously guided past these difficulties through the influence of my "Invisible Counselors."

My original purpose in conducting Council meetings with imaginary beings, was solely that of impressing my own subconscious mind, through the principle of auto-suggestion, with certain characteristics which I desired to acquire. In more recent years, my experimentation has taken on an entirely different trend. I now go to my imaginary counselors with every difficult problem which confronts me and my clients. The results are often astonishing, although I do not depend entirely on this form of Counsel.

You, of course, have recognized that this chapter covers a subject with which a majority of people are not familiar. The Sixth Sense is a subject that will be of great interest and benefit to the person whose aim is to accumulate vast wealth, but it need not claim the attention of those whose desires are more modest.

Henry Ford, undoubtedly understands and makes practical use of the sixth sense. His vast business and financial operations make it necessary for him to understand and use this principle. The late Thomas A. Edison understood and used the sixth sense in connection with the development of inventions, especially those involving basic patents, in connection with which he had no human experience and no accumulated knowledge to guide him, as was the case while he was working on the talking machine, and the moving picture machine.

Nearly all great leaders, such as Napoleon, Bismark, Joan of Are, Christ, Buddha, Confucius, and Mohammed, understood, and probably made use of the sixth sense almost continuously. The major portion of their greatness consisted of their knowledge of this principle.

The sixth sense is not something that one can take off and put on at will. Ability to use this great power comes slowly, through application of the other principles outlined in this book. Seldom does any individual come into workable knowledge of the sixth sense before the age of forty. More often the knowledge is not available until one is well past fifty, and this, for the reason that the spiritual forces, with which the sixth sense is so closely related, do not mature and become usable except through years of meditation, selfexamination, and serious thought.

No matter who you are, or what may have been your purpose in reading this book, you can profit by it without understanding the principle described in this chapter. This is especially true if your major purpose is that of accumulation of money or other material things.

The chapter on the sixth sense was included, because the book is designed for the purpose of presenting a complete philosophy by which individuals may unerringly guide themselves in attaining whatever they ask of life. The starting point of all achievement is DESIRE. The finishing point is that brand of KNOWLEDGE which leads to understanding—understanding of self, understanding of others, understanding of the laws of Nature, recognition and understanding of HAPPINESS.

This sort of understanding comes in its fullness only through familiarity with, and use of the principle of the sixth sense, hence that principle had to be included as a part of this philosophy, for the benefit of those who demand more than money.

Having read the chapter, you must have observed that while reading it, you were lifted to a high level of mental stimulation. Splendid! Come back to this again a month from now, read it once more, and observe that your mind will soar to a still higher level of stimulation. Repeat this experience from time to time, giving no concern as to how much or how little you learn at the time, and eventually you will find yourself in possession of a power that will enable you to throw off discouragement, master fear, overcome procrastination, and draw freely upon your imagination. Then you will have felt the touch of that unknown "something" which has been the moving spirit of every truly great thinker leader, artist, musician, writer, statesman. Then you will be in position to transmute your DESIRES into their physical or financial counterpart as easily as you may lie down and quit at the first sign of opposition.

FAITH VS. FEAR!

Previous chapters have described how to develop FAITH, through Auto-suggestion, Desire and the Subconscious. The next chapter presents detailed instructions for the mastery of FEAR.

Here will be found a full description of the six fears which are the cause of all discouragement, timidity, procrastination, indifference, indecision, and the lack of ambition, self-reliance, initiative, self-control, and enthusiasm.

Search yourself carefully as you study these six enemies, as they may exist only in your subconscious mind, where their presence will be hard to detect.

Remember, too, as you analyze the "Six Ghosts of Fear," that they are nothing but ghosts because they exist only in one's mind.

Remember, also, that ghosts—creations of uncontrolled imagination—have caused most of the damage people have done to their own minds, therefore, ghosts can be as dangerous as if they lived and walked on the earth in physical bodies.

The Ghost of the Fear of Poverty, which seized the minds of millions of people in 1929, was so real that it caused the worst business depression this country has ever known. Moreover, this particular ghost still frightens some of us out of our wits.

CHAPTER FIFTEEN

HOW TO OUTWIT THE SIX GHOSTS OF FEAR:
Take Inventory of Yourself,
As You Read This Closing Chapter,
and Find out How Many of the "Ghosts" Are
Standing in Your Way

BEFORE you can put any portion of this philosophy into successful use, your mind must be prepared to receive it. The preparation is not difficult. It begins with study, analysis, and understanding of three enemies which you shall have to clear out. These are INDECISION, DOUBT, and FEAR!

The Sixth Sense will never function while these three negatives, or any of them remain in your mind. The members of this unholy trio are closely related; where one is found, the other two are close at hand.

INDECISION is the seedling of FEAR! Remember this, as you read. Indecision crystalizes into DOUBT, the two blend and become FEAR! The "blending" process often is slow. This is one reason why these three enemies are so dangerous. They germinate and grow *without their presence being observed.*

The remainder of this chapter describes an end which must be attained before the philosophy, as a whole, can be put into practical use. It also analyzes a condition which has, but lately, reduced huge numbers of people to poverty, and it states a truth which must be understood by all who accumulate riches, whether measured in terms of money or a state of mind of far greater value than money.

The purpose of this chapter is to turn the spotlight of attention upon the cause and the cure of the six basic fears. Before we can master an enemy, we must know its name, its habits, and its place of abode. As you read, analyze yourself carefully, and determine which, if any, of the six common fears have attached themselves to you.

Do not be deceived by the habits of these subtle enemies. Sometimes they remain hidden in the subconscious mind, where they are difficult to locate, and still more difficult to eliminate.

THE SIX BASIC FEARS

There are six basic fears, with some combination of which every human suffers at one time or another. Most people are fortunate if they do not suffer from the entire six. Named in the order of their most common appearance, they are:—

The fear of POVERTY
The fear of CRITICISM   } at the bottom of most of one's worries
The fear of ILL HEALTH

The fear of LOSS OF LOVE OF SOMEONE
The fear of OLD AGE
The fear of DEATH

All other fears are of minor importance, they can be grouped under these six headings.

The prevalence of these fears, as a curse to the world, runs in cycles. For almost six years, while the depression was on, we floundered in the cycle of FEAR OF POVERTY. During the world-war, we were in the cycle of FEAR OF DEATH. Just following the war, we were in the cycle of FEAR OF ILL HEALTH, as evidenced by the epidemic of disease which spread itself all over the world.

Fears are nothing more than states of mind. One's state of mind is subject to control and direction. Physicians, as everyone knows, are less subject to attack by disease than ordinary laymen, for the reason that physicians DO NOT FEAR DISEASE. Physicians, without fear or hesitation, have been known to physically contact hundreds of people, daily, who were suffering from such contagious diseases as small-pox, without becoming infected. Their immunity against the disease consisted, largely, if not solely, in their absolute lack of FEAR.

Man can create nothing which he does not first conceive in the form of an impulse of thought. Following this statement, comes another of still greater importance, namely, MAN'S THOUGHT IMPULSES BEGIN IMMEDIATELY TO TRANSLATE THEMSELVES INTO THEIR PHYSICAL EQUIVALENT, WHETHER THOSE THOUGHTS ARE VOLUNTARY OR INVOLUNTARY. Thought impulses which are picked up through the ether, by mere chance (thoughts which have been released by other minds) may determine one's financial, business, professional, or social destiny just as surely as do the thought impulses which one creates by intent and design.

We are here laying the foundation for the presentation of a fact of great importance to the person who does not understand why some people appear to be "lucky" while others of equal or greater ability, training, experience, and brain capacity, seem destined to ride with misfortune. This fact may be explained by the statement that *every human being has the ability to completely control his own mind,* and with this control, obviously, every person may open his mind to the tramp thought impulses which are being released by other brains, or close the doors tightly and admit only thought impulses of his own choice.

Nature has endowed man with absolute control over but one thing, and that is THOUGHT. This fact, coupled with the additional fact that everything which man creates, begins in the form of a thought, leads one very near to the principle by which FEAR may be mastered.

If it is true that ALL THOUGHT HAS A TENDENCY TO CLOTHE ITSELF IN ITS PHYSICAL EQUIVALENT (and this is true, beyond any reasonable room for doubt), it is equally true that thought impulses of fear and poverty cannot be translated into terms of courage and financial gain.

The people of America began to think of poverty, following the Wall Street crash of 1929. Slowly, but surely that mass thought was crystalized into its physical equivalent, which was known as a "depression." This had to happen, it is in conformity with the laws of Nature.

THE FEAR OF POVERTY

There can be no compromise between POVERTY and RICHES! The two roads that lead to poverty and riches travel in opposite directions. If you want riches, you must refuse to accept any circumstance that leads toward poverty. (The word "riches" is here used in its broadest sense, meaning financial, spiritual, mental and material estates). The starting point of the path that leads to riches is DESIRE. In chapter one, you received full instructions for the proper use of DESIRE. In this chapter, on FEAR, you have complete instructions for preparing your mind to make practical use of DESIRE.

Here, then, is the place to give yourself a challenge which will definitely determine how much of this philosophy you have absorbed. Here is the point at which you can turn prophet and foretell, accurately, what the future holds in store for you. If, after reading this chapter, you are willing to accept poverty, you may as well make up your mind to receive poverty. This is one decision you cannot avoid.

If you demand riches, determine what form, and how much will be required to satisfy you. You know the road that leads to riches. You have been given a road map which, if followed, will keep you on that road. If you neglect to make the start, or stop before you arrive, no one will be to blame, but YOU. This responsibility is yours. No alibi will save you from accepting the responsibility if you now fail or refuse to demand riches of Life, because the acceptance calls for but one thing—incidentally, the only thing you can control—and that is a STATE OF MIND. A state of mind is something that one assumes. It cannot be purchased, it must be created.

Fear of poverty is a state of mind, nothing else! But it is sufficient to destroy one's chances of achievement in any undertaking, a truth which became painfully evident during the depression.

This fear paralyzes the faculty of reason, destroys the faculty of imagination, kills off self-reliance, undermines enthusiasm, discourages initiative, leads to uncertainty of purpose, encourages procrastination, wipes out enthusiasm and makes self-control an impossibility. It takes the charm from one's personality, destroys the possibility of accurate thinking, diverts concentration of effort, it masters persistence turns the will-power into nothingness, destroys ambition, beclouds the memory and invites failure in every conceivable form, it kills love and assassinates the finer emotions of the heart, discourages friendship and invites disaster in a hundred forms, leads to sleeplessness, misery and unhappiness—and all this despite the obvious truth that we live in a world of over-abundance of every thing the heart could desire, with nothing standing between us and our desires, excepting lack of a definite purpose.

The Fear of Poverty is, without doubt, the most destructive of the six basic fears. It has been placed at the head of the list, because it is the most difficult to master. Considerable courage is required to state the truth about the origin of this fear, and still greater courage to accept the truth after it has been stated. The fear of poverty grew out of man's inherited tendency to PREY UPON HIS FELLOW MAN ECONOMICALLY. Nearly all animals lower than man are motivated by instinct, but their capacity to "think" is limited, therefore, they prey upon one another physically. Man, with his superior sense of intuition, with the capacity to think and to reason, does not cat his fellowman bodily, he gets more satisfaction out of "eating" him FINANCIALLY. Man is so avaricious that every conceivable law has been passed to safeguard him from his fellowman.

Of all the ages of the world, of which we know anything, the age in which we live seems to be one that is outstanding because of man's money-madness. A man is considered less than the dust of the earth, unless he can display a fat bank account; but if he has money—NEVER MIND HOW HE ACQUIRED IT—he is a "king" or a "big shot"; he is above the law, he rules in politics, he dominates in business, and the whole world about him bows in respect when he passes.

Nothing brings man so much suffering and humility as POVERTY! Only those who have experienced poverty understand the full meaning of this.

It is no wonder that man *fears* poverty. Through a long line of inherited experiences man has learned, for sure, that some men cannot be trusted, where matters of money and earthly possessions are concerned. This is a rather stinging indictment, the worst part of it being that it is TRUE.

The majority of marriages are motivated by the wealth possessed by one, or both of the contracting parties. It is no wonder, therefore, that the divorce courts are busy.

So eager is man to possess wealth that he will acquire it in whatever manner he can—through legal methods if possible—through other methods if necessary or expedient.

Self-analysis may disclose weaknesses which one does not like to acknowledge. This form of examination is essential to all who demand of Life more than mediocrity and poverty. Remember, as you check yourself point by point, that you are both the court and the jury, the prosecuting attorney and the attorney for the defense, and that you are the plaintiff and the defendant, also, that you are on trial. Face the facts squarely. Ask yourself definite questions and demand direct replies. When the examination is over, you will know more about yourself. If you do not feel that you can be an impartial judge in this self-examination, call upon someone who knows you well to serve as judge while you cross-examine yourself. You are after the truth. *Get it, no matter at what cost even though it may temporarily embarrass you!*

The majority of people, if asked what they fear most, would reply, "I fear nothing." The reply would be inaccurate, because few people realize that they are bound, handicapped, whipped spiritually and physically through some form of fear. So subtle and deeply seated is the emotion of fear that one may go through life burdened with it, never recognizing its presence. Only a courageous analysis will disclose the presence of this universal enemy. When you begin such an analysis, search deeply into your character. Here is a list of the symptoms for which you should look:

SYMPTOMS OF THE FEAR OF POVERTY

INDIFFERENCE. Commonly expressed through lack of ambition; willingness to tolerate poverty; acceptance of whatever compensation life may offer without protest; mental and physical laziness; lack of initiative, imagination, enthusiasm and self-control.

INDECISION. The habit of permitting others to do one's thinking. Staying "on the fence."

DOUBT. Generally expressed through alibis and excuses designed to cover up, explain away, or apologize for one's failures, sometimes expressed in the form of envy of those who are successful, or by criticising them.

WORRY. Usually expressed by finding fault with others, a tendency to spend beyond one's income, neglect of personal appearance, scowling and frowning; intemperance in the use of alcoholic drink, sometimes through the use of narcotics; nervousness, lack of poise, self-consciousness and lack of self-reliance.

OVER-CAUTION. The habit of looking for the negative side of every circumstance, thinking and talking of possible failure instead of concentrating upon the means of succeeding. Knowing all the roads to disaster, but never searching for the plans to avoid failure. Waiting for "the right time" to begin putting ideas and plans into action, until the waiting becomes a permanent habit. Remembering those who have failed, and forgetting those who have succeeded. Seeing the hole in the doughnut, but overlooking the doughnut. Pessimism, leading to indigestion, poor elimination, autointoxication, bad breath and bad disposition.

PROCRASTINATION. The habit of putting off until tomorrow that which should have been done last year. Spending enough time in creating alibis and excuses to have done the job. This symptom is closely related to over-caution, doubt and worry. Refusal to accept responsibility when it can be avoided. Willingness to compromise rather than put up a stiff fight. Compromising with difficulties instead of harnessing and using them as stepping stones to advancement. Bargaining with Life for a penny, instead of demanding prosperity, opulence, riches, contentment and happiness. Planning what to do IF AND WHEN OVERTAKEN BY FAILURE, INSTEAD OF BURNING ALL BRIDGES AND MAKING RETREAT IMPOSSIBLE. Weakness of, and often total lack of self-confidence, definiteness of purpose, self-control, initiative, enthusiasm, ambition, thrift and sound reasoning ability. EXPECTING POVERTY INSTEAD OF DEMANDING RICHES. Association with those who accept poverty instead of seeking the company of those who demand and receive riches.

MONEY TALKS!

Some will ask, "why did you write a book about money? Why measure riches in dollars, alone?" Some will believe, and rightly so, that there are other forms of riches more desirable than money. Yes, there are riches which cannot be measured in terms of dollars, but there are millions of people who will say, "Give me all the money I need, and I will find everything else I want."

The major reason why I wrote this book on how to get money is the fact that the world has but lately passed through an experience that left millions of men and women paralyzed with the FEAR OF POVERTY. What this sort of fear does to one was well described by Westbrook Pegler, in the New York World-Telegram, viz:—

> "Money is only clam shells or metal discs or scraps of paper, and there are treasures of the heart and soul which money cannot buy, but most people, being broke, are unable to keep this in mind and sustain their spirits. When a man is down and out and on the street, unable to get any job at all, something happens to his spirit which can be observed in the droop of his shoulders, the set of his hat, his walk and his gaze. He cannot escape a feeling of inferiority among people with regular employment, even though he knows they are definitely not his equals in character, intelligence or ability.
>
> "These people—even his friends—feel, on the other hand, a sense of superiority and regard him, perhaps unconsciously, as a casualty. He may borrow for a time, but not enough to carry on in his accustomed way, and he cannot continue to borrow very long. But borrowing in itself, when a man is borrowing merely to live, is a depressing experience, and the money lacks the power of earned money to revive his spirits. Of course, none of this applies to bums or habitual ne'er-do-wells, but only to men of normal ambitions and self-respect.
>
> ### "WOMEN CONCEAL DESPAIR.
>
> "Women in the same predicament must be different. We somehow do not think of women at all in considering the down-and-outers. They are scarce in the breadlines, they rarely are seen begging on the streets, and they are not recognizable in crowds by the same plain signs which identify busted men. Of course, I do not mean

the shuffling hags of the city streets who are the opposite number of the confirmed male bums. I mean reasonably young, decent and intelligent women. There must be many of them, but their despair is not apparent. Maybe they kill themselves.

"When a man is down and out he has time on his hands for brooding. He may travel miles to see a man about a job and discover that the job is filled or that it is one of those jobs with no base pay but only a commission on the sale of some useless knickknack which nobody would buy, except out of pity. Turning that down, he finds himself back on the street with nowhere to go but just anywhere. So he walks and walks. He gazes into store windows at luxuries which are not for him, and feels inferior and gives way to people who stop to look with an active interest. He wanders into the railroad station or puts himself down in the library to ease his legs and soak up a little heat, but that isn't looking for a job, so be gets going again. He may not know it, but his aimlessness would give him away even if the very lines of his figure did not. He may be well dressed in the clothes left over from the days when he had a steady job, but the clothes cannot disguise the droop.

"MONEY MAKES DIFFERENCE.

"He sees thousands of other people, bookkeepers or clerks or chemists or wagon hands, busy at their work and envies them from the bottom of his soul. They have their independence, their self-respect and manhood, and he simply cannot convince himself that he is a good man, too, though he argue it out and arrive at a favorable verdict hour after hour.

"It is just money which makes this difference in him. With a little money he would be himself again.

"Some employers take the most shocking advantage of people who are down and out. The agencies hang out little colored cards offering miserable wages to busted men—$12 a week, $15 a week. An $18 a week job is a plum, and anyone with $25 a week to offer does not hang the job in front of an agency on a colored card. I have a want ad clipped from a local paper demanding a clerk, a good, clean penman, to take telephone orders for a sandwich shop from 11 A.M. to 2 P.M. for $8 a month—not $8 a week but $8 a month. The ad says also, 'State religion.' Can you imagine the brutal effrontery of anyone who demands a good, clean penman for 11 cents an hour inquiring into the victim's religion? But that is what busted people are offered."

THE FEAR OF CRITICISM

Just how man originally came by this fear, no one can state definitely, but one thing is certain—he has it in a highly developed form. Some believe that this fear made its appearance about the time that politics became a "profession." Others believe it can be traced to the age when women first began to concern themselves with "styles" in wearing apparel.

This author, being neither a humorist nor a prophet, is inclined to attribute the basic fear of criticism to that part of man's inherited nature which prompts him not only to take away his fellowman's goods and wares, but to justify his action by CRITICISM of his fellowman's character. It is a well known fact that a thief will criticize the man from whom he steals—that politicians seek office, not by displaying their own virtues and qualifications, but by attempting to besmirch their opponents.

The fear of criticism takes on many forms, the majority of which are petty and trivial. Baldheaded men, for example, are bald for no other reason than their fear of criticism. Heads become bald because of the tight fitting bands of hats which cut off the circulation from the roots of the hair. Men wear hats, not because they actually need them, but mainly because "everyone is doing it." The individual falls into line and does likewise, lest some other individual CRITICISE him. Women seldom have bald heads, or even thin hair, because they wear hats which fit their heads loosely, the only purpose of the hats being adornment.

But, it must not be supposed that women free from the fear of criticism. If any woman claims to be superior to man with reference to this fear, ask her to walk down the street wearing a hat of the vintage of 1890.

The astute manufacturers of clothing have not been slow to capitalize this basic fear of criticism, with which all mankind has been cursed. Every season the styles in many articles of wearing apparel change. Who establishes the styles? Certainly not the purchaser of clothing, but the manufacturer. Why does he change the styles so often? The answer is obvious. He changes the styles so he can sell more clothes.

For the same reason the manufacturers of automobiles (with a few rare and very sensible exceptions) change styles of models every season. No man wants to drive an automobile which is not of the latest style, although the older model may actually be the better car.

We have been describing the manner in which people behave under the influence of fear of criticism as applied to the small and petty things of life. Let us now examine human behavior when this fear affects people in connection with the more important events of human relationship. Take for example practically any person who has reached the age of "mental maturity" (from 35 to 40 years of age, as a general average), and if you could read the secret thoughts of his mind, you would find a very decided disbelief in most of the fables taught by the majority of the dogmatists and theologians a few decades back.

Not often, however, will you find a person who has the courage to openly state his belief on this subject. Most people will, if pressed far enough, tell a lie rather than admit that they do not believe the stories associated with that form of religion which held people in bondage prior to the age of scientific discovery and education.

Why does the average person, even in this day of enlightenment, shy away from denying his belief in the fables which were the basis of most of the religions a few decades ago? The answer is, "because of the fear of criticism." Men and women have been burned at the stake for daring to express disbelief in ghosts. It is no wonder we have inherited a consciousness which makes us fear criticism. The time was, and not so far in the past, when criticism carried severe punishments—it still does in some countries.

The fear of criticism robs man of his initiative, destroys his power of imagination limits his individuality, takes away his self-reliance, and does him damage in a hundred other ways. Parents often do their children irreparable injury by criticising them. The mother of one of my boyhood chums used to punish him with a switch almost daily, always completing the job with the statement, "You'll land in the penitentiary before you are twenty." He was sent to a reformatory at the age of seventeen.

Criticism is the one form of service, of which everyone has too much. Everyone has a stock of it which is handed out, gratis, whether called for or not. One's nearest relatives often are the worst offenders. It should be recognized as a crime (in reality it is a crime of the worst nature), for any parent to build inferiority complexes in the mind of a child, through unnecessary criticism. Employers who understand human nature, get the best there is in men, not by criticism, but by constructive suggestion. Parents may accomplish the same results with their children. Criticism will plant FEAR in the human heart, or resentment, but it will not build love or affection.

SYMPTOMS OF THE FEAR OF CRITICISM

This fear is almost as universal as the fear of poverty, and its effects are just as fatal to personal achievement, mainly because this fear destroys initiative, and discourages the use of imagination. The major symptoms of the fear are:

SELF-CONSCIOUSNESS. Generally expressed through nervousness, timidity in conversation and in meeting strangers, awkward movement of the hands and limbs, shifting of the eyes.

LACK OF POISE. Expressed through lack of voice control, nervousness in the presence of others, poor posture of body, poor memory.

PERSONALITY. Lacking in firmness of decision, personal charm, and ability to express opinions definitely. The habit of side-stepping issues instead of meeting them squarely. Agreeing with others without careful examination of their opinions.

INFERIORITY COMPLEX. The habit of expressing self-approval by word of mouth and by actions, as a means of covering up a feeling of inferiority. Using "big words" to impress others, (often without knowing the real meaning of the words). imitating others in dress, speech and manners. Boasting of imaginary achievements. This sometimes gives a surface appearance of a feeling of superiority.

EXTRAVAGANCE. The habit of trying to "keep up with the Joneses," spending beyond one's income.

LACK OF INITIATIVE. Failure to embrace opportunities for self-advancement, fear to express opinions, lack of confidence in one's own ideas, giving evasive answers to questions asked by superiors, hesitancy of manner and speech, deceit in both words and deeds.

LACK OF AMBITION. Mental and physical laziness, lack of self-assertion, slowness in reaching decisions, easily influenced by others, the habit of criticising others behind their backs and flattering them to their faces, the habit of accepting defeat without protest, quitting an undertaking when opposed by others, suspicious of other people without cause, lacking in tactfulness of manner and speech, unwillingness to accept the blame for mistakes.

THE FEAR OF ILL HEALTH

This fear may be traced to both physical and social heredity. It is closely associated, as to its origin, with the causes of fear of Old Age and fear of Death, because it leads one closely to the border of "terrible worlds" of which man knows not, but concerning which he has been taught some discomforting stories. The opinion is somewhat general, also, that certain unethical people engaged in the business of "selling health" have had not a little to do with keeping alive the fear of ill health.

In the main, man fears ill health because of the terrible pictures which have been planted in his mind of what may happen if death should overtake him. He also fears it because of the economic toll which it may claim.

A reputable physician estimated that 75% of all people who visit physicians for professional service are suffering with hypochondria (imaginary illness). It has been shown most convincingly that the fear of disease, even where there is not the slightest cause for fear, often produces the physical symptoms of the disease feared.

Powerful and mighty is the human mind! It builds or it destroys.

Playing upon this common weakness of fear of ill health, dispensers of patent medicines have reaped fortunes. This form of imposition upon credulous humanity became so prevalent some twenty years ago that Carriers' Weekly Magazine conducted a bitter campaign against some of the worst offenders in the patent medicine business.

During the "flu" epidemic which broke out during the world war, the mayor of New York City took drastic steps to check the damage which people were doing themselves through their inherent fear of ill health. He called in the newspaper men and said to them, "Gentlemen, I feel it necessary to ask you not to publish any *scare headlines* concerning the 'flu' epidemic. Unless you cooperate with me, we will have a situation which we cannot control." The newspapers quit publishing stories about the "flu," and within one month the epidemic had been successfully checked.

Through a series of experiments conducted some years ago, it was proved that people may be made ill by suggestion. We conducted this experiment by causing three acquaintances to visit the "victims," each of whom asked the question, "What ails you? You look terribly ill." The first questioner usually provoked a grin, and a nonchalant "Oh, nothing, I'm alright," from the victim. The second questioner usually was answered with the statement, "I don't know exactly, but I do feel badly." The third questioner was usually met with the frank admission that the victim was actually feeling ill.

Try this on an acquaintance if you doubt that it will make him uncomfortable, but do not carry the experiment too far. There is a certain religious sect whose members take vengeance upon their enemies by the "hexing" method. They call it "placing a spell" on the victim.

There is overwhelming evidence that disease sometimes begins in the form of negative thought impulse. Such an impulse may be passed from one mind to another, by suggestion, or created by an individual in his own mind.

A man who was blessed with more wisdom than this incident might indicate, once said "When anyone asks me how I feel, I always want to answer by knocking him down."

Doctors send patients into new climates for their health, because a change of "mental attitude" is necessary. The seed of fear of ill health lives in every human mind. Worry, fear, discouragement, disappointment in love and business affairs, cause this seed to germinate and grow. The recent business depression kept the doctors on the run, because every form of negative thinking may cause ill health.

Disappointments in business and in love stand at the head of the list of causes of fear of ill health. A young man suffered a disappointment in love which sent him to a hospital. For months he hovered between life and death. A specialist in suggestive therapeutics was called in. The specialist changed nurses, placing him in charge of a very *charming young woman* who began (by pre-arrangement with the doctor) to make love to him the first day of her arrival on the job. Within three weeks the patient was discharged from the hospital, still suffering, but with an entirely different malady. HE WAS IN LOVE AGAIN. The remedy was a hoax, but the patient and the nurse were later married. Both are in good health at the time of this writing.

SYMPTOMS OF THE FEAR OF ILL HEALTH

The symptoms of this almost universal fear are:

AUTO-SUGGESTION. The habit of negative use of self-suggestion by looking for, and expecting to find the symptoms of all kinds of disease. "Enjoying" imaginary illness and speaking of it as being real. The habit of trying all "fads" and "isms" recommended by others as having therapeutic value. Talking to others of operations, accidents and other forms of illness. Experimenting with diets, physical exercises, reducing systems, without professional guidance. Trying home remedies, patent medicines and "quack" remedies.

HYPOCHONDRIA. The habit of talking of illness, concentrating the mind upon disease, and expecting its appearance until a nervous break occurs. Nothing that comes in bottles can cure this condition. It is brought on by negative thinking and nothing but positive thought can affect a cure. Hypochondria, (a medical term for imaginary disease) is said to do as much damage on occasion, as the disease one fears might do. Most so-called cases of "nerves" come from imaginary illness.

EXERCISE. Fear of ill health often interferes with proper physical exercise, and results in over-weight, by causing one to avoid outdoor life.

SUSCEPTIBILITY. Fear of ill health breaks down Nature's body resistance, and creates a favorable condition for any form of disease one may contact.

The fear of ill health often is related to the fear of Poverty, especially in the case of the hypochondriac, who constantly worries about the possibility of having to pay doctor's bills, hospital bills, etc. This type of person spends much time preparing for sickness, talking about death, saving money for cemetery lots, and burial expenses, etc.

SELF-CODDLING. The habit of making a bid for sympathy, using imaginary illness as the lure. (People often resort to this trick to avoid work). The habit of feigning illness to cover plain laziness, or to serve as an alibi for lack of ambition.

INTEMPERANCE. The habit of using alcohol or narcotics to destroy pains such as headaches, neuralgia, etc., instead of eliminating the cause.

The habit of reading about illness and worrying over the possibility of being stricken by it. The habit of reading patent medicine advertisements.

THE FEAR OF LOSS OF LOVE

The original source of this inherent fear needs but little description, because it obviously grew out of man's polygamous habit of stealing his fellowman's mate, and his habit of taking liberties with her whenever he could.

Jealousy, and other similar forms of dementia praecox grow out of man's inherited fear of the loss of love of someone. This fear is the most painful of all the six basic fears. It probably plays more havoc with the body and mind than any of the other basic fears, as it often leads to permanent insanity.

The fear of the loss of love probably dates back to the stone age, when men stole women by brute force. They continue to steal females, but their technique has changed. Instead of force, they now use persuasion, the promise of pretty clothes, motorcars, and other "bait" much more effective than physical force. Man's habits are the same as they were at the dawn of civilization, but he expresses them differently.

Careful analysis has shown that women are more susceptible to this fear than men. This fact is easily explained. Women have learned, from experience, that men are polygamous by nature, that they are not to be trusted in the hands of rivals.

SYMPTOMS OF THE FEAR OF LOSS OF LOVE

The distinguishing symptoms of this fear are:—

JEALOUSY. The habit of being suspicious of friends and loved ones without any reasonable evidence of sufficient grounds. (Jealousy is a form of dementia praecox which sometimes becomes violent without the slightest cause). The habit of accusing wife or husband of infidelity without grounds. General suspicion of everyone, absolute faith in no one.

FAULT FINDING. The habit of finding fault with friends, relatives, business associates and loved ones upon the slightest provocation, or without any cause whatsoever.

GAMBLING. The habit of gambling, stealing, cheating, and otherwise taking hazardous chances to provide money for loved ones, with the belief that love can be bought. The habit of spending beyond one's means, or incurring debts, to provide gifts for loved ones, with the object of making, a favorable showing. Insomnia, nervousness, lack of persistence, weakness of will, lack of self-control, lack of self-reliance, bad temper.

THE FEAR OF OLD AGE

In the main, this fear grows out of two sources. First, the thought that old age may bring with it POVERTY. Secondly, and by far the most common source of origin, from false and cruel teachings of the past which have been too well mixed with "fire and brimstone," and other bogies cunningly designed to enslave man through fear.

In the basic fear of old age, man has two very sound reasons for his apprehension—one growing out of his distrust of his fellowman, who may seize whatever worldly goods he may possess, and the other arising from the terrible pictures of the world beyond, which were planted in his mind, through social heredity before he came into full possession of his mind.

The possibility of ill health, which is more common as people grow older, is also a contributing cause of this common fear of old age. Eroticism also enters into the cause of the fear of old age, as no man cherishes the thought of diminishing sex attraction.

The most common cause of fear of old age is associated with the possibility of poverty. "Poorhouse" is not a pretty word. It throws a chill into the mind of every person who faces the possibility of having to spend his declining years on a poor farm.

Another contributing cause of the fear of old age, is the possibility of loss of freedom and independence, as old age may bring with it the loss of both physical and economic freedom.

SYMPTOMS OF THE FEAR OF OLD AGE

The commonest symptoms of this fear are:—

> The tendency to slow down and develop an inferiority complex at the age of mental maturity, around the age of forty, falsely believing one's self to be "slipping" because of age. (The truth is that man's most useful years, mentally and spiritually, are those between forty and sixty).
>
> The habit of speaking apologetically of one's self as "being old" merely

because one has reached the age of forty, or fifty instead of reversing the rule and expressing gratitude for having reached the age of wisdom and understanding.

The habit of killing off initiative, imagination, and self-reliance by falsely believing one's self too old to exercise these qualities. The habit of the man or woman of forty dressing with the aim of trying to appear much younger, and affecting mannerisms of youth; thereby inspiring ridicule by both friends and strangers.

THE FEAR OF DEATH

To some this is the cruelest of all the basic fears. The reason is obvious. The terrible pangs of fear associated with the thought of death, in the majority of cases, may be charged directly to religious fanaticism. So-called "heathen" are less afraid of death than the more "civilized." For hundreds of millions of years man has been asking the still unanswered questions, "whence" and "whither." Where did I come from, and where am I going?

During the darker ages of the past, the more cunning and crafty were not slow to offer the answer to these questions, FOR A PRICE. Witness, now, the major source of origin of the FEAR OF DEATH.

"Come into my tent, embrace my faith, accept my dogmas, and I will give you a ticket that will admit you straightaway into heaven when you die," cries a leader of sectarianism. "Remain out of my tent," says the same leader, "and may the devil take you and burn you throughout eternity."

ETERNITY is a long time. FIRE is a terrible thing. The thought of eternal punishment, with fire, not only causes man to fear death, it often causes him to lose his reason. It destroys interest in life and makes happiness impossible.

During my research, I reviewed a book entitled "A Catalogue of the Gods," in which were listed the *30,000 gods* which man has worshiped. Think of it! Thirty thousand of them, represented by everything from a crawfish to a man. It is little wonder that men have become frightened at the approach of death.

While the religious leader may not be able to provide safe conduct into heaven, nor, by lack of such provision, allow the unfortunate to descend into hell, the possibility of the latter seems so terrible that the very thought of it lays hold of the imagination in such a realistic way that it paralyzes reason, and sets up the fear of death.

In truth, NO MAN KNOWS, and no man has ever known, what heaven or hell is like, nor does any man know if either place actually exists. This very lack of positive knowledge opens the door of the human mind to the charlatan so he may enter and control that mind with his stock of legerdemain and various brands of pious fraud and trickery.

The fear of DEATH is not as common now as it was during the age when there were no great colleges and universities. Men of science have turned the spotlight of truth upon the world, and this truth is rapidly freeing men and women from this terrible fear of DEATH. The young men and young women who attend the colleges and universities are not easily impressed by "fire" and "brimstone." Through the aid of biology, astronomy, geology, and other related sciences, the fears of the dark ages which gripped the minds of men and destroyed their reason have been dispelled.

Insane asylums are filled with men and women who have gone mad, because of the FEAR OF DEATH.

This fear is useless. Death will come, no matter what anyone may think about it. Accept it as a necessity, and pass the thought out of your mind. It must be a necessity, or it would not come to all. Perhaps it is not as bad as it has been pictured.

The entire world is made up of only two things, ENERGY and MATTER. In elementary physics we learn that neither matter nor energy (the only two realities known to man) can be created nor destroyed. Both matter and energy can be transformed, but neither can be destroyed.

Life is energy, if it is anything. If neither energy nor matter can be destroyed, of course life cannot be destroyed. Life, like other forms of energy, may be passed through various processes of transition, or change, but it cannot be destroyed. Death is mere transition.

If death is not mere change, or transition, then nothing comes after death except a long, eternal, peaceful sleep, and sleep is nothing to be feared. Thus you may wipe out, forever, the fear of Death.

SYMPTOMS OF THE FEAR OF DEATH

The general symptoms of this fear are:—

> The habit of THINKING about dying instead of making the most of LIFE, due, generally, to lack of purpose, or lack of a suitable occupation. This fear is more prevalent among the aged, but sometimes the more youthful are victims of it. The greatest of all remedies for the fear of death is a BURNING DESIRE FOR ACHIEVEMENT, backed by useful service to others. A busy person seldom has time to think about dying. He finds life too thrilling to worry about death. Sometimes the fear of death is closely associated with the Fear of Poverty, where one's death would leave loved ones poverty-stricken. In other cases, the fear of death is caused by illness and the consequent breaking down of physical body resistance. The commonest causes of the fear of death are: ill-health, poverty, lack of appropriate occupation, disappointment over love, insanity, religious fanaticism.

OLD MAN WORRY

Worry is a state of mind based upon fear. It works slowly, but persistently. It is insidious and subtle. Step by step it "digs itself in" until it paralyzes one's reasoning faculty, destroys self-confidence and initiative. Worry is a form of sustained fear caused by indecision therefore it is a state of mind which can be controlled.

An unsettled mind is helpless. Indecision makes an unsettled mind. Most individuals lack the willpower to reach decisions promptly, and to stand by them after they have been made, even during normal business conditions. During periods of economic unrest (such as the world recently experienced), the individual is hand-icapped, not alone by his inherent nature to be slow at reaching decisions, but he is influenced by the indecision of others around him who have created a state of "mass indecision."

During the depression the whole atmosphere, all over the world, was filled with "Fearenza" and "Worryitis," the two mental disease germs which began to spread themselves after the Wall Street frenzy in 1929. There is only one known antidote for these germs; it is the habit of prompt and firm DECISION. Moreover, it is an antidote which every individual must apply for himself.

We do not worry over conditions, once we have reached a decision to follow a definite line of action.

I once interviewed a man who was to be electrocuted two hours later. The con-demned man was the calmest of some eight men who were in the death-cell with him. His calmness prompted me to ask him how it felt to know that he was going into eternity in a short while. With a smile of confidence on his face, he said, "It feels fine. Just think, brother, my troubles will soon be over. I have had nothing but trouble all my life. It has been a hardship to get food and clothing. Soon I will not need these things. I have felt fine ever since I learned FOR CERTAIN that I must die. I made up my mind then, to accept my fate in good spirit."

As he spoke he devoured a dinner of proportions sufficient for three men, eat-ing every mouthful of the food brought to him, and apparently enjoying it as much as if no disaster awaited him. DECISION gave this man resignation to his fate? Decision can also prevent one's acceptance of undesired circumstances.

The six basic fears become translated into a state of worry, through indecision. Relieve yourself, forever of the fear of death, by reaching a decision to accept death as an inescapable event. Whip the fear of poverty by reaching a decision to get along with whatever wealth you can accumulate WITHOUT WORRY. Put your foot upon the neck of the fear of criticism by reaching a decision NOT TO WORRY about what other people think, do, or say. Eliminate the fear of old age by reach-ing a decision to accept it, not as a handicap, but as a great blessing which carries with it wisdom, self-control, and understanding not known to youth. Acquit your-self of the fear of ill health by the decision to forget symptoms. Master the fear of loss of love by reaching a decision to get along without love, if that is necessary.

Kill the habit of worry, in all its forms, by reaching a general, blanket decision that nothing which life has to offer is worth the price of worry. With this decision will come poise, peace of mind, and calmness of thought which will bring happiness.

A man whose mind is filled with fear not only destroys his own chances of intelligent action, but, he transmits these destructive vibrations to the minds of all who come into contact with him, and destroys, also their chances.

Even a dog or a horse knows when its master lacks courage; moreover, a dog or a horse will pick up the vibrations of fear thrown off by its master, and behave accordingly. Lower down the line of intelligence in the animal kingdom, one finds this same capacity to pick up the vibrations of fear. A honey-bee immediately senses fear in the mind of a person—for reasons unknown, a bee will sting the person whose mind is releasing vibrations of fear, much more readily than it will molest the person whose mind registers no fear.

The vibrations of fear pass from one mind to another just as quickly and as surely as the sound of the human voice passes from the broadcasting station to the receiving set of a radioand BY THE SELF-SAME MEDIUM.

Mental telepathy is a reality. Thoughts pass from one mind to another, voluntarily, whether or not this fact is recognized by either the person releasing the thoughts, or the persons who pick up those thoughts.

The person who gives expression, by word of mouth, to negative or destructive thoughts is practically certain to experience the results of those words in the form of a destructive "kick-back." The release of destructive thought impulses, alone, without the aid of words, produces also a "kickback" in more ways than one. First of all, and perhaps most important to be remembered, the person who releases thoughts of a destructive nature, must suffer damage through the breaking down of the faculty of creative imagination. Secondly, the presence in the mind of any destructive emotion develops a negative personality which repels people, and often converts them into antagonists. The third source of damage to the person who entertains or releases negative thoughts, lies in this significant fact—these thought-impulses are not only damaging to others, but they IMBED THEMSELVES IN THE SUBCONSCIOUS MIND OF THE PERSON RELEASING THEM, and there become a part of his character.

One is never through with a thought, merely by releasing it. When a thought is released, it spreads in every direction, through the medium of the ether, but it also, plants itself *permanently* in the subconscious mind of *the person releasing it.*

Your business in life is, presumably to achieve success. To be successful, you must find peace of mind, acquire the material needs of life, and above all, attain HAPPINESS. All of these evidences of success begin in the form of thought impulses.

You may control your own mind, you have the power to feed it whatever thought impulses you choose. With this privilege goes also the responsibility of using it constructively. You are the master of your own earthly destiny just as surely as you have the power to control your own thoughts. You may influence, direct, and eventually control your own environment, making your life what you want it to be—or, you may neglect to exercise the privilege which is yours, to make your life to order, thus casting yourself upon the broad sea of "Circumstance" where you will be tossed hither and yon, like a chip on the waves of the ocean.

THE DEVIL'S WORKSHOP
THE SEVENTH BASIC EVIL

In addition to the Six Basic Fears, there is another evil by which people suffer. It constitutes a rich soil in which the seeds of failure grow abundantly. It is so subtle that its presence often is not detected. This affliction cannot properly be classed as a fear. IT IS MORE DEEPLY SEATED AND MORE OFTEN FATAL THAN ALL OF THE SIX FEARS. For want of a better name, let us call this evil SUSCEPTIBILITY TO NEGATIVE INFLUENCES.

Men who accumulate great riches always protect themselves against this evil! The poverty stricken never do! Those who succeed in any calling must prepare their minds to resist the evil. If you are reading this philosophy for the purpose of accumulating riches, you should examine yourself very carefully, to determine whether you are susceptible to negative influences. If you neglect this self-analysis, you will forfeit your right to attain the object of your desires.

Make the analysis searching. After you read the questions prepared for this self-analysis, hold yourself to a strict accounting in your answers. Go at the task as carefully as you would search for any other enemy you knew to be awaiting you in ambush and deal with your own faults as you would with a more tangible enemy.

You can easily protect yourself against highway robbers, because the law provides organized cooperation for your benefit, but the "seventh basic evil" is more difficult to master, because it strikes when you are not aware of its presence, when you are asleep, and while you are awake. Moreover, its weapon is intangible, because it consists of merely—a STATE OF MIND. This evil is also dangerous because it strikes in as many different forms as there are human experiences. Sometimes it enters the mind through the well-meant words of one's own relatives. At other times, it bores from within, through one's own mental attitude. Always it is as deadly as poison, even though it may not kill as quickly.

HOW TO PROTECT YOURSELF AGAINST NEGATIVE INFLUENCES

To protect yourself against negative influences, whether of your own making, or the result of the activities of negative people around you, recognize that you have a WILL-POWER, and put it into constant use, until it builds a wall of immunity against negative influences in your own mind.

Recognize the fact that; you, and every other human being, are, by nature, lazy, indifferent, and susceptible to all suggestions which harmonize with your weaknesses.

Recognize that you are, by nature, susceptible to all the six basic fears, and set up, habits for the purpose of counteracting all these fears.

Recognize that negative influences often work on you through your subconscious mind, therefore they are difficult to detect, and keep your mind closed against all people who depress or discourage you in any way.

Clean out your medicine chest, throw away all pill bottles, and stop pandering to colds, aches, pains and imaginary illness.

Deliberately seek the company of people who influence you to THINK AND ACT FOR YOURSELF.

Do not EXPECT troubles as they have a tendency not to disappoint.

Without doubt, the most common weakness of all human beings is the habit of leaving their minds open to the negative influence of other people. This weakness is all the more damaging, because most people do not recognize that they are cursed by it, and many who acknowledge it, neglect or refuse to correct the evil until it becomes an uncontrollable part of their daily habits.

To aid those who wish to see themselves as they really are, the following list of questions has been prepared. Read the questions and state your answers aloud, so you can hear your own voice. This will make it easier for you to be truthful with yourself.

SELF-ANALYSIS TEST QUESTIONS

Do you complain often of "feeling bad," and if so, what is the cause?

Do you find fault with other people at the slightest provocation?

Do you frequently make mistakes in your work, and if so, why?

Are you sarcastic and offensive in your conversation?

Do you deliberately avoid the association of anyone, and if so, why?

Do you suffer frequently with indigestion? If so, what is the cause?

Does life seem futile and the future hopeless to you? If so, why?

Do you like your occupation? If not, why?

Do you often feel self-pity, and if so why?

Are you envious of those who excel you?

To which do you devote most time, thinking of SUCCESS, or of FAILURE?

Are you gaining or losing self-confidence as you grow older?

Do you learn something of value from all mistakes?

Are you permitting some relative or acquaintance to worry you? If so, why?

Are you sometimes "in the clouds" and at other times in the depths of
   despondency?

Who has the most inspiring influence upon you? What is the cause?

Do you tolerate negative or discouraging influences which you can avoid?

Are you careless of your personal appearance? If so, when and why?

Have you learned how to "drown your troubles" by being too busy to be annoyed
   by them?

Would you call yourself a "spineless weakling" if you permitted others to do your
   thinking for you?

Do you neglect internal bathing until auto-intoxication makes you ill-tempered
   and irritable?

How many preventable disturbances annoy you, and why do you tolerate them?

Do you resort to liquor, narcotics, or cigarettes to "quiet your nerves"? If so, why
   do you not try will-power instead?

Does anyone "nag" you, and if so, for what reason?

Do you have a DEFINITE MAJOR PURPOSE, and if so, what is it, and what plan
   have you for achieving it?

Do you suffer from any of the Six Basic Fears? If so, which ones?

Have you a method by which you can shield yourself against the negative influence of others?

Do you make deliberate use of auto-suggestion to make your mind positive?

Which do you value most, your material possessions, or your privilege of controlling your own thoughts?

Are you easily influenced by others, against your own judgment?

Has today added anything of value to your stock of knowledge or state of mind?

Do you face squarely the circumstances which make you unhappy, or sidestep the responsibility?

Do you analyze all mistakes and failures and try to profit by them or, do you take the attitude that this is not your duty?

Can you name three of your most damaging weaknesses? What are you doing to correct them?

Do you encourage other people to bring their worries to you for sympathy?

Do you choose, from your daily experiences, lessons or influences which aid in your personal advancement?

Does your presence have a negative influence on other people as a rule?

What habits of other people annoy you most?

Do you form your own opinions or permit yourself to be influenced by other people?

Have you learned how to create a mental state of mind with which you can shield yourself against all discouraging influences?

Does your occupation inspire you with faith and hope?

Are you conscious of possessing spiritual forces of sufficient power to enable you to keep your mind free from all forms of FEAR?

Does your religion help you to keep your own mind positive?

Do you feel it your duty to share other people's worries? If so, why?

If you believe that "birds of a feather flock together" what have you learned about yourself by studying the friends whom you attract?

What connection, if any, do you see between the people with whom you associate most closely, and any unhappiness you may experience?

Could it be possible that some person whom you consider to be a friend is, in reality, your worst enemy, because of his negative influence on your mind?

By what rules do you judge who is helpful and who is damaging to you?

Are your intimate associates mentally superior or inferior to you?

How much time out of every 24 hours do you devote to:

    a. your occupation

    b. sleep

    c. play and relaxation

    d. acquiring useful knowledge

    e. plain waste

Who among your acquaintances,

    a. encourages you most

    b. cautions You most

    c. discourages you most

    d. helps you most in other ways

What is your greatest worry? Why do you tolerate it?

When others offer you free, unsolicited advice, do you accept it without question, or analyze their motive?

What, above all else, do you most DESIRE? Do you intend to acquire it? Are you willing to subordinate all other desires for this one? How much time daily do you devote to acquiring it?

Do you change your mind often? If so, why? Do you usually finish everything you begin?

Are you easily impressed by other people's business or professional titles, college degrees, or wealth? Are you easily influenced by what other people think or say of you?

Do you cater to people because of their social or financial status?

Whom do you believe to be the greatest person living? In what respect is this person superior to yourself?

How much time have you devoted to studying and answering these questions? (At least one day is necessary for the analysis and the answering of the entire list.)

If you have answered all these questions truthfully, you know more about yourself than the majority of people. Study the questions carefully, come back to them once each week for several months, and be astounded at the amount of additional knowledge of great value to yourself, you will have gained by the simple method of answering the questions truthfully. If you are not certain concerning the answers to some of the questions, seek the counsel of those who know you well, especially those who have no motive in flattering you, and see yourself through their eyes. The experience will be astonishing.

You have ABSOLUTE CONTROL over but one thing, and that is your thoughts. This is the most significant and inspiring of all facts known to man! It reflects man's Divine nature. This Divine prerogative is the sole means by which you may control your own destiny if you fail to control your own mind, you may be sure you will control nothing else.

If you must be careless with your possessions, let it be in connection with material things. *Your mind is your spiritual estate!* Protect and use it with the care to which Divine Royalty is entitled. You were given a WILL-POWER for this purpose.

Unfortunately, there is no legal protection against those who, either by design or ignorance, poison the minds of others by negative suggestion. This form of destruction should be punishable by heavy legal penalties, because it may and often does destroy one's chances of acquiring material things which are protected by law.

Men with negative minds tried to convince Thomas A. Edison that he could not build a machine that would record and reproduce the human voice, "because" they said, "no one else bad ever produced such a machine." Edison did not believe them. He knew that the mind could produce ANYTHING THE MIND COULD CONCEIVE AND BELIEVE, and that knowledge was the thing that lifted the great Edison above the common herd.

Men with negative minds told F. W. Woolworth, he would go "broke" trying to run a store on five and ten cent sales. He did not believe them. He knew that he could do anything, within reason, if he backed his plans with faith. Exercising his right to keep other men's negative suggestions out of his mind, he piled up a fortune of more than a hundred million dollars.

Men with negative minds told George Washington he could not hope to win against the vastly superior forces of the British, but he exercised his Divine right to BELIEVE, therefore this book was published under the protection of the Stars and Stripes, while the name of Lord Cornwallis has been all but forgotten.

Doubting Thomases scoffed scornfully when Henry Ford tried out his first crudely built automobile on the streets of Detroit. Some said the thing never would become practical. Others said no one would pay money for such a contraption. FORD SAID, "I'LL BELT THE EARTH WITH DEPENDABLE MOTOR CARS," AND HE DID! His decision to trust his own judgment has already piled up a fortune far greater than the next five generations of his descendents can squander. For the benefit of those seeking vast riches, let it be remembered that practically the sole difference between Henry Ford and a majority of the more than one hundred thousand men who work for him, is this—FORD HAS A MIND AND CONTROLS IT, THE OTHERS HAVE MINDS WHICH THEY DO NOT TRY TO CONTROL.

Henry Ford has been repeatedly mentioned, because he is an astounding example of what a man with a mind of his own, and a will to control it, can accomplish. His record knocks the foundation from under that time-worn alibi, "I never had a chance." Ford Dever had a chance, either, but be CREATED AN OPPORTUNITY AND BACK IT WITH PERSISTENCE UNTIL IT MADE HIM RICHER THAN CROESUS.

Mind control is the result of self-discipline and habit. You either control your mind or it controls you. There is no half-way compromise. The most practical of all methods for controlling the mind is the habit of keeping it busy with a definite purpose, backed by a definite plan. Study the record of any man who achieves noteworthy success, and you will observe that he has control over his own mind, moreover, that he exercises that control and directs it toward the attainment of definite objectives. Without this control, success is not possible.

"FIFTY-SEVEN" FAMOUS ALIBIS
By Old Man IF

People who do not succeed have one distinguishing trait in common. They know *all the reasons for failure,* and have what they believe to be air-tight alibis to explain away their own lack of achievement.

Some of these alibis are clever, and a few of them are justifiable by the facts. But alibis cannot be used for money. The world wants to know only one thing— HAVE YOU ACHIEVED SUCCESS?

A character analyst compiled a list of the most commonly used alibis. As you read the list, examine yourself carefully, and determine how many of these alibis, if any, are your own property. Remember, too, the philosophy presented in this book makes every one of these alibis obsolete.

IF I didn't have a wife and family...

IF I had enough "pull"...

IF I had money...

IF I had a good education...

IF I could get a job...

IF I had good health...

IF I only had time...

IF times were better...

IF other people understood me...

IF conditions around me were only different...

IF I could live my life over again...

IF I did not fear what "THEY" would say...

IF I had been given a chance...

IF I now had a chance...

IF other people didn't "have it in for me"...

IF nothing happens to stop me...

IF I were only younger...

IF I could only do what I want...

IF I had been born rich...

IF I could meet "the right people"...

IF I had the talent that some people have...

IF I dared assert myself...

IF I only had embraced past opportunities...

IF people didn't get on my nerves...

IF I didn't have to keep house and look after the children...

IF I could save some money...

IF the boss only appreciated me...

IF I only had somebody to help me...

IF my family understood me...

IF I lived in a big city...

IF I could just get started...

IF I were only free...

IF I had the personality of some people...

IF I were not so fat...

IF my talents were known...

IF I could just get a "break"...

IF I could only get out of debt...

IF I hadn't failed...

IF I only knew how...

IF everybody didn't oppose me...

IF I didn't have so many worries...

IF I could marry the right person...

IF people weren't so dumb...

IF my family were not so extravagant...

IF I were sure of myself...

IF luck were not against me...

IF I had not been born under the wrong star...

IF it were not true that "what is to be will be"...

IF I did not have to work so hard...

IF I hadn't lost my money...

IF I lived in a different neighborhood...

IF I didn't have a "past"...

IF I only had a business of my own...

IF other people would only listen to me...

IF * * * and this is the greatest of them all * * *

I had the courage to see myself as I really am, I would *find out what is wrong with me, and correct it,* then I might have a chance to profit by my mistakes and learn something from the experience of others, for I know that there is something WRONG with me, or I would now be where I *WOULD HAVE BEEN IF I* had spent more time analyzing my weaknesses, and less time building alibis to cover them.

Building alibis with which to explain away failure is a national pastime. The habit is as old as the human race, and *is fatal to success!* Why do people cling to their pet alibis? The answer is obvious. They defend their alibis because THEY

CREATE them! A man's alibi is the child of his own imagination. It is human nature to defend one's own brainchild.

Building alibis is a deeply rooted habit. Habits are difficult to break, especially when they provide justification for something we do. Plato had this truth in mind when he said, "The first and best victory is to conquer self. To be conquered by self is, of all things, the most shameful and vile."

Another philosopher had the same thought in mind when he said, "It was a great surprise to me when I discovered that most of the ugliness I saw in others, was but a reflection of my own nature."

"It has always been a mystery to me," said Elbert Hubbard, "why people spend so much time deliberately fooling themselves by creating alibis to cover their weaknesses. If used differently, this same time would be sufficient to cure the weakness then no alibis would be needed."

In parting, I would remind you that "Life is a checkerboard, and the player opposite you is TIME. If you hesitate before moving, or neglect to move promptly, your men will be wiped off the board by TIME. You are playing against a partner who will not tolerate INDECISION!"

Previously you may have had a logical excuse for not having forced Life to come through with whatever you asked, but that alibi is now obsolete, because you are in possession of the Master Key that unlocks the door to Life's bountiful riches.

The Master Key is intangible, but it is powerful! It is the privilege of creating, *in your own mind*, a BURNING DESIRE for a definite form of riches. There is no penalty for the use of the Key, but there is a price you must pay if you do not use it. The price is FAILURE. There is a reward of stupendous proportions if you put the Key to use. It is the satisfaction that comes to all who *conquer self and force Life to pay whatever is asked.*

The reward is worthy of your effort. Will you make the start and be convinced?

"If we are related," said the immortal Emerson, "we shall meet." In closing, may I borrow his thought, and say, "If we are related, we have, through these pages, met."

THE END

BOOK TWO:

THE SCIENCE OF GETTING RICH

W. D. WATTLES

CONTENTS

PREFACE

This book is pragmatical, not philosophical; a practical manual, not a treatise upon theories. It is intended for the men and women whose most pressing need is for money; who wish to get rich first, and philosophize afterward. It is for those who have, so far, found neither the time, the means, nor the opportunity to go deeply into the study of metaphysics, but who want results and who are willing to take the conclusions of science as a basis for action, without going into all the processes by which those conclusions were reached.

It is expected that the reader will take the fundamental statements upon faith, just as he would take statements concerning a law of electrical action if they were promulgated by a Marconi or an Edison; and, taking the statements upon faith, that he will prove their truth by acting upon them without fear or hesitation. Every man or woman who does this will certainly get rich; for the science herein applied is an exact science, and failure is impossible. For the benefit, however, of those who wish to investigate philosophical theories and so secure a logical basis for faith, I will here cite certain authorities.

The monistic theory of the universe—the theory that One is All, and that All is One; that one Substance manifests itself as the seeming many elements of the material world—is of Hindu origin, and has been gradually winning its way into the thought of the western world for two hundred years. It is the foundation of all the Oriental philosophies, and of those of Descartes, Spinoza, Leibnitz, Schopenhauer, Hegel, and Emerson.

The reader who would dig to the philosophical foundations is advised to read Hegel and Emerson; and he will do well to read "The Eternal News," a very excellent pamphlet published by J. J. Brown, 300 Cathcart Road, Govanhill, Glasgow, Scotland. He may also find some help in a series of articles written by the author, which were published in *Nautilus* (Holyoke, Mass.) during the spring and summer of 1909, under the title "What is Truth?"

In writing this book I have sacrificed all other considerations to plainness and simplicity of style, so that all might understand. The plan of action laid down herein was deduced from the conclusions of philosophy; it has been thoroughly tested, and bears the supreme test of practical experiment; it works. If you wish to know how the conclusions were arrived at, read the writings of the authors mentioned above; and if you wish to reap the fruits of their philosophies in actual practice, read this book and do exactly as it tells you to do.

THE AUTHOR

CHAPTER ONE

THE RIGHT TO BE RICH

WHATEVER may be said in praise of poverty, the fact remains that it is not possible to live a really complete or successful life unless one is rich. No man can rise to his greatest possible height in talent or soul development unless he has plenty of money; for to unfold the soul and to develop talent he must have many things to use, and he cannot have these things unless he has money to buy them with.

Man develops in mind, soul, and body by making use of things, and society is so organized that man must have money in order to become the possessor of things; therefore, the basis of all advancement for man must be the science of getting rich.

The object of all life is development; and everything that lives has an inalienable right to all the development it is capable of attaining.

Man's right to life means his right to have the free and unrestricted use of all the things which may be necessary to his fullest mental, spiritual, and physical unfoldment; or, in other words, his right to be rich.

In this book, I shall not speak of riches in a figurative way; to be really rich does not mean to be satisfied or contented with a little. No man ought to be satisfied with a little if he is capable of using and enjoying more. The purpose of Nature is the advancement and unfoldment of life; and every man should have all that can contribute to the power, elegance, beauty, and richness of life; to be content with less is sinful.

The man who owns all he wants for the living of all the life he is capable of living is rich; and no man who not plenty of money can have all he wants. Life has advanced so far, and become so complex, that even the most ordinary man or woman requires a great amount of wealth in order to live in a manner that even approaches completeness. Every person naturally wants to become all that he is capable of becoming; this desire to realize innate possibilities is inherent in human nature; we cannot help wanting to be all that we can be. Success in life is becoming what you want to be; you can become what you want to be only by making use of things, and you can have the free use of things only as you become rich enough to buy them. To understand the science of getting rich is therefore the most essential of all knowledge.

There is nothing wrong in wanting to get rich. The desire for riches is really the desire for a richer, fuller, and more abundant life; and that desire is praiseworthy. The man who does not desire to live more abundantly is abnormal, and so the man who does not desire to have money enough to buy all he wants is abnormal.

There are three motives for which we live; we live for the body, we live for the mind, and we live for the soul. No one of these is better or holier than the other; all are alike desirable, and no one of the three—body, mind, or soul—can live fully if either of the others is cut short of full life and expression. It is not right or noble to live only for the soul and deny mind or body; and it is wrong to live for the intellect and deny body and soul.

We are all acquainted with the loathsome consequences of living for the body and denying both mind and soul; and we see that real life means the complete expression of all that man can give forth through body, mind, and soul. Whatever he may say, no man can be really happy or satisfied unless his body is living fully in every function, and unless the same is true of his mind and his soul. Wherever there is unexpressed possibility, or function not performed, there is unsatisfied desire. Desire is possibility seeking expression, or function seeking performance.

Man cannot live fully in body without good food, comfortable clothing, and warm shelter; and without freedom from excessive toil. Rest and recreation are also necessary to his physical life.

He cannot live fully in mind without books and time to study them, without opportunity for travel and observation, or without intellectual companionship.

To live fully in mind he must have intellectual recreations, and must surround himself with all the objects of art and beauty he is capable of using and appreciating.

To live fully in soul, man must have love; and love is denied expression by poverty.

Man's highest happiness is found in the bestowal of benefits on those he loves; love finds its most natural and spontaneous expression in giving. The man who has nothing to give cannot fill his place as a husband or father, as a citizen, or as a man. It is in the use of material things that man finds full life for his body, develops his mind, and unfolds his soul. It is therefore of supreme importance to him that he should be rich.

It is perfectly right that you should desire to be rich; if you are a normal man or woman you cannot help doing so. It is perfectly right that you should give your best attention to the Science of Getting Rich, for it is the noblest and most necessary of all studies. If you neglect this study, you are derelict in your duty to yourself, to God, and to humanity; for you can render God and humanity no greater service than to make the most of yourself.

CHAPTER TWO

THERE IS A SCIENCE OF GETTING RICH

THERE is a Science of getting rich, and it is an exact science, like algebra or arithmetic. There are certain laws which govern the process of acquiring riches; once these laws are learned and obeyed by any man, he will get rich with mathematical certainty.

The ownership of money and property comes as a result of doing things in a certain way; those who do things in this Certain Way, whether on purpose or accidentally, get rich; while those who do not do things in this Certain Way, no matter how hard they work or how able they are, remain poor.

It is a natural law that like causes always produce like effects; and, therefore, any man or woman who learns to do things in this Certain Way will infallibly get rich.

That the above statement is true is shown by the following facts:—

Getting rich is not a matter of environment, for if it were, all the people in certain neighborhoods would become wealthy; the people of one city would all be rich, while those of other towns would all be poor; or the inhabitants of one state would roll in wealth, while those of an adjoining state would be in poverty.

But everywhere we see rich and poor living side by side, in the same environment, and often engaged in the same vocations. When two men are in the same locality, and in the same business, and one gets rich while the other remains poor, it shows that getting rich is not, primarily, a matter of environment. Some environments may be more favorable than others, but when two men in the same business are in the same neighborhood, and one gets rich while the other fails, it indicates that getting rich is the result of doing things in a Certain Way.

And further, the ability to do things in this Certain Way is not due solely to the possession of talent, for many people who have great talent remain poor, while others who have very little talent get rich.

Studying the people who have got rich, we find that they are an average lot in all respects, having no greater talents and abilities than other men. It is evident that they do not get rich because they possess talents and abilities that other men have not, but because they happen to do things in a Certain Way.

Getting rich is not the result of saving, or "thrift"; many very penurious people are poor, while free spenders often get rich.

Nor is getting rich due to doing things which others fail to do; for two men in the same business often do almost exactly the same things, and one gets rich while the other remains poor or becomes a bankrupt.

From all these things, we must come to the conclusion that getting rich is the result of doing things in a Certain Way.

If getting rich is the result of doing things in a Certain Way, and if like causes always produce like effects, then any man or woman who can do things in that way can become rich, and the whole matter is brought within the domain of exact science.

The question arises here, whether this Certain Way may not be so difficult that only a few may follow it. This cannot be true, as we have seen, so far as natural ability is concerned. Talented people get rich, and blockheads get rich; intellectually brilliant people get rich, and very stupid people get rich; physically strong people get rich, and weak and sickly people get rich.

Some degree of ability to think and understand is, of course, essential; but in so far as natural ability is concerned, any man or woman who has sense enough to read and understand these words can certainly get rich.

Also, we have seen that it is not a matter of environment. Location counts for something; one would not go to the heart of the Sahara and expect to do successful business.

Getting rich involves the necessity of dealing with men, and of being where there are people to deal with; and if these people are inclined to deal in the way you want to deal, so much the better. But that is about as far as environment goes.

If anybody else in your town can get rich, so can you; and if anybody else in your state can get rich, so can you.

Again, it is not a matter of choosing some particular business or profession. People get rich in every business, and in every profession; while their next door neighbors in the same vocation remain in poverty.

It is true that you will do best in a business which you like, and which is congenial to you; and if you have certain talents which are well developed, you will do best in a business which calls for the exercise of those talents.

Also, you will do best in a business which is suited to your locality; an ice-cream parlor would do better in a warm climate than in Greenland, and a salmon fishery will succeed better in the Northwest than in Florida, where there are no salmon.

But, aside from these general limitations, getting rich is not dependent upon your engaging in some particular business, but upon your learning to do things in a Certain Way. If you are now in business, and anybody else in your locality is getting rich in the same business, while you are *not* getting rich, it is because you are not doing things in the same Way that the other person is doing them.

No one is prevented from getting rich by lack of capital. True, as you get capital the increase becomes more easy and rapid; but one who has capital is already rich, and does not need to consider how to become so. No matter how poor you may be, if you begin to do things in the Certain Way you will begin to get rich; and you will begin to have capital. The getting of capital is a part of the process of getting rich; and it is a part of the result which invariably follows the doing of things in the Certain Way.

You may be the poorest man on the continent, and be deeply in debt; you may have neither friends, influence, nor resources; but if you begin to do things in this Way, you must infallibly begin to get rich, for like causes must produce like effects. If you have no capital, you can get capital; if you are in the wrong business, you can get into the right business; if you are in the wrong location, you can go to the right location; and you can do so *by beginning in your present business and in your present location* to do things in the Certain Way which causes success.

CHAPTER THREE

IS OPPORTUNITY MONOPOLIZED?

No man is kept poor because opportunity has been taken away from him; because other people have monopolized the wealth, and have put a fence around it. You may be shut off from engaging in business in certain lines, but there are other channels open to you. Probably it would be hard for you to get control of any of the great railroad system; that field is pretty well monopolized. But the electric railway business is still in its infancy, and offers plenty of scope for enterprise; and it will be but a very few years until traffic and transportation through the air will become a great industry, and in all its branches will give employment to hundreds of thousands, and perhaps to millions, of people. Why not turn your attention to the development of aerial transportation, instead of competing with J. J. Hill and others for a chance in the steam railway world?

It is quite true that if you are a workman in the employ of the steel trust you have very little chance of becoming the owner of the plant in which you work; but it is also true that if you will commence to act in a Certain Way, you can soon leave the employ of the steel trust; you can buy a farm of from ten to forty acres, and engage in business as a producer of foodstuffs. There is great opportunity at this time for men who will live upon small tracts of land and cultivate the same intensively; such men will certainly get rich. You may say that if is impossible for you to get the land, but I am going to prove to you that it is not impossible, and that you can certainly get a farm if you will go to work in a Certain Way.

At different periods the tide of opportunity sets in different directions, according to the needs of the Whole, and the particular stage of social evolution which has been reached. At present, in America, it is setting toward agriculture and the allied industries and professions. To-day, opportunity is open before the farmer in his line more than before the factory worker in his line. It is open before the business man who supplies the farmer more than before the one who supplies the factory worker; and before the professional man who waits upon the farmer more than before the one who serves the working class.

There is abundance of opportunity for the man who will go with the tide, instead of trying to swim against it.

So the factory workers, either as individuals or as a class, are not deprived of opportunity. The workers are not being "kept down" by their masters; they are not being "ground" by the trusts and combinations of capital. As a class, they are where they are because they do not do things in a Certain Way. If the workers of America chose to do so, they could follow the example of their brothers in Belgium and, other countries, and establish great department stores and co-operative industries; they could elect men of their own class to office, and pass laws favoring the, development of such co-operative industries; and in a few years they could take peaceable possession of the industrial field.

The working class may become the master class whenever they will begin to do things in a Certain Way; the law of wealth is the same for them as it is for all others. This they must learn; and they will remain where they are as long as they continue to do as they do. The individual worker, however, is not held down by the ignorance or the mental slothfulness of his class; he can follow the tide of opportunity to riches, and this book will tell him how.

No one is kept in poverty by a shortness in the supply of riches; there is more than enough for all. A palace as large as the capitol at Washington might be built for every family on earth from the building material in the United States alone; and under intensive cultivation, this country would produce wool, cotton, linen, and silk enough to clothe each person in the world finer than Solomon was arrayed in all his glory; together with food enough to feed them all luxuriously. The visible supply is practically inexhaustible; and the invisible supply really IS inexhaustible.

Everything you see on earth is made from one original substance, out of which all things proceed.

New forms are constantly being made, and older ones are dissolving; but all are shapes assumed by One Thing.

There is no limit to the supply of Formless Stuff, or Original Substance. The universe is made out of it; but it was not all used in making the universe. The spaces in, through, and between the forms of the visible universe are permeated and filled with the Original Substance; with the Formless Stuff; with the raw material of all things. Ten thousand times as much as has been made might still be made, and even then we should not have exhausted the supply of universal raw material.

No man, therefore, is poor because nature is poor, or because there is not enough to go around.

Nature is an inexhaustible storehouse of riches; the supply will never run short. Original Substance is alive with creative energy, and is constantly producing more forms. When the supply of building material is exhausted, more will be produced; when the soil is exhausted so that foodstuffs and materials for clothing will no longer grow upon it, it will be renewed or more soil will be made. When all the gold and silver has been dug from the earth, if man is still in such a stage of social development that he needs gold and silver, more will be produced from the Formless. The Formless Stuff responds to the needs of man; it will not let him be without any good thing.

This is true of man collectively; the race as a whole is always abundantly rich, and if individuals are poor, it is because they do not follow the Certain Way of doing things which makes the individual man rich.

The Formless Stuff is intelligent; it is stuff which thinks. It is alive, and is always, impelled toward more life.

It is the natural and inherent impulse of life to seek to live more; it is the nature of intelligence to enlarge itself, and of consciousness to seek to extend its boundaries and find fuller expression. The universe of forms has been made by Formless Living Substance, throwing itself into form in order to express itself more fully.

The universe is a great Living Presence, always moving inherently toward more life and fuller functioning.

Nature is formed for the advancement of life; its impelling motive is the increase of life. For this cause, everything which can possibly minister to life is bountifully provided; there can be no lack unless God is to contradict himself and nullify his own works.

You are not kept poor by lack in the supply of riches; it is a fact which I shall demonstrate a little farther on that even the resources of the Formless Supply are at the command of the man or woman who will act and think in a Certain Way.

CHAPTER FOUR

THE FIRST PRINCIPLE IN THE SCIENCE
OF GETTING RICH

Thought is the only power which can produce tangible riches from the Formless Substance. The stuff from which all things are made is a substance which thinks, and thought of form in this substance produces the form.

Original Substance moves according to its thoughts; every form and process you see in nature is the visible expression of a thought in Original Substance. As the Formless Stuff thinks of a form, it takes that form; as it thinks of a motion, it makes that motion. That is the way all things were created. We live in a thought world, which is part of a thought universe.

The thought of a moving universe extended throughout Formless Substance, and the Thinking Stuff moving according to that thought, took the form of systems of planets, and maintains that form. Thinking Substance takes the form of its thought, and moves according to the thought. Holding the idea of a circling system of suns and worlds, it takes the form of these bodies, and moves them as it thinks. Thinking the form of a slow-growing oak tree, it moves accordingly, and produces the tree, though centuries may be required to do the work. In creating, the Formless seems to move according to the lines of motion it has established; the thought of an oak tree does not cause the instant formation of a full-grown tree, but it does start in motion the forces which will produce the tree, along established lines of growth.

Every thought of form, held in thinking Substance, causes the creation of the form, but always, or at least generally, along lines of growth and action already established.

The thought of a house of a certain construction, if it were impressed upon Formless Substance, might not cause the instant formation of the house; but, it would cause the turning of creative energies already working in trade and commerce into such channels as to result in the speedy building of the house. And if there were no existing channels through which the creative energy could work, then the house would be formed directly from primal substance, without waiting for the slow processes of the organic and inorganic world.

No thought of form can be impressed upon Original Substance without causing the creation of the form.

Man is a thinking center, and can originate thought. All the forms that man fashions with his hands must first exist in his thought; he cannot shape a thing until he has thought that thing.

And so far man has confined his efforts wholly to the work of his hands; he has applied manual labor to the, world of forms, seeking to change or modify those already existing. He has never thought of trying to cause the creation of new forms by impressing his thoughts upon Formless Substance.

When man has a thought-form he takes material from the forms of nature, and makes an image of the form which is in his mind. He has, so far, made little or no effort to co-operate with Formless Intelligence; to work "with the Father." He has not dreamed that he can "do what he seeth the Father doing." Man reshapes and modifies existing forms by manual labor; he has given no attention to the question whether he may not produce things from Formless Substance by communicating his thoughts to it. We propose to prove that he may do so; to prove that any man or woman may do so, and to show how. As our first step, we must lay down three fundamental propositions

First, we assert that there is one original formless stuff, or substance, from which all things are made. All the seemingly many elements are but, different presentations of one element; all the many forms found in organic and inorganic nature are but different shapes, made from the same stuff. And this stuff is thinking stuff; a thought held in it produces the form of the thought. Thought, in thinking substance, produces shapes. Man is a thinking center, capable of original thought; if man can communicate his thought to original thinking substance, he can cause the creation, or formation, of the thing he thinks about. To summarize this: —

There is a thinking stuff from which all things are made, and which, in its original state, permeates, penetrates, and fills the interspaces of the universe.

A thought, in this substance, produces the thing that is imaged by the thought.

Man can form things in his thought, and, by impressing his thought upon formless substance, can cause the thing he thinks about to be created.

It may be asked if I can prove these statements; and without going into details, I answer that I can do so, both by logic and experience.

Reasoning back from the phenomena of form and thought, I come to one original thinking substance; and reasoning forward from this thinking substance, I come to man's power to cause the formation of the thing he thinks about.

And by experiment, I find the reasoning true; and this is my strongest proof.

If one man who reads this book gets rich by doing what it tells him to do, that is evidence in support of my claim; but if every man who does what it tells him to do gets rich, that is positive proof until some one goes through the process and fails. The theory is true until the process fails; and this process will not fail, for every man who does exactly what this books tells him to do will get rich.

I have said that men get rich by doing things in a Certain Way; and in order to do so, men must become able to think in a certain way.

A man's way of doing things is the direct result of the way he thinks about things.

To do things in the way you want to do them, you will have to acquire the ability to think the way you want to think; this is the first step toward getting rich.

To think what you want to think is to think TRUTH, regardless of appearances.

Every man has the natural and inherent power to think what he wants to think, but it requires far more effort to do so than it does to think the thoughts which are suggested by appearances. To think according to appearances is easy; to think truth regardless of appearances is laborious, and requires the expenditure of more power than any other work man is called upon to perform.

There is no labor from which most people shrink as they do from that of sustained and consecutive thought; it is the hardest work in the world. This is especially true when truth is contrary to appearances. Every appearance in the visible world tends to produce a corresponding form in the mind which observes it; and this can only be prevented by holding the thought of the TRUTH.

To look upon the appearance of disease will produce the form of disease in your own mind, and ultimately in your body, unless you hold the thought of the truth, which is that there is no disease; it is only an appearance, and the reality is health.

To look upon the appearances of poverty will produce corresponding forms in your won mind, unless you hold to the truth that there is no poverty; there is only abundance.

To think health when surrounded by the appearances of disease, or to think riches when in the midst of appearances of poverty, requires power; but he who acquires this power becomes a MASTER MIND. He can conquer fate; he can have what he wants.

This power can only be acquired by getting hold of the basic fact which is behind all appearances; and that fact is that there is one Thinking Substance, from which and by which all things are made.

Then we must grasp the truth that every thought held in this substance becomes a form, and that man can so impress his thoughts upon It as to cause them to take form and become visible things.

Then we realize this, we lose all doubt and fear, for we know that we can create what we want to create; we can get what we want to have, and can become what we want to be. As a first step toward getting rich, you must believe the three fundamental statements given previously in this chapter; and in order to emphasize them, I repeat them here:—

There is a thinking stuff from which all things are made, and which, in its original state, permeates, penetrates, and fills the interspaces of the universe.

A thought, in this substance, produces the thing that is imaged by the thought.

Man can form things in his thought, and, by impressing his thought upon formless substance, can cause the thing he thinks about to be created.

You must lay aside all other concepts of the universe than this monistic one; and you must dwell upon this until it is fixed in your mind, and has become your habitual thought. Read these creed statements over and over again; fix every word upon your memory, and meditate upon them until you firmly believe what they say. If a doubt comes to you, cast it aside as a sin. Do not listen to arguments against this idea; do not go to churches or lectures where a contrary concept of things is taught or preached. Do not read magazines or books which teach a different idea; if you get mixed up in your faith, all your efforts will be in vain.

Do not ask why these things are true, nor speculate as to how they can be true; simply take them on trust.

The science of getting rich begins with the absolute acceptance of this faith.

CHAPTER FIVE

INCREASING LIFE

You must get rid of the last vestige of the old idea that there is a Deity whose will it is that you should be poor, or whose purposes may be served by keeping you in poverty.

The Intelligent Substance which is All, and in all, and which lives in All and lives in you, is a consciously Living Substance. Being a consciously living substance, It must have the natural and inherent desire of every living intelligence for increase of life. Every living thing must continually seek for the enlargement of its life, because life, in the mere act of living, must increase itself.

A seed, dropped into the ground, springs into activity, and in the act of living produces a hundred more seeds; life, by living, multiplies itself. It is forever Becoming More; it must do so, if it continues to be at all.

Intelligence is under this same necessity for continuous increase. Every thought we think makes it necessary for us to think another thought; consciousness is continually expanding. Every fact we learn leads us to the learning of another fact; knowledge is continually increasing. Every talent we cultivate brings to the mind the desire to cultivate another talent; we are subject to the urge of life, seeking expression, which ever drives us on to know more, to do more, and to be more.

In order to know more, do more, and be more we must have more; we must have things to use, for we learn, and do, and become, only by using things. We must get rich, so that we can live more.

The desire for riches is simply the capacity for larger life seeking fulfillment; every desire is the effort of an unexpressed possibility to come into action. It is power seeking to manifest which causes desire. That which makes you want more money is the same as that which makes the plant grow; it is Life, seeking fuller expression.

The One Living Substance must be subject to this inherent law of all life; it is permeated with the desire to live more; that is why it is under the necessity of creating things.

The One Substance desires to live more in you; hence it wants you to have all the things you can use.

It is the desire of God that you should get rich. He wants you to get rich because he can express himself better through you if you have plenty of things to use in giving him expression. He can live more in you if you have unlimited command of the means of life.

The universe desires you to have everything you want to have.

Nature is friendly to your plans.

Everything is naturally for you.

Make up your mind that this is true.

It is essential, however, that your *purpose should harmonize with the purpose that is in All*.

You must want real life, not mere pleasure or sensual gratification. Life is the performance of function; and the individual really lives only when he performs every function, physical, mental, and spiritual, of which he is capable, without excess in any.

You do not want to get rich in order to live swinishly, for the gratification of animal desires; that is not life. But the performance of every physical function is a part of life, and no one lives completely who denies the impulses of the body a normal and healthful expression.

You do not want to get rich solely to enjoy mental pleasures, to get knowledge, to gratify ambition, to outshine others, to be famous. All these are a legitimate part of life, but the man who lives for the pleasures of the intellect alone will only have a partial life, and he will never be satisfied with his lot.

You do not want to get rich solely for the good of others, to lose yourself for the salvation of mankind, to experience the joys of philanthropy and sacrifice. The joys of the soul are only a part of life; and they are no better or nobler than any other part.

You want to get rich in order that you may eat, drink, and be merry when it is time to do these things; in order that you may surround yourself with beautiful things, see distant lands, feed your mind, and develop your intellect; in order that you may love men and do kind things, and be able to play a good part in helping the world to find truth.

But remember that extreme altruism is no better and no nobler than extreme selfishness; both are mistakes.

Get rid of the idea that God wants you to sacrifice yourself for others, and that you can secure his favor by doing so; God requires nothing of the kind.

What he wants is that you should make the most of yourself, for yourself, and for others; and *you can help others more by making the most of yourself than in any other way*.

You can make the most of yourself only by getting rich; so it is right and praiseworthy that you should give your first and best thought to the work of acquiring wealth.

Remember, however, that the desire of Substance is for all, and its movements must be for more life to, all; it cannot be made to work for less life to any, because it is equally in all, seeking riches and life.

Intelligent Substance will make things for you, but it will not take things away from some one else and give them to you.

You must get rid of the thought of competition. You are to create, not to compete for what is already created.

You do not have to take anything away from any one.

You do not have to drive sharp bargains.

You do not have to cheat, or to take advantage. You do not need to let any man work for you for less than he earns.

You do not have to covet the property of others, or to look at it with wishful eyes; no man has anything of which you cannot have the like, and that without taking what he has away from him.

You are to become a creator, not a competitor; you are going to get what you want, but in such a way that when you get it every other man will have more than he has now.

I am aware that there are men who get a vast amount of money by proceeding in direct opposition to the statements in the paragraph above, and may add a word of explanation here. Men of the plutocratic type, who become very rich, do so sometimes purely by their extraordinary ability on the plane of competition; and sometimes they unconsciously relate themselves to Substance in its great purposes and movements for the general racial upbuilding through industrial evolution. Rockefeller, Carnegie, Morgan, *et al.*, have been the unconscious agents of the Supreme in the necessary work of systematizing and organizing productive industry; and in the end, their work will contribute immensely toward increased life for all. Their day is nearly over; they have organized production, and *will soon be succeeded by the agents of the multitude, who will organize the machinery of distribution.*

The multi-millionaires are like the monster reptiles of the prehistoric eras; they play a necessary part in the evolutionary process, but the same Power which produced them will dispose of them. And it is well to bear in mind that they have never been really rich; a record of the private lives of most of this class will show that they have really been the most abject and wretched of the poor.

Riches secured on the competitive plane are never satisfactory and permanent; they are yours to-day, and another's to-morrow. Remember, if you are to become rich in a scientific and certain way, you must rise entirely out of the competitive thought. You must never think for a moment that the supply is limited. Just as soon as you begin to think that all the money is being "cornered" and controlled by bankers and others, and that you must exert yourself to get laws passed to stop this process, and so on; in that moment you drop into the competitive mind, and your power to cause creation is gone for the time being; and what is worse, you will probably arrest the creative movements you have already instituted.

KNOW that there are countless millions of dollars' worth of gold in the mountains of the earth, not yet brought to light; and know that if there were not, more would be created from Thinking Substance to supply your needs.

KNOW that the money you need will come, even if it is necessary for a thousand men to be led to the discovery of new gold mines to-morrow.

Never look at the visible supply; look always at the limitless riches in Formless Substance, and KNOW that they are coming to you as fast as you can receive and use them. Nobody, by cornering the visible supply, can prevent you from getting what is yours.

So never allow yourself to thin for an instant that all the best building spots will be taken before you get ready to build your house, unless you hurry. Never worry about the trusts and combines, and get anxious for fear they will soon come to own the whole earth. Never get afraid that you will lose what you want because some other person "beats you to it." That cannot possibly happen; you are not seeking anything that is possessed by anybody else; you are causing what you want to be created from Formless Substance, and the supply is without limits. Stick to the formulated statement:—

There is a thinking stuff from which all things are made, and which, in its original state, permeates, penetrates, and fills the interspaces of the universe.

A thought, in this substance, produces the thing that is imaged by the thought.

Man can form things in his thought, and, by impressing his thought upon formless substance, can cause the thing he thinks about to be created.

CHAPTER SIX

HOW RICHES COME TO YOU

When I say that you do not have to drive sharp bargains, I do not mean that you do not have to drive any bargains at all, or that you are above the necessity for having any dealings with your fellow men. I mean that you will not need to deal with them unfairly; you do not have to get something for nothing, *but can give to every man more than you take from him.*

You cannot give every man more in cash market value than you take from him, but you can give him more in use value than the cash value of the thing you take from him. The paper, ink, and other material in this book may not be worth the money you paid for it; but if the ideas suggested by it bring you thousands of dollars, you have not been wronged by those who sold it to you; they have given you a great use value for a small cash value.

Let us suppose that I own a picture by one of the great artists, which, in any civilized community, is worth thousands of dollars. I take it to Baffin Bay, and by "salesmanship" induce an Eskimo to give a bundle of furs worth $500 for it. I have really wronged him, for he has no use for the picture; it has no use value to him; it will not add to his life.

But suppose I give him a gun worth $50 for his furs; then he has made a good bargain. He has use for the gun; it will get him many more furs and much food; it will add to his life in every way; it will make him rich.

When you rise from the competitive to the creative plane, you can scan your business transactions very strictly, and if you are selling any man anything which does not add more to his life than the thing he gives in exchange, you can afford to stop it. You do not have to beat anybody in business. And if you are in a business which does beat people, get out of it at once.

Give every man more in use value than you take from him in cash value; then you are adding to the life of the world by every business transaction.

If you have people working for you, you must take from them more in cash value than you pay them in wages; but *you can so organize your business that it will be filled with the principle of advancement,* and so that each employee who wishes to do so may advance a little every day.

You can make your business do for your employees what this book is doing for you. You can so conduct your business that it will be a sort of ladder, by which every employee who will take the trouble may climb to riches himself; and given the opportunity, if he will not do so it is not your fault.

And finally, because you are to cause the creation of your riches from Formless Substance which permeates all your environment, it does not follow that they are to take shape from the atmosphere and come into being before your eyes.

If you want a sewing machine, for instance, I do not mean to tell you that you are to impress the thought of a sewing machine on Thinking Substance until the machine is formed without hands, in the room where you sit, or elsewhere. But if you want a sewing machine, hold the mental image of it with the most positive certainty that it is being made, or is on its way to you. After once forming the thought, have the most absolute and unquestioning faith that the sewing machine is coming; never think of it, or speak of it, in any other way than as being sure to arrive. Claim it as already yours.

It will be brought to you by the power of the Supreme Intelligence, acting upon the minds of men. If you live in Maine, it may be that a man will be brought from Texas or Japan to engage in some transaction which will result in your getting what you want.

If so, the whole matter will be as much to that man's advantage as it is to yours.

Do not forget for a moment that the Thinking Substance is through all, in all, communicating with all, and can influence all. The desire of Thinking Substance for fuller life and better living has caused the creation of all the sewing machines already made; and it can cause the creation of millions more, and will, whenever men set it in motion by desire and faith, and by acting in a Certain Way.

You can certainly have a sewing machine in your house; and it is just as certain that you can have any other thing or things which you want, and which you will use for the advancement of your own life and the lives of others.

You need not hesitate about asking largely; "it is your Father's pleasure to give you the kingdom," said Jesus.

Original Substance wants to live all that is possible in you, and wants you to have all that you can or will use for the living of the most abundant life.

If you fix upon your consciousness the fact that the desire you feel for the possession of riches is one with the desire of Omnipotence for more complete expression, your faith becomes invincible.

Once I saw a little boy sitting at a piano, and vainly trying to bring harmony out of the keys; and I saw that he was grieved and provoked by his inability to play real music. I asked him the cause of his vexation, and he answered, "I can feel the music in me, but I can't make my hands go right." The music in him was the URGE of Original Substance, containing all the possibilities of all life; all that there is of music was seeking expression through the child.

God, the One Substance, is trying to live and do and enjoy things through humanity. He is saying, "I want hands to build wonderful structures, to play divine harmonies, to paint glorious pictures; I want feet to run my errands, eyes to see my beauties, tongues to tell mighty truths and to sing marvelous songs," and so on.

All that there is of possibility is seeking expression through men. God wants those who can play music to have pianos and every other instrument, and to have the means to cultivate their talents to the fullest extent; He wants those who can appreciate beauty to be able to surround themselves with beautiful things; He wants those who can discern truth to have every opportunity to travel and observe; He wants those who can appreciate dress to be beautifully clothed, and those who can appreciate good food to be luxuriously fed.

He wants all these things because it is Himself that enjoys and appreciates them; it is God who wants to play, and, sing, and enjoy beauty, and proclaim truth, and wear fine clothes, and eat good foods.

"It is God that worketh in you to will and to do," said Paul.

The desire you feel for riches is the Infinite, seeking to express Himself in you as He sought to find expression in the little boy at the piano.

So you need not hesitate to ask largely.

Your part is to focalize and express the desires of God.

This is a difficult point with most people; they retain something of the old idea that poverty and self-sacrifice are pleasing to God. They look upon poverty as a part of the plan, a necessity of nature. They have the idea that God, has finished His work, and made all that He can make, and that the majority of men must stay poor because there is not enough to go around. They hold to so much of this erroneous thought that they feel ashamed to ask for wealth; they try not to want more than a very modest competence, just enough to make them fairly comfortable.

I recall now the case of one student who was told that he must get in mind a clear picture of the things he desired, so that the creative thought of them might be impressed on Formless Substance. He was a very poor man, living in a rented house, and having only what he wanted from day to day; and he could not grasp the fact that all wealth was his. So, after thinking the matter over, he decided that he might reasonably ask for a new rug for the floor of his best room, and an anthracite coal stove to heat the house during the cold weather. Following the instructions given in this book, he obtained these things in a few months; and then it dawned upon him that he had not asked enough. He went though the house in which he lived, and planned all the improvements he would like to make in it; he mentally added a bay window here and a room there, until it was complete in his mind as his ideal home; and then he planned its furnishings.

Holding the whole picture in his mind, he began living in the Certain Way, and moving toward what he wanted; and he owns the house now, and is rebuilding it after the form of his mental image. And now, with still larger faith, he is going on to get greater things. It has been unto him according to his faith, and it is so with you and with all of us.

CHAPTER SEVEN

GRATITUDE

The illustrations given in the last chapter will have conveyed to the reader the fact that the first step toward getting rich is to convey the idea of your wants to the Formless Substance.

This is true, and you will see that in order to do so it becomes necessary to relate yourself to the Formless Intelligence in a harmonious way.

To secure this harmonious relation is a matter of such primary and vital importance that I shall give some space to its discussion here, and give you instructions which, if you will follow them, will be certain to bring you into perfect unity of mind with God.

The whole process of mental adjustment and atonement can be summed up in one word, *gratitude*.

First, you believe that there is one Intelligent Substance, from which all things proceed; second, you believe that this Substance gives you everything you desire; and third, you relate yourself to It by a feeling of deep and profound gratitude.

Many people who order their lives rightly in all other ways are kept in poverty by their lack of gratitude. Having received one gift from God, they cut the wires which connect them with Him by failing to make acknowledgment.

It is easy to understand that the nearer we live to the source of wealth, the more wealth we shall receive; and it is easy also to understand that the soul that is always grateful lives in closer touch with God than the one which never looks to Him in thankful acknowledgment.

The more gratefully we fix our minds on the Supreme when good things come to us, the more good things we will receive, and the more rapidly they will come; and the reason simply is that the mental attitude of gratitude draws the mind into closer touch with the source from which the blessings come.

If it is a new thought to you that gratitude brings your whole mind into closer harmony with the creative energies of the universe, consider it well, and you will see that it is true. The good things you already have come to you along the line of obedience to certain laws. Gratitude will lead your mind out along the ways by which things come; and it will keep you in close harmony with creative thought and prevent you from falling into competitive thought.

Gratitude alone can keep you looking toward the All, and prevent you from falling into the error of thinking of the supply as limited; and to do that would be fatal to your hopes.

There is a Law of Gratitude, and it is absolutely necessary that you should observe the law, if you are to get the results you seek.

The law of gratitude is the natural principle that action and reaction are always equal, and in opposite directions.

The grateful outreaching of your mind in thankful praise to the Supreme *is a liberation or expenditure of force; it cannot fail to reach that to which it is addressed, and the reaction is an instantaneous movement toward you.*

"Draw nigh unto God, and He will draw nigh unto you." That is a statement of psychological truth.

And if your gratitude is strong and constant, the reaction in Formless Substance will be strong and continuous; the movement of the things you want will be always toward you. Notice the grateful attitude that Jesus took; how He always seems to be saying, "I thank Thee, Father, that Thou hearest me." You cannot exercise much power without gratitude; for it is gratitude that keeps you connected with Power.

But the value of gratitude does not consist solely in getting you more blessings in the future. Without gratitude you cannot long keep from dissatisfied thought regarding things as they are.

The moment you permit your mind to dwell with dissatisfaction upon things as they are, you begin to lose ground. You fix attention upon the common, the ordinary the poor, and the squalid and mean; and your mind takes the form of these things. Then you will transmit these forms or mental images to the Formless, and the common, the poor, the squalid, and mean will come to you.

To permit your mind to dwell upon the inferior is to become inferior and to surround yourself with inferior things.

On the other hand, to fix your attention on the best is to surround yourself with the best, and to become the best.

The Creative Power within us makes us into the image of that to which we give our attention.

We are Thinking Substance, and thinking substance always takes the form of that which it thinks about.

The grateful mind is constantly fixed upon the best; therefore it tends to become the best; it takes the form or character of the best, and will receive the best.

Also, faith is born of gratitude. The grateful mind continually expects good things, and expectation becomes faith. The reaction of gratitude upon one's own mind produces faith; and every outgoing wave of grateful thanksgiving increases faith. He who has no feeling of gratitude cannot long retain a living faith; and without a living faith you cannot get rich by the creative method, as we shall see in the following chapters.

It is necessary, then, to cultivate the habit of being grateful for every good thing that comes to you; and to give thanks continuously.

And because all things have contributed to your advancement, you should include all things in your gratitude.

Do not waste time thinking or talking about the shortcomings or wrong actions of plutocrats or trust magnates. Their organization of the world has made your opportunity; all you get really comes to you because of them.

Do not rage against corrupt politicians; if it were not for Politicians we should fall into anarchy, and your opportunity would be greatly lessened.

God has worked a long time and very patiently to bring us up to where we are in industry and government, and He is going right on with His work. There is not the least doubt that He will do away with plutocrats, trust magnates, captains of industry, and politicians as soon as they can be spared; but in the meantime, behold they are all very good. Remember, that they are all helping to arrange the lines of transmission along which your riches will come to you, and be grateful to them all. This will bring you into harmonious relations with the good in everything, and the good in everything will move toward you.

CHAPTER EIGHT

THINKING IN THE CERTAIN WAY

Turn back to chapter VI., and read again the story of the man who formed a mental image of his house, and you will get a fair idea of the initial step toward getting rich. You must form a clear and definite mental picture of what you want; you cannot transmit an idea unless you have it yourself.

You must have it before you can give it; and many people fail to impress Thinking Substance because they have themselves only a vague and misty concept of the things they want to do, to have, or to become.

It is not enough that you should have a general desire for wealth "to do good with"; everybody has that desire.

It is not enough that you should have a wish to travel, see things, live more, etc. Everybody has those desires also. If you were going to send a wireless message to a friend, you would not send the letters of the alphabet in their order, and let him construct the message for himself; nor would you take words at random from the dictionary. You would send a coherent sentence; one which meant something. When you try to impress your wants upon Substance, remember that it must be done by a coherent statement; you must know what you want, and be definite.

You can never get rich, or start the creative power into action, by sending out unformed longings and vague desires.

Go over your desires just as the man I have described went over his house; see just what you want, and get a clear mental picture of it as you wish it to look when you get it.

That clear mental picture you must have continually in mind, as the sailor has in mind the port toward which he is sailing the ship; you must keep your face toward it all the time. You must no more lose sight of it than the steersman loses sight of the compass.

It is not necessary to take exercises in concentration, nor to set apart special times for prayer and affirmation, nor to "go into silence," nor to do occult stunts of any kind. These things are well enough, but all you need is to know what you want, and to want it badly enough so that it will stay in your thoughts.

Spend as much of your leisure time as you can in contemplating your picture, but no one needs to take exercises to concentrate his mind on a thing which he really wants; it is the things you do not really care about which require effort to fix your attention upon them.

And unless you really want to get rich, so that the desire is strong enough to hold your thoughts directed to the purpose as the magnetic pole holds the needle of the compass, it will hardly be worth while for you to try to carry out the instructions given in this book.

The methods herein set forth are for people whose desire for riches is strong enough to overcome mental laziness and the love of ease, and make them work.

The more clear and definite you make your picture, then, and the more you dwell upon it, bringing out all its delightful details, the stronger your desire will be; and the stronger your desire, the easier it will be to hold your mind fixed upon the picture of what you want.

Something more is necessary, however, than merely to see the picture clearly. If that is all you do, you are only a dreamer, and will have little or no power for accomplishment.

Behind your clear vision must be the purpose to realize it; to bring it out in tangible expression.

And behind this purpose must be an invincible and unwavering FAITH that the thing is already yours; that it is "at hand" and you have only to take possession of it.

Live in the new house, mentally, until it takes form around you physically. In the mental realm, enter at once into full enjoyment of the things you want.

"Whatsoever things ye ask for when ye pray, believe that ye receive them, and ye shall have them," said Jesus.

See the things you want as if they were actually around you all the time; see yourself as owning and using them. Make use of them in imagination just as you will use them when they are your tangible possessions. Dwell upon your mental picture until it is clear and distinct, and then take the Mental Attitude of Ownership toward everything in that picture. Take possession of it, in mind, in the full faith that it is actually yours. Hold to this mental ownership do not waver for an instant in the faith that it is real.

And remember what was said in a preceding chapter about gratitude; be as thankful for it all the time as you expect to be when it has taken form. The man who can sincerely thank God for the things which as yet he owns only in imagination, has real faith. He will get rich; he will cause the creation of whatsoever he wants.

You do not need to pray repeatedly for the things you want; it is not necessary to tell God about it everyday.

"Use not vain repetitions as the heathen do," said Jesus to His pupils, "for your Father knoweth that ye have need of these things before ye ask Him."

Your part is to intelligently formulate your desire for the things which make for a larger life, and to get these desires arranged into a coherent whole; and then to impress this Whole Desire upon the Formless Substance, which the power and the will to bring you what you want.

You do not make this impression by repeating strings of words; you make it by holding the vision with unshakable PURPOSE to attain it, and with steadfast FAITH that you do attain it.

The answer to prayer is not according to your faith while you are talking, but according to your faith while you are working.

You cannot impress the mind of God by having a special Sabbath day set apart to tell Him what you want, and then forgetting Him during the rest of the week. You cannot impress Him by having special hours to go into your closet and pray, if you then dismiss the matter from your mind until the hour of prayer comes again.

Oral prayer is well enough, and has its effect, especially upon yourself, in clarifying your vision and strengthening your faith; but it is not your oral petitions which get you what you want. In order to get rich you do not need a "sweet hour of prayer"; you need to "pray without ceasing." And by prayer I mean holding steadily to your vision, with the purpose to cause its creation into solid form, and the faith that you are doing so.

"Believe that ye *receive* them."

The whole matter turns on receiving, once you have clearly formed your vision. When you *have* formed it, it is well to make an oral statement, addressing the Supreme in reverent prayer; and from that moment you must, in mind, receive what you ask for. Live in the new house; wear the fine clothes; ride in the automobile; go on the journey, and confidently plan for greater journeys. Think and speak of all the things you have asked for in terms of actual present ownership. Imagine an environment, and a financial condition exactly as you want them, and live all the time in that imaginary environment, and financial condition. Mind, however, that you do not do this as a mere dreamer and castle builder; hold to the FAITH that the imaginary is being realized, and to the PURPOSE to realize it. Remember that it is faith and purpose in the use of the imagination which make the difference between the scientist and the dreamer. And having learned this fact, it is here that you must learn the proper use of the Will.

CHAPTER NINE

HOW TO USE THE WILL

To set about getting rich in a scientific way, you do not try to apply your will power to anything outside of yourself.

You have no right to do so, anyway.

It is wrong to apply your will to other men and women, in order to get them to do what you wish done.

It is as flagrantly wrong to coerce people by mental power as it is to coerce them by physical power. If compelling people by physical force to do things for you reduces them to slavery, compelling them by mental means accomplishes exactly the same thing; the only difference is in methods. If taking things from people by physical force is robbery, then taking things by mental force is robbery also; there is no difference in principle.

You have no right to use your will power upon another person, even "for his own good"; for you do not know what is for his good.

The science of getting rich does not require you to apply power or force to any other person in any way whatsoever. There is not the slightest necessity for doing so; indeed, any attempt to use your will upon others will only tend to defeat your purpose.

You do not need to apply your will to things, in order to compel them to come to you.

That would simply be trying to coerce God, and would be foolish and useless, as well as irreverent.

You do not have to compel God to give you good things, any more than you have to use your will power to make the sun rise.

You do not have to use your will power to conquer an unfriendly deity, or to make stubborn and rebellious forces do your bidding.

Substance is friendly to you, and is more anxious to give you what you want than you are to get it.

To get rich, you need only to use your will power upon yourself.

When you know what to think and do, then you must use your will to compel yourself to think and do the right things. That is the legitimate use of the will in getting what you want—to use it in holding yourself to the right course. Use your will to keep yourself thinking and acting in the Certain Way.

Do not try to project your will, or your thoughts, or your mind out into space, to "act" on things or people.

Keep your mind at home; it can accomplish more there than elsewhere.

Use your mind to form a mental image of what you want, and to hold that vision with faith and purpose; and use your will to keep your mind working in the Right Way.

The more steady and continuous your faith and purpose, the more rapidly you will get rich, because you will make only POSITIVE impressions upon Substance; and you will not neutralize or offset them by negative impressions.

The picture of your desires, held with faith and purpose, is taken up by the Formless, and permeates it to great distances,—throughout the universe, for all I know.

As this impression spreads, all things are set moving toward its realization; every living thing, every inanimate thing, and the things yet uncreated are stirred toward bringing into being that which you want. All force begins to be exerted in that direction; all things begin to move toward you. The minds of people, every-where, are influenced toward doing the things necessary to the fulfilling of your desires; and they work for you, unconsciously.

But you can check all this by starting a negative impression in the Formless Substance. Doubt or unbelief is as certain to start a movement away from you as faith and purpose are to start one toward you. It is not understanding this that most people who try to make use of "mental science" in getting rich make their failure. Every hour and moment you spend in giving heed to doubts and fears, every hour you spend in worry, every hour in which your soul is possessed by unbelief, sets a current away from you in the whole domain of intelligent Substance. All the prom-ises are unto them that believe, and unto them only. Notice how insistent Jesus was upon this point of belief; and now you know the reason why.

Since belief is all important, it behooves you to guard your thoughts; and as your beliefs will be shaped to a very great extent by the things you observe and think about, it is important that you should command your attention.

And here the will comes into use; for it is by your will that you determine upon what things your attention shall be fixed.

If you want to become rich, you must not make a study of poverty.

Things are not brought into being by thinking about their opposites. Health is never to be attained by studying disease and thinking about disease; righteousness is not to be promoted by studying sin and thinking about sin; and no one ever got rich by studying poverty and thinking about poverty.

Medicine as a science of disease has increased disease; religion as a science of sin has promoted sin, and economics as a study of poverty will fill the world with wretchedness and want.

Do not talk about poverty; do not investigate it, or concern yourself with it. Never mind what its causes are; you have nothing to do with them. What concerns you is the cure.

Do not spend your time in charitable work, or charity movements; all charity only tends to perpetuate the wretchedness it aims to eradicate.

I do not say that you should be hardhearted or unkind, and refuse to hear the cry of need; but you must not try to eradicate poverty in any of the conventional ways. Put poverty behind you, and put all that pertains to it behind you, and "make good."

Get rich; that is the best way you can help the poor.

And you cannot hold the mental image which is to make you rich if you fill your mind with pictures of poverty. Do not read books or papers which give circumstantial accounts of the wretchedness of the tenement dwellers, of the horrors of child labor, and so on. Do not read anything which fills your mind with gloomy images of want and suffering.

You cannot help the poor in the least by knowing about these things; and the wide-spread knowledge of them does not tend at all to do away with poverty.

What tends to do away with poverty is not the getting of pictures of poverty into your mind, but getting pictures of wealth into the minds of the poor.

You are not deserting the poor in their misery when you refuse to allow your mind to be filled with pictures of that misery.

Poverty can be done away with, not by increasing the number of well-to-do people who think about poverty, but by increasing the number of poor people who purpose with faith to get rich.

The poor do not need charity; they need inspiration. Charity only sends them a loaf of bread to keep them alive in their wretchedness, or gives them an entertainment to make them forget for an hour or two; but inspiration will, cause them to rise out of their misery. If you want to help the poor, demonstrate to them that they can become rich; prove it by getting rich yourself.

The only way in which poverty will ever be banished from this world is by getting a large and constantly increasing number of people to practice the teachings of this book.

People must be taught to become rich by creation, not by competition.

Every man who becomes rich by competition throws down behind him the ladder by which he rises, and keeps others down; but every man who gets rich by creation opens a way for thousands to follow him, and inspires them to do so.

You are not showing hardness of heart or an unfeeling disposition when you refuse to pity poverty, see poverty, read about poverty, or think or talk about it, or to listen to those who do talk about it. Use your will power to keep your mind OFF the subject of poverty, and to keep it fixed with faith and purpose ON the vision of what you want.

CHAPTER TEN

FURTHER USE OF THE WILL

You cannot retain a true and clear vision of wealth if you are constantly turning your attention to opposing pictures, whether they be external or imaginary.

Do not tell of your past troubles of a financial nature, if you have had them; do not think of them at all. Do not tell of the poverty of your parents, or the hardships of your early life; to do any of these things is to mentally class yourself with the poor for the time being, and it will certainly check the movement of things in your direction.

"Let the dead bury their dead," as Jesus said.

Put poverty and all things that pertain to poverty completely behind you.

You have accepted a certain theory of the universe as being correct, and are resting all your hopes of happiness on its being correct; and what can you gain by giving heed to conflicting theories?

Do not read religious books which tell you that the world is soon coming to an end; and do not read the writings of muck-rakers and pessimistic philosophers who tell you that it is going to the devil.

The world is not going to the devil; it is going to God.

It is a wonderful Becoming.

True, there may be a good many things in existing conditions which are disagreeable; but what is the use of studying them when they are certainly passing away, and when the study of them only tends to check their passing and keep them with us? Why give time and attention to things which are being removed by evolutionary growth, when you can hasten their removal only by promoting the evolutionary growth as far as your part of it goes?

No matter how horrible in seeming may be the conditions in certain countries, sections, or places, you waste your time and destroy your own changes by considering them.

You should interest yourself in the world's becoming rich.

Think of the riches the world is coming into, instead of the poverty it is growing out of; and bear in mind that the only way in which you can assist the world in growing rich is by growing rich yourself through the creative method—not the competitive one.

Give your attention wholly to riches; ignore poverty.

Whenever you think or speak of those who are poor, think and speak of them as those who are becoming rich; as those who are to be congratulated rather than pitied. Then they and others will catch the inspiration, and begin to search for the way out.

Because I say that you are to give your whole time and mind and thought to riches, it does not follow that you are to be sordid or mean.

To become really rich is the noblest aim you can have in life, for it includes everything else.

On the competitive plane, the struggle to get rich is a Godless scramble for power over other men; but when we come into the creative mind, all this is changed.

All that is possible in the way of greatness and soul unfoldment, of service and lofty endeavor, comes by way of getting rich; all is made possible by the use of things.

If you lack for physical health, you will find that the attainment of it is conditional on your getting rich.

Only those who are emancipated from financial worry, and who have the means to live a care-free existence and follow hygienic practices, can have and retain health.

Moral and spiritual greatness is possible only to those who are above the competitive battle for existence; and only those who are becoming rich on the plane of creative thought are free from the degrading influences of competition. If your heart is set on domestic happiness, remember that love flourishes best where there is refinement, a high level of thought, and freedom from corrupting influences; and these are to be found only where riches are attained by the exercise of creative thought, without strife or rivalry.

You can aim at nothing so great or noble, I repeat, as to become rich; and you must fix your attention upon your mental picture of riches, to the exclusion of all that may tend. to dim or obscure the vision.

You must learn to see the underlying TRUTH in all things; you must see beneath all seemingly wrong conditions the Great One Life ever moving forward toward fuller expression and more complete happiness.

It is the truth that there is no such thing as poverty; that there is only wealth.

Some people remain in poverty because they are ignorant of the fact that there is wealth for them; and these can best be taught by showing them the way to affluence in your own person and practice.

Others are poor because, while they feel that there is a way out, they are too intellectually indolent to put forth the mental effort necessary to find that way and travel it; and for these the very best thing you can do is to arouse their desire by showing them the happiness that comes from being rightly rich.

Others still are poor because, while they have some notion of science, they have become so swamped and lost in the maze of metaphysical and occult theories that they do not know which road to take. They try a mixture of many systems and fail in all. For these, again, the very best thing to do is to show the right way in your own person and practice; an ounce of doing things is worth a pound of theorizing.

The very best thing you can do for the whole world is to make the most of yourself.

You can serve God and man in no more effective way than by getting rich; that is, if you get rich by the creative method, and not by the competitive one.

Another thing. We assert that this book gives in detail the principles of the science of getting rich; and if that is true, you do not need to read any other book upon the subject. This may sound narrow and egotistical, but consider: there is no more scientific method of computation in mathematics than by addition, subtraction, multiplication, and division; no other method is possible. There can be but one shortest distance between two points. There is only one way to think scientifically, and that is to think in the way that leads by the most direct and simple route to the goal. No man has yet formulated a briefer or less complex "system" than the one set forth herein; it has been stripped of all non-essentials. When you commence on this, lay all others aside; put them out of your mind altogether.

Read this book every day; keep it with you; commit it to memory, and do not think about other "systems" and theories. If you do, you will begin to have doubts, and to be uncertain and wavering in your thought; and then you will begin to make failures.

After you have made good and become rich, you may study other systems as much as you please; but until you are quite sure that you have gained what you want, do not read anything on this line but this book, unless it be the authors mentioned in the Preface.

And read only the most optimistic comments on the world's news; those in harmony with your picture.

Also, postpone your investigations into the occult. Do not dabble in Theosophy, Spiritualism, or kindred studies. It is very likely that the dead still live, and are near; but if they are, let them alone; mind your own business.

Wherever the spirits of the dead may be, they have their own work to do, and their own problems to solve; and we have no right to interfere with them. We cannot help them, and it is very doubtful whether they can help us, or whether we have any right to trespass upon their time if they can. Let the dead and the hereafter alone, and solve your own problem; get rich. If you begin to mix with the occult, you will start mental cross-currents which will surely bring your hopes to shipwreck. Now, this and the preceding chapters have brought us to the following statement of basic facts:—

There is a thinking stuff from which all things are made, and which, in its original state, permeates, penetrates, and fills the interspaces of the universe.

A thought, in this substance, produces the thing that is imaged by the thought.

Man can form things in his thought, and, by impressing his thought upon formless substance, can cause the thing he thinks about to be created.

In order to do this, man must pass from the competitive to the creative mind; he must form a clear mental picture of the things he wants, and hold this picture in his thoughts with the fixed PURPOSE to get what he wants, and the unwavering FAITH that he does get what he wants, closing his mind against all that may tend to shake his purpose, dim his vision, or quench his faith.

And in addition to all this, we shall now see that he must live and act in a Certain Way.

CHAPTER ELEVEN

ACTING IN THE CERTAIN WAY

Thought is the creative power, or the impelling force which causes the creative power to act; thinking in a Certain Way will bring riches to you, but you must not rely upon thought alone, paying no attention to personal action. That is the rock upon which many otherwise scientific metaphysical thinkers meet shipwreck—the failure to connect thought with personal action.

We have not yet reached the stage of development, even supposing such a stage to be possible, in which man can create directly from Formless Substance without nature's processes or the work of human hands; man must not only think, but his personal action must supplement his thought.

By thought you can cause the gold in the hearts of the mountains to be impelled toward you; but it will not mine itself, refine itself, coin itself into double eagles, and come rolling along the roads seeking its way into your pocket.

Under the impelling power of the Supreme Spirit, men's affairs will be so ordered that some one will be led to mine the gold for you; other men's business transactions will be so directed that the gold will be brought toward you, and you must so arrange your own business affairs that you may be able to receive it when it comes to you. Your thought makes all things, animate and inanimate, work to bring you what you want; but your personal activity must be such that you can rightly receive what you want when it reaches you. You are not to take it as charity, nor to steal it; you must give every man more in use value than he gives you in cash value.

The scientific use of thought consists in forming a clear and distinct mental image of what you want; in holding fast to the purpose to get what you want; and in realizing with grateful faith that you *do* get what you want.

Do not try to "project" your thought in any mysterious or occult way, with the idea of having it go out and do things for you; that is wasted effort, and will weaken your power to think with sanity.

The action of thought in getting rich is fully explained in the preceding chapters; your faith and purpose positively impress your vision upon Formless Substance, which has THE SAME DESIRE FOR MORE LIFE THAT YOU HAVE; and this vision, received from you, sets all the creative forces at work IN AND THROUGH THEIR REGULAR CHANNELS OF ACTION, but directed toward you.

It is not your part to guide or supervise the creative process; all you have to do with that is to retain your vision, stick to your purpose, and maintain your faith and gratitude.

But you must act in a Certain Way, so that you can appropriate what is yours when it comes to you; so that you can meet the things you have in your picture, and put them in their proper places as they arrive.

You can readily see the truth of this. When things reach you, they will be in the hands of other men, who will ask an equivalent for them.

And you can only get what is yours by giving the other man what is his.

Your pocketbook is not going to be transformed into a Fortunatus's purse, which shall be always full of money without effort on your part.

This is the crucial point in the science of getting rich; right here, where thought and personal action must be combined. There are very many people who, consciously or unconsciously, set the creative forces in action by the strength and persistence of their desires, but who remain poor because they do not provide for the reception of the thing they want when it comes.

By thought, the thing you want is brought to you; by action you receive it.

Whatever your action is to be, it is evident that you must act NOW. You cannot act in the past, and it is essential to the clearness of your mental vision that you dismiss the past from your mind. You cannot act in the future, for the future is not here yet. And you cannot tell how you will want to act in any future contingency until that contingency has arrived.

Because you are not in the right business, or the right environment now, do not think that you must postpone action until you get into the right business or environment. And do not spend time in the present taking thought as to the best course in possible future emergencies; have faith in your ability to meet any emergency when it arrives.

If you act in the present with your mind on the future, your present action will be with a divided mind, and will not be effective.

Put your whole mind into present action.

Do not give your creative impulse to Original Substance, and then sit down and wait for results; if you do, you will never get them. Act now. There is never any time but now, and there never will be any time but now. If you are ever to begin to make ready for the reception of what you want, you must begin now.

And your action, whatever it is, must most likely be in your present business or employment, and must be upon the persons and things in your present environment.

You cannot act where you are not; you cannot act where you have been, and you cannot act where you are going to be; you can act only where you are.

Do not bother as to whether yesterday day's work was well done or ill done; do to-day's work well.

Do not try to do to-morrow's work now; there will be plenty of time to do that when you get to it.

Do not try, by occult or mystical means, to act on people or things that are out of your reach.

Do not wait for a change of environment before you act; get a change of environment by action.

You can so act upon the environment in which you are now, as to cause yourself to be transferred to a better environment.

Hold with faith and purpose the vision of yourself in the better environment, but act upon your present environment with all your heart, and with all your strength, and with all your mind.

Do not spend any time in day dreaming or castle building; hold to the one vision of what you want, and act NOW.

Do not cast about seeking some new thing to do, or some strange, unusual, or remarkable action to perform as a first step toward getting rich. It is probable that your actions, at least for some time to come, will be those you have been performing for some time past; but you are to begin now to perform these actions in the Certain Way, which will surely make you rich.

If you are engaged in some business, and feel that it is not the right one for you, do not wait until you get into the right business before you begin to act.

Do not feel discouraged, or sit down and lament because you are misplaced. No man was ever so misplaced but that he could find the right place, and no man ever became so involved in the wrong business but that he could get into the right business.

Hold the vision of yourself in the right business, with the purpose to get into it, and the faith that you will get into it, and are getting into it; but ACT in your present business. Use your present business as the means of getting a better one, and use your present environment as the means of getting into a better one. Your vision of the right business, if held with faith and purpose, will cause the Supreme to move the right business toward you; and your action, if performed in the Certain Way, will cause you to move toward the business.

If you are an employee, or wage earner, and feel that you must change places in order to get what you want, do not "project" your thought into space and rely upon it to get you another job. It will probably fail to do so.

Hold the vision of yourself in the job you want, while you ACT with faith and purpose on the job you have, and you will certainly get the job you want.

Your vision and faith will set the creative force in motion to bring it toward you, and your action will cause the forces in your own environment to move you toward the place you want. In closing this chapter, we will add another statement to our syllabus:—

There is a thinking stuff from which all things are made, and which, in its original state, permeates, penetrates, and fills the interspaces of the universe.

A thought, in this substance, produces the thing that is imaged by the thought.

Man can form things in his thought, and, by impressing his thoughts upon formless substance, can cause the thing he thinks about to be created.

In order to do this, man must pass from the competitive to the creative mind; he must form a clear mental picture of the things he wants, and hold this picture in his thoughts with the fixed PURPOSE to get what he wants, and the unwavering FAITH that he does get what he wants, closing his mind to all that may tend to shake his purpose, dim his vision, or quench his faith.

That he may receive what he wants when it comes, man must act NOW upon the people and things in his present environment.

CHAPTER TWELVE

EFFICIENT ACTION

You must use your thought as directed in previous chapters, and begin to do what you can do where you are; and you must do ALL that you can do where you are.

You can advance only by being larger than your present place; and no man is larger than his present place who leaves undone any of the work pertaining to that place.

The world is advanced only by those who more than fill their present places.

If no man quite filled his present place, you can see that there must be a going backward in everything. Those who do not quite fill their present places are a dead weight upon society, government, commerce, and industry; they must be carried along by others at a great expense. The progress of the world is retarded only by those who do not fill the places they are holding; they belong to a former age and a lower stage or plane of life, and their tendency is toward degeneration. No society could advance if every man was smaller than his place; social evolution is guided by the law of physical and mental evolution. In the animal world, evolution is caused by excess of life.

When an organism has more life than can be expressed in the functions of its own plane, it develops the organs of a higher plane, and a new species is originated.

There never would have been new species had there not been organisms which more than filled their places. The law is exactly the same for you; your getting rich depends upon your applying this principle to your own affairs.

Every day is either a successful day or a day of failure; and it is the successful days which get you what you want.

If every day is a failure, you can never get rich; while if every day is a success, you cannot fail to get rich.

If there is something that may be done to-day, and you do not do it, you have failed in so far as that thing is concerned; and the consequences may be more disastrous than you imagine.

You cannot foresee the results of even the most trivial act; you do not know the workings of all the forces that have been set moving in your behalf. Much may be depending on your doing some simple act; it may be the very thing which is to open the door of opportunity to very great possibilities. You can never know all the combinations which Supreme Intelligence is making for you in the world of things and of human affairs; your neglect or failure to do some small thing may cause a long delay in getting what you want.

Do, every day, ALL that can be done that day.

There is, however, a limitation or qualification of the above that you must take into account.

You are not to overwork, nor to rush blindly into your business in the effort to do the greatest possible number of things in the shortest possible time.

You are not to try to do to-morrow's work to-day, nor to do a week's work in a day.

It is really not the number of things you do, but the EFFICIENCY of each separate action that counts.

Every act is, in itself, either a success or a failure.

Every act is, in itself, either effective or inefficient.

Every inefficient act is a failure, and if you spend your life in doing inefficient acts, your whole life will be a failure.

The more things you do, the worse for you, if all your acts are inefficient ones.

On the other hand, every efficient act is a success in itself, and if every act of your life is an efficient one, your whole life MUST be a success.

The cause of failure is doing too many things in an inefficient manner, and not doing enough things in an efficient manner.

You will see that it is a self-evident proposition that if you do not do any inefficient acts, and if you do a sufficient number of efficient acts, you will become rich. If, now, it is possible for you to make each act an efficient one, you see again that the getting of riches is reduced to an exact science, like mathematics.

The matter turns, then, on the question whether you can make each separate act a success in itself. And this you can certainly do.

You can make each act a success, because All Power is working with you; and All Power cannot fail.

Power is at your service; and to make each act efficient you have only to put power into it.

Every action is either strong or weak; and when every one is strong, you are acting in the Certain Way which will make you rich.

Every act can be made strong and efficient by holding your vision while you are doing it, and putting the whole power of your FAITH and PURPOSE into it.

It is at this point that the people fail who separate mental power from personal action. They use the power of mind in one place and at one time, and they act in another place and at another time. So their acts are not successful in themselves; too many of them are inefficient. But if All Power goes into every act, no matter how commonplace, every act will be a success in itself; and as in the nature of things every success opens the way to other successes, your progress toward what you want, and the progress of what you want toward you, will become increasingly rapid.

Remember that successful action is cumulative in its results. Since the desire for more life is inherent in all things, when a man begins to move toward larger life more things attach themselves to him, and the influence of his desire is multiplied.

Do, every day, all that you can do that day, and do each act in an efficient manner.

In saying that you must hold your vision while you are doing each act, however trivial or commonplace, I do not mean to say that it is necessary at all times to see the vision distinctly to its smallest details. It should be the work of your leisure hours to use your imagination on the details of your vision, and to contemplate them until they are firmly fixed upon your memory.

If you wish speedy results, spend practically all your spare time in this practice.

By continuous contemplation you will get the picture of what you want, even to the smallest details, so firmly fixed upon your mind, and so completely transferred to the mind of Formless Substance, that in your working hours you need only to mentally refer to the picture to stimulate your faith and purpose, and cause your best effort to be put forth. Contemplate your picture in your leisure hours until your consciousness is so full of it that you can grasp it instantly. You will become so enthused with its bright promises that the mere thought of it will call forth the strongest energies of your whole being.

Let us again repeat our syllabus, and by slightly changing the closing statements bring it to the point we have now reached.

There is a thinking stuff from which all things are made, and which, in its original state, permeates, penetrates, and fills the interspaces of the universe.

A thought, in this substance, produces the thing that is imaged by the thought.

Man can form things in his thought, and, by impressing his thought upon formless substance, can cause the thing he thinks about to be created.

In order to do this, man must pass from the competitive to the creative mind; he must form a clear mental picture of the things he wants, and do with faith and purpose, all that can be done each day, doing each separate thing in an efficient manner.

CHAPTER THIRTEEN

GETTING INTO THE RIGHT BUSINESS

Success, in any particular business, depends for one thing upon your possessing in a well-developed state the faculties required in that business.

Without good musical faculty no one can succeed as a teacher of music; without well-developed mechanical faculties no one can achieve great success in any of the mechanical trades; without tact and the commercial faculties no one can succeed in mercantile pursuits. But to possess in a well-developed state the faculties required in your particular vocation does not insure getting rich. There are musicians who have remarkable talent, and who yet remain poor; there are blacksmiths, carpenters, and so on who have excellent mechanical ability, but who do not get rich; and there are merchants with good faculties for dealing with men who nevertheless fail.

The different faculties are tools; it is essential to have good tools, but it is also essential that the tools should be used in the Right Way. One man can take a sharp saw, a square, a good plane, and so on, and build a handsome article of furniture; another man can take the same tools and set to work to duplicate the article, but his production will be a batch. He does not know how to use good tools in a successful way.

The various faculties of your mind are the tools with which you must do the work which is to make you rich; it will be easier for you to succeed if you get into a business for which you are well equipped with mental tools.

Generally speaking, you will do best in that business which will use your strongest faculties; the one for which you are naturally "best fitted." But there are limitations to this statement, also. No man should regard his vocation as being irrevocably fixed by the tendencies with which he was born.

You can get rich in ANY business, for if you have not the right talent for it you can develop that talent; it merely means that you will have to make your tools as you go along, instead of confining yourself to the use of those with which you were born. It will be EASIER for you to succeed in a vocation for which you already have the talents in a well-developed state; but you CAN succeed in any vocation, for you can develop any rudimentary talent, and there is no talent of which you have not at least the rudiment.

You will get rich most easily in point of effort, if you do that for which you are best fitted; but you will get rich most satisfactorily if you do that which you WANT to do.

Doing what you want to do is life; and there is no real satisfaction in living if we are compelled to be forever doing something which we do not like to do, and can never do what we want to do. And it is certain that you can do what you want to do; the desire to do it is proof that you have within you the power which can do it.

Desire is a manifestation of power.

The desire to play music is the power which can play music seeking expression and development; the desire to invent mechanical devices is the mechanical talent seeking expression and development.

Where there is no power, either developed or undeveloped, to do a thing, there is never any desire to do that thing; and where there is strong desire to do a thing, it is certain proof that the power to do it is strong, and only requires to be developed and applied in the Right Way.

All things else being equal, it is best to select the business for which you have the best developed talent; but if you have a strong desire to engage in any particular line of work, you should select that work as the ultimate end at which you aim.

You can do what you want to do, and it is your right and privilege to follow the business or a vocation which will be most congenial and pleasant.

You are not obliged to do what you do not like to do, and should not do it except as a means to bring you to the doing of the thing you want to do.

If there are past mistakes whose consequences have placed you in an undesirable business or environment, you may be obliged for some time to do what you do not like to do; but you can make the doing of it pleasant by knowing that it is making it possible for you to come to the doing of what you want to do.

If you feel that you are not in the right vocation, do not act too hastily in trying to get into another one. The best way, generally, to change business or environment is by growth.

Do not be afraid to make a sudden and radical change if the opportunity is presented, and you feel after careful consideration that it is the right opportunity; but never take sudden or radical action when you are in doubt as to the wisdom of doing so.

There is never any hurry on the creative plane; and there is no lack of opportunity.

When you get out of the competitive mind you will understand that you never need to act hastily. No one else is going to beat you to the thing you want to do; there is enough for all. If one place is taken, another and a better one will be opened for you a little farther on; there is plenty of time. When you are in doubt, wait. Fall back on the contemplation of your vision, and increase your faith and purpose; and by all means, in times of doubt and indecision, cultivate gratitude.

A day or two spent in contemplating the vision of what you want, and in earnest thanksgiving that you are getting it, will bring your mind into such close relationship with the Supreme that you will make no mistake when you do act.

There is a mind which knows all there is to know; and you can come into close unity with this mind by faith and the purpose to advance in life, if you have deep gratitude.

Mistakes come from acting hastily, or from acting in fear or doubt, or in forgetfulness of the Right Motive, which is more life to all, and less to none.

As you go on in the Certain Way, opportunities will come to you in increasing number; and you will need to be very steady in your faith and purpose, and to keep in close touch with the All Mind by reverent gratitude.

Do all that you can do in a perfect manner every day, but do it without haste, worry, or fear. Go as fast as you can, but never hurry.

Remember that in the moment you begin to hurry you cease to be a creator and become a competitor; you drop back upon the old plane again.

Whenever you find yourself hurrying, call a halt; fix your attention on the mental image of the thing you want, and begin to give thanks that you are getting it. The exercise of GRATITUDE will never fail to strengthen your faith and renew your purpose.

CHAPTER FOURTEEN

THE IMPRESSION OF INCREASE

Whether you change your vocation or not, your actions for the present must be those pertaining to the business in which you are now engaged.

You can get into the business you want by making constructive use of the business you are already established in; by doing your daily work in a Certain Way.

And in so far as your business consists in dealing with other men, whether personally or by letter, the key-thought of all your efforts must be to convey to their minds the impression of increase.

Increase is what all men and all women are seeking; it is the urge of the Formless Intelligence within them, seeking fuller expression.

The desire for increase is inherent in all nature; it is the fundamental impulse of the universe. All human activities are based on the desire for increase; people are seeking more food, more clothes, better shelter, more luxury, more beauty, more knowledge, more pleasure—increase in something, more life.

Every living thing is under this necessity for continuous advancement; where increase of life ceases, dissolution and death set in at once.

Man instinctively knows this, and hence he is forever seeking more. This law of perpetual increase is set forth by Jesus in the parable of the talents; only those who gain more retain any; from him who hath not shall be taken away even that which he hath.

The normal desire for increased wealth is not an evil or a reprehensible thing; it is simply the desire for more abundant life; it is aspiration.

And because it is the deepest instinct of their natures, all men and women are attracted to him who can give them more of the means of life.

In following the Certain Way as described in the foregoing pages, you are getting continuous increase for yourself, and you are giving it to all with whom you deal.

You are a creative center, from which increase is given off to all.

Be sure of this, and convey assurance of the fact to every man, woman, and child with whom you come in contact. No matter how small the transaction, even if it be only the selling of a stick of candy to a little child, put into it the thought of increase, and make sure that the customer is impressed with the thought.

Convey the impression of advancement with everything you do, so that all people shall receive the impression that you are an Advancing Man, and that you advance all who deal with you. Even to the people whom you meet in a social way, without any thought of business, and to whom you do not try to sell anything, give the thought of increase.

You can convey this impression by holding the unshakable faith that you, yourself, are in the Way of Increase; and by letting this faith inspire, fill, and permeate every action.

Do everything that you do in the firm conviction that you are an advancing personality, and that you are giving advancement to everybody.

Feel that you are getting rich, and that in so doing you are making others rich, and conferring benefits on all.

Do not boast or brag of your success, or talk about it unnecessarily; true faith is never boastful.

Wherever you find a boastful person, you find one who is secretly doubtful and afraid. Simply feel the faith, and let it work out in every transaction; let every act and tone and look express the quiet assurance that you are getting rich; that you are already rich. Words will not be necessary to communicate this feeling to others; they will feel the sense of increase when in your presence, and will be attracted to you again.

You must so impress others that they will feel that in associating with you they will get increase for themselves. See that you give them a use value greater than the cash value you are taking from them.

Take an honest pride in doing this, and let everybody know it; and you will have no lack of customers. People will go where they are given increase; and the Supreme, which desires increase in all, and which knows all, will move toward you men and women who have never heard of you. Your business will increase rapidly, and you will be surprised at the unexpected benefits which will come to you. You will be able from day to day to make larger combinations, secure greater advantages, and to go on into a more congenial vocation if you desire to do so.

But in doing all this, you must never lose sight of your vision of what you want, or your faith and purpose to get what you want.

Let me here give you another word of caution in regard to motives.

Beware of the insidious temptation to seek for power over other men.

Nothing is so pleasant to the unformed or partially developed mind as the exercise of power or dominion over others. The desire to rule for selfish gratification has been the curse of the world. For countless ages kings and lords have drenched the earth with blood in their battles to extend their dominions; this not to seek more life for all, but to get more power for themselves.

To-day, the main motive in the business and industrial world is the same; men marshal their armies of dollars, and lay waste the lives and hearts of millions in the same mad scramble for power over others. Commercial kings, like political kings, are inspired by the lust for power.

Jesus saw in this desire for mastery the moving impulse of that evil world He sought to overthrow. Read the twenty-third chapter of Matthew, and see how He pictures the lust of the Pharisees to be called "Master," to sit in the high places, to domineer over others, and to lay burdens on the backs of the less fortunate; and note how He compares this lust for dominion with the brotherly seeking for the Common Good to which He calls His disciples.

Look out for the temptation to seek for authority, to become a "master," to be considered as one who is above the common herd, to impress others by lavish display, and so on.

The mind that seeks for mastery over others is the competitive mind; and the competitive mind is not the creative one. In order to master your environment and your destiny, it is not at all necessary that you should rule over your fellow men; and indeed, when you fall into the world's struggle for the high places, you begin to be conquered by fate and environment, and your getting rich becomes a matter of chance and speculation.

Beware of the competitive mind! No better statement of the principle of creative action can be formulated than the favorite declaration of the late "Golden Rule" Jones of Toledo: "What I want for myself, I want for everybody."

CHAPTER FIFTEEN

THE ADVANCING MAN

What I have said in the last chapter applies as well to the professional man and the wage-earner as to the man who is engaged in mercantile business.

No matter whether you are a physician, a teacher, or a clergyman, if you can give increase of life to others and make them sensible of the fact, they will be attracted to you, and you will get rich. The physician who holds the vision of himself as a great and successful healer, and who works toward the complete realization of that vision with faith and purpose, as described in former chapters, will come into such close touch with the Source of Life that he will be phenomenally successful; patients will come to him in throngs.

No one has a greater opportunity to carry into effect the teachings of this book than the practitioner of medicine; it does not matter to which of the various schools he may belong, for the principle of healing is common to all of them, and may be reached by all alike. The Advancing Man in medicine, who holds to a clear mental image of himself as successful, and who obeys the laws of faith, purpose, and gratitude, will cure every curable case he undertakes, no matter what remedies he may use.

In the field of religion, the world cries out for the clergyman who can teach his hearers the true science of abundant life. He who masters the details of the science of getting rich, together with the allied sciences of being well, of being great, and of winning love, and who teaches these details from the pulpit, will never lack for a congregation. This is the gospel that the world needs; it will give increase of life, and men will hear it gladly, and will give liberal support to the man who brings it to them.

What is now needed is a demonstration of the science of life from the pulpit. We want preachers who can not only tell us how, but who in their own persons will show us how. We need the preacher who will himself be rich, healthy, great, and beloved, to teach us how to attain to these things; and when he comes he will find a numerous and loyal following.

The same is true of the teacher who can inspire the children with the faith and purpose of the advancing life. He will never be "out of a job." And any teacher who has this faith and purpose can give it to his pupils; he cannot help giving it to them if it is part of his own life and practice.

What is true of the teacher, preacher, and physician is true of the lawyer, dentist, real estate man, insurance agent—of everybody.

The combined mental and personal action I have described is infallible; it cannot fail. Every man and woman who follows these instructions steadily, perseveringly, and to the letter, will get rich. The law of the Increase of Life is as mathematically certain in its operation as the law of gravitation; getting rich is an exact science.

The wage-earner will find this as true of his case as of any of the others mentioned. Do not feel that you have no chance to get rich because you are working where there is no visible opportunity for advancement, where wages are small and the cost of living high. Form your clear mental vision of what you want, and begin to act with faith and purpose.

Do all the work you can do, every day, and do each piece of work in a perfectly successful manner; put the power of success, and the purpose to get rich, into everything that you do.

But do not do this merely with the idea of currying favor with your employer, in the hope that he, or those above you, will see your good work and advance you; it is not likely that they will do so.

The man who is merely a "good" workman, filling his place to the very best of his ability, and satisfied with that, is valuable to his employer; and it is not to the employer's interest to promote him; he is worth more where he is.

To secure advancement, something more is necessary than to be too large for your place.

The man who is certain to advance is the one who is too big for his place, and who has a clear concept of what he wants to be; who knows that he can become what he wants to be, and who is determined to BE what he wants to be.

Do not try to more than fill your present place with a view to pleasing your employer; do it with the idea of advancing yourself. Hold the faith and purpose of increase during work hours, after work hours, and before work hours. Hold it in such a way that every person who comes in contact with you, whether foreman, fellow workman, or social acquaintance, will feel the power of purpose radiating from you; so that every one will get the sense of advancement and increase from you. Men will be attracted to you, and if there is no possibility for advancement in your present job, you will very soon see an opportunity to take another job.

There is a Power which never fails to present opportunity to the Advancing Man who is moving in obedience to law.

God cannot help helping you, if you act in a Certain Way; He must do so in order to help Himself.

There is nothing in your circumstances or in the industrial situation that can keep you down. If you cannot get rich working for the steel trust, you can get rich on a ten-acre farm; and if you begin to move in the Certain Way, you will certainly escape from the "clutches" of the steel trust and get on to the farm or wherever else you wish to be.

If a few thousands of its employees would enter upon the Certain Way, the steel trust would soon be in a bad plight; it would have to give its workingmen more opportunity, or go out of business. Nobody has to work for a trust; the trusts can keep men in so-called hopeless conditions only so long as there are men who are too ignorant to know of the science of getting rich, or too intellectually slothful to practice it.

Begin this way of thinking and acting, and your faith and purpose will make you quick to see any opportunity to better your condition.

Such opportunities will speedily come, for the Supreme, working in All, and working for you, will bring them before you.

Do not wait for an opportunity to be all that you want to be; when an opportunity to be more than you are now is presented and you feel impelled toward it, take it. It will be the first step toward a greater opportunity.

There is no such thing possible in this universe as a lack of opportunities for the man who is living the advancing life.

It is inherent in the constitution of the cosmos that all things shall be for him and work together for his good; and he must certainly get rich if he acts and thinks in the Certain Way. So let wage-earning men and women study this book with great care, and enter with confidence upon the course of action it prescribes; it will not fail.

CHAPTER SIXTEEN

SOME CAUTIONS, AND
CONCLUDING OBSERVATIONS

Many people will scoff at the idea that there is an exact science of getting rich; holding the impression that the supply of wealth is limited, they will insist that social and governmental institutions must be changed before even any considerable number of people can acquire a competence.

But this is not true.

It is true that existing governments keep the masses in poverty, but this is because the masses do not think and act in the Certain Way.

If the masses begin to move forward as suggested in this book, neither governments nor industrial systems can check them; all systems must be modified to accommodate the forward movement.

If the people have the Advancing Mind, have the Faith that they can become rich, and move forward with the fixed purpose to become rich, nothing can possibly keep them in poverty.

Individuals may enter upon the Certain Way at any time, and under any government, and make themselves rich; and when any considerable number of individuals do so under any government, they will cause the system to be so modified as to open the way for others.

The more men who get rich on the competitive plane, the worse for others; the more who get rich on the creative plane, the better for others.

The economic salvation of the masses can only be accomplished by getting a large number of people to practice the scientific method set down in this book, and become rich. These will show others the way, and inspire them with a desire for real life, with the faith that it can be attained, and with the purpose to attain it.

For the present, however, it is enough to know that neither the government under which you live nor the capitalistic or competitive system of industry can keep you from getting rich. When you enter upon the creative plane of thought you will rise above all these things and become a citizen of another kingdom.

But remember that your thought must be held upon the creative plane; you are never for an instant to be betrayed into regarding the supply as limited, or into acting on the moral level of competition.

Whenever you do fall into old ways of thought, correct yourself instantly; for when you are in the competitive mind, you have lost the co-operation of the Mind of the Whole.

Do not spend any time in planning as to how you will meet possible emergencies in the future, except as the necessary policies may affect your actions to-day. You are concerned with doing to-day's work in a perfectly successful manner, and not with emergencies which may arise to-morrow; you can attend to them as they come.

Do not concern yourself with questions as to how you shall surmount obstacles which may loom upon your business horizon, unless you can see plainly that your course must be altered to-day in order to avoid them.

No matter how tremendous an obstruction may appear at a distance, you will find that if you go on in the Certain Way it will disappear as you approach it, or that a way over, through, or around it will appear.

No possible combination of circumstances can defeat a man or woman who is proceeding to get rich along strictly scientific lines. No man or woman who obeys the law can fail to get rich, any more than one can multiply two by two and fail to get four.

Give no anxious thought to possible disasters, obstacles, panics, or unfavorable combinations of circumstances; it is time enough to meet such things when they present themselves before you in the immediate present, and you will find that every difficulty carries with it the wherewithal for its overcoming.

Guard your speech. Never speak of yourself, your affairs, or of anything else in a discouraged or discouraging way.

Never admit the possibility of failure, or speak in a way that infers failure as a possibility.

Never speak of the times as being hard, or of business conditions as being doubtful. Times may be hard and business doubtful for those who are on the competitive plane, but they can never be so for you; you can create what you want, and you are above fear.

When others are having hard times and poor business, you will find your greatest opportunities.

Train yourself to think of and to look upon the world as a something which is Becoming, which is growing; and to regard seeming evil as being only that which is undeveloped. Always speak in terms of advancement; to do otherwise is to deny your faith, and to deny your faith is to lose it.

Never allow yourself to feel disappointed. You may expect to have a certain thing at a certain time, and not get it at that time; and this will appear to you like failure.

But if you hold to your faith you will find that the failure is only apparent.

Go on in the certain way, and if you do not receive that thing, you will receive something so much better that you will see that the seeming failure was really a great success.

A student of this science had set his mind on making a certain business combination which seemed to him at the time to be very desirable, and he worked for some weeks to bring it about. When the crucial time came, the thing failed in a perfectly inexplicable way; it was as if some unseen influence had been working secretly against him. He was not disappointed; on the contrary, he thanked God that his desire had been overruled, and went steadily on with a grateful mind. In a few weeks an opportunity so much better came his way that he would not have made the first deal on any account; and he saw that a Mind which knew more than he knew had prevented him from losing the greater good by entangling himself with the lesser.

That is the way every seeming failure will work out for you, if you keep your faith, hold to your purpose, have gratitude, and do, every day, all that can be done that day, doing each separate act in a successful manner.

When you make a failure, it is because you have not asked for enough; keep on, and a larger thing than you were seeking will certainly come to you. Remember this.

You will not fail because you lack the necessary talent to do what you wish to do. If you go on as I have directed, you will develop all the talent that is necessary to the doing of your work.

It is not within the scope of this book to deal with the science of cultivating talent; but it is as certain and simple as the process of getting rich.

However, do not hesitate or waver for fear that when you come to any certain place you will fail for lack of ability; keep right on, and when you come to that place, the ability will be furnished to you. The same source of ability which enabled the untaught Lincoln to do the greatest work in government ever accomplished by a single man is open to you; you may draw upon all the mind there is for wisdom to use in meeting the responsibilities which are laid upon you. Go on in full faith.

Study this book. Make it your constant companion until you have mastered all the ideas contained in it. While you are getting firmly established in this faith, you will do well to give up most recreations and pleasures; and to stay away from places where ideas conflicting with these are advanced in lectures or sermons. Do not read pessimistic or conflicting literature, or get into arguments upon the matter. Do very little reading, outside of the writers mentioned in the Preface. Spend most of your leisure time in contemplating your vision, and in cultivating gratitude, and in reading this book. It contains all you need to know of the science of getting rich; and you will find all the essentials summed up in the following chapter.

CHAPTER SEVENTEEN

SUMMARY OF THE
SCIENCE OF GETTING RICH

There is a thinking stuff from which all things are made, and which, in its original state, permeates, penetrates, and fills the interspaces of the universe.

A thought in this substance produces the thing that is imaged by the thought.

Man can form things in his thought, and by impressing his thought upon formless substance can cause the thing he thinks about to be created.

In order to do this, man must pass from the competitive to the creative mind; otherwise he cannot be in harmony with the Formless Intelligence, which is always creative and never competitive in spirit.

Man may come into full harmony with the Formless Substance by entertaining a lively and sincere gratitude for the blessings it bestows upon him. Gratitude unifies the mind of man with the intelligence of Substance, so that man's thoughts are received by the Formless. Man can remain upon the creative plane only by uniting himself with the Formless Intelligence through a deep and continuous feeling of gratitude.

Man must form a clear and definite mental image of the things he wishes to have, to do, or to become; and he must hold this mental image in his thoughts, while being deeply grateful to the Supreme that all his desires are granted to him. The man who wishes to get rich must spend his leisure hours in contemplating his Vision, and in earnest thanksgiving that the reality is being given to him. Too much stress cannot be laid on the importance of frequent contemplation of the mental image, coupled with unwavering faith and devout gratitude. This is the process by which the impression is given to the Formless, and the creative forces set in motion.

The creative energy works through the established channels of natural growth, and of the industrial and social order. All that is included in his mental image will surely be brought to the man who follows the instructions given above, and whose faith does not waver. What he wants will come to him through the ways of established trade and commerce.

In order to receive his own when it shall come to him, man must be active; and this activity can only consist in more than filling his present place. He must keep in mind the Purpose to get rich through the realization of his mental image. And he must do, every day, all that can be done that day, taking care to do each act in a successful manner. He must give to every man a use value in excess of the cash value he receives, so that each transaction makes for more life; and he must so hold the Advancing Thought that the impression of Increase will be communicated to all with whom he comes in contact.

The men and women who practice the foregoing instructions will certainly get rich; and the riches they receive will be in exact proportion to the definiteness of their vision, the fixity of their purpose, the steadiness of their faith and the depth of their gratitude.

BOOK THREE:

THE
MASTER KEY

CHARLES F. HAANEL

CONTENTS

FOREWORD

Nature compels us all to move through life. We could not remain stationary however much we wished.

Every right-thinking person wants not merely to move through life like a sound-producing, perambulating plant, but to develop—to improve—and to continue the development mentally to the close of physical life.

This development can occur only through the improvement of the quality of individual thought and the ideals, actions and conditions that arise as a consequence.

Hence a study of the creative processes of thought and how to apply them is of supreme importance to each one of us. This knowledge is the means whereby the evolution of human life on earth may be hastened and uplifted in the process.

Humanity ardently seeks "The Truth" and explores every avenue to it. In this process it has produced a special literature, which ranges the whole gamut of thought from the trivial to the sublime—up from Divination, through all the Philosophies, to the final lofty Truth of "The Master Key."

"The Master Key" is here given to the world as a means of tapping the great cosmic intelligence and attracting from it that which corresponds to the ambitions and aspirations of each reader.

Every thing and institution we see around us, created by human agency, had first to exist as a thought in some human mind. Thought therefore is constructive. Human thought is the spiritual power of the cosmos operating through its creature man. "The Master Key" instructs the reader how to use that power, and use it both constructively and creatively. The things and conditions we desire to become realities we must first create in thought. "The Master Key" explains and guides the process.

There is, at the present time, a great ferment of unrest in the world. This does not necessarily imply the imminence of either war or revolution. Revolutions and wars are not deliberately planned in advance. They occur spontaneously, either from an explosion or collapse of economic conditions due to wrong thinking, or from an absence of any thought at all, or from a delay in the application of right thought. Whatever some may think, it is not at this moment a war or an economic or social revolution for which a troubled world is yearning. What the world consciously or subconsciously desires is neither the overthrow nor fusion of nations or classes, but a rapid adjustment of consuming to producing power, viz., a speeding up of the process of social evolution to the point where the standards of life correspond to new demands. These demands are created by the open-eyed participation of all in the life of an intenser age, and by the spread of an improved education in the schools and universities, through books, the press, the stage and the screen.

It is not possible to reverse the aspiration of Humanity. Hence the decision has to be made whether this evolution should be stemmed or whether it should be helped: if helped, it is important that the ethic which is to lead Humanity onward should be lofty, practical and one that modern people can understand.

"The Master Key" is this ethic.

"The Master Key" reveals the wisdom of the ages, and expounds it with that simple lucid power which arises from inspiration.

The author, Mr. Charles F. Haanel, inspired himself, is able to inspire the reader. Through the multiplication of similarly inspired individuals in all countries the potentiality exists now to create deliberately a growing community of interests, and to improve national and world conditions more quickly than in the past, by a process of harmonious collaboration.

The power of human thought as taught by "The Master Key" is the only human power which is greater than the power of arms. The dawn of the age of thought does not mean the end of the use of might; it implies the end of the abuse of might; it means the use of the common power solely for purposes beneficial to the individual, to the nation, and to the world.

More than 200,000 individuals are already "Master Key" adepts. They are creating new conditions in the New World and form a body of "Master Key" thought which is an example and friendly invitation to thinking people in our own British Empire and other lands.

"The Master Key" teaching has hitherto been published in the form of a Correspondence Course Of 24 lessons, delivered to students one per week for 24 weeks. The reader, who now receives the whole 24 parts at one time, is warned not to attempt to read the book like a novel, but to treat it as a course of study and conscientiously to imbibe the meaning of each part—reading and re-reading one part only per week—before proceeding to the next. Otherwise the later parts will tend to be misunderstood and the reader's time and money will be wasted.

The exercises create a power similar to that which other devout people find in prayer. They should be faithfully performed in the silence, this "silence" being a room, study, or private office where conversation and movement do not obtrude to distract the attention.

Used as thus instructed "The Master Key" will make of the reader a greater, better personality, and a better citizen, equipped with a new power to achieve any worthy personal purpose and a new ability to enjoy life's beauty and wonder.

F. H. BURGESS.

LONDON,
30th, November, 1933.

INTRODUCTION
Part One

Before any environment, successful or otherwise, can be created, action of some kind is necessary, and before any action is possible, there must be thought of some kind, either conscious or unconscious, and as thought is a product of mind, it becomes evident that Mind is the creative centre from which all activities proceed.

It is not expected that any of the inherent laws which govern the modern business world as it is at present constituted can be suspended or repealed by any force on the same plane, but it is axiomatic that a higher law may overcome a lower one. Tree life causes the sap to ascend, not by repealing the law of gravity but by surmounting it.

To control circumstances a knowledge of certain scientific principles of mind-action is required. Such knowledge is a most valuable asset. It may be gained by degrees and put into practice as fast as learned. Power over circumstances is one of its fruits; health, harmony and prosperity are assets upon its balance sheet. It costs only the labour of harvesting its great resources.

The naturalist who spends much of his time in observing visible phenomena is constantly creating power in that portion of his brain set apart for observation. The result is that he becomes very much more expert and skilful in knowing what he sees, and grasping an infinite number of details at a glance, than does his unobserving friend. He has reached this facility by exercise of his brain. He deliberately chose to enlarge his brain power in the line of observation, so he deliberately exercised that special faculty, over and over, with increasing attention and concentration. Now we have the result—a man learned in the lore of observation far above his fellows. Or, on the other hand, one can, by stolid inaction, allow the delicate brain matter to harden and ossify until his whole life is barren and fruitless.

Every thought tends to become a material thing. Our desires are seed thoughts that have a tendency to sprout and grow and blossom and bear fruit. We are sowing these seeds every day. What shall the harvest be? Each of us to-day is the result of his past thinking. Later we shall be the result of what we are now thinking. We create our own character, personality and environment by the thought which we originate, or entertain. Thought seeks its own. The law of mental attraction is an exact parallel to the law of atomic affinity. Mental currents are as real as electric, magnetic or heat currents. We attract the currents with which we are in harmony—are we selecting those which will be conducive to our success? This is the important question.

Lines of least resistance are formed by the constant action of the mind. The activity of the brain reacts upon the particular faculty of the brain employed. The latent power of the mind is developed by constant exercise. Each form of its activity becomes more perfect by practice. Exercises for the development of the mind present a variety of motives for consideration. They involve the development of the perceptive faculties, the cultivation of the emotions, the quickening of the imagination, the symmetrical unfoldment of the intuitive faculty, which without being able to give a reason frequently impels or prohibits choice, and finally the power of the mind may be cultivated by the development of the moral character.

"The greatest man," said Seneca, "is he who chooses right with invincible determination." The greatest power of the mind, then, depends upon its exercise in moral channels and therefore requires that every conscious mental effort should involve a moral end. A developed moral consciousness modifies consideration of motives, and increases the force and continuity of actions; consequently the well developed symmetrical character necessitates good physical, mental and moral health, and this combination creates initiative, power, resistless force, and necessarily success.

It will be found that Nature is constantly seeking to express Harmony in all things, is forever trying to bring about an harmonious adjustment, for every discord, every wound, every difficulty; therefore when thought is harmonious, nature begins to create the material conditions, the possession of which is necessary in order to make up an harmonious environment.

When we understand that mind is the great creative power, what does not become possible? With Desire as the great creative energy, can we not see why Desire should be cultivated, controlled and directed in our lives and destinies? Men and women of strong mentality, who dominate those around them, and often those far removed from them, really emanate currents charged with power which, coming in contact with the minds of others, causes the desires of the latter to be in accord with the mind of the strong individuality. Great masters of men possess this power to a marked degree. Their influence is felt far and near, and they secure compliance with their wishes by making others "want" to act in accord with them. In this way men of strong Desire and Imagination may and do exert powerful influence over the minds of others, leading the latter in the way desired. The magnetic persons attract, allure and draw. They are emotional, and capture the will of others.

No man is ever created without the inherent power in himself to help himself. The personality that understands its own intellectual and moral power of conquest will certainly assert itself. It is this truth which an enfamined world craves to-day. The possibility of asserting a slumbering intellectual courage that dearly discerns, and a moral courage that grandly undertakes is open to all. There is a divine potency in every human being.

We speak of the sun as "rising" and "setting" though we know that this is simply an appearance of motion. To our senses the earth is apparently standing still, and yet we know it is revolving rapidly. We speak of a bell as a "sounding body," yet we know that all that the bell can do is to produce vibrations in the air. When these vibrations come at the rate of sixteen a second they cause a sound to be heard in the mind. It is possible for the mind to hear vibrations up to the rate of 38,000 a second. When the number increases beyond this all is silence again; so that we know that the sound is not in the bell; it is in our own mind.

We speak and even think of the sun as "giving light," yet we know it is simply giving forth energy which produces vibrations in the ether at the rate of four hundred trillion a second, causing what are termed light waves, so that we know that what we call light is simply a mode of motion, and the only light that there is, is the sensation caused in the mind by the motion of these waves. When the number of vibrations increases, the light changes in colour, each change in colour being caused by shorter and more rapid vibrations; so that although we speak of the rose as being red, the grass as being green, or the sky as being blue, we know that these colours exist only in our minds, and are the sensation experienced by us as the result of the vibrations of light. When the vibrations are reduced below four hundred trillion a second, they no longer affect us as light but we experience the sensation of heat.

So we have come to know that appearances exist for us only in our consciousness. Even time and space become annihilated, time being only the experience of succession, there being no past or future except as a thought relation to the present. In the last analysis, therefore, we know that one principle governs and controls all there is. Every atom is forever conserved; whatever is parted with must inevitably be received somewhere. It cannot perish and it only exists for use. It can go only where it is attracted, and therefore required. We can receive only what we give, and we may give only to those who can receive; and it remains with us to determine our rate of growth and the degree of harmony that we shall express.

The laws under which we live are designed solely for our advantage. These laws are immutable and we cannot escape from their operation. All the great eternal forces act in solemn silence, but it is in our power to place ourselves, in harmony with them and thus express a life of comparative peace and happiness

Difficulties, inharmonies, obstacles, indicate that we are either refusing to give out what we no longer need, or refusing to accept what we require. Growth is attained through an exchange of the old for the new, of the good for the better; it is a conditional or reciprocal action, for each of us is a complete thought entity and the completeness makes it possible for us to receive only as we give. We cannot obtain what we lack if we tenaciously cling to what we have.

The Principle of Attraction operates to bring to us only what may be to our advantage. We are able consciously to control our conditions as we come to sense the purpose of what we attract, and are able to extract from each experience only what we require for our further growth. Our ability to do this determines the degree of harmony or happiness we attain.

The ability to appropriate what we require for our growth continually increases as we reach higher planes and broader visions, and the greater our ability to know what we require, the more certain we shall be to discern its presence, to attract it and to absorb it. Nothing may reach us except what is necessary for our growth. All conditions and experiences that come to us do so for our benefit. Difficulties and obstacles will continue to come until we absorb their wisdom and gather from them the essentials of further growth. That we reap what we sow, is mathematically exact. We gain permanent strength exactly to the extent of the effort required to overcome our difficulties.

The inexorable requirements of growth demand that we exert the greatest degree of attraction for what is perfectly in accord with us. Our highest happiness will be best attained through our understanding of and conscious cooperation with natural laws.

Our mind-forces are often bound by the paralysing suggestions that come to us from the crude thinking of the race, and which are accepted and acted upon without question. Impressions of fear, of worry, of disability and of inferiority are given us daily. These are sufficient reasons in themselves why men achieve so little—why the lives of multitudes are so barren of results, when all the time there are possibilities within them which need only the liberating touch of appreciation and wholesome ambition to expand into real greatness.

Women, perhaps even more than men, have been subject to these conditions. This is true because of their finer susceptibilities making them more open to thought-vibrations from other minds, and because the flood of negative and repressive thoughts has been aimed more especially at them.

But it is being overcome. Florence Nightingale overcame it when she rose in the Crimea to heights of tender sympathy and executive before unknown among women, Clara Barton, the head of the Red Cross, overcame it when she wrought a similar work in the armies of the Union. Jenny Lind overcame it when she showed her ability to command enormous financial rewards while at the same time gratifying the passionate desire of her nature and reaching the front rank of her day in musical art. And there is a long list of women singers, philanthropists, writers and actresses who have proved themselves capable of reaching the greatest literary, dramatic, artistic and sociological achievement.

Women as well as men are beginning to do their own thinking. They have awakened to some conception of their possibilities. They demand that if life holds any secrets, these shall be disclosed. At no previous time has the influence and potency of thought received such careful and discriminating investigation. While a few seers have grasped the great fact that mind is the universal substance, the basis of all things, never before has this vital truth penetrated the more general consciousness. Many minds are now striving to give this wonderful truth definite utterance. Modern science has taught us that light and sound are simply different intensities of motion, and this may lead to discoveries of forces within man that could not have been conceived of until this revelation was made.

A new era has dawned, and now, standing in its light, man sees something of the vastness of the meaning of life—something of its grandeur. Within that life is the germ of infinite potencies. One feels convinced that man's possibility of attainment cannot be measured, that boundary lines to his onward march are unthinkable. Standing on this height he finds that he can draw new power to himself from the infinite energy of which he is a part.

INTRODUCTION
Part Two

Some men seem to attract success, power, wealth, attainment, with very little conscious effort; others conquer with great difficulty; still others fail altogether to reach their ambitions, desires and ideals. Why is this so? Why should some men realize their ambitions easily, others with difficulty, and still others not at all? The cause cannot be physical, else the most perfect men, physically, would be the most successful. The difference, therefore, must be mental—must be in the mind; hence mind must be the creative force, must constitute the sole difference between men. It is mind, therefore, which overcomes, environment and every other obstacle in the path of men.

It is the actualizing of interior quality through the creative power of thought which has given us great leaders like Alexander, Napoleon, Cromwell, Marlborough and Washington; captains of industry like Carnegie, Morgan, Rockefeller and Leverhulme; inventors like Stephenson, Morse, Marconi, Edison, Tesla, and hosts of others. If, then, the only difference between men lies in their ability to think, to use and control their thought, to develop it—if the secret of all success, all power, all attainment is the creative power of mind, the force of thought—surely the ability of think correctly should become the paramount object of every man.

When the creative power of thought is fully understood, its effect will be seen to be marvellous. But such results cannot be secured without proper application, diligence and concentration. The student will find that the laws governing in the mental and spiritual world are as fixed and infallible as in the material world. To secure the desired results, then, it is necessary to know the law and to comply with it. A proper compliance with the law will be found to produce the desired result with invariable exactitude. The student who learns that power comes from within, that he is weak only because he has depended on help from outside, and who unhesitatingly throws himself on his own thought, instantly rights himself, stands erect, assumes a dominant attitude, and works miracles.

Scientists tell us that we live in the universal ether. This is formless, of itself, but it is pliable, and forms about us, in us and around us, according to our thought and word. We set it into activity by that which we think. Then that which manifests to us objectively is that we have thought or said.

Thought is governed by law. The reason we have not manifested more faith is because of lack of understanding. We have not understood that everything works in exact accordance with definite law. The law of thought is as definite as the law of mathematics, or the law of chemistry, or the law of electricity, or the law of gravitation. When we begin to understand that happiness, health, success, prosperity and every other condition or environment are results, and that these results are created by right thinking, either consciously or unconsciously, we shall realize the importance of a working knowledge of the laws governing thought.

Those coming into a conscious realization of the power of thought find themselves in possession of the best that life can give; substantial things of a higher order become theirs, and these sublime realities are so constituted that they can be made tangible parts of daily personal life. They realize a world of higher power, and keep that power constantly working. This power is inexhaustible, limitless, and they are therefore carried forward from victory to victory. Obstacles that seem insurmountable are overcome. Enemies are changed to friends, conditions are overcome, elements transformed, fate is conquered.

The supply of good is inexhaustible, and the demand can be made along whatever lines we may desire. This is the mental law of demand and supply.

Our circumstances and environment are formed by our thoughts. We have, perhaps, been creating these conditions unconsciously. If they are unsatisfactory, the remedy is to consciously alter our mental attitude and see our circumstances adjust themselves to the new mental condition. There is nothing strange or supernatural about this; it is simply the Law of Being. The thoughts which take root in the mind will certainly produce fruit after their kind. The greatest schemer cannot "gather grapes of thorns, or figs of thistles." To improve our conditions we must first improve ourselves. Our thoughts and desires will be the first to show improvement.

To be in ignorance of the laws governing in the mental world is to be like a child playing with fire, or a man manipulating powerful chemicals without a knowledge of their nature and relations. This is universally true, because Mind is the one great cause which produces all conditions in the lives of men and women.

Admitting that you agree with everything that has been stated, thus far, and most persons will take no exception to anything that has been said, it still remains to make a practical application of the law.

In order to take advantage of this law, and put ourselves into harmonious relationship with it, so that the benefit may be made manifest in our lives, it is necessary to see that the conditions are all met for its proper operation. We may know the laws governing electricity, we may have all the proper mechanism, the lamps, the wires, the switches, and we may even know how to generate the power, but if the connections are, not properly made, we can work the switch till doomsday and no light will appear; so with the law of attraction—it is in operation all the time, everywhere, something is constantly being created, something is appearing, everything is continually changing, but to take advantage of this process, it is just as necessary to comply with the law as it is in the case of electricity or gravitation.

Mind is creative and operates through the law of attraction. We are not to try to influence any to do what we think they should do. Each individual has a right to choose for himself, but aside from this we would be operating under the law of force, which is destructive in its nature and just the opposite of the law of attraction. A little reflection will convince you that all of the great laws of nature operate in silence and that the underlying principle is the law of attraction. It is only destructive processes such as earthquakes and catastrophies, that employ force. Nothing good is ever accomplished in that way.

To be successful, attention must invariably be directed to the creative plane; it must never seek to deprive. You do not wish to take anything away from any one else, you want to create something for yourself, and what you want for yourself you are perfectly willing that everyone else should have.

You know that it is not necessary to take from one to give to another, but that the supply for all is abundant. Nature's storehouse of wealth is inexhaustible and if there seems to be a lack of supply anywhere it is only because the channels of distribution are as yet imperfect.

Abundance is a natural law of the universe. The evidence of this law is conclusive; we see it on every hand. Everywhere Nature is lavish—wasteful, extravagant. Nowhere is economy observed in any created thing. Profusion is manifested in everything. The millions and millions of trees and flowers and plants and animals and the vast scheme of reproduction where the process of creating and recreating is for ever going on, all indicates the lavishness with which Nature has made provision for man. That there is an abundance for everyone is evident, but that many seem to have been separated from this supply is also evident; they have not yet come into a realization of the Universality of all substance, and that mind is the active principle which starts causes in motion whereby we are related to the things we desire.

It is evident, therefore, that he who fails to fully investigate and take advantage of the wonderful progress which is being made, in this last and greatest science, will soon be as far behind as the man who would refuse to acknowledge and accept the benefits which have accrued to mankind through an understanding of the laws of electricity.

Of course, mind creates negative conditions just as readily as favorable conditions, and when we consciously or unconsciously visualize every kind of lack, limitation and discord, we create these conditions; this is what many are unconsciously doing all the time.

This law as well as every other law is no respecter of persons, but is in constant operation and is relentlessly bringing to each individual exactly what he has created; in other words, "Whatsoever a man soweth that shall he also reap."

Abundance, therefore, depends upon a recognition of the laws of Abundance, and the fact that Mind is not only the creator, but the only creator of all there is. Certainly nothing can be created, before we know that it can be created and then make the proper effort. There is no more Electricity in the world to-day than there was fifty years ago, but until someone recognized the law by which it could be made of service, we received no benefit; now that the law is understood, practically the whole world is lit by it. So with the law of Abundance; it is only those who recognize the law and place themselves in harmony with it, who share in its benefits.

A recognition of the law of abundance develops certain mental and moral qualities, among which are Courage, Loyalty, Tact, Sagacity, Individuality and Constructiveness. These are all modes of thought, and as all thought is creative, they manifest in objective conditions corresponding with the mental condition. This is necessarily true because the ability of the individual to think is his ability to act upon the Universal mind and bring it into manifestation, it is the process whereby the individual becomes a channel for the differentiation of the Universal. Every thought is a cause and every condition an effect.

This principle endows the individual with seemingly transcendental possibilities, among which is the mastery of conditions through the creation and recognition of opportunities. This creation of opportunity implies the existence or creation of the necessary qualities or talents which are thought forces and which result in a consciousness of power which future events cannot disturb. It is this organization of victory or success within the mind, this consciousness of power within which constitutes the responsive harmonious action whereby we are related to the objects and purposes which we seek. This is the law of attraction in action; this law being the common property of all, can be exercised by any one having sufficient knowledge of its operation.

Courage is that power of the mind which manifests in the love of mental conflict; it is a noble and lofty sentiment, it is equally fitted to command or obey. Both require courage. It often has a tendency to conceal itself. There are men and women, too, who apparently exist only to do what is pleasing to others, but when the time comes and the latent will is revealed, we find under the velvet glove an iron hand and no mistake about it. True courage is cool, calm and collected, and is never foolhardy, quarrelsome ill natured or contentious.

Accumulation is the power to reserve and preserve a part of the supply which we are constantly receiving, so as to be in position to take advantage of the larger opportunities which will come as soon as we are ready for them. Has it not been said, "To him that hath shall be given." All successful businessmen have this quality well developed. James J. Hill, who recently died leaving an estate of over £12,000,000 said: "If you want to know whether you are destined to be a success or a failure in life, you can easily find out. The test is simple and it is infallible. Are you able to save money? If not, drop out. You will lose. You may think not, but you will lose as sure as you live. The seed of success is not in you." This is very good so far as it goes, but any one who knows the biography of James J. Hill, knows that he acquired his £12,000,000 by following the exact methods we have given. In the fast place, he started with nothing; he had to use his imagination to idealize the vast railroad which he projected across the western prairies. He then had to come into a recognition of the law of abundance in order to provide the ways and means for materializing it unless he had followed out this program he would never have had anything to save.

Accumulativeness acquires momentum; the more you accumulate the more you desire and the more you desire the more you accumulate, so that it is but a short time until the action and reaction acquire a momentum that cannot be stopped. It must, however, never be confounded with selfishness, miserliness or penuriousness; they are perversions and will make any true progress impossible.

Constructiveness is the creative instinct of the mind. It will be readily seen that every successful businessman must be able to plan, develop or construct. In the business world it is usually referred to as initiative. It is not enough to go along in the beaten path. New ideas must be developed, new ways of doing things. It manifests in building, designing, planning, inventing, discovering, improving. It is a most valuable quality and must be constantly encouraged and developed. Every individual possesses it in some degree, because he is a centre of consciousness in that Infinite and Eternal Energy from which all things proceed.

Water manifests on three planes, as ice, as water and as steam; it is all the same compound, the only difference is the temperature, but no one would try to drive an engine with ice; convert it into steam and it easily takes up the load. So with your energy; if you want it to act on the creative plane, you will have to begin by melting the ice with the fire of imagination, and you will find that the stronger the fire and the more ice you melt, the more fire, the more powerful your thought will become, and the easier it will be for you to materialize your desire.

Sagacity is the ability to perceive and cooperate with Natural Law. True Sagacity avoids trickery and deceit as it would the leprosy; it is the product of that deep insight which enables one to penetrate into the heart of things and understand how to set causes in motion which will inevitably create successful conditions.

Tact is a very subtle and at the same time a very important factor in business success. It is very similar to intuition. To possess tact one must have a fine feeling, must instinctively know what to say or what to do. In order to be tactful one must possess Sympathy and Understanding, that understanding which is so rare, for all men see and hear and feel, but how desperately few "understand." Tact enables one to foresee what is about to happen and calculate the result of actions. Tact enables us to feel when we are in the presence of physical, mental and moral cleanliness, for these are to-day invariably demanded as the price of success.

Loyalty is one of the strongest links which bind men of strength and character. It is one which can never be broken with impunity. The man who would lose his right hand rather than betray a friend will never lack friends. The man who will stand in silent guard, until death, if need be, beside the shrine of confidence or friendship of those who have allowed him to enter will find himself linked with a current of cosmic power which will attract desirable conditions only. It is inconceivable that such a one should ever meet with lack of any kind.

Individuality is the power to unfold our own latent possibilities, to be a law unto ourselves, to be interested in the race rather than the goal. Strong men care nothing for the flock of imitators who trot complacently behind them. They derive no satisfaction in the mere leading of large numbers, or the plaudits of the mob. This pleases only petty natures and inferior minds. Individuality glories more in the unfolding of the power within than in the servility of the weakling.

Individuality is a real power inherent in all and the development and consequent expression of this power enables one to assume the responsibility of directing his own footsteps rather than stampeding after some self-assertive bellwether.

Truth is the imperative condition of all well-being. To be sure, to know the truth and to stand confidently on it is a satisfaction beside which no other is comparable. Truth is the underlying verity, the condition precedent to every business or social relation. Truth is the only solid ground in a world of conflict, doubt and danger.

Every act not in harmony with Truth, whether through ignorance or design, cuts the ground from under our feet, leads to discord, inevitable loss, and confusion, for while the humblest mind can accurately foretell the result of every correct action, the greatest, most profound and penetrating mind loses its way hopelessly and can form no conception of the results due to a departure from correct principles.

Those who establish within themselves the requisite elements of true success have established confidence, organized victory, and it only remains for them to take such steps from time to time as the newly awakened thought force will direct, and herein rests the magical secret of all power.

Less than ten per cent. of our mental processes is conscious, the other ninety per cent. is subconscious and unconscious, so that he who would depend upon his conscious thought alone for results is less than ten per cent efficient. Those who are accomplishing anything worth while are those who are enabled to take advantage of this greater storehouse of mental wealth. It is in the vast domain of the sub-conscious mind that great truths are hidden, and it is here that thought finds its creative power, its power to correlate with its object, to bring out of the unseen the seen.

Those familiar with the laws of Electricity understand the principle that electricity must always pass from a higher to a lower potentiality and can therefore make whatever application of the power they desire. Those not familiar with this law can effect nothing; and so with the law governing in the Mental World, those who understand that Mind penetrates all things, is Omnipresent and is responsive to every demand, can make use of the law and can control conditions, circumstances and environment; the uninformed cannot use it because they do not know it.

The fruit of this knowledge is, as it were, a gift of the Gods; it is the "truth" that makes men free, not only free from every lack and limitation, but free from sorrow, worry and care, and is it not wonderful to realize that this law is no respecter of persons, that it makes no difference what your habit of thought may be the way has been prepared.

With the realization that this mental power controls and directs every other power which exists, that it can be cultivated and developed, that no limitation can be placed upon its activity, it will become apparent that it is the greatest fact in the world, the remedy for every ill, the solution for every difficulty, the gravitation of every desire, in fact, that it is the Creator's magnificent provision for human emancipation.

INTRODUCTION
Part Three

The scientific spirit now dominates every field of effort, relations of cause and effect are no longer ignored.

The discovery of a reign of law marked an epoch in human progress. It eliminated the element of uncertainty and caprice from men's lives, and substituted law, reason and certitude.

Men now understand that for every result there is an adequate and definite cause, so that when a given result is desired, they seek the condition by which alone this result may be attained.

The basis upon which all law rests was discovered by inductive reasoning which consists of comparing a number of separate instances with one another until the common factor which gives rise to them all is seen.

It is this method of study to which the civilized nations owe the greater part of their prosperity and the more valuable part of their knowledge; it has lengthened life, it has mitigated pain, it has spanned rivers, it has brightened night with the splendour of day, extended the range of vision, accelerated motion, annihilated distance, facilitated intercourse, and enabled men to descend into the sea and to soar in the air, what wonder then that men to extend the blessings of this system of study to their method of thinking, so that when it became plainly evident that certain results followed a particular method of thinking it only remained to classify these results.

This method is scientific and it is the only method by which we shall be permitted to retain that degree of liberty and freedom which we have been accustomed to look upon as an inalienable right, because a people is safe at home and in the world only if national preparedness means such things as growing surplus of health, accumulated efficiency in public and private business of whatever sort, continuous advance in the science and art of acting together, and the increasingly dominant endeavor to make all of these and all other aspects of national development centre and revolve about ascending life, single and collective, for which science, art and ethics furnish guidance and controlling motives.

The Master Key is based on absolute scientific truth and will unfold the possibilities that lie dormant in the individual, and teach how they may be brought into powerful action, to increase the person's effective capacity, bringing added energy, discernment, vigour and mental elasticity. The student who gains an understanding of the mental laws which are unfolded will come into the possession of an ability to secure results hitherto undreamed of, and which has rewards hardly to be expressed in words.

It explains the correct use of both the receptive and active elements of the mental nature, and instructs the student in the recognition of opportunity; it strengthens the will and reasoning powers, and teaches the cultivation and best uses of imagination, desire, the emotions and the intuitional faculty. It gives initiative, tenacity of purpose, wisdom of choice, intelligent sympathy and a thorough enjoyment of life on its higher planes.

The Master Key teaches the use of Mind Power, true Mind Power, not any of the substitutes and perversions; it has nothing to do with Hypnotism, Magic or any of the more or less fascinating deceptions by which many are led to think that something can be had for nothing.

The Master Key cultivates and develops the understanding which will enable you to control the body and thereby the health. It improves and strengthens the Memory. It develops Insight, the kind of Insight which is so rare, the kind which is the distinguishing characteristic of every successful business man, the kind which enables men to see the possibilities as well as the difficulties in every situation, the kind which enables men to discern opportunity close at hand, for thousands fail to see opportunities almost within their grasp while they are industriously working with situations which under no possibility can be made to realize any substantial return.

The Master Key develops Mental Power which means that others instinctively recognize that you are a person of force, of character—that they want to do what you want them to do; it means that you attract men and things to you; that you are what some people call "lucky," that "things" come your way; that you have come into an understanding of the fundamental laws of Nature, and have put yourself in harmony with them; that you are in tune with the Infinite; that you understand the law of attraction, the Natural laws of growth, and the Psychological laws on which all advantages in the social and business world rest.

Mental Power is creative power, it gives you the ability to create for yourself; it does not mean the ability to take something away from some one else. Nature never does things that way. Nature makes two blades of grass grow where one grew before, and Mind Power enables men to do the same thing.

The Master Key develops insight and sagacity, increased independence, the ability and disposition to be helpful; it destroys distrust, depression, fear, melancholia, and every form of lack, limitation and weakness, including pain and disease; it awakens buried talents, supplies initiative, force, energy, vitality—it awakens an appreciation of the beautiful in Art, Literature and Science.

It has changed the lives of thousands of men and women, by substituting definite principles for uncertain and hazy methods—and principles are the foundation upon which every system of efficiency must rest.

Elbert Gary, the chairman of the United States Steel Corporation said: "The services of advisors, instructors, efficiency experts in successful management are indispensable to most business enterprises of magnitude, but I deem the recognition and adoption of right principles of vastly more importance." The Master Key teaches right principles, and suggests methods for making a practical application of the principles; in that it differs from every other course of study. It teaches that the only possible value which can attach to any principle is in its application. Many read books, take home study courses, attend lectures all their lives without ever making any progress in demonstrating the value of the principles involved. The Master Key suggests methods by which the value of the principles taught may be demonstrated and put in actual practice in the daily experience.

There is a change in the thought of the world. This change is silently transpiring in our midst, and is more important than any which the world has undergone since the downfall of Paganism.

The present revolution in the opinions of all classes of men, the highest and most cultured of men as well as those of the laboring class, stands unparalleled in the history of the world.

Science has of late made such vast discoveries, has revealed such an infinity of resources, has unveiled such enormous possibilities and such unsuspected forces, that scientific men more and more hesitate to affirm certain theories as established and indubitable or to deny certain other theories as absurd or impossible, and so a new civilization is being born; customs, creeds, and cruelty are passing; vision, faith and service are taking their place. The fetters of tradition are being melted off from humanity, and as the dross of materialism is being consumed, thought is being liberated and truth is rising full orbed before an astonished multitude.

The whole world is on the eve of a new consciousness, a new power and a new realization of the resources within the self. The last century saw the most magnificent material progress in history. The present century will produce the greatest progress in mental and spiritual power.

Physical Science has resolved matter into molecules, molecules into atoms, atoms into energy, and it has remained for Sir Ambrose Fleming, in an address before the Royal institution, to resolve this energy into mind. He says: "In its ulti-mate essence, energy may be incomprehensible by us except as an exhibition of the direct operation of that which we call Mind or Will."

Let us see what are the most powerful forces in Nature. In the mineral world everything is solid and fixed. In the animal and vegetable kingdom it is in a state of flux, forever changing, always being created and recreated. In the atmosphere we find heat, light and energy. Each realm becomes finer and more spiritual as we pass from the visible to the invisible, from the coarse to the fine, from the low potential-ity to high potentiality. When we reach the invisible we find energy, in its purest and most volatile state.

And as the most powerful forces of Nature are the invisible forces, so we find that the most powerful forces of man are his invisible forces, his spiritual force, and the only way in which the spiritual force can manifest is through the process of thinking. Thinking is the only activity which the spirit possesses, and thought is the only product of thinking.

Addition and subtraction are therefore spiritual transactions; reasoning is a spiritual process; ideas are spiritual conceptions; questions are spiritual search-lights and logic, argument and philosophy is spiritual machinery.

Every thought brings into action certain physical tissue, parts of the brain, nerve or muscle. This produces an actual physical change in the construction of the tissue. Therefore it is only necessary to have a certain number of thoughts on a given subject in order to bring about a complete change in the physical organiza-tion of a man.

This is the process by which failure is changed to success. Thoughts of courage, power, inspiration, harmony, are substituted for thoughts of failure, despair, lack, limitation and discord, and as these thoughts take root, the physical tissue is changed and the individual sees life in a new light, old things have actu-ally passed away, all things have become new, he is born again, this time born of the spirit, life has a new meaning for him, he is reconstructed and is filled with joy, confidence, hope, energy. He sees opportunities for success to which he was hereto-fore blind. He recognizes possibilities which before had no meaning for him. The thoughts of success with which he has been impregnated are radiated to those around him, and they in turn help him onward and upward; he attracts to him new and successful associates, and this in turn changes his environment; so that by this simple exercise of thought, a man changes not only himself, but his environment, circumstances and conditions.

You will see, you must see, that we are at the dawn of a new day; that the pos-sibilities are so wonderful, so fascinating, so limitless as to be almost bewildering. A century ago any man with an airplane or even a Gatling gun could have annihi-lated a whole army equipped with the implements of warfare then in use. So it is at present. Any man with a knowledge of the possibilities contained in the Master Key has an inconceivable advantage over the multitude.

THE MASTER KEY
PSYCHOLOGICAL CHART

It is a psychological fact that ninety per cent. of our mental power is never or seldom used. Therefore, most men have the power to achieve ten times as much as they ever accomplish.

This chart will tell you exactly where you stand, what you are accomplishing and what you can accomplish if you make the necessary effort.

Copy the following table out and fill it in as instructed below:

Mental Product	%
Health	%
Time Efficiency	%
Creative Power	%
Concentration	%
Total	%
Divide by 5—Average	%

The first test is your Mental product. What is it worth? Are you getting full value for it? What you get for your mental product depends entirely upon your ability to sell it to the best advantage. The chances are that many men with no more ability than yourself are being paid ten, twenty or fifty times more than you are, for a product no better than yours. If so, there is a reason, and this chart will explain it.

Estimate the value of what you have to sell, your knowledge, your experience, your loyalty, your energy, and if you are marketing it at its full rate value give yourself 100 per cent.; if you are only getting one-half of what it is worth give yourself fifty per cent., but be fair; do not underestimate the value of what you have to offer; remember that loss leads to greater loss and most loss comes from self-depreciation. Cause and effect do not operate somewhere, sometimes, but everywhere, always. This is an invariable law, so that whatever we receive, good or bad, is the result of a definite cause and reaches us either as a penalty or a reward.

And remember this, your ability to sell your mental product as the rate of 5 per cent. annually on £100,000 does not depend upon ability or knowledge either; you may be selling your product for £400 a year, and it may be more valuable than that of many who are being paid at the rate of £5,000 a year. The reason is plain. Knowledge does not apply itself; you are allowing it to remain in static form; you must convert it into dynamic form by applying creative power and concentration. The lack of concentrated, intelligent, charted effort may be costing you £4,000 a year.

Next, take Health. If you eat well, sleep well, take a reasonable amount of recreation, and can attend to your business, profession or household duties without any consideration for or thought of the state of your health, give yourself 100 per cent.; but if your body needs constant attention, if you have to be continually worried about what to eat or what not to eat, if you cannot sleep, or if you have aches or pains of any description, deduct from the 100 per cent. If you think your health is 90 per cent. of what it should be, give yourself 90 per cent., or if you are only 50 per cent. efficient, put it down—be absolutely fair.

Remember that your physical body is maintained through a process of continuous destruction and reconstruction. Life is simply an exchange of the old for the new, and health is only the equilibrium which nature maintains during the process of creating new tissue and eliminating the old or waste tissue.

Birth and death are constantly taking place in our body, new cells are constantly being formed by the process of converting food, water and air into living tissue. Every action of the brain, every movement of a muscle means the destruction and consequent death of some of these cells and the accumulation of these dead, unused and waste cells is what causes pain, suffering and disease. The symptoms depend upon what organs are being taxed in their effort to eliminate the waste matter.

An understanding of these laws and a consequent knowledge as to how to preserve an equilibrium between the new cells which are being created and the old cells which are being eliminated is the secret of perfect health.

Next in importance comes Time Efficiency, because time is all that we have, and what we accomplish depends entirely upon what use we make of our time. If you work eight hours, sleep eight hours, and use eight hours for recreation, study and self-improvement and all the time is fully utilized, give yourself 100 per cent.

But if any part of the eight hours which should be sold at a profit is spent in idleness, or gossip, or any form of mental dissipation; if any part of this time is wasted, or worse than wasted by allowing your thought to rest on critical, discordant or inharmonious subjects of any kind, cut down your percentage accordingly. If you fall asleep the minute your head touches the pillow, all right, but if you spend from fifteen minutes to an hour trying to get to sleep, cut your percentage down again. If your sleep is disturbed by dreams or fear or worry of any kind, cut your percentage down again.

If you jump up early and feel refreshed and vigorous, if you bathe and make your toilet without the loss of any unnecessary time, well and good, but if you idle or dream or fritter away from fifteen minutes to a half-hour needlessly, cut your percentage down again. If you spend the rest of your time in good healthy recreation, which benefits you, both physically and mentally, well and good; you are acquiring capital which will have a cash value, but if you let the time get away from you with nothing to show for it, you are not better physically, mentally or morally; if the time has gone and left nothing of value, then it has been lost for it may leave something detrimental, something which will prove a handicap in your race for success. Here again you must be fair with yourself and give yourself exactly the percentage to which you are entitled.

Next comes your Creative Power. If most persons whom you meet do what you want them to do; if they feel toward you as you wish them to feel; if they think what you want them to think, give yourself 100 per cent., because everything we get must come from others; there is no other channel by which success can reach us. This creative power must be unconsciously exercised, it must be your personality; if, however, you have to make a tremendous effort when you wish to accomplish something, if you have to exert will power, if you must fret and worry and stew over the result of an important interview, cut your percentage down to 50 per cent. or 40 per cent. or even less, because you do not understand the principle involved.

When you understand there will be no cause for anxiety; you will know, because in the first place you will never want or expect anyone to do anything except what is best for them; you will understand that every transaction must benefit both parties. When you understand these laws, when the principles become a vital part of your life, when they are involved in your mental attitude, you will have found the Master Key and all doors will be open to you, because you will understand that every event, every condition, every thing was first an idea, and that just to the extent that you grew quiet, and focused your attention on that idea, stilling all the activities of the mind, and eliminating all other thoughts from your consciousness, will the various phases and possibilities of the idea develop; and just in accordance with the definiteness with which you picture that idea, and the extent with which the idea takes possession of you will the creative power do its work, and the creative power will eventually take control and direct every activity of both mind and body and will begin to shape every condition related to the idea, so that sooner or later the idea will come forth in definite tangible form. If you understand this thoroughly, and have demonstrated it time and time again, so that you can mould and shape and determine conditions, I say again, give yourself 100 per cent.

Next comes Concentration. Can you concentrate? Do you know what it means to concentrate? Can you direct the thought to any problem which may arise, for five minutes, ten minutes or fifteen minutes, to the absolute exclusion of everything else? Can you unravel, disintegrate, take the problem apart, see every phase of it, see the cause which brought it about, see the solution, see it definitely, conclusively, and finally and know that your solution is correct? Can you then dismiss the matter and turn your attention to something else without ever recurring to the matter again? If you can do this, give yourself 100 per cent. If, however, you are haunted by fears, troubles, anxieties. If, when you have no problem to solve, you make one for yourself, by drawing on your imagination; if you are afraid of what this one says, or the other one thinks, or someone else does, then cut down your percentage, because if you knew how to concentrate you would not be afraid of anyone or anything; you would be in possession of a power which would make every other known power sink into insignificance. Be careful to give yourself exactly the percentage to which you feel you are entitled.

Now strike an average. See where you stand. If you are a little above the average, your chart will be something like this:

Mental Product	50%
Health	80%
Time Efficiency	80%
Creative Power	50%
Concentration	10%
	270%
Divide by 5—Average	54%

Assuming that you are earning £1,000 a year and that you feel that your mental product should be worth £2,000 a year, which is the basis for your calculation, then any method which would assist you to increase your earning power to £2,000 a year would be worth £1,000 a year to you.

Again, any method which would bring you health, efficiency in your time, efficiency in your creative power, or increase your ability to concentrate, would be worth at least £1,000 a year. Many have found that the Master Key teaching does all of this and much more.

ADVICE

Remember—
> *Fully to understand grand and beautiful thought requires, perhaps, as much time as to conceive it.*

> JOUBERT

If you wish to enjoy the utmost practical benefit form "The Master Key"— go slowly.

Transfuse into your mind the contents of one part only, each week for twenty-four weeks.

Realize the meaning of every phrase.

Consult "The Master Key" constantly, as your perpetual help and stimulus.

Each time you read the work you will get a better understanding of the eternal cosmic principles.

Tell others of "The Master Key" so that more and more people may reciprocate with you, as conscious adepts in harmony.

PART ONE

Tells upon what possession is based, explains the cause of all gain, explains the cause of loss as well as all other experiences in life. It explains how power is secured. It tells of a world within and how this world is governed. It explains how the solution for every problem in life may be found. It tells how practical men and women find the courage, power, hope, enthusiasm and confidence by which they are given the intelligence and wisdom to make their dreams come true. It tells how more efficiency is obtained and retained and how our future may be placed under our own control instead of being at the mercy of any capricious or uncertain external power. It explains the cause of every condition, the reason for every experience, the origin of all power, and why all power is absolutely under our own control.

Would you bring into your life more power? Get the power consciousness. More health? Get the health consciousness. More happiness? Get the happiness consciousness. Live the spirit of these things until they become yours by right. It will then become impossible to keep them from you. The things of the world are fluid to a power within man by which he rules them.

You need not acquire this power. You already have it. But you want to understand it; you want to use it; you want to control it; you want to impregnate yourself with it, so that you can go forward and carry the world before you.

Day by day, as you go on and on, as you gain momentum, as your inspiration deepens, as your plans crystallize, as you gain understanding, you will come to realize that this world is no dead pile of stones and timber, but that it is a living thing. It is made up of the beating hearts of humanity. It is a thing of life and beauty.

It is evident that it requires understanding to work with material of this description, but those who come into this understanding are inspired by a new light, a new force, they gain confidence and greater power each day, they realize their hopes and their dreams come true, life has a deeper, fuller, clearer meaning than before.

✻

1. That much gathers more is true on every plane of existence, and that loss leads to greater loss is equally true.

2. Mind is creative, and conditions, environmental and all experiences in life are the result of our habitual or predominant mental attitude.

3. The attitude of mind necessarily depends upon what we think. Therefore, the secret of all power, all achievement and all possession depends upon our method of thinking.

4. This is true because we must "be" before we can "do," and we can "do" only to the extent that we "are" and what we "are" depends upon what we "think."

5. We cannot express powers that we do not possess. The only way by which we may secure possession of power is to become conscious of power, and we can never become conscious of power until we learn that all power is from within.

6. There is a world within—a world of thought and feeling and power; of light and life and beauty and, although invisible, its forces are mighty.

7. The world within is governed by mind. When we discover this world we shall find the solution for every problem, the cause for every effect; and since the world within is subject to our control, all laws, of power and possession are also within our control.

8. The world without is a reflection of the world within. What appears without is what has been found within. In the world within may be found infinite Wisdom, infinite Power, infinite Supply of all that is necessary, waiting for unfoldment, development and expression. If we recognize these potentialities in the world within they will take form within the world without.

9. Harmony in the world within will be reflected in the world without by harmonious conditions, agreeable surroundings, the best of everything. It is the foundation of health, and a necessary essential to all greatness, all power, all attainment, all achievement and all success.

10. Harmony in the world within means the ability to control our thoughts, and to determine for ourselves how any experience is to affect us.

11. Harmony in the world within results in optimism and affluence; affluence within results in affluence without.

12. The world without reflects the circumstances and the conditions of the consciousness within.

13. If we find wisdom in the world within, we shall have the understanding to discern the marvellous possibilities that are latent in this world within, and we shall be given the power to make these possibilities manifest in the world without.

14. As we become conscious of the wisdom ill the world within we mentally take possession of this wisdom, and by taking mental possession we come into actual possession of the power and wisdom necessary to bring into manifestation the essentials necessary for our most complete and harmonious development.

15. The world within is the practical world in which the men and women of power generate courage, hope, enthusiasm, confidence, trust and faith, by which they are given the fine intelligence to see the vision and the practical skill to make the vision real.

16. Life is an unfoldment, not accretion. What comes to us in the world without is what we already possess in the world within.

17. All possession is based on consciousness. All gain is the result of an accumulative consciousness. All loss is the result of a scattering consciousness.

18. Mental efficiency is contingent upon harmony; discord means confusion; therefore, he who would acquire power must be in harmony with Natural Law.

19. We are related to the world without by the objective mind. The brain is the organ of this mind, and the cerebrospinal system of nerves puts us in conscious communication with every part of the body. This system of nerves responds to every sensation of light, heat, odor, sound and taste.

20. When this mind thinks correctly, when it understands the truth, when the thoughts sent through the cerebro-spinal nervous system to the body are constructive, these sensations are pleasant, harmonious.

21. The result is that we build strength, vitality and all constructive forces into our body, but it is through this same objective mind that all distress, sickness, lack, limitation and every form of discord and inharmony is admitted to our lives. It is

therefore through the objective mind, by wrong thinking, that we are related to all destructive forces.

22. We are related to the world within by the subconscious mind. The solar plexus is the organ of this mind; the sympathetic system of nerves presides over all subjective sensations, such as joy, fear, love, emotion, respiration, imagination and all other subconscious phenomena. It is through the subconscious that we are connected with the Universal Mind and brought into relation with the Infinite constructive forces of the Universe.

23. It is the co-ordination of these two centres of our being, and the understanding of their functions, which is the great secret of life. With this knowledge we can bring the objective and subjective minds into conscious co-operation and thus co-ordinate the finite and the infinite. Our future is entirely within our own control. It is not at the mercy of any capricious or uncertain external power.

24. All agree that there is but one Principle or Consciousness pervading the entire Universe, occupying all space, and being essentially the same in kind at every point of its presence. It is all powerful, all wisdom and always present. All thoughts and things are within Itself. It is all in all.

25. There is but one consciousness in the universe able to think, and when it thinks its thoughts become objective things to it. As this Consciousness is omnipresent it must be present within every individual; each individual must be a manifestation of that Omnipotent, Omnisscient and Omnipresent Consciousness.

26. As there is only one Consciousness in the Universe that is able to think it necessarily follows that your consciousness is identical with the Universal Consciousness, or, in other words, all mind is one mind. There is no dodging this conclusion.

27. The consciousness that focuses in your brain cells is the same consciousness which focuses in the brain cells of every other individual. Each individual is but the individualization of the Universal, the Cosmic Mind.

28. The Universal Mind is static or potential energy; it simply is; it can manifest only through the individual, and the individual can manifest only through the Universal. They are one.

29. The ability of the individual to think is his ability to act on the Universal and bring it into manifestation. Human consciousness consists only in the ability of man to think. Walker says, " Mind in itself is believed to be a subtle form of static energy, from which arises the activities called 'thought' which is the dynamic phase of mind. Mind is static energy, thought is dynamic energy—the two phases of the same thing." Thought is therefore the vibratory force formed by converting static mind into dynamic mind.

30. As the sum of all attributes is contained in the Universal Mind, which is Omnipotent, Omniscient and Omnipresent, these attributes must be present at all times in their potential form in every individual. Therefore, when the individual thinks, the thought is compelled by its nature to embody itself in an objectivity or condition which will correspond with its origin.

31. Every thought is therefore a cause, and every condition an effect; for this reason it is absolutely essential that you control your thoughts so as to bring forth only desirable conditions.

32. All power is from within, and is absolutely under your control; it comes through exact knowledge and by the voluntary exercises of exact Principles.

33. It should be plain that when you acquire a thorough understanding of this law, and are able to control your thought processes, you can apply it to any condition; in other words, you will have come into conscious co-operation with omnipotent law, which is the fundamental basis of all things.

34. The Universal Mind is the life principle of every atom which is in existence; every atom is continually striving to manifest more life; all are intelligent, and all are seeking to carry out the purpose for which they were created.

35. A majority of mankind lives in the world without; few have found the world within, and yet it is the world within that makes the world without; it is therefore creative and everything which you find in your world without has been created by you in the world within.

36. The Master Key will bring you into a realization of power which will be yours when you understand this relation between the world without and the world within. The world within is the cause, the world without the effect; to change the effect you must change the cause.

37. You will at once see that this is a radically new and different idea; most men try to change effects by working with effects. They fail to see that this is simply changing one form of distress for another. To remove discord, we must remove the cause, and this cause can be found only in the world within.

38. All growth is from within. This is evident in all nature. Every plant, every animal, every human being is a living testimony to this great law, and the error of the ages is in looking for strength or power from without.

39. The world within is the Universal fountain of supply, and the world without is the outlet to the stream. Our ability to receive depends upon our recognition of this Universal Fountain, this Infinite Energy of which each individual is an outlet, and so is one with every other individual.

40. Recognition is a mental process, mental action is therefore the interaction of the individual upon the Universal Mind, and as the Universal Mind is the intelligence which pervades all space and animates all living things, this mental action and reaction is the law of causation, but the principle of causation does not obtain in the individual but in the Universal Mind. It is not an objective faculty but a subjective process, and the results are seen in an infinite variety of conditions and experiences.

41. In order to express life there must be mind; nothing can exist without mind. Everything which exists is some manifestation of this one basic substance from which and by which all things have been created and are continually being re-created.

42. We live in a fathomless sea of plastic mind substance. This substance is ever alive and active. It is sensitive to the highest degree. It takes form according to the mental demand. Thought forms the mould or matrix from which the substance expresses.

43. Remember that it is in the application alone that the value consists, and that a practical understanding of this law will substitute abundance for poverty, wisdom for ignorance, harmony for discord and freedom for tyranny, and certainly there can be no greater blessing than these from a material and social standpoint.

44. Now make the application; Select a room where you can be alone and undisturbed; sit erect, comfortably, but do not lounge; let your thoughts roam where they will but be perfectly still for from fifteen minutes to half an hour; continue this for three or four days or for a week until you secure full control of your physical being.

45. Many will find this extremely difficult; others will conquer with ease, but it is absolutely essential to secure complete control of the body before you are ready to progress. In Part Two you will receive instructions for the next step; till the meantime you must have mastered this one.

❋

1. *What is the world without in its relation to the world within?*
   The world without is a reflection of the world within.
2. *Upon what does all possession depend?*
   All possession is based on consciousness.
3. *How is the individual related to the objective world?*
   The individual is related to the objective world by the objective mind; the brain is the organ of this mind.
4. *How is he related to the Universal Mind?*
   He is related to the Universal Mind by the subconscious mind; the Solar Plexus is the organ of this mind.
5. *What is the Universal Mind?*
   The Universal Mind is the life principle of every atom which is in existence.
6. *How can the Individual act on the Universal?*
   The ability of the individual to think is his ability to act upon the Universal and bring it into manifestation.
7. *What is the result of this action and interaction?*
   The result of this action and inter-action is cause and effect; every thought is a cause, and every condition an effect.
8. *How are harmonious and desirable conditions secured?*
   Harmonious and desirable conditions are obtained by right thinking.

9. *What is the cause of all discord, inharmony, lack and limitation?*

   Discord, inharmony, lack and limitation are the result of wrong thinking.

10. *What is the source of all power?*

   The source of all power is the world within, the Universal Fountain of Supply, the Infinite Energy of which each individual is an outlet.

Those who have finished by making all others think with them have usually been those who began by daring to think for themselves.

                                                              —Colton.

PART TWO

Tells how and why the operations of the mind are carried on by two parallel modes of activity, the one conscious and the other subconscious. It explains why the thought processes of the subconscious are the theatre of the most important mental phenomena, why ease and perfection depend entirely upon the degree in which we cease to depend upon the consciousness. It explains the origin of all great, noble, brilliant thoughts and ideas, why we find ourselves sometimes endowed with tact, instinct, courage, sagacity and inspiration. In fact, it tells of a vast mental storehouse in which ninety per cent. of our thought processes originate; it explains also how this vast mental storehouse may be placed under the supervision and in the keeping of the conscious mind. It tells why those who are familiar with the laws governing in this larger mental domain are enabled to accomplish, to achieve, to become writers, authors, artists, ministers, captains of industry, and why all others must necessarily remain less than ten per cent. efficient.

Our difficulties are largely due to confused ideas and ignorance of our true interests. The great task is to discover the laws of Nature to which we are to adjust ourselves. Clear thinking and moral insight are therefore of in calculable value. All processes, even those of thought, rest on solid foundations.

The keener the sensibilities, the more acute the judgment, the more delicate the taste, the more refined the moral feelings, the more subtle the intelligence, the loftier the aspiration—the purer and more intense are the gratifications which existence yields. Hence it is that the study of the best that has been thought in the world gives supreme pleasure.

The powers, uses and possibilities of the mind under the new interpretations are incomparably more wonderful than the most extravagant accomplishment, or even dreams of material progress. Thought is energy. Active thought is active energy; concentrated thought is concentrated energy. Thought concentrated on a definite purpose becomes power. This is the power which is being used by those who do not believe in the virtue of poverty, or the beauty of self-denial. They perceive that this is the talk of weaklings.

The ability to receive and manifest this power depends upon the ability to recognize the Infinite Energy ever dwelling in man, constantly creating and re-creating his body and mind, and ready at any moment to manifest through him in any needful manner. In exact proportion to the recognition of this truth will be the manifestation in the outer life of the individual.

Part Two explains the method by which this is accomplished

✳

1. The operations of the mind are produced by two parallel modes of activity, the one conscious, and the other subconscious. Prof. Davidson Says: "He who thinks to illuminate the whole range of mental action by the light of his own consciousness is not unlike one who should go about to illuminate the universe with a rushlight."

2. The subconscious, logical processes are carried on with a certainty and regularity that would be impossible if there existed the possibility of error our mind is so designed that it prepares for as the most important foundations of cognition, whilst we have not the slightest apprehension of the *modus operandi*.

3. The subconscious soul, like a benevolent stranger, works and makes provision for our benefit, pouring only the mature fruit into our lap; thus ultimate analysis of thought processes shows that the subconscious is the theatre of the most important mental phenomena.

4. It is through the subconscious that Shakespeare must have perceived, without effort, great truths that are hidden from the conscious mind of the student; that Phidias fashioned marble and bronze; that Raphael painted Madonnas and Beethoven composed symphonies.

5. Ease and perfection depend entirely upon the degree in which we cease to depend upon the consciousness; playing the piano, skating, operating the typewriter, the skilled trades, depend for their perfect execution on the process of the subconscious mind. The marvel of playing a brilliant piece on the piano, while at the same time conducting a vigorous conversation, shows the greatness of our subconscious powers.

6. We are all aware how dependent we are upon the subconscious, and the greater, the nobler, the more brilliant our thoughts are, the more it is obvious to ourselves that the origin lies beyond our ken. We find ourselves endowed with tact, instinct, sense of the beautiful in art, music, etc., of whose origin or dwelling place we are wholly unconscious.

7. The value of the subconscious is enormous; it inspires us; it warns us; it furnishes us with names, facts and scenes from the storehouse of memory. It directs our thoughts, tastes, and accomplishes tasks so intricate that no conscious mind, even if it had the power, has the capacity for.

8. We can walk at will; we can raise the arm whenever we choose to do so; we can give our attention through eye or ear to any subject at pleasure. On the other hand, we cannot stop our heartbeats nor the circulation of the blood, nor the growth of stature, nor the formation of nerve and muscle tissue, nor the building of the bones, nor many other important vital processes.

9. If we compare these two sets of action, the one decreed by the will of the moment, and the other proceeding in majestic, rhythmic course, subject to no vacillation, but constant at every moment, we stand in awe of the latter, and ask to have the mystery explained. We see at once that these are the vital processes of our physical life, and we cannot avoid the inference that these all-important functions are designedly withdrawn from the domain of our outward will with its variations and transitions, and placed under the direction of a permanent and dependable power within us.

10. Of these two powers, the outward and changeable has been termed the "Conscious Mind," or the "Objective Mind" (dealing with outward objects). The interior power is called the "Subconscious Mind," or the "Subjective Mind," and besides its work on the mental plane it controls the regular functions that make physical life possible.

11. It is necessary to have a clear understanding of their respective functions on the mental plane, as well as of certain other basic principles. Perceiving and operating through the five physical senses, the conscious mind deals with the impressions and objects of the outward life.

12. It has the faculty of discrimination, carrying with it the responsibility of choice. It has the power of reasoning whether inductive, deductive, analytical or

syllogistic, and this power may be developed to a high degree. It is the seat of the will, with all the energies that flow therefrom.

13. Not only can it impress other minds, but it can direct the subconscious mind. In this way the conscious mind becomes the responsible ruler and guardian of the subconscious mind. It is this high function that can completely reverse conditions in your life.

14. It is often true that conditions of fear, worry, poverty, disease, disharmony and evils of all kinds dominate us by reason of false suggestions accepted by the unguarded subconscious mind. All this the trained conscious mind can entirely prevent by its vigilant protective action. It may properly be called "the watchman at the gate" of the great subconscious domain.

15. One writer has expressed the chief distinction between the two phases of mind thus:

"Conscious mind is reasoning will. Subconscious mind is instinctive desire, the result of past reasoning will."

16. The subconscious mind draws just and accurate inferences from premises furnished from outside sources. Where the premise is true, the subconscious mind reaches a faultless conclusion, but where the premise or suggestion is an error the whole structure falls. The subconscious mind does not engage in the process of proving. It relies upon the conscious mind, "the watchman at the gate," to guard it from mistaken impressions.

17. Receiving any suggestions as true, the subconscious mind at once proceeds to act thereon in the whole domain of its tremendous field of work. The conscious mind can suggest either truth or error. If the latter, it is at the cost of wide-reaching peril to the whole being.

18. The conscious mind ought to be on duty during every waking hour. When the "watchman" is "off guard," or when its calm judgment is suspended, under a variety of circumstances, then the subconscious mind is unguarded and left open to suggestion from all sources. During the wild excitement of panic, or during the height of anger, or the impulses of the irresponsible mob, or at any other time of unrestrained passion, the conditions are most dangerous. The subconscious mind is then open to the suggestion of fear, hatred, selfishness, greed, self-depreciation and other negative forces, derived from surrounding persons or circumstances. The result is usually unwholesome in the extreme, with effects that may endure to distress it for a long time. Hence the great importance of guarding the subconscious mind from false impressions.

19. The subconscious mind perceives by intuition. Hence its processes are rapid. It does not wait for the slow methods of conscious reasoning. In fact, it cannot employ them.

20. The subconscious mind never sleeps, never rests, any more than does your heart, or your blood. It has been found that by plainly stating to the subconscious mind certain specific things to be accomplished, forces are set in operation that lead to the result desired. Here, then, is a source of power that places us in

290 THE SECRET TO GETTING RICH TRILOGY

touch with Omnipotence. Herein is a deep principle that is well worth our most earnest study.

21. The operation of this law is interesting. Those who put it into operation find that when they go out to meet the person with whom they anticipate a difficult interview, lo! something has been there before them and dissolved the supposed differences; everything is changed ; all is harmonious; they find that when some difficult business problem presents itself they can afford to make delay and something suggests the proper solution; everything is properly arranged; in fact, those who have learned to trust the subconscious find that they have infinite resources at their command.

22. The subconscious mind is the seat of our principles and our aspirations. It is the fount of our artistic and altruistic ideals. These instincts can only be overthrown by an elaborate and gradual process of undermining the innate principles.

23. The subconscious mind cannot argue controversially. Hence, if it has accepted wrong suggestions, the sure method of over coming them is by the use of a strong counter suggestion, frequently repeated, which the mind must accept, thus eventually forming new and healthy habits of thought and life, for the subconscious mind is the seat of Habit. That which we do over and over becomes mechanical; it is no longer an act of judgment, but has worn its deep grooves in the subconscious mind. This is favorable for us if the habit is wholesome and right. If it is harmful and wrong, the remedy is to recognize the omnipotence of the subconscious mind and suggest present actual freedom. The subconscious being creative and one with our divine source will at once create the freedom suggested.

24. To sum up: The normal functions of the subconscious on the physical side have to do with the regular and vital processes, with the preservation of life and the restoration of health; with the care of offspring, which includes an instinctive desire to preserve all life and improve conditions generally.

25. On the mental side, it is the storehouse of memory; it harbors the wonderful thought messengers, who work, unhampered by time or space; it is the fountain of the practical initiative and constructive forces of life: It is the seat of habit.

26. On the spiritual side, it is the source of ideals, of aspiration, of the imagination, and is the channel through which we recognize our Divine Source, and in proportion as we recognize this divinity do we come into an understanding of the source of power.

27. Someone may ask: "How can the subconscious change conditions?" The reply is, because the subconscious is a part of the Universal Mind and a part must be the same in kind and quality as the whole; the only difference is one of degree. The whole, as we know, is creative; in fact, it is the only creator there is; consequently we find that mind is creative, and as thought is the only activity which the mind possesses thought must necessarily be creative also.

28. But we shall find that there is a vast difference between simply thinking and directing our thought consciously, systematically and constructively; when we

do this we place our mind in harmony with the Universal Mind, we come in tune with the Infinite, we set in operation the mightiest force in existence, the creative power of the Universal Mind. This, as everything else, is governed by natural law, and this law is the "Law of Attraction," which is that Mind is creative, and will automatically correlate with its object and bring it into manifestation.

29. In Part One I gave you an exercise for the purpose of securing control of the physical body; if you have accomplished this you are ready to advance. This time you will begin to control your thought. Always take the same room, the same chair, and the same position, if possible. In some cases it is not convenient to take the same room: in this case simply make the best use of such conditions as may be available. Now be perfectly still as before, but inhibit all thought; this will give you control over all thoughts of care, worry and fear, and will enable you to entertain only the kind of thoughts you desire. Continue this exercise until you gain complete mastery.

30. You will not be able to do this for more than a few moments at a time, but the exercise is valuable, because it will be a very practical demonstration of the great number of thoughts that are constantly trying to gain access to your mental world.

31. In Part Three, you will receive instructions for an exercise that may be a little more interesting, but it is necessary that you master this one first.

*

11. *What are the two modes of mental activity?*
   Conscious and subconscious.
12. *Upon what do ease and perfection depend?*
   Ease and perfection depend entirely upon the degree in which we cease to depend upon the conscious mind.
13. *What is the value of the subconscious?*
   It is enormous; it guides us, warns us, it controls the vital processes and is the seat of memory.
14. *What are some of the functions of the conscious mind?*
   It has the faculty of discrimination; it has the power of reasoning; it is the seat of the will and may impress the subconscious.
15. *How has the distinction between the conscious and subconscious been expressed?*
   "Conscious mind is reasoning will. Subconscious mind is instinctive desire, the result of past reasoning will."
16. *What method is necessary in order to impress the subconscious?*
   Mentally state what is wanted.
17. *What will be the result?*
   If the desire is in harmony with the forward movement of the great Whole, forces will be set in motion that will bring about the result.

18. *What is the result of the operation of this law?*
    Our environment reflects conditions corresponding to the predominant mental attitude which we entertain.
19. *What name has been given to this law?*
    The Law of Attraction.
20. *How is the law stated ?*
    Thought is a creative energy, and will automatically correlate with its object and bring it into manifestation.

Cause and effect is as absolute and undeviating in the hidden realm of thought as in the world of visible and material things.
Mind is the master weaver, both of the interior garment of character and the outer garment of circumstance.

–James Allen.

ADVICE

Remember—
Fully to understand grand and beautiful thought requires, perhaps, as much time as to conceive it.

JOUBERT

If you wish to enjoy the utmost practical benefit form "The Master Key"—go slowly.

Transfuse into your mind the contents of one part only, each week for twenty-four weeks.

Realize the meaning of every phrase.

Consult "The Master Key" constantly, as your perpetual help and stimulus.

Each time you read the work you will get a better understanding of the eternal cosmic principles.

Tell others of "The Master Key" so that more and more people may reciprocate with you, as conscious adepts in harmony.

PART THREE

Tells why the necessary action and interaction of the conscious and subconscious minds requires two corresponding systems of nerves. It explains how the connection is made between these two systems of nerves. It explains and tells of a central point in the body for the distribution of energy. How this energy is distributed. How the distribution of this energy gives the individual pleasant sensations, how the interruption of this distribution brings discord, disharmony and lack and limitation of every kind. It tells of an arch enemy which must be destroyed, and tells how to destroy it. It tells what determines the experiences in life with which we are to meet, and why these experiences are under our own control. One enthusiastic reader says of this Part: "This document in my opinion is the greatest single document beneficial to mankind ever written in the history of the world; it is the first time that I have come into a true understanding of the Silent Powers that dominate and determine one's success."

You have found that the Individual may act on the Universal, and that the result of this action and interaction is cause and effect.

Thought, therefore, is the cause, and the experiences with which you meet in life are the effect.

Eliminate, therefore, any possible tendency to complain of conditions as they have been, or as they are, because it rests with you to change them and make them what you would like them to be.

Direct your efforts to a realization of the mental resources, always at your command, from which all real and lasting power comes.

Persist in this practice till you come to a realization of the fact that there can be no failure in the accomplishment of any proper object in life if you but understand your power and persist in your object, because the mind forces are ever ready to lend themselves to a purposeful will in the effort to crystallize thought and desire into actions, events and conditions.

Whereas in the beginning each function of life and each action is the result of conscious thought, the habitual actions become automatic and the thought that controls them passes into the realm of the subconscious; yet it is just as intelligent as before. It is necessary that it become automatic or subconscious in order that the self-conscious mind may attend to other things. The new actions will, however, in their turn, become habitual, then automatic, then subconscious in order that the mind again may be freed from this detail and advanced to still other activities.

When you realize this, you will have found a source of power that will enable you to cope with any situation in life that may develop.

＊

1. The necessary interaction of the conscious and subconscious mind requires a similar interaction between the corresponding systems of nerves. Judge Troward indicates the very beautiful method in which this interaction is effected. He says: The cerebro-spinal system is the organ of the conscious mind, and the sympathetic is the organ of the subconscious. The cerebro-spinal is the channel through which we receive conscious perception from the physical senses, and exercise control over the movements of the body. This system of nerves has its centre in the brain.

2. The Sympathetic System has its centre in a ganglionic mass at the back of the stomach known as the Solar Plexus, and is the channel of that mental action which unconsciously supports the vital functions of the body.

3. The connection between the two systems is made by the vagus nerve, which passes out of the cerebral region as a portion of the voluntary system to the thorax, sending out branches to the heart and lungs, and finally passing through the

diaphragm it loses its outer coating and becomes identified with the nerves of the Sympathetic System, so forming a connecting link between the two and making man physically a single entity.

4. We have seen that every thought is received by the brain, which is the organ of the conscious; it is here subjected to our power of reasoning. When the objective mind has been satisfied that the thought is true it is sent to the Solar Plexus, or the brain of the subjective mind, to be made into our flesh, to be brought into the world as a reality. It is then no longer susceptible to any argument whatever. The subconscious mind cannot argue; it only acts. It accepts the conclusions of the objective mind as final.

5. The Solar Plexus has been likened to the sun of the body, because it is a central point of distribution for the energy that the body is constantly generating. This energy is very real energy, and this sun is a very real sun, and the energy is being distributed by very real nerves to all parts of the body, and is thrown off in an atmosphere that envelops the body.

6. If this radiation is sufficiently strong the person is called magnetic; he is said to be filled with personal magnetism. Such a person may wield an immense power for good. His presence alone will often bring comfort to the troubled minds with which he comes in contact.

7. When the Solar Plexus is in active operation and is radiating life, energy and vitality to every part of the body, and to everyone whom he meets, the sensations are pleasant, the body is filled with health and all with whom he comes in contact experience a pleasant sensation.

8. If there is any interruption of this radiation the sensations are unpleasant, the flow of life and energy to some part of the body is stopped, and this is the cause of every ill to the human race, physical, mental or environmental.

9. Physical because the sun of the body is no longer generating sufficient energy to vitalize some part of the body; mental because the conscious mind is dependent upon the subconscious mind for the vitality necessary to support its thought, and environmental because the connection between the subconscious mind and the Universal mind is being interrupted.

10. The Solar Plexus is the point at which the part meets with the whole, where the finite becomes Infinite, where the Uncreate becomes create, the Universal becomes individualized, the Invisible becomes visible. It is the point at which life appears, and there is no limit to the amount of life an individual may generate from this Solar centre.

11. This centre of energy is Omnipotent because it is the point of contact with all life and all intelligence. It can therefore accomplish whatever it is directed to accomplish, and herein lies the power of the conscious mind; the subconscious can and will carry out such plans and ideas as may be suggested to it by the conscious mind.

12. Conscious thought, then, is master of this sun centre from which the life and energy of the entire body flows, and the quality of the thought which we enter-

tain determines the quality of the thought which this sun will radiate, and the character of the thought which our conscious mind entertains will determine the character of the thought which this sun will radiate, and the nature of the thought which our conscious mind entertains will determine the nature of thought which this sun will radiate, and consequently will determine the nature of the experience which will result.

13. It is evident, therefore, that all we have to do is let our light shine; the more energy we can radiate, the more rapidly shall we be enabled to transmute undesirable conditions into sources of pleasure and profit. The important question, then, is how to let this light shine; how to generate this energy.

14. Non-resistant thought expands the Solar Plexus; resistant thought contracts it. Pleasant thought expands it; unpleasant thought contracts it. Thoughts of courage, power, confidence and hope all produce a corresponding state, but the one arch enemy of the Solar Plexus which must be absolutely destroyed before there is any possibility of letting any light shine is fear. This enemy must be completely destroyed; he must be eliminated; he must be expelled forever; he is the cloud which hides the sun; which causes a perpetual gloom.

15. It is this personal devil which makes men fear the past, the present and the future; fear themselves, their friends and their enemies; fear everything and everybody. When fear is effectually and completely destroyed, your light will shine, the clouds will disperse and you will have found the source of power, energy and life.

16. When you find that you are really one with the Infinite power, and when you can consciously realize this power by a practical demonstration of your ability to overcome any adverse condition by the power of your thought, you will have nothing to fear; fear will have been destroyed and you will have come into possession of your birthright.

17. It is our attitude of mind towards life that determines the experiences with which we are to meet; if we expect nothing we shall have nothing; if we demand much we shall receive the greater portion. The world is harsh only as we fail to assert ourselves. The criticism of the world is bitter only to those who cannot compel room for their ideas. It is fear of this criticism that causes many ideas to fail to see the light of day.

18. But the man who knows that he has a Solar Plexus will not fear criticism or anything else; he will be too busy radiating courage, confidence, and power; he will anticipate success by his mental attitude; he will pound barriers to pieces and leap over the chasm of doubt and hesitation which fear places in his path.

19. A knowledge of our ability to consciously radiate health, strength and harmony will bring us into a realization that there is nothing to fear because we are in touch with Infinite Strength.

20. This knowledge can be gained only by making a practical application of this information. We learn by doing; through practice the athlete becomes powerful.

21. As the following statement is of considerable importance, I will put it in several ways, so that you cannot fail to get the full significance of it. If you are reli-

giously inclined, I would say, you can let your light shine. If your mind has a bias towards physical science, I would say you can wake the Solar Plexus; or, if you prefer the strictly scientific interpretation, I will say that you can impress your subconscious mind.

22. I have already told you what the result of this impression will be. It is the method in which you are now interested. You have already learned that the subconscious is intelligent and that it is creative, and responsive to the will of the conscious mind. What, then, is the most natural way of making the desired impression? Mentally, concentrate on the object of your desire; when you are concentrating you are impressing the subconscious.

23. This is not the only way, but it is a simple and effective way, and the most direct way, and consequently the way in which the best results are secured. It is the method which is producing such extraordinary results that many think that miracles are being accomplished.

24. It is the method by which every great inventor, every great financier, every great statesman has been enabled to convert the subtle and invisible force of desire, faith and confidence into actual, tangible, concrete facts in the objective world.

25. The subconscious mind is a part of the Universal mind. The Universal is the creative principle of the Universe, a part must be the same in kind and quality as the whole. This means that this creative power is absolutely unlimited; it is not bound by precedent of any kind, and consequently has no prior existing pattern by which to apply its constructive principle.

26. We have found that the subconscious mind is responsive to our conscious will, which means that the unlimited creative power of the Universal Mind is within the control of the conscious mind of the individual.

27. When making a practical application of this principle, in accordance with the exercises given in subsequent Parts, it is well to remember that it is not necessary to outline the method by which the subconscious will produce the results you desire. The finite cannot inform the Infinite. You are simply to say what you desire, not how you are to obtain it.

28. You are the channel by which the undifferentiated is being differentiated, and this differentiation is being accomplished by appropriation. It only requires recognition to set causes in motion which will bring about results in accordance with your desire, and this is accomplished because the Universal can act only through the individual, and the individual can act only through the Universal; they are one.

29. For your next exercise I will ask you to go one step further. I want you to not only be perfectly still, and inhibit all thought as far as possible, but relax, let go, let the muscles take their normal condition; this will remove all pressure from the nerves and eliminate that tension which so frequently produces physical exhaustion.

30. Physical relaxation is a voluntary exercise of the will and the exercise will be found to be of great value, as it enables the blood to circulate freely to and from the brain and body.

31. Tension leads to mental unrest and abnormal mental activity of the mind; it produces worry, care, fear and anxiety. Relaxation is therefore an absolute necessity in order to allow the mental faculties to exercise the greatest freedom.

32. Make this exercise as thorough and complete as possible, mentally determine that you will relax every muscle and nerve, until you feel quiet and restful and at peace with yourself and the world.

33. The Solar Plexus will then be ready to function and you will be surprised at the result.

We judge of a man's wisdom by his hope, knowing that the perception of the inexhaustibleness of Nature is an immortal youth.

—Emerson.

❋

21. *What system of nerves is the organ of The Conscious Mind?*
    The Cerebro-spinal.
22. *What system of nerves is the organ of the subconscious mind?*
    The sympathetic.
23. *What is the central point of distribution for the energy that the body is constantly generating?*
    The solar plexus.
24. *How may this distribution be interrupted?*
    By resistant, critical or discordant thoughts, but especially by fear.
25. *What is the result of such interruption?*
    Every ill with which the human race is afflicted.
26. *How may this energy be controlled and directed?*
    By conscious thought.
27. *How may fear be completely eliminated?*
    By an understanding and recognition of the true source of all power.
28. *What determines the experiences with which we meet in life?*
    Our predominant mental attitude.
29. *How may we awake the solar plexus?*
    Mentally concentrate upon the condition that we desire to see manifested in our lives.
30. *What is the creative principle of the Universe?*
    The Universal Mind.

Mind in itself is believed to be a subtle form of static energy, from which arises the activities called "thought," which is the dynamic phase of mind. Mind is static energy, thought is dynamic energy—the two phases of the same thing.

—Walker.

PART FOUR

This Part tells what it is which controls that which you call yourself. "You" are not your body; the body is simply the physical instrument that the ego uses to carry out its purpose. "You" are not your mind; this is simply another instrument that the ego uses to think, reason and plan. When you say "'I' go" you tell the body where to go, when you say "'I' think" you tell the mind what to think. When you come into a realization of the true nature of the "I" you will enjoy a sense of power that nothing else can give, because you will come to know what you are, who you are, what you want, and how to get it.

This Part will show you why what you think, or do, or feel, is an indication of what you are.

Thought is energy, and energy is power, and it is because all the religions, sciences and philosophies with which the world has heretofore been familiar have been based upon the manifestation of this energy instead of the energy itself, that the world has been limited to effects, while causes have been ignored or misunderstood.

For this reason we have God and the Devil in religion, positive and negative in science, and good and bad in philosophy.

The Master Key reverses the process; it is interested only in cause, and the letters received from readers tell a marvellous story; they indicate conclusively that adepts are finding the cause whereby they may secure for themselves health, harmony, abundance, and whatever else may be necessary for their welfare and happiness.

Life is expressive and it is our business to express ourselves harmoniously and constructively. Sorrow, misery, unhappiness, disease and poverty are not necessities and we are constantly eliminating them.

But this process of eliminating consists in rising above and beyond limitation of any kind. He who has strengthened and purified his thought need not concern himself about microbes, and he who has come into an understanding of the law of abundance will go at once to the source of supply.

It is thus that fate, fortune and destiny will be controlled as readily as a captain controls his ship, or an engineer his train.

❋

1. The "I" of you is not the physical body; that is simply an instrument which the "I" uses to carry out its purposes; the "I" cannot be the Mind, for the mind is simply another instrument which the "I" uses with which to think, reason, and plan.

2. The "I" must be something that controls and directs both the body and the mind; something that determines what they shall do and how they shall act. When you come into a realization of the true nature of this "I" you will enjoy a sense of power that you have never before known.

3. Your personality is made up of countless individual characteristics, peculiarities, habits and traits of character; these are the result of your former method of thinking, but they have nothing to do with the real "I."

4. When you say "I think," the "I" tells the mind what it shall think; when you say "I go," the "I" tells the physical body where it shall go; the real nature of this "I" is spiritual, and is the source of the real power which comes to men and women when they come into a realization of their true nature.

5. The greatest and most marvellous power which this "I" has been given is the power to think, but few people know how to think constructively, or correctly, consequently they achieve only indifferent results. Most people allow their thoughts to dwell on selfish purposes, the inevitable result of an infantile mind. When a mind becomes mature, it understands that the germ of defeat is in every selfish thought.

6. The trained mind knows that every transaction must benefit every person who is in any way connected with the transaction, and any attempt to profit by the weakness, ignorance or necessity of another will inevitably operate to his disadvantage.

7. This is because the individual is a part of the Universal. A part cannot antagonize any other part, but, on the contrary, the welfare of each part depends upon a recognition of the interests of the whole.

8. Those who recognize this principle have a great advantage in the affairs of life. They do not wear themselves out. They can eliminate vagrant thoughts with facility. They can readily concentrate to the highest possible degree on any subject. They do not waste time or money upon objects that can be of no possible benefit to them.

9. If you cannot do these things it is because you have thus far not made the necessary effort. Now is the time to make the effort. The result will be exactly in proportion to the effort expended. One of the strongest affirmations that you can use for the purpose of strengthening the will and realizing your power to accomplish is, "I can be what I will to be."

10. Every time you repeat it realize who and what this "I" is; try to come into a thorough understanding of the true nature of the "I"; if you do you will become invincible; that is, provided that your objects and purposes are constructive and are therefore in harmony with the creative principle of the Universe.

11. If you make use of this affirmation, use it continuously, night and morning, and as often during the day as you think of it, and continue to do so until it becomes a part of you; form the habit.

12. Unless you do this, you had better not start at all, because modern Psychology tells us that when we start something and do not complete it, or make a resolution and do not keep it, we are forming the habit of failure; absolute, ignominious failure. If you do not intend to do a thing, do not start; if you do start, see it through even if the heavens fall; if you make up your mind to do something, do it; let nothing, no one interfere; the "I" in you has determined, the thing is settled; the die is cast, there is no longer any argument.

13. If you carry out this idea, beginning with small things which you know you can control and gradually increase the effort, but never under any circumstances allowing your "I" to be overruled, you will find that you can eventually control yourself, and many men and women have found to their sorrow that it is easier to control a kingdom than to control themselves.

14. But when you have learned to control yourself you will have found the "World Within" which controls the world without; you will have become irre-

sistible; men and things will respond to your every wish without any apparent effort on your part.

15. This is not so strange or impossible as it may appear when you ember that the "World Within" is controlled by the "I" and that this "I" is a part or one with the Infinite "I" which is the Universal Energy or Spirit, usually called God.

16. This is not a mere statement or theory made for the purpose of confirming or establishing an idea, but it is a fact which has been accepted by the best religious thought as well as the best scientific thought.

17. Herbert Spencer says: "Amid all the mysteries by which we are surrounded, nothing is more certain that that we are ever in the presence of an infinite and Eternal Energy from which all things proceed."

18. Lyman Abbott, in an address delivered before the Alumni of Bangor Theological Seminary, said: "We are coming to think of God as dwelling *in* man rather than as operating on men from without."

19. Science goes a little way in its search and stops. Science finds the ever-present Eternal Energy, but Religion finds the Power behind this energy and locates it within man. But this is by no means a new discovery; the Bible says exactly the same thing, and the language is just as plain and convincing: "Know ye not that ye are the temple of the living God?" Here, then, is the secret of the wonderful creative power of the " World Within."

20. Here is the secret of power, of mastery. To overcome does not mean to go without things. Self-denial is not success. We cannot give unless we get; we cannot be helpful unless we are strong. The Infinite is not a bankrupt and we who are the representatives of Infinite power should not be bankrupts either, and if we wish to be of service to others we must have power and more power, but to get it we must give it; we must be of service.

21. The more we give the more we shall get; we must become a channel whereby the Universal can express activity. The Universal is constantly seeking to express itself, to be of service, and it seeks the channel whereby it can find the greatest activity, where it can do the most good, where it can be of greatest service to mankind.

22. The Universal cannot express through you as long as you are busy with your plans, your own purposes; quiet the senses, seek inspiration, focus the mental activity on the within, dwell in the consciousness of your unity with Omnipotence. "Still water runs deep"; contemplate the multitudinous opportunities to which you have spiritual access by the Omnipresence of power.

23. Visualize the events, circumstances and conditions that these spiritual connections may assist in manifesting. Realize the fact that the essence and soul of all things is spiritual and that the spiritual is the real, because it is the life of all there is; when the spirit is gone, the life is gone; it is dead; it has ceased to exist.

24. These mental activities pertain to the world within, to the world of cause; and conditions and circumstances that result are the effect. It is thus that you

become a creator. This is important work, and the higher, loftier, grander and more noble ideals which you can conceive, the more important the work will become.

25. Overwork or overplay or overbodily activity of any kind produces conditions of mental apathy and stagnation which makes it impossible to do the more important work which results in a realization of conscious power. We should, therefore, seek the Silence frequently. Power comes through repose; it is in the Silence that we can be still, and when we are still we can think, and thought is the secret of all attainment.

26. Thought is a mode of motion and is carried by the law of vibration the same as light or electricity. It is given vitality by the emotions through the law of love; it takes form and expression by the law of growth; it is a product of the spiritual "I" hence its Divine, spiritual, and creative nature.

27. From this it is evident that in order to express power, abundance or any other constructive purpose, the emotions must be called upon to give feeling to the thought so that it will take form. How may this purpose be accomplished? This is the vital point; how may we develop the faith, the courage, the feeling, which will result in accomplishment?

28. The reply is, by exercise; mental strength is secured in exactly the same way that physical strength is secured, by exercise. We think something, perhaps with difficulty the first time; we think the same thing again, and it becomes easier this time; we think it again and again; it then becomes a mental habit. We continue to think the same thing; finally it becomes automatic; we can no longer help thinking this thing; we are now positive of what we think; there is no longer any doubt about it. We are sure; we know.

29. In Part Three I asked you to relax, to let go physically. Now I am going to ask you to let go mentally. If you practised the previous exercise fifteen or twenty minutes a day in accordance with the instructions, you can no doubt relax physically; and anyone who cannot consciously do this quickly and completely is not a master of himself. He has not obtained freedom; he is still a slave to conditions. But I shall assume that you have mastered the exercise and are ready to take the next step, which is mental freedom.

30. Now after taking your usual position, remove all tension by completely relaxing, then mentally let go of all adverse conditions, such as hatred, anger, worry, jealousy, envy, sorrow, trouble or disappointment of any kind.

31. You may say that you cannot "let go" of these things, but you can; you can do so by mentally determining to do so, by voluntary intention and persistence.

32. The reason that some cannot do this is because they allow themselves to be controlled by the emotions instead of by their intellect. But the will guided by the intellect will gain the victory. You will not succeed the first time you try, but practice makes perfect, in this as in everything else, and you must succeed in dismissing, eliminating and completely destroying these negative and destructive thoughts; because they are the seed that is constantly germinating into discordant conditions of every conceivable kind and description.

There is nothing truer than that the quality of thought that we entertain correlates certain externals in the outside world. This is the Law from which there is no escape. And it is this Law, this correlative of the thought with its object, that from time immemorial has led the people to believe in special providence.

—Wilmans.

PART FIVE

This Part tells how the subconscious processes are continually at work, and it tells how we may consciously direct this work instead of being mere passive recipients of its activity. It tells how we may have a vision of the destination to be reached the dangers and pitfalls to be avoided. It tells how "the word has become flesh," how we are constantly creating and recreating ourselves. It tells of a mental home which each of us is building for ourselves, the importance of this home where the material is secured the character of the furnishing, how and why many of us need a mental house-cleaning in case we wish to realize our ideas. It tells of the conditions by which we may come into an inheritance of health, harmony and prosperity, and the condition is one that demands no sacrifice except the loss of our limitations, our servitudes and our weaknesses, and costs only the labour of harvesting its great resources.

After studying this Part carefully, you will see that every conceivable force or object or fact is the result of mind in action.

Mind in action is thought, and thought is creative. Men are thinking now as they never thought before. Therefore, this is a creative age, and the world is awarding its richest prizes to the thinkers.

Matter is powerless, passive, inert. Mind is force, energy power. Mind shapes and controls matter. Every form which matter takes is but the expression of some pre-existing thought.

But thought works no magic transformations; it obeys natural laws; it sets in motion natural forces; it releases natural energies; it manifests in your conduct and actions, and these in turn react upon your friends and acquaintances, and eventually upon the whole of your environment.

You can originate thought, and, since thoughts are creative, you can create for yourselves the things you desire.

❋

1. At least ninety per cent. of our mental life is subconscious, so that those who fail to make use of this mental power live within very narrow limits.

2. The subconscious can and will solve any problem for us if we know how to direct it. The subconscious processes are always at work; the only question is, are we to be simply passive recipients of this activity, or are we to consciously direct the work? Shall we have a vision of the destination to be reached, the dangers to be avoided, or shall we simply drift?

3. We have found that mind pervades every part of the physical body and is always capable of being directed or impressed by authority coming from the objective or the more dominant portion of the mind.

4. The mind, which pervades the body, is largely the result of heredity, which, in turn, is simply the result of all the environments of all past generations on the responsive and ever moving life forces. An understanding of this fact will enable us to use our authority when we find some undesirable trait of character manifesting.

5. We can consciously use all the desirable characteristics with which we have been provided and we can repress and refuse to allow the undesirable ones to manifest.

6. Again, this mind that pervades our physical body is not only the result of hereditary tendencies, but is the result of home, business and social environment, where countless thousands of impressions, ideas, prejudices and similar thoughts have been received. Much of this has been received from others, the result of opin-

ions, suggestions or statements; much of it is the result of our own thinking, but nearly all of it has been accepted with little or no examination or consideration.

7. The idea seemed plausible, the conscious received it, passed it on to the sub-conscious, where it was taken up by the Sympathetic System and passed on to be built into our physical body. "The word has become flesh."

8. This, then, is the way we are constantly creating and re-creating ourselves; we are to-day the result of our past thinking, and we shall be what we are thinking today, the Law of Attraction is bringing to us, not the things we should like, or the things we wish for, or the things some one else has, but it brings us our own, the things which we have created by our thought processes, whether consciously or unconsciously. Unfortunately, many of us are creating these things unconsciously.

9. If either of us were building a home for ourselves, how careful we would be in regard to the plans; how we should study every detail; how we should watch the material and select only the best of everything; and yet how careless we are when it comes to building our Mental Home, which is infinitely more important than any physical home, as everything which can possibly enter into our lives depends upon the character of the material which enters into the construction of our Mental Home.

10. What is the character of this material? We have seen that it is the result of the impressions that we have accumulated in the past and stored away in our sub-conscious Mentality. If these impressions have been of fear, of worry, of care, of anxiety; if they have been despondent, negative, doubtful, then the texture of the material that we are weaving today will be of the same negative material. Instead of being of any value, it will be mildewed and rotten and will bring us only more toil and care and anxiety. We shall be forever busy trying to patch it up and make it appear at least genteel.

11. But if we have stored away nothing but courageous thought, if we have been optimistic, positive, and have immediately thrown any kind of negative thought on the scrap heap, have refused to have anything to do with it, have refused to associate with it or become identified with it in any way, what then is the result? Our mental material is now of the best kind we can weave any kind of mate-rial we want we can use any colour we wish; we know that the texture is firm, that the material is solid, that it will not fade, and we have no fear, no anxiety concern-ing the future; there is nothing to cover, there are no patches to hide.

12. These are psychological facts; there is no theory or guesswork about these thinking processes; there is nothing secret about them; in fact, they are so plain that every one can understand them. The thing to do is to have a mental house-cleaning, and to have this house-cleaning every day, and keep the house clean. Mental, moral and physical cleanliness are absolutely indispensable if we are to make progress of any kind.

13. When this mental house-cleaning process has been completed, the mate-rial that is left will be suitable for the making of the kind of ideals or mental images which we desire to realize.

14. There is a fine estate awaiting a claimant, its broad acres, with abundant crops, running water and fine timber, stretch away as far as the eye can see. There is a mansion, spacious and cheerful, with rare pictures, a well-stocked library, rich hangings, and every comfort and luxury. All the heir has to do is to assert his heirship, take possession, and use the property. He must use it; he must not let it decay; for use is the condition on which he holds it. To neglect it is to lose possession.

15. In the domain of mind and spirit, in the domain of practical power, such an estate is yours. You are the heir! You can assert your heirship, and possess, and use this rich inheritance. Power over circumstances is one of its fruits, health, harmony and prosperity are assets upon its balance sheet. It offers you poise and peace. It costs you only the Labour of studying and harvesting its great resources. It demands no sacrifice, except the loss of your limitations, your servitudes, your weakness. It clothes you with self-honour, and puts a scepter in your hands.

16. To gain this estate, three processes are necessary: You must earnestly desire it. You must assert your claim. You must take possession.

17. You admit that those are not burdensome conditions.

18. You are familiar with the subject of heredity. Darwin, Huxley, Haeckel, and other physical scientists have piled evidence mountain high that heredity is a law attending progressive creation. It is progressive heredity which gives man his erect attitude, his power of motion, the organs of digestion, blood circulation, nerve force, muscular force, bone structure and a host of other faculties on the physical side. There are even more impressive facts concerning heredity of mind force. All these constitute what may be called your human heredity.

19. But there is a heredity that the physical scientists have not compassed. It lies beneath and antecedent to all their researches. At a point where they throw up their hands in despair, saying they cannot account for what they see, this divine heredity is found in full sway.

20. It is the benignant force that decrees primal creation. It thrills down from the Divine, direct into every created being. It originates life, which the physical scientist has not done, nor ever can do. It stands out among all forces supreme, unapproachable. No human heredity measures up to it.

21. This Infinite Life flows through you; is you. Its doorways are but the faculties that comprise your consciousness. To keep open these doors is the Secret of Power. Is it not worthwhile to make the effort?

22. The great fact is, that the source of life and all power is from within. Persons, circumstances and events may suggest need and opportunities, but the insight, strength and power to answer these needs will be found within.

23. Avoid counterfeits. Build firm foundations for your consciousness upon forces that flow direct from the Infinite source, the Universal Mind of which you are the image and likeness.

24. Those who have come into possession of this inheritance are never quite the same again. They have come into possession of a sense of power hitherto

undreamed of. They can never again be timid, weak, vacillating, or fearful. They are indissolubly connected with Omnipotence. Something in them has been aroused; they have suddenly discovered that they possess a tremendous latent ability of which they were heretofore entirely unconscious.

25. This power is from within, but we cannot receive it unless we give it. Use is the condition upon which we hold this inheritance. We are each of us but the channel through which the Omnipotent power is being differentiated into form; unless we give out the channel is obstructed and we can receive no more. This is true on every plane of existence and in every field of endeavor and all walks of life. The more we give, the more we get. The athlete who wishes to get strong must make use of the strength he has, and the more he gives the more he will get. The financier who wishes to make money must make use of the money he has, for only by using it can he get more.

26. The merchant who does not keep his goods going out will soon have none coming in; the business which fails to give efficient service will soon lack customers; the barrister who fails to get results will soon lack clients, and so it goes everywhere; power is contingent upon a proper use of the power already in our possession; what is true in every field of endeavor, every experience in life, is true of the power from which every other power known among men is begotten—spiritual power. Take away the spirit and what is left? Nothing.

27. If then the spirit is all there is, upon the recognition of this fact must depend the ability to demonstrate all power, whether physical, mental or spiritual.

28. All possession is the result of the accumulative attitude of mind, or the money consciousness; this is the magic wand which will enable you to receive the idea, and it will formulate plans for you to execute, and you will find as much pleasure in the execution as in the satisfaction of attainment and achievement.

29. Now, go to your room, take the same seat, the same position as heretofore, arid mentally select a place which has pleasant associations. Make a complete mental picture of it, see the buildings, the grounds, the trees, friends, associations, everything complete. At first you will find yourself thinking of everything under the sun, except the ideal upon exercises every day without fail.

Relation and connection are not somewhere and some time, but everywhere and always.

—Emerson.

✳

41. *What proportion of our mental life is subconscious?*
    At least ninety per cent.
42. *Is this vast mental storehouse generally utilized?*
    No.
43. *Why not?*

Few understand or appreciate the fact that it is an activity that they may consciously direct.

44. *Where has the conscious mind received its governing tendencies?*

    From heredity—which means that it is the result of all the environments of all past generations.

45. *What is the law of attraction bringing to us?*

    Our "Own."

46. *What is our " Own"?*

    What we inherently are, and is the result of our past thinking, both conscious and subconscious.

47. *Of what is the material with which we construct our mental home composed?*

    The thoughts that we entertain.

48. *What is the Secret of Power?*

    A recognition of the omnipresence of omnipotence.

49. *Where does it originate?*

    All life and all power is from within.

50. *Upon what is the possession of power contingent?*

    Upon a proper use of the power already in our possession.

The key to every man is his thought. Sturdy and defying though he look, he has a helm which he obeys, which is the idea after which all his facts are classified. He can only be reformed by showing him a new idea which commands his own.

—Emerson.

PART SIX

Tells of the unlimited possibilities of the Universal Mind, which is the life principle of every atom in existence, and explains how this mind is differentiated in form. It tells of the most marvellous piece of mechanism that has ever been constructed and tells how the effect that will be produced depends entirely upon the "mechanism to which it is attached." It tells why we should all become familiar with the mechanism so as to secure the effects that we desire. The power to which it can be attached is unlimited, and we can accordingly secure any effect we desire when we become familiar with the mechanism, and understand how to make the proper connections. An understanding of this part will enable you to plan courageously and execute fearlessly, because you will have come into a knowledge of the source of all power and this will determine your course in life, bringing you into contact with all that is strongest and best and most desirable.

This Part will give you an excellent understanding of the most wonderful piece of mechanism that has ever been created. A mechanism whereby you may create for yourself Health, Strength, Success, Prosperity or any other condition which you desire. Necessities are demands, and demands create action, and actions bring about results. The process of evolution is constantly building our tomorrows out of our to-days. Individual development, like Universal development, must be gradual with an ever-increasing capacity and volume.

The knowledge that if we infringe upon the rights of others we become moral thorns and find ourselves entangled at every turn of the road, should be an indication that success is contingent upon the highest moral ideal, which is "The greatest good to the greatest number."

Aspiration, desire and harmonious relations constantly and persistently maintained will accomplish results. The greatest hindrance is erroneous and fixed ideas.

To be in tune with eternal truth we must possess poise and harmony within. In order to receive intelligence the receiver must be in tune with the transmitter.

Thought is a product of Mind, and Mind is creative, but this does not mean that the Universal will change its *modus operandi* to suit us or our ideas, but it does mean that we can come into harmonious relationship with the Universal, and when we have accomplished this we may ask anything to which we are entitled, and the way will be made plain.

✳

1. The Universal Mind is so wonderful that it is difficult to understand its utilitarian powers and possibilities and its unlimited creative effects.

2. We have found that this Mind is not only all intelligence but all substance. How, then, is it to be differentiated in form? How are we to secure the effect that we desire?

3. Ask any electrician what the effect of electricity will be and he will reply that "Electricity is a form of motion and its effect will depend upon the mechanism to which it is attached." Upon this mechanism will depend whether we shall have heat, light, power, music or any of the other marvellous demonstrations of power to which this vital energy has been harnessed.

4. What effect can be produced by thought? The reply is that thought is mind in motion (just as wind is air in motion), and its effect will depend entirely on the "mechanism to which it is attached."

5. Here, then, is the secret of all mental power; it depends entirely on the mechanism that we attach.

6. What is this mechanism? You know something of the mechanism that has

been invented by Edison, Bell, Marconi and other electrical wizards, by which place and space and time have become only figures of speech, but did you ever stop to think that the mechanism which has been given you for transforming the Universal, Omnipresent Potential Power was invented by a greater inventor than Edison?

7. We are accustomed to examining the mechanism of the implements that we use for tilling the soil, and we try to get an understanding of the mechanism of the motorcar that we drive, but most of us are content to remain in absolute ignorance of the greatest piece of mechanism that has ever come into existence, the brain of man.

8. Let us examine the wonders of this mechanism; perhaps we shall thereby get a better understanding of the various effects of which it is the cause.

9. In the first place, there is the great mental world in which we live and move and have our being; this world is omnipotent, omniscient and omnipresent; it will respond to our desire in direct ratio to our purpose and faith; the purpose must be in accordance with the law of our being, that is, it must be creative or constructive; our faith must be strong enough to generate a current of sufficient strength to bring our purpose into manifestation. "As thy faith is, so be it unto thee," bears the stamp of scientific test.

10. The effects which are produced in the world without are the result of the action and reaction of the individual upon the universal; that is the process which we call thinking; the brain is the organ through which this process is accomplished. Think of the wonder of it all. Do you love music, flowers, literature, art, or are you inspired by the thought of ancient or modern genius? Remember, every beauty to which you respond must have its corresponding outline in your brain before you can appreciate it.

11. There is not a single virtue or principle in the storehouse of nature which the brain cannot express. The brain is an embryonic world, ready to develop at any time as necessity may arise. If you can comprehend that this is a scientific truth and one of the wonderful laws of nature, it will be easier for you to get an understanding of the mechanism by which these extraordinary results are being accomplished.

12. The nervous system has been compared to an electric circuit with its battery of cells in which force is originated, and its white matter to insulated wires by which the current is conveyed; it is through these channels that every impulse or desire is carried through the mechanism.

13. The spinal cord is the great motor and sensory pathway by which messages are conveyed to and from the brain; then, there is the blood supply plunging through the veins and arteries, renewing our energy and strength, the perfectly arranged structure upon which the entire physical body rests, and, finally, the delicate and beautiful skin, clothing the entire mechanism in a mantle of beauty.

14. This then is the "Temple of the living God" and the individual "I" is given control, and upon his understanding of the mechanism that is within his control will the result depend.

15. Every thought sets the brain cells in action; at first the substance upon which the thought is directed fails to respond, but if the thought is sufficiently refined and concentrated, the substance finally yields and expresses perfectly.

16. This influence of the mind can be exerted upon any part of the body, causing the elimination of any undesirable effect.

17. A perfect conception and understanding of the laws governing in the mental world cannot fail to be of inestimable value in the transaction of business, as it develops the power of discernment and gives a dearer understanding and appreciation of facts.

18. The man who looks within instead of without cannot fail to make use of the mighty forces which will eventually determine his course in life and so bring him into vibration with all that is best, strongest and most desirable.

19. Attention or concentration is probably the most important essential in the development of mind culture. The possibilities of attention when properly directed are so startling that they would hardly appear credible to the uninitiated. The cultivation of attention is the distinguishing characteristic of every successful man or woman, and is the very highest personal accomplishment that can be acquired.

20. The power of attention can be more readily understood by comparing it with a sun glass in which the rays of sunlight are focused; they possess no particular strength as long as the glass is moved about and the rays but let the glass be held perfectly still and let the rays be focused on one spot for any length of time, the effect will become immediately apparent.

21. So with the power of thought; let power be dissipated by scattering the thought from one object to another, and no result is apparent; but focus this power through attention or concentration on any single purpose for any length of time and nothing becomes impossible.

22. A very simple remedy for a very complex situation, some will say. All right, try it, you who have had no experience in concentrating the thought on a definite purpose or object. Choose any single object and concentrate your attention on it for a definite purpose for even ten minutes; you cannot do it; the mind will wander a dozen times and it will be necessary to bring it back to the directed from one place to another original purpose, and each time the effect will have been lost and at the end of the ten minutes nothing will have been gained, because you have not been able to hold your thought steadily to the purpose.

23. It is, however, through attention that you will finally be able to overcome obstacles of any kind that appear in your path onward and upward, and the only way to acquire this wonderful power is by practice—practice makes perfect, in this as in anything else.

24. In order to cultivate the power of attention bring a photograph with you to the same seat in the same room in the same position as heretofore. Examine it closely at least ten minutes, note the expression of the eyes, the form of the features, the clothing, the way the hair is arranged; in fact, note every detail shown on

the photograph carefully. Now cover it and close your eyes and try to see it mentally; if you can see every detail perfectly and can form a good mental image of the photograph, you are to be congratulated; if not, repeat the process until you can.

25. This step is simply for the purpose of preparing the soil; in Part Seven we shall be ready to sow the seed.

26. It is by such exercises as these that you will finally be able to control your mental moods, your attitude, your consciousness.

27. Great organizers are learning to withdraw from the multitude more and more, that they may have more time for planning, thinking and generating the right mental moods.

28. Successful businessmen are constantly demonstrating the fact that it pays to keep in touch with the thought of other successful business men.

29. A single idea may be worth thousands of pounds, and these ideas can only come to those who are receptive, who are prepared to receive them, who are in a successful frame of mind.

30. Men are learning to place themselves in harmony with the Universal Mind; they are learning the unity of all things; they are learning the basic methods and principles of thinking, and this is changing conditions and multiplying results.

31. They are finding that circumstances and environment follow the trend of mental and spiritual progress; they find that growth follows knowledge; action follows inspiration; opportunity follows perception; always the spiritual first, then the transformation into the infinite and illimitable possibilities of achievement.

32. As the individual is but the channel for the differentiation of the Universal, these possibilities are necessarily inexhaustible.

33. Thought is the process by which we may absorb the Spirit of Power, and hold the result in our inner consciousness until it becomes a part of our ordinary consciousness. The method of accomplishing this result by the persistent practice of a few fundamental principles, as explained in this Book, is the Master-Key that unlocks the storehouse of Universal Truth.

34. The two great sources of human suffering at present are bodily disease and mental anxiety. These may be readily traced to the infringement of some Natural Law. This is, no doubt owing to the fact that so far knowledge has largely remained partial, but the clouds of darkness which have accumulated through long ages are beginning to roll away and with them many of the miseries that attend imperfect information.

That a man can change himself, improve himself, re-create himself, control his environment, and master his own destiny is the conclusion of every mind that is wide awake to the power of right thought in constructive action.

—Larsen.

❋

51. *What are some of the effects which can be produced by electricity?*
Heat, light, power, music.

52. *Upon what do these various effects depend?*
Upon the mechanism to which the electricity is attached.

53. *What is the result of the action and interaction of the individual mind upon the Universal?*
The conditions and experiences with which we meet.

54. *How may these conditions be changed?*
By changing the mechanism by which the Universal is differentiated in form.

55. *What is this mechanism?*
The brain.

56. *How may it be changed?*
By the process we call thinking. Thoughts produce brain cells, and these cells respond to the corresponding thought in the Universal.

57. *Of what value is the power of concentration?*
It is the very highest personal accomplishment which can be acquired, and the distinguishing characteristic of every successful man or woman.

58. *How may it be acquired?*
By faithfully practising the exercises outlined in this System.

59. *Why is this so important?*
Because it will enable us to control our thoughts, and since thoughts are causes conditions must be effects; if we can control the cause we can also control the effect.

60. *What is changing conditions and multiplying results in the objective world?*
Men are learning the basic methods of constructive thinking.

"This above all: To thine own self be true, And it must follow, as the night the day, Thou canst not then be false to any man."

ADVICE

Remember—
  Fully to understand grand and beautiful thought requires, perhaps, as much
  time as to conceive it.
                                                        –JOUBERT

If you wish to enjoy the utmost practical benefit form "The Master Key"—
go slowly.

Transfuse into your mind the contents of one part only, each week for twenty-
four weeks.

Realize the meaning of every phrase.

Consult "The Master Key" constantly, as your perpetual help and stimulus.

Each time you read the work you will get a better understanding of the eternal
cosmic principles.

Tell others of "The Master Key" so that more and more people may reciprocate
with you, as conscious adepts in harmony.

PART SEVEN

This Part tells of a method by which you may construct the mould or model from which your future will emerge it tells how you may make it grand and beautiful; it explains that you an not limited as to cost or material, that no one can place any limitation on it but yourself. It explains that in the construction of this model, there is much work to be done, that no one can do the work but yourself, but it tells you what to do and how to do it, it suggests methods and plans which if faithfully and persistently carried out will result in conditions exactly in accordance with the purpose and thought. It tells of millions of faithful helpers that will come to your aid if you are faithful in your work, and it tells why some who are apparently faithfully endeavoring to realize their ideal seem to fail. It is sometimes just as important to know what not to do as what to do.

Through all the ages man has believed in an invisible power, through which and by which all things have been created and are continually being re-created.

We may personalize this power and call it God, or we may think of it as the essence or spirit, which permeates all things, but in either case the effect is the same.

So far as the individual is concerned, the objective, the physical, the visible, is the personal, that which can be cognized by the senses. It consists of body, brain and nerves. The subjective is the spiritual, the invisible, the impersonal.

The personal is conscious because it is a personal entity. The impersonal being the same in kind and quality as ail other Being, is not conscious of itself and has therefore been termed the subconscious.

The personal, or conscious, has the power of will and choice, and can therefore exercise discrimination in the selection of methods whereby to bring about the solution of difficulties.

The impersonal, or spiritual, being a part or one with the source and origin of all power, can necessarily exercise no such choice, but, on the contrary, it has Infinite resources at its command. It can and does bring about results by methods concerning which the human or individual mind can have no possible conception.

You will therefore see that it is your privilege to depend upon the human will, with all its limitations and misconceptions or you may utilize the potentialities of Infinity by making use of the subconscious mind. Here, then, is the scientific explanation of the wonderful power that has been put within your control, if you but understand, appreciate and recognize it.

One method of consciously utilizing this omnipotent power is outlined in Part Seven.

*

1. Visualization is the process of making mental images, and the image is the mould or model that will serve as a pattern from which your future will emerge.

2. Make the pattern clear, and make it beautiful; do not be afraid; make it grand; remember that no limitation can be placed upon you by anyone but yourself; you are not limited as to cost or material; draw on the Infinite for your supply, construct it in your imagination; it will have to be there before it will ever appear anywhere else.

3. Make the image clear and clean-cut, hold it firmly in the mind and you will gradually and constantly bring the thing nearer to you. You can be what "you will to be."

4. This is another psychological fact that is well known, but unfortunately, reading about it will not bring about any result that you may have in mind; it will

not even help you to form the mental image, much less bring it into manifestation. Work is necessary, labour, hard mental labour, the kind of effort that so few are willing to put forth.

5. The first step is idealization. It is likewise the most important step, because it is the plan on which you are going to build. It must be solid; it must be permanent. The architect, when he plans a grand building, has every line and detail pictured in advance. The engineer, when he spans a chasm, first ascertains the strength requirements of a million separate parts.

6. They see the end before a single step is taken; so you are to picture in your mind what you want; you are sowing the seed, but before sowing any seed you want to know what the harvest is to be. This is Idealization. If you are not sure, return to the chair daily until the picture becomes plain; it will gradually unfold; first the general plan will be dim, but it will take shape, the outline will take form, then the details, and you will gradually develop the power by which you will be enabled to formulate plans which will eventually materialize in the objective world. You will come to know what the future holds for you.

7. Then comes the process of visualization. You must see the picture more and more complete, see the detail, and, as the details begin to unfold, the ways and means for bringing it into manifestation will develop. One thing will lead to another. Thought will lead to action, action will develop methods, methods will develop friends, and friends will bring about circumstances, and, finally, the third step, or Materialization, will have been accomplished.

8. We all recognize that the Universe must have been thought into shape before it ever could have become a material fact. And if we are willing to follow along the lines of the Great Architect of the Universe, we shall find our thoughts taking form, just as the Universe took concrete form. It is the same mind operating through the individual. There is no difference in kind or quality, the only difference is one of degree.

9. The architect visualizes his building, he sees it as he wishes it to be. His thought becomes a plastic mould from which the building will eventually emerge, a high one or a low one, a beautiful one or a plain one; his vision takes form on paper and eventually the necessary material is utilized and the building stands complete.

10. The inventor visualizes his idea in exactly the same manner. For instance, Nikola Tesla, he with the giant intellect, one of the greatest inventors of all ages, the man who has brought forth the most amazing realities, always visualizes his inventions before attempting to work them out. He does not rush to embody them in form and then spend his time in correcting defects. Having first built up the idea in his imagination, he holds it there as a mental picture, to be reconstructed and improved by his thought. "In this way," he writes in the *Electrical Experimenter*, "I am enabled to rapidly develop and perfect a conception with out touching anything. When I have gone so far as to embody in the invention every possible improvement I can think of, and see no fault anywhere, I put into concrete form

the product of my brain. Invariably my device works as I conceived it should; in twenty years there has not been a single exception."

11. If you can conscientiously follow these directions, you will develop Faith, the kind of Faith that is the "Substance of things hoped for, the evidence of things not seen"; you will develop confidence, the kind of confidence that leads to endurance and courage; you will develop the power of concentration which will enable you to exclude all thoughts except the ones which are associated with your purpose.

12. The law is that thought will manifest in form, and only one who knows how to be the divine thinker of his own thoughts can ever take a Master's place and speak with authority.

13. Clearness and accuracy are obtained only by repeatedly having the image in mind. Each repeated action renders the image more dear and accurate than the preceding, and in proportion to the dearness and accuracy of the image will the outward manifestation be. You must build it firmly and securely in your mental world, the world within, before it can take form in the world without, and you can build nothing of value, even in the mental world, unless you have the proper material. When you have the material you can build anything you wish, but make sure of your material. You cannot make broadcloth from shoddy.

14. This material will be brought out by millions of silent mental workers and fashioned into the form of the image that you have in mind.

15. Think of it! You have over five million of these mental workers, ready and in active use; brain cells they are called. Besides this, there is another reserve force of at least an equal number, ready to be called into action at the slightest need. Your power to think, then, is almost unlimited, and this means that your power to create the kind of material that is necessary to build for yourself any kind of environment that you desire is practically unlimited.

16. In addition to these millions of mental workers, you have billions of mental workers in the body, every one of which is endowed with sufficient intelligence to understand and act upon any message or suggestion given. These cells are all busy creating and re-creating the body, but, in addition to this, they are endowed with psychic activity whereby they can attract to themselves the substance necessary for perfect development.

17. They do this by the same law and in the same manner that every form of life attracts to itself the necessary material for growth. The oak, the rose, the lily, all require certain material for their most perfect expression and they secure it by silent demand, the Law of Attraction, the most certain way for you to secure what you require for your most complete development.

18. Make the Mental Image; make it clear, distinct, perfect; hold it firmly; the ways and means will develop; supply will follow the demand; you will be led to do the right thing at the right tune and in the right way. Earnest Desire will bring about Confident Expectation, and this in turn must be reinforced by Firm Demand.

These three cannot fail to bring about Attainment, because the Earnest Desire is the feeling, the Confident Expectation is the thought, and the Firm Demand is the will, and, as we have seen, feeling gives vitality to thought and the will holds it steadily until the law of Growth brings it into manifestation.

19. Is it not wonderful that man has such tremendous power within himself, such transcendental faculties concerning which he had no conception? Is it not strange that we have always been taught to look for strength and power "without"? We have been taught to look everywhere but "within," and whenever this power manifested in our lives we were told that it was something supernatural.

20. There are many who have come to an understanding of this wonderful power, and who make serious and conscientious efforts to realize health, power and other conditions, and seem to fail. They do not seem able to bring the Law into operation. The difficulty in nearly every case is that they are dealing with externals. They want money, power, health and abundance, but they fail to realize that these are effects and can come only when the cause is found.

21. Those who will give no attention to the world without, will seek only to ascertain the truth, will look only for wisdom, will find that this wisdom will unfold and disclose the source of all power, that it will manifest in thought and purpose which will create the external conditions desired. This truth will find expression in noble purpose and courageous action.

22. Create ideals only, give no thought to external conditions, make the world within beautiful and opulent and the world without will express and manifest the condition that you have made within. You will come into a realization of your power to create ideals and these ideals will be projected into the world of effect.

23. For instance, a man is in debt. He will be continually thinking about the debt, concentrating on it, and as thoughts are causes the result is that he not only fastens the debt closer to him, but actually creates more debt. He is putting the great law of Attraction into operation with the usual and inevitable result—Loss leads to greater "Loss."

24. What, then, is the correct principle? Concentrate on the things you want, not on the things you do not want. Think of abundance; idealize the methods and plans for putting the Law of Abundance into operation. Visualize the condition which the Law of Abundance creates; this will result in manifestation.

25. If the law operates perfectly to bring about poverty, lack and every form of limitation for those who are continually entertaining thoughts of lack and fear, it will operate with the same certainty to bring about conditions of abundance and opulence for those who entertain thoughts of courage and power.

26. This is a difficult problem for many; we are too anxious; we manifest anxiety, fear, distress; we want to do something; we want to help; we are like a child who has just planted a seed and every fifteen minutes goes out and stirs up the earth to see if it is growing. Of course, under such circumstances, the seed will never germinate, and yet this is exactly what many of us do in the mental world.

27. We must plant the seed and leave it undisturbed. This does not mean that we are to sit down and do nothing, by no means; we will do more and better work than we have ever done before, new channels will constantly be provided, new doors will open; all that is necessary is to have an open mind, be ready to act when the time comes.

28. Thought force is the most powerful means of obtaining knowledge, and if concentrated on any subject will solve the problem. Nothing is beyond the power of human comprehension, but in order to harness thought force and make it do your bidding, work is required.

29. Remember that thought is the fire that creates the steam that turns the wheel of fortune, upon which your experiences depend.

30. Ask yourself a few questions and then reverently await the response. Do you not now and then feel the self within you? Do you assert this self or do you follow the majority? Remember that majorities are always led, they never lead. It was the majority that fought, tooth and nail, against the steam engine, the power loom and every other advance or improvement ever suggested.

31. For your next exercise visualize your friend, see him exactly as you last saw him, see the room, the furniture, recall the conversation, now see his face, see it distinctly, now talk to him about some subject of mutual interest; see his expression change, watch him smile. Can you do this? All right, you can; then arouse his interest, tell him a story of adventure, see his eyes light up with the spirit of fun or excitement. Can you do all of this? If so, your imagination is good, you are making excellent progress.

❋

61. *What is visualization?*
    The process of making mental pictures.
62. *What is the result of this method of thought?*
    By holding the image or picture in mind, we can gradually but surely bring the thing nearer to us. We can be what we will to be.
63. *What is Idealization?*
    It is a process of visualizing or idealizing the plans that will eventually materialize in our objective world.
64. *Why are clearness and accuracy necessary?*
    Because "seeing" creates "feeling" and "feeling" creates "being." First the mental, then the emotional, then the illimitable possibilities of achievement.
65. *How are they obtained?*
    Each repeated action renders the image more accurate than the former one.
66. *How is the material for the construction of your mental image secured?*

By millions of mental workers. Brain cells they are called.

67. *How are the necessary conditions for bringing about the materialization of your ideal in the objective world secured?*

    By the Law of Attraction. The natural law by which all conditions and experiences are brought about.

68. *What three steps are necessary in order to bring this law into operation?*

    Earnest Desire, Confident Expectation, Firm Demand.

69. *Why do many fail?*

    Because they concentrate on loss, disease and disaster. The law is operating perfectly; the things they fear are coming upon them.

70. *What is the alternative?*

    Concentrate on the ideals that you desire to see manifested in your life.

Man is mind, and evermore he takes the tool of thought, and shaping what he wills, brings forth, a thousand joys, a thousand ills. He thinks in secret and it comes to pass, Environment is but his looking glass.

                                                                —James Allen.

PART EIGHT

This Part tells of the creative principle of the Universe, what it is, how it takes form and how it is brought into manifestation. This principle being the underlying principle of all existence must necessarily be governed by an immutable law. It tells how the character, health and circumstances of the individual are formed, and suggests methods whereby desirable conditions and circumstances may be created. It tells how and why and when the material from which your future is to emerge is secured. It suggests methods and exercises by which you may secure complete control of the power that governs in this mighty field of action. Mighty because it is the most important work which any individual can undertake. We are making our future now, to-day, when it comes we shall have to accept what is given. It will be too late to change it, but we can dominate it, control it, make it what we want it to be, and this Part explains how.

In this Part you will find that you may freely choose what you think, but the result of your thought is governed by an immutable law. Is not this a wonderful thought? Is it not wonderful to know that our lives are not subject to caprice or variability of any kind? That they are governed by law. This stability is our opportunity, because by complying with the law we can secure the desired effect with invariable precision.

It is the Law that makes the Universe one grand paean of Harmony. If it were not for law, the Universe would be a Chaos instead of a Cosmos.

Here, then, is the secret of the origin of both good and evil: this is all of the good and evil there ever was or ever will be.

Let me illustrate. Thought results in action. If your thought is constructive and harmonious, the result will be good: if your thought is destructive or inharmonious, the result will be evil.

There is therefore but one law, one principle, one cause, one Source of Power, and good and evil are simply words that have been coined to indicate the result of our action, or our compliance or non-compliance with this law.

The importance of this is well illustrated in the lives of Emerson and Carlyle. Emerson loved the good and his life was a symphony of peace and harmony; Carlyle hated the bad, and his life was a record of perpetual discord and disharmony.

Here we have two grand men, each intent upon achieving the same ideal, but one makes use of constructive thought and is therefore in harmony with Natural Law, the other makes use of destructive thought and therefore brings upon himself discord of every kind and character.

It is evident therefore that we are to hate nothing, not even the "bad," because hatred is destructive, and we shall soon find that by entertaining destructive thought we are sowing the "wind" and shall reap the "whirlwind."

*

1. Thought contains a vital principle, because it is the creative principle of the Universe and by its nature will combine with other similar thoughts.

2. As the one purpose of life is growth, all principle underlying existence must contribute to give it effect. Thought, therefore, takes form and the law of growth eventually brings it into manifestation.

3. You may freely choose what you think, but the result of your thought is governed by an immutable law. Any line of thought persisted in cannot fail to produce its result in the character, health and circumstances of the individual. Methods whereby we can substitute habits of constructive thinking for those which we have found produce only undesirable effects are therefore of primary importance.

4. We all know that this is by no means easy. Mental habits are difficult to control, but it can be done and the way to do it is to begin at once to substitute constructive thought for destructive thought. Form the habit of analyzing every thought. If it is necessary, if its manifestation in the objective will be a benefit, not only to yourself, but to all whom it may affect in any way, keep it; treasure it; it is of value; it is in tune with the Infinite it will grow and develop and produce fruit an hundredfold. On the other hand, it will be well for you to keep this quotation from George Matthews Adams in mind, "Learn to keep the door shut, keep out of your mind, out of your office, and out of your world, every element that seeks admittance with no definite helpful end in view."

5. If your thought has been critical or destructive, and has resulted in any condition of discord or disharmony in your environment, it may be necessary for you to cultivate a mental attitude that will be conducive to constructive thought.

6. The imagination will be found to be a great assistance in this direction; the cultivation of the imagination leads to the development of the ideal out of which your future will emerge.

7. The imagination gathers up the material by which the Mind weaves the fabric in which your future is to be clothed.

8. Imagination is the light by which we can penetrate new worlds of thought and experience.

9. Imagination is the mighty instrument by which every discoverer, every inventor, opened the way from precedent to experience. Precedent said, "It cannot be done"; experience said, "It is done."

10. Imagination is a plastic power, moulding the things of sense into new forms and ideals.

11. Imagination is the constructive form of thought which must precede every constructive form of action.

12. A builder cannot build a structure of any kind until he has first received the plans from the architect, and the architect must get them from his imagination.

13. The Captain of Industry cannot build a giant corporation which may co-ordinate hundreds of smaller firms and thousands of employees, and utilize millions of capital until he has first created the entire work in his imagination. Objects in the material world are as clay in the potter's hand; it is in the Master Mind that the real things are created, and it is by the use of the imagination that the work is done. In order to cultivate the imagination it must be exercised. Exercise is necessary to cultivate mental muscle as well as physical muscle. It must be supplied with nourishment or it cannot grow.

14. Do not confuse Imagination with Fancy, or that form of daydreaming in which some people like to indulge. Daydreaming is a form of mental dissipation that may lead to mental disaster.

15. Constructive imagination means mental labour, by some considered to be the hardest kind of labour, but, if so, it yields the greatest returns, for all the great

things in life have come to men and women who had the capacity to think, to imagine, and to make their dreams come true.

16. When you have become thoroughly conscious of the fact that Mind is the only creative principle, that it is Omnipotent, Omniscient and Omnipresent, and that you can consciously come into harmony with this Omnipotence through your power of thought, you will have taken a long step in the right direction.

17. The next step is to place yourself in position to receive this power. As it is Omnipresent, it must be within you. We know that this is so because we know that all power is from within, but it must be developed, unfolded, cultivated; in order to do this we must be receptive, and this receptivity is acquired just as physical strength is gained, by exercise.

18. The law of attraction will certainly and unerringly bring to you the conditions, environment, and experiences in life, corresponding with your habitual, characteristic, predominant mental attitude. Not what you think once in a while when you are in church, or have just read a good book, but your predominant mental attitude is what counts.

19. You cannot entertain weak, harmful, negative thoughts ten hours a day and expect to bring about beautiful, strong and harmonious conditions by ten minutes of strong, positive, creative thought.

20. Real power comes from within. All power that anybody can possibly use is within man, only waiting to be brought into visibility by his first recognizing it, and then affirming it as his, working it into his consciousness until he becomes one with it.

21. People say that they desire abundant life, and so they do, but so many interpret this to mean that if they will exercise their muscles or breathe scientifically, eat certain foods in certain ways, drink so many glasses of water every day, of just a certain temperature, keep out of droughts, they will attain the abundant life they seek. The result of such methods is but indifferent. However, when man awakens to the truth, and affirms his oneness with all Life, he finds that he takes on the clear eye, the elastic step, the vigor of youth; he finds that he has discovered the source of all power.

22. All mistakes are but the mistakes of ignorance. Knowledge gaining and consequent power is what determines growth and evolution. The recognition and demonstration of knowledge is what constitutes power, and this power is spiritual power, and this spiritual power is the power that lies at the heart of all things; it is the soul of the universe.

23. This knowledge is the result of man's ability to think; thought is therefore the germ of man's conscious evolution. When man ceases to advance in his thoughts and ideals, his forces immediately begin to disintegrate and his countenance gradually registers these changing conditions.

24. Successful men make it their business to hold ideals of the conditions that they wish to realize. They constantly hold in mind the next step necessary to the ideal for which they are striving. Thoughts are the materials with which they build,

and the imagination is their mental work-shop. Mind is the ever moving force with which they secure the persons and circumstances necessary to build their success structure, and imagination is the matrix in which all great things are fashioned.

25. If you have been faithful to your ideal, you will hear the call when circumstances are ready to materialize your plans and results will correspond in the exact ratio of your fidelity to your ideal. The ideal steadily held is what predetermines and attracts the necessary conditions for its fulfillment.

26. It is thus that you may weave a garment of spirit and power into the web of your entire existence; it is thus that you may lead a charmed life and be for ever protected from all harm; it is thus that you may become a positive force whereby conditions of opulence and harmony may be attracted to you.

27. This is the leaven that is gradually permeating the general consciousness and is largely responsible for the conditions of unrest that are everywhere evident.

28. In your last exercise you created a mental image, you brought it from the invisible into the visible; now I want you to take an object and follow it back to its origination, see of what it really consists. If you do this you will develop imagination, insight, perception, and sagacity. These come not by the superficial observation of the multitude, but by a keen analytical observation that sees below the surface.

29. It is the few who know that the things which they see are only effects, and understand the causes by which these effects were brought into existence.

30. Take the same position as heretofore and visualize a Battleship; see the grim, monster floating on the surface of the water; there appears to be no life anywhere about; all is silence; you know that by far the largest part of the vessel is under water; out of sight; you know that the ship is as large and as heavy as a twenty-story skyscraper or the National Gallery; you know that there are hundreds of men ready to spring to their appointed task instantly; you know that every department is in charge of able, trained, skilled officers who have proven themselves competent to take charge of this marvellous piece of mechanism; you know that although it lies apparently oblivious to everything else, it has eyes which see everything for miles around, and nothing is permitted to escape its watchful vision; you know that while it appears quiet, submissive and innocent, it is prepared to hurl a steel projectile weighing thousands of pounds at an enemy many miles away; this and much more you can bring to mind with comparatively no effort whatever. But how did the battleship come to be where it is; how did it come into existence in the first place? All of this you want to know if you are a careful observer.

31. Follow the great steel plates through the foundries, see the thousands of men employed in their production; go still further back, and see the ore as it comes from the mine, see it loaded on barges or trucks, see it melted and properly treated; go back still further and see the architect and engineers who planned the vessel; let the thought carry you back still further in order to determine why they planned the vessel; you will see that you are now so far back that the vessel is something intangible, it no longer exists, it is now only a thought existing in the brain of the architect; but from where did the order come to plan the vessel? Probably from the Sec-

retary of War or the First Lord of the Admiralty; probably this vessel was planned long before war was thought of, and Parliament or Congress had to pass a bill appropriating the money; possibly there was opposition, and speeches for or against the bill. Whom do these Members of Parliament or these Congressmen represent? They represent you and me, so that our line of thought begins with the Battleship and ends with ourselves, and we find in the last analysis that our own thought is responsible for this and many other things, of which we seldom think, and a little further reflection will develop the most important fact of all, and that is, if someone had not discovered the law by which this tremendous mass of steel and iron could be made to float upon the water, instead of immediately going to the bottom, the battleship could not have come into existence at all.

32. This law is that, " the specific gravity of any substance is the weight of any volume of it, compared with an equal volume of water." The discovery of this law revolutionized every kind of ocean travel, commerce and warfare, and made the existence of the battleship possible.

33. You will find exercises of this kind invaluable. When the thought has been trained to look below the surface everything takes on a different appearance, the insignificant becomes significant, the uninteresting interesting; the things which we supposed to be of no importance are seen to be the only really vital things in existence.

●

71. *What is the imagination?*
A form of constructive thought. The light by which we penetrate new worlds of thought and experience. The mighty instrument by which every inventor or discoverer opened the way from precedent to experience.

72. *What is the result of imagination?*
The cultivation of the imagination leads to the development of the ideal out of which your future will emerge.

73. *How may it be cultivated?*
By exercise; it must be supplied with nourishment or it cannot live.

74. *How does imagination differ from day dreaming?*
Day dreaming is a form of mental dissipation, while imagination is a form of constructive thought which must precede every constructive action.

75. *What are mistakes?*
The result of ignorance.

76. *What is knowledge?*
The result of a man's ability to think.

77. *What is the power with which successful men build?*
Mind is the ever moving force with which they secure the persons and circumstances necessary to complete their plans.

78. *What pre-determines the result?*
   The ideal held steadily in mind attracts the necessary conditions for its fulfillment.

79. *What is the result of a keen analytical observation?*
   The development of imagination, insight, perception and sagacity.

80. *To what do these lead?*
   Opulence and harmony.

LOOK TO THIS DAY.

For it is Life, the very Life of Life.
In Its brief course lie all the Verities
   and
Realities of your existence;
   The Bliss of Growth;
   The Glory of Action;
   The Splendour of Beauty;
For Yesterday is but a Dream,
   And To-morrow is only a Vision;
   But To-day well lived makes every
Yesterday a Dream of Happiness, and
Every Tomorrow a Vision of Hope.
   Look well, therefore, to This Day!

—From the Sanscrit.

ADVICE

Remember—
   Fully to understand grand and beautiful thought requires, perhaps, as much
   time as to conceive it.
   –JOUBERT

If you wish to enjoy the utmost practical benefit form "The Master Key"— go slowly.

Transfuse into your mind the contents of one part only, each week for twenty-four weeks.

Realize the meaning of every phrase.

Consult "The Master Key" constantly, as your perpetual help and stimulus.

Each time you read the work you will get a better understanding of the eternal cosmic principles.

Tell others of "The Master Key" so that more and more people may reciprocate with you, as conscious adepts in harmony.

PART NINE

This part tells of the fundamental principle the imperative condition, the immutable law underlying every successful business relation or social condition. It tells of the law by which you may make yourself irresistible, by which you may sweep away every form of word disharmony and doubt. It tells the secret of the solution to every problem. It explains that there are only three things that all mankind requires for complete happiness and development. It tells what they are and how they may be had.

THE MASTER KEY: PART NINE 333

In this Part you may learn to fashion the tools by which you may build for yourself any condition you desire.

If you wish to change conditions, you must change yourself. Your whims, your wishes, your fancies, your ambitions may be thwarted at every step, but your inmost thoughts will find expression just as certainly as the plant springs from the seed.

Suppose, then, we desire to change conditions, how are we to bring this about? The reply is simple: By the law of growth. Cause and effect are as absolute and undeviating in the hidden realm of thought as in the world of material things.

Hold in mind the condition desired; affirm it as an already existing fact. This indicates the value of a powerful affirmation. By constant repetition it becomes a part of ourselves. We are actually changing ourselves; we are making ourselves what we want to be.

Character is not a thing of chance, but it is the result of continued effort. If you are timid, vacillating, self-conscious, or if you are over-anxious or harassed by thoughts of fear or impending danger, remember that it is axiomatic that "two things cannot exist in the same place at the same time." Exactly the same thing is true in the mental and spiritual world; so that your remedy is plainly to substitute thoughts of courage, power, self-reliance and confidence, for those of fear, lack and limitation.

The easiest and most natural way to do this is to select an affirmation that seems to fit your particular case. The positive thought will destroy the negative as certainly as light destroys darkness, and the results will be just as effectual.

Act is the blossom of thought, and conditions are the result of action, so that you constantly have in your possession the tools by which you will certainly and inevitably make or unmake yourself, and joy or suffering will be the reward

*

1. There are only three things that can possibly be desired in the "world without" and each of them can be found in the "world within." The secret of finding them is simply to apply the proper "mechanism" of attachment to the omnipotent power to which each individual has access.

2. The three things which all mankind desires and which are necessary for his highest expression and complete development are Health, Wealth and Love. All will admit that Health is absolutely essential; no one can be happy if the physical body is in pain. All will not so readily admit that Wealth is necessary, but must admit that a sufficient supply at least is necessary, and what would be considered sufficient for one, would be considered absolute and painful lack for another; and as Nature provides not only enough but abundantly, wastefully, lavishly, we realize

that any lack or limitation is only the limitation which has been made by an artificial method of distribution.

3. All will probably admit that Love is the third, or some will say the first, essential necessary to the happiness of mankind; at any rate, those who possess all three, Health, Wealth and Love, find nothing else which can be added to their cup of happiness.

4. We have found that the Universal substance is "All Health," "All Substance" and "All Love" and that the mechanism of attachment whereby we can consciously connect with this Infinite supply is in our method of thinking. To think correctly is therefore to enter into the "Secret Place of the Most High."

5. What shall we think? If we know this we shall have found the proper mechanism of attachment that will relate us to "Whatsoever things we desire." This mechanism may seem very simple when I give it to you, but read on; you will find that it is in reality the "Master-Key," the "Aladdin's lamp," if you please; you will find that it is the foundation, the imperative condition, the absolute law of well-doing, which means, well-being.

6. To think correctly, accurately, we must know the "Truth." The truth then is the underlying principle in every business or social relation. It is a condition precedent to every right action. To know the truth, to be sure, to be confident, affords a satisfaction beside which no other is at all comparable; it is the only solid ground in a world of doubt, conflict and danger.

7. To know the Truth, is to be in harmony with the Infinite and Omnipotent power. To know the truth is, therefore, to connect yourself with a power which is irresistible and which will sweep away every kind of discord, disharmony, doubt or error, because the "Truth is mighty and will prevail."

8. The humblest intellect can readily foretell the result of any action when he knows that it is based on truth, but the mightiest intellect, the most profound and penetrating mind loses its way hopelessly and can form no conception of the results which may ensue when his hopes are based on a premise which he knows to be false.

9. Every action which is not in harmony with Truth, whether through ignorance or design, will result in discord, and eventual loss in proportion to its extent and character.

10. How then are we to know the truth in order to attach this mechanism that will relate us to the Infinite?

11. We can make no mistake about this if we realize that Truth is the vital principle of the Universal Mind and is Omnipresent. For instance, if you require health, a realization of the fact that the "I" in you is spiritual and that all spirit is one; that wherever a part is the whole must be, will bring about a condition of health, because every cell in the body must manifest the truth as you see it. If you see sickness they will manifest sickness; if you see perfection they must manifest perfection. The affirmation, "I am whole, perfect, strong, powerful, loving, harmonious

and happy," will bring about harmonious conditions. The reason for this is because the affirmation is in strict accordance with the Truth, and when truth appears every form of error or discord must necessarily disappear.

12. You have found that the "I" is spiritual, it must necessarily then always be no less than perfect. The affirmation, "I am whole, perfect, strong, powerful, loving, harmonious and happy" is therefore an exact scientific statement.

13. Thought is a spiritual activity and spirit is creative, therefore the result of holding this thought in mind must necessarily bring about conditions in harmony with the thought.

14. If you require Wealth a realization of the fact that the "I" in you is one with the Universal mind which is all substance, and is Omnipotent, will assist you in bringing into operation the law of attraction which will bring you into vibration with those forces which make for success and bring about conditions of power and affluence in direct proportion with the character and purpose of your affirmation.

15. Visualization is the mechanism of the attachment that you require. Visualization is a very different process from seeing; seeing is physical, and is therefore related to the objective world, the "world without," but Visualization is a product of the imagination, and is therefore a product of the subjective mind, the "world within." It therefore possesses vitality; it will grow. The thing visualized will manifest itself in form. The mechanism is perfect; it was created by the Master Architect who "doeth all things well," but unfortunately sometimes the operator is inexperienced or inefficient, but practice and determination will overcome this defect.

16. If you require Love try to realize that the only way to get love is by giving it, that the more you give the more you will get, and the only way in which you can give it, is to fill yourself with it, until you become a magnet. The method was explained in another Part.

17. He who has learned to bring the greatest spiritual truths into touch with the so-called lesser life has discovered the secret of solution of his problems quickened, made more thoughtful, by his nearness of approach to great ideas, great events, great natural objects, and great men. Lincoln is said to have begotten in all who came near him the feeling awakened when one approaches a mountain, and this sense asserts itself most keenly when one comes to realize that he understands the things that are eternal, including the power of Truth.

18. It is sometimes an inspiration to hear from some one who has actually put these principles to the test, someone who has demonstrated them in his own life. I am today in receipt of a letter from a Mr. Andrews; he says:

"Dear Friend:

You will find my experience published in the March issue of 'Nautilus,' and you are at liberty to make any extracts from or reference to it that may suit your purpose.

Sincerely yours,

Frederick Andrews,

Oddfellows Building,
        Indianapolis, Ind."

19. "I was about thirteen years old when Dr. T.W. Marsee, since passed over, said to my mother: 'There is no possible chance, Mrs. Andrews. I lost my little boy the same way, after doing everything for him that it was possible to do. I have made a special study of these cases, and I know there is no possible chance for him to get well.'

20. "She turned to him and said: 'Doctor, what would you do if he were your boy?' and he answered, 'I would fight, fight as long as there is a breath of life to fight for.'

21. "That was the beginning of along drawn-out battle, with many ups and downs, the doctors all agreeing that there was no chance for a cure, though they encouraged and cheered us the best they could.

22. "But at last the victory came, and I have grown from a little, crooked, twisted cripple, going about on my hands and knees, to a strong, straight, well formed man.

23. "Now, I know you want the formula, and I will give it to you as briefly and quickly as I can.

24. "I built up an affirmation for myself taking the qualities I most needed, and a for myself over and over again, 'I am whole, perfect, strong, powerful, loving, harmonious and happy.' I kept up this affirmation, always the same, never varying, till I could wake up in the night and find myself repeating, 'I am whole, perfect, strong, powerful, loving, harmonious and happy.' It was the last thing on my lips at night and the first thing in the morning.

25. "Not only did I affirm it for myself, but for others that I knew needed it. I want to emphasize this point. Whatever you desire for yourself, affirm it for others, and it will help you both. We reap what we sow. If we send out thoughts of love and health, they return to us like bread cast upon the waters; but if we send out thoughts of fear, worry, jealousy, anger, hate, etc., we will reap the results in our own lives.

26. "It used to be said that man is built completely anew every seven years, but some scientists now declare that we build ourselves entirely over again every eleven months: so we are really only eleven months old. If we build the defects back into our bodies year after year, we have no one to blame but ourselves.

27. "Man is the sum total of his own thoughts; so the question is, how are we going to entertain only the good thoughts and reject the evil ones? At first we can't keep the evil thoughts from coming, but we can keep from entertaining them. The only way to do this is to forget them—which means, get something for them. This is where the ready-made affirmation comes in.

28. "When a thought of anger, jealousy, fear or worry creeps in, just start your affirmation going. The way to fight darkness is with light—the only way to fight cold is with heat—the way to overcome evil is with good. For myself, I never could

find any help in denials. Affirm the good, and the bad will vanish.

–Frederick Andrews."

29. If there is anything you require, it will be well for you to make use of this affirmation; it cannot be improved upon. Use it just as it is; take it into the silence with you, until it sinks into your sub-consciousness, so that you use it anywhere, in your car, on the tram, in the office, at home; this is the advantage of spiritual methods; they are always available. Spirit is omnipresent, ever ready; all that is required is a proper recognition of its omnipotence, and a willingness or desire to become the recipient of its beneficent effects.

30. If our predominant mental attitude is one of power, courage, kindliness and sympathy, we shall find that our environment will reflect conditions in correspondence with these thoughts; if it is weak, critical, envious and destructive, we shall find our environment reflecting conditions corresponding to these thoughts.

31. Thoughts are causes and conditions are effects. Herein is the explanation of the origin of both good and evil. Thought is creative and will automatically correlate with its object. This is a Cosmological law, the law of Attraction, the law of Cause and Effect; the recognition and application of this law will determine both beginning and end; it is the law by which in all ages and in all times the people were led to believe in the power of prayer. "As thy faith is, so be it unto thee," is simply another, a shorter and a better way of stating it.

32. Your next exercise is to visualize a plant; take a flower, the one you most admire, bring it from the unseen into the seen, plant the tiny seed, water it, care for it, place it where it will get the direct rays of the morning sun, see the seed burst; it is now a living thing, something which is alive and beginning to search for the means of subsistence. See the roots penetrating the earth, watch them shoot out in all directions and remember that they are living cells dividing and subdividing, and that they will soon number millions, that each cell is intelligent, that it knows what it wants and knows how to get it. See the stem shoot forward and upward, watch it burst through the surface of the earth, see it divide and form branches, see how perfect and symmetrical each branch is formed, see the leaves begin to form, and then the tiny stems, each one holding aloft a bud, and as you watch you see the bud begin to unfold and your favorite flower comes to view; and now if you will concentrate intently you will become conscious of a fragrance; it is the fragrance of the flower as the breeze gently sways the beautiful creation which you have visualized.

33. When you are enabled to make your vision clear and complete you will be enabled to enter into the spirit of a thing; it will become very real to you; you will be learning to concentrate and the process is the same, whether you are concentrating on health, a favorite flower, an ideal, a complicated business proposition or any other problem of life.

34. Every success has been accomplished by persistent concentration upon the object in view.

In the end, thought rules the world. There are times when impulses and passions are more powerful, but they soon expend themselves; while mind, acting constantly, is ever ready to drive them back and work when their energy is exhausted.

—J. McCosh.

*

81. *What is the imperative condition of all well-being?*
    Well doing.
82. *What is the condition precedent to every right action?*
    Right thinking.
83. *What is the underlying condition necessary in every business transaction or social relation?*
    To know the Truth.
84. *What is the result of a knowledge of the Truth?*
    We can readily foretell the result of any action that is based upon a true premise.
85. *What is the result of any action based upon a false premise?*
    We can form no conception of the results that may ensue.
86. *How may we know the Truth?*
    By a realization of the fact that Truth is the vital principle of the Universe and is therefore omnipresent.
87. *What is the nature of Truth?*
    It is spiritual.
88. *What is the secret of the solution to every problem?*
    To apply spiritual Truth.
89. *What is the advantage of spiritual methods?*
    They are always available.
90. *What are the necessary requirements?*
    A recognition of the omnipotence of spiritual power and a desire to become the recipient of its beneficent effects.

Thought means life, since those who do not think do not live in any high or real sense. Thinking makes the man.

—A. B. Alcott.

PART TEN

This Part tells of the Law of Abundance. It shows that Nature has provided an abundance for all, and why some seem to be separated from this supply. It tells of a connecting link between the individual and the supply, explains the Law of Attraction, the law by which your "own" is brought to you. It tells why every experience in life is the result of this law. It tells why and how you attract the things to you that make up the sum total of your existence. It tells how you may place yourself in harmony with this law and thereby assist in bringing about desirable conditions in your health, environment, or finances. It shows that this Law of Attraction is fundamental and eternal and that there is no escape from the result of its operation. A knowledge of this Law is absolutely essential to those desiring to make permanent progress.

If you get a thorough understanding of the thought contained in Part Ten, you will have learned that nothing happens without a definite cause. You will be enabled to formulate your plans in accordance with exact knowledge. You will know how to control any situation by bringing adequate causes into play. When you win, as you will, you will know exactly why.

The ordinary man, who has no definite knowledge of cause and effect, is governed by his feelings or emotions. He thinks chiefly to justify his action. If he fails as a businessman, he says that luck is against him. If he dislikes music, he says that music is an expensive luxury. If he is a poor clerk, he says that he could succeed better at some outdoor work. If he lacks friends, he says his individuality is too fine to be appreciated.

He never thinks this problem through to the end. In short, he does not know that every effect is the result of a certain definite cause, but he seeks to console himself with explanations and excuses. He thinks only in self-defense.

On the contrary, the man who understands that there is no effect without an adequate cause thinks impersonally. He gets down to absolute facts regardless of consequences. He is free to follow the path of truth wherever it may lead. He sees the issue clear to the end, and he meets the requirements fully and fairly, and the result is that the world gives him all that it has to give, in friendship, honour, love and approval.

❋

1. Abundance is a natural law of the Universe. The evidence of this law is conclusive; we see it on every hand. Everywhere Nature is lavish, wasteful, extravagant. Nowhere is economy observed in any created thing. Profusion is manifested in everything. The millions and millions of trees and flowers and plants and animals and the vast scheme of reproduction where the process of creating and recreating is for ever going on, all indicate the lavishness with which Nature has made provision for man. That there is an abundance for everyone is evident, but that many fail to participate in this abundance is also evident; they have not yet come into a realization of the Universality of all substance, and that mind is the active principle whereby we are related to the things we desire.

2. All wealth is the offspring of power; possessions are of value only as they confer power. Events are significant only as they affect power; all things represent certain forms and degrees of power.

3. Knowledge of cause and effect as shown by the laws governing electricity, chemical affinity and gravitation, enables man to plan courageously and execute fearlessly. These laws are called Natural Laws, because they govern in the physical

world, but all power is not physical power; there is also mental power, and there is moral and spiritual power.

4. Spiritual power is superior because it exists on a higher plane. It has enabled man to discover the law by which these wonderful forces of Nature could be harnessed and made to do the work of hundreds and thousands of men. It has enabled man to discover laws whereby time and space have been annihilated and now apparently the law of gravitation is to be overcome.

The operation of this law is dependent upon spiritual contact, as Henry Drummond well says:

5. "In the physical world as we know it, there exists the organic and the inorganic. The inorganic or the mineral world is absolutely cut off from the plant or animal world; the passage is hermetically sealed. These barriers have never yet been crossed. No change of substance, no modification of environment, no chemistry, no electricity, no form of energy, no evolution of any kind can ever endow a single atom of the mineral world with the attribute of Life.

6. "Only by the bending down into this dead world of some living form can those dead atoms be gifted with the properties of vitality; without this contact with life they remain fixed in the inorganic sphere for ever. Huxley says that the doctrine of Biogenesis or life only from life is victorious all along the line, and Tyndall is compelled to say: 'I affirm that no shred of trustworthy evidence exists to prove that life in our day has ever appeared independent of antecedent life.'

7. "Physical laws may explain the inorganic, Biology explains and accounts for the development of the organic, but of the point of contact Science is silent. A similar passage exists between the Natural world and the Spiritual world; this passage is hermetically sealed on the natural side. The door is closed; no man can open it, no organic change, no mental energy, no moral effort, no progress of any kind can enable any human being to enter the spiritual world."

8. But as the plant reaches down into the mineral world and touches it with the mystery of Life, so the Universal Mind reaches down into the human mind and endows it with new, strange, wonderful and even marvellous qualities. All men or women who have ever accomplished anything in the world of industry, commerce or art have accomplished because of this process.

9. Thought is the connecting link between the Infinite and the finite, between the Universal and the individual. We have seen that there is an impassable barrier between the organic and the inorganic and that the only way that matter can unfold is to be impregnated with life; as a seed reaches down into the mineral world and begins to unfold and reach out, the dead matter begins to live, a thousand invisible fingers begin to weave a suitable environment for the new arrival, and as the law of growth begins to take effect, we see the process continue until the Lily finally appears, and even " Solomon in all his glory was not arrayed like one of these."

10. Even so, a thought is dropped into the invisible substance of the Universal Mind, that substance from which all things are created, and as it takes root, the law

of growth begins to take effect and we find that conditions and environment are but the objective form of our thought.

11. The law is that Thought is an active vital form of dynamic energy that has the power to correlate with its object and bring it out of the invisible substance from which all things are created into the visible or objective world. This is the law by which, and through which, all things come into manifestation; it is the Master Key by which you are admitted into the Secret Place of the Most High and are "given dominion over all things." With an understanding of this law you may "decree a thing and it shall be established unto thee."

12. It could not be otherwise; if the soul of the Universe as we know it, is the Universal Spirit, then the Universe is simply the condition which the Universal Spirit has made for itself. We are simply individualized spirit and are creating the conditions for our growth in exactly the same way.

13. This creative power depends upon our recognition of the potential power of spirit or mind and must not be confused with Evolution. Creation is the calling into existence of that which does not exist in the objective world. Evolution is simply the unfolding of potentialities involved in things that already exist.

14. In taking advantage of the wonderful possibilities opened up to us through the operation of this law, we must remember that we ourselves contribute nothing to its efficacy as the Great Teacher said: "It is not I that doeth the works, but the Father that dwelleth in me, He doeth the work." We must take exactly the same position; we can do nothing to assist in the manifestation, we simply comply with the law, and the All-originating Mind will bring about the result.

15. The great error of the present day is the idea that Man has to originate the intelligence whereby the Infinite can proceed to bring about a specific purpose or result. Nothing of this kind is necessary; the Universal Mind can be depended upon to find the ways and means for bringing about any necessary manifestation. We must, however, create the ideal, and this ideal should be perfect.

16. We know that the laws governing Electricity have been formulated in such a way that this invisible power can be controlled and used for our benefit and comfort in thousands of ways. We know that messages are carried around the world, that ponderous machinery does its bidding, that it now illuminates practically the whole world, but we know, too, that if we consciously or ignorantly violate its law by touching a live wire, when it is not properly insulated, the result will be unpleasant and possibly disastrous. A lack of understanding of the laws governing in the invisible world has the same result, and many are suffering the consequences all the time.

17. It has been explained that the law of causation depends upon polarity, a circuit must be formed; this circuit cannot be formed unless we operate in harmony with the law. How shall we operate in harmony with the law unless we know what the law is? How shall we know what the Law is? By study, by observation.

18. We see the law in operation everywhere; all nature testifies to the operation of the law by silently, constantly expressing itself in the law of growth. Where

there is growth, there must be life; where there is life there must be harmony, so that everything that has life is constantly attracting to itself the conditions and the supply that are necessary for its most complete expression.

19. If your thought is in harmony with the creative Principle of nature, it is in tune with the Infinite Mind, and it will form the circuit, it will not return to you void; but it is possible for you to think thoughts that are not in tune with the Infinite, and there is no polarity, the circuit is not formed. What, then, is the result? What is the result when a dynamo is generating electricity? The circuit is cut off and there is no outlet. The dynamo stops.

20. It will be exactly the same with you, if you entertain thoughts which are not in accordance with the Infinite and cannot therefore be polarized; there is no circuit, you are isolated, the thoughts cling to you, harass you, worry you, and finally bring about disease and possibly death; the physician may not diagnose the case exactly in this way, he may give it some fancy name which has been manufactured for the various ills which are the result of wrong thinking, but the cause is the same nevertheless.

21. Constructive thought must necessarily be creative, but creative thought must be harmonious, and this eliminates all destructive or competitive thought.

22. Wisdom, strength, courage and all harmonious conditions are the result of power and we have seen that all power is from within; likewise, every lack, limitation or adverse circumstance is the result of weakness, and weakness is simply absence of power; it comes from nowhere, it is nothing—the remedy then is simply to develop power, and this is accomplished in exactly the same manner that all power is developed—by exercise.

23. This exercise consists in making an application of your knowledge. Knowledge will not apply itself. You must make the application. Abundance will not come to you out of the sky, neither will it drop into your lap, but a conscious realization of the law of attraction and the intention to bring it into operation for a certain, definite and specific purpose, and the will to carry out this purpose will bring about the materialization of your desire by a natural law of transference. If you are in business, it will increase and develop along regular channels, possibly new or unusual channels of distribution will be opened and when the law becomes fully operative you will find that the things you seek are seeking you.

24. For your next exercise select a blank space on the wall, or any other convenient spot, from where you usually sit, mentally draw a black horizontal line about six inches long, try to see the line as plainly as though it were painted on the wall; now mentally draw two vertical lines connecting with this horizontal line at either end; now draw another horizontal line connecting with the two vertical lines; now you have a square. Try to see the square perfectly; when you can do so draw a circle within the square; now place a point in the centre of the circle; now draw the point towards you about ten inches; now you have a cone on a square base; you will remember that your work was all in black; change it to white, to red, to yellow.

25. If you can do this, you are making excellent progress and will soon be enabled to concentrate on any problem you may have in mind.

When any object or purpose is clearly held in thought, its precipitation, in tangible and visible form, is merely a question of time. The vision always precedes and itself determines the realization.

—Lillian Whiting.

❋

91. *What is Wealth?*
   Wealth is the offspring of power.
92. *Of what value are possessions?*
   Possessions are of value only as they confer power.
93. *Of what value is a knowledge of cause and effect?*
   It enables men to plan courageously and execute fearlessly.
94. *How does life originate in the inorganic world?*
   Only by the introduction of some living form. There is no other way.
95. *What is the, connecting link between the finite and the Infinite?*
   Thought is the connecting link.
96. *Why is that so?*
   Because the Universal can manifest only through the individual.
97. *Upon what does causation depend?*
   Upon polarity; a circuit must be formed; the Universal is the positive side of the battery of life, the individual is the negative, and thought forms the circuit.
98. *Why do many fail to secure harmonious conditions?*
   They do not understand the law; there is no polarity; they have not formed the circuit.
99. *What is the remedy ?*
   A conscious recognition of the law of attraction with the intention of bringing it into existence for a definite purpose.
100. *What will be the result?*
   Thought will correlate with its object and bring it into manifestation, because thought is a product of the spiritual man, and spirit is the creative Principle of the Universe.

A vivid thought brings the power to paint it; and in proportion to the depths of its source is the force of its projection.

—Emerson.

ADVICE

Remember—
  Fully to understand grand and beautiful thought requires, perhaps, as much
  time as to conceive it.
                                                    –JOUBERT

If you wish to enjoy the utmost practical benefit form "The Master Key"—
  go slowly.

Transfuse into your mind the contents of one part only, each week for twenty-
  four weeks.

Realize the meaning of every phrase.

Consult "The Master Key" constantly, as your perpetual help and stimulus.

Each time you read the work you will get a better understanding of the eternal
  cosmic principles.

Tell others of "The Master Key" so that more and more people may reciprocate
  with you, as conscious adepts in harmony.

PART ELEVEN

This Part tells of the means by which we have discovered that the infinitely small as well as the infinitely large is in the last analysis nothing but force, motion, life and mind. It tells of the process by which we have become familiar with the vast organization by which we are identified with the complex operations of Nature. It gives concise directions for making use of the creative power of the Universe, the power by which all things are brought into existence. It shows how this marvellous power may be utilized, directed and made available for the solution of every human problem.

Your life is governed by law, by actual, immutable principles that never vary. Law is in operation at all times, in all places.

Fixed laws underlie all human actions. For this reason, men who control giant industries are enabled to determine with absolute precision just what percentage of every hundred thousand people will respond to any given set of conditions.

It is well, however, to remember that while every effect is the result of a cause, the effect in turn becomes a cause, which creates other effects, which in turn create still other causes; so that when you put the law of attraction into operation you must remember that you are starting a train of causation for good or otherwise which may have endless possibilities.

We frequently hear it said, "A very distressing situation came into my life, which could not have been the result of my thought, as I certainly never entertained any thought which could have such a result." We fail to remember that like attracts like in the mental world, and that the thought which we entertain brings to us certain friendships, companionships of a particular kind, and these in turn bring about conditions and environment, which in turn are responsible for the conditions of which we complain.

✳

1. Inductive reasoning is the process of the objective mind by which we compare a number of separate instances with one another until we see the common factor that gives rise to them all.

2. Induction proceeds by comparison of facts; it is this method of studying nature that has resulted in the discovery of a reign of law that has marked an epoch in human progress.

3. It is the dividing line between superstition and intelligence; it has eliminated the elements of uncertainty and caprice from men's lives and substituted law, reason and certitude.

4. It is the "Watchman at the Gate" mentioned in a former Part.

5. When, by virtue of this principle, the world to which the senses were accustomed, has been revolutionized; when the sun has been arrested in his course, the apparently flat earth has been shaped into a ball and set whirling around him; when the inert matter has been resolved into active elements, and the universe presents itself wherever we direct the telescope and microscope, full of force, motion and life; we are constrained to ask by what possible means the delicate forms of organization in the midst of it are kept in order and repair.

6. Like poles and like forces repel themselves or remain impenetrable to each other, and this cause seems in general sufficient to assign a proper place and dis-

tance to stars, men and forces. As men of different virtues enter into partnership, so do opposite poles attract each other; elements that have no property in common like acids and gases cling to each other in preference and a general exchange is kept up between the surplus and the demand.

7. As the eye seeks and receives satisfaction from colours complementary to those which are given, so do need, want and desire, in the largest sense, induce, guide and determine action.

8. It is our privilege to become conscious of the principle and act in accordance with it. Cuvier sees a tooth belonging to an extinct race of animals. This tooth wants a body for the performance of its function, and it defines the peculiar body it stands in need of with such precision that Cuvier is able to reconstruct the frame of this animal.

9. Perturbations are observed in the motions of Uranus. Adams and Leverrier need another star at a certain place to keep the solar system in order, and Neptune appears in the place and at the hour appointed.

10. The instinctive wants of the animal and the intellectual wants of Cuvier; the wants of nature and of the minds of Leverrier and Adams were alike, and thus the results; here the thoughts of an existence, there an existence. A well-defined lawful want, therefore, furnishes the reason for the more complex operations of nature.

11. Having recorded correctly the answers furnished by nature and stretched our senses with the growing science over her surface; having joined hands with the levers that move the earth; we become conscious of such a close, varied and deep contact with the world without, that our wants and purposes become no less identified with the harmonious operations of this vast organization, than the life, liberty and happiness of the citizen are identified with the existence of his government.

12. As the interests of the individual are protected by the arms of the country, added to his own; and his needs produce certain supply in the degree that they are felt more universally and steadily; in the same manner does conscious citizenship in the Kingdom of nature secure us from the annoyances of subordinate agents by our alliance with superior powers; and by our conformity with the fundamental laws of resistance or inducement offered to mechanical or chemical agents, we distribute the labour to be performed between them and man to the best advantage of inventor and user.

13. If Plato could have witnessed the pictures executed by the sun with the assistance of the photographer, or a hundred similar illustrations of what man does by induction, he would perhaps have been reminded of the intellectual midwifery of his master and, in his own mind might have arisen the vision of a land where all manual, mechanical labour and repetition is assigned to the power of nature, where our wants are satisfied by purely mental operations set in motion by the will, and where the supply is created by the demand.

14. However distant that land may appear, induction has taught men to make strides towards it and has surrounded him with benefits which are, at the same time, rewards for past fidelity and incentives for more assiduous devotion.

15. Induction is also an aid in concentrating and strengthening our faculties for the remainder of the journey, giving unerring solution for individual as well as universal problems, by the mere operations of mind in the purest form.

16. Here we find a method, the spirit of which is, to believe that what is sought has been accomplished, in order to accomplish it: a method, bequeathed upon us by the same Plato who, outside of this sphere, could never find how the ideas became realities.

17. This conception is also elaborated by Swedenborg in his doctrine of correspondences. And a still greater teacher has said, "What things so ever ye desire, when ye pray, believe that ye receive them, and ye shall have them." (Mark xi. 24 R.V.) The differences of the tense in this passage is remarkable.

18. We are first to believe that our desire has already been fulfilled, its accomplishment will then follow. This is a concise direction for making use of the creative power of thought by impressing on the Universal subjective mind the particular thing that we desire as an already existing fact.

19. We are thus thinking on the plane of the absolute and eliminating all consideration of conditions or limitation and are planting a seed which, if left undisturbed, will finally germinate into external fruition.

20. To review: Inductive reasoning is the process of the objective mind, by which we compare a number of separate instances with one another until we see the common factor that gives rise to them all. We see people in every civilized country on the globe, securing results by some process which they do not seem to understand themselves, and to which they usually attach more or less mystery. Our reason is given to us for the purpose of ascertaining the law by which these results are accomplished.

21. The operation of this thought process is seen in those fortunate natures that possess everything that others must acquire by toil, who never have a struggle with conscience because they always act correctly, and can never comport themselves otherwise than with tact, learn everything easily, complete everything they begin with a happy knack, live in eternal harmony with themselves, without ever reflecting much what they do, or ever experiencing difficulty or toil.

22. The fruit of this thought is, as it were, a gift of the gods, but a gift that few as yet realize, appreciate, or understand. The recognition of the marvellous power that is possessed by the mind under proper conditions and the fact that this power can be utilized, directed, and made available for the solution of every human problem is of transcendental importance.

23. All truth is the same, whether stated in modern scientific terms or in the language of apostolic times. There are timid souls who fail to realize that the very completeness of truth requires various statement—that no one human formula will show every side of it.

24. Change, emphasis, new language, novel interpretations, unfamiliar perspectives, are not, as some suppose, signs of departure from truth, but on the con-

trary they are evidence that the truth is being apprehended in new relations to human needs, and is becoming more generally understood.

25. The truth must be told to each generation and to every people in new and different terms, so that when the Great Teacher said—"Believe that ye receive and ye shall receive," or when Paul said—"Faith is the substance of things not seen," or when modern science says—"The law of attraction is that law by which thought correlates with its object," each statement, when subjected to analysis, is found to contain exactly the same truth. The only difference being in the form of presentation.

26. We are standing on the threshold of a new era. The time has arrived when man has learned the secrets of mastery and the way is being prepared for a new social order, more wonderful than anything ever heretofore dreamed of. The conflict of modern science with theology, the study of comparative religions, the tremendous power of new social movements, all of these are but clearing the way for the new order. They may have destroyed traditional forms that have become antiquated and impotent, but nothing of value has been lost.

27. A new faith has been born, a faith that demands a new form of expression, and this faith is taking form in a deep consciousness of power that is being manifested in the present spiritual activity found on every hand.

28. The spirit which sleeps in the mineral, breathes in the vegetable, moves in the animal, and reaches its highest development in man is the Universal Mind, and it behoves us to span the gulf between being and doing, theory and practice by demonstrating our understanding of the dominion which we have been given.

29. By far the greatest discovery of all the centuries is the power of thought. The importance of this discovery has been a little slow in reaching the general consciousness, but it has arrived, and already in every field of research the importance of this greatest of all great discoveries is being demonstrated.

30. You ask in what does the creative power of thought consist? It consists in creating ideas, and these in turn objectify themselves by appropriating, inventing, observing, discerning, discovering, analyzing, ruling, governing, combining and applying matter and force. It can do this because it is an intelligent creative power.

31. Thought reaches its loftiest activity when plunged into its own mysterious depth; when it breaks through the narrow compass of self and passes from truth to truth to the region of eternal light, where all which is, was or eve, will be, melt into one grand harmony.

32. From this process of self contemplation comes inspiration which is creative intelligence, and which is undeniably superior to every element, force or law of nature, because it can understand, modify, govern and apply them to its own ends and purposes and therefore possess them.

33. Wisdom begins with the dawn of reason, and reason is but an understanding of the knowledge and principles whereby we may know the true meaning of things. Wisdom, then, is illuminated reason, and this wisdom leads to humility, for humility is a large part of Wisdom.

34. We all know many who have achieved the seemingly impossible, who have realized life-long dreams, who have changed everything, including themselves. We have sometimes marvelled at the demonstration of an apparently irresistible power, which seemed to be ever available just when it was most needed. But it is all clear now. All that is required is an understanding of certain definite fundamental principles and their proper application.

35. For your next exercise, concentrate on the quotation taken from the Bible, "Whatsoever things ye desire, when ye pray, believe that ye receive them and ye shall have them." Notice that there is no limitation, "Whatsoever things" is very definite and implies that the only limitation which is placed upon us is in our ability to think, to be equal to the occasion, to rise to the emergency, to remember that Faith is not a shadow, but a substance, "the substance of things hoped for, the evidence of things not seen.

✻

101. *What is inductive reasoning?*
It is the process of the objective mind by which we compare a number of separate instances with each other until we see the common factor which gives rise to them all.

102. *What has this method of studying accomplished?*
It has resulted in the discovery of a reign of law that has marked an epoch in human progress.

103. *What is it that guides and determines action?*
It is need, want and desire which in the largest sense induce, guide and determine action.

104. *What is the formula for the unerring solution of every individual problem?*
We are to believe that our desire has already been fulfilled; its accomplishment will then follow.

105. *What great Teachers advocated it?*
Jesus, Plato, Swedenborg.

106. *What is the result of the operation of this thought process?*
We are thinking on the plane of the absolute and planting a seed, which if left undisturbed will germinate into fruition.

107. *Why is it scientifically exact?*
Because it is Natural Law.

108. *What is Faith?*
"Faith is the substance of things hoped for, the evidence of things unseen."

109. *What is the Law of Attraction?*
The Law by which Faith is brought into manifestation.

110. *What importance do you attach to an understanding of this law?*

It has eliminated the elements of uncertainty and caprice from men's lives and substituted law, reason and certitude.

Death is but the natural process whereby all material forms are thrown into the crucible for reproduction in fresh diversity.

PART TWELVE

This Part tells of numerous counterfeits and perversions by which many are led to think that something can be had for nothing. There is no royal road to success, we must give before we can get; if we cannot give money, we must give service, we must give time and thought, the Law of Compensation demands an eye for an eye. It tells how we may create the implements by which we may put into operation the laws by which we can gain access to the unlimited resources of Nature.

In the fourth paragraph you will find the following statement: "You must first have the knowledge of your power; second, the courage to dare; third, the faith to do."

If you concentrate upon the thoughts given; if you give them your entire attention, you will find a world of meaning in each sentence, and will attract to yourself other thoughts in harmony with them, and you will soon grasp the full significance of the vital knowledge upon which you are concentrating.

Knowledge does not apply itself; we as individuals must make the application, and the application consists in fertilizing the thought with a living purpose.

The time and thought which most persons waste in aimless effort would accomplish wonders if properly directed with some special object in view. In order to do this, it is necessary to centre your mental force upon a specific thought and hold it there, to the exclusion of all other thoughts. If you have ever looked through the focusing screen of a camera, you found that when the object was not in focus, the impression was indistinct and possibly blurred, but when the proper focus was obtained the picture was clear and distinct. This illustrates the power of concentration. Unless you can concentrate upon the object that you have in view, you will have but a hazy, indifferent, vague, indistinct and blurred outline of your ideal and the results will be in accordance with your mental picture.

❋

1. There is no purpose in life that cannot be best accomplished through a scientific understanding of the creative power of thought.

2. The power to think is common to all. Man is, because he thinks. Man's power to think is infinite; consequently his creative power is unlimited.

3. We know that thought is building for us the thing we think of and actually bringing it nearer, yet we find it difficult to banish fear, anxiety or discouragement, all of which are powerful thought forces, and which continually send the things we desire further away, so that it is often one step forward and two steps backward.

4. The only way to keep from going backward is to keep going forward. Eternal vigilance is the price of success. There are three steps, and each one is absolutely essential. You must first have the knowledge of your power; second, the courage to dare; third, the faith to do.

5. With this as a basis you can construct an ideal business, an ideal home, ideal friends, ideal environment. You are not restricted as to material or cost. Thought is omnipotent and has the power to draw on the Infinite bank of Primary substance for all that it requires. Infinite resources are therefore at your command.

6. But your ideal must be sharp, clear-cut, definite; to have one ideal to-day, another to-morrow, and a third next week, means to scatter your forces and accomplish nothing; your result will be a meaningless and chaotic combination of wasted material.

7. Unfortunately this is the result that many are securing, and the cause is self evident. If a sculptor started out with a piece of marble and a chisel and changed his ideal every fifteen minutes, what result could he expect? And why should you expect any different result in moulding the greatest and most plastic of all sub-stances, the only real substance?

8. The result of this indecision and negative thought is often found in the loss of material wealth. Supposed independence that required many years of toil and effort suddenly disappears. It is often found then that money and property are not independence at all. On the contrary, the only independence is found to be a prac-tical working knowledge of the creative power of thought.

9. This practical working method cannot come to you, until you learn that the only real power which you can have, is the power to adjust yourself to Divine and unchangeable principles. You cannot change the Infinite, but you can come into an understanding of Natural laws. The reward of this understanding is a conscious realization of your ability to adjust your thought faculties to the Universal Thought that is Omnipresent. Your ability to co-operate with this Omnipotence will indicate the degree of success with which you meet.

10. The power of thought has many counterfeits which are more or less fasci-nating, but the results are harmful instead of helpful.

11. Of course, worry, fear and all negative thoughts produce a crop after their kind; those who harbor thoughts of this kind must inevitably reap exactly what they have sown.

12. Again, there are the Phenomena seekers who gormandize on tile so-called proofs and demonstrations obtained at materializing seances. They throw open their mental doors and soak themselves in the most poisonous currents which can be found in the psychic world. They do not seem to understand that it is the abil-ity to become negative, receptive and passive, and thus drain themselves of all their vital force, which enables them to bring about these vibratory thought forms.

13. There are also the Hindu worshippers, who see in the materializing phe-nomena which are performed by the so-called adepts, a source of power, forgetting, or never seeming to realize that as soon as the will is withdrawn the forms wither, and the vibratory forces of which they are composed vanish.

14. Telepathy, or thought transference, has received considerable attention, but as it requires a negative mental state on the part of the receiver, the practice is harmful. A thought may be sent with the intention of hearing or seeing, but it will bring the penalty attached to the inversion of the principle involved.

15. Hypnotism is positively dangerous to the subject as well as the operator. No one familiar with the laws governing in the mental world would think of

attempting to dominate the will of another, for by so doing he will gradually but surely divest himself of his own power.

16. All of these perversions have their temporary satisfaction and for some a keen fascination, but there is an infinitely greater fascination in a true understanding of the world of power within, a power which increases with use; is permanent instead of fleeting; which not only is potent as a remedial agency to bring about the remedy for past error or results of wrong thinking, but is a prophylactic agency protecting us from all manner and form of danger, and finally is an actual creative force with which we can build new conditions and new environment.

17. The law is, that thought will correlate with its object and bring forth in the material world the correspondence of the thing thought or produced in the mental world. We then discern the absolute necessity of seeing that every thought has the inherent germ of truth in order that the law of growth will bring into manifestation good, for good alone can confer any permanent power.

18. The principle that gives the thought the dynamic power to correlate with its object, and therefore to master every adverse human experience, is the law of attraction, which is another name for love. This is an eternal and fundamental principle, inherent in all things, in every system of Philosophy, in every Religion and in every Science. There is no getting away from the law of love. It is feeling that imparts vitality to thought. Feeling is desire, and desire is love. Thought impregnated with love becomes invincible.

19. We find this truth emphasized wherever the power of thought is understood. The Universal Mind is not only Intelligence, but it is substance, and this substance is the attractive force which brings electrons together by the law of attraction so that they form atoms; the atoms in turn are brought together by the same law and form molecules; molecules take objective forms; and so we find that the law of love is the creative force behind every manifestation, not only of atoms but of worlds, of the Universe, of everything of which the imagination can form any conception.

20. It is the operation of this marvellous of attraction which has caused men in all and all times to believe that there must be some personal being who responded to their petitions and desires, and manipulated events in order to comply with their requirements.

21. It is the combination of Thought and Love that forms the irresistible force, called the law of attraction. All natural laws are irresistible, the law of Gravitation, or Electricity, or any other law operates with mathematical exactitude. There is no variation, it is only the channel of distribution which may be imperfect. If a bridge falls, we do not attribute the collapse to any variation of the law of gravitation. If a light fails us, we do not conclude that the laws governing electricity cannot be depended upon, and if the law of attraction seems to be imperfectly demonstrated by an inexperienced or uninformed person, we are not to conclude that the greatest and most infallible law upon which the entire system of creation depends has been suspended. We should rather conclude that a little more understanding of the

law is required, for the same reason that a correct solution of a difficult problem in Mathematics is not always readily and easily obtained.

22. Things are created in the mental or spiritual world before they appear in the outward act or event. By the simple process of governing our thought forces to-day, we help create the events that will come into our lives in future, perhaps even to-morrow. Educated desire is the most potent means of bringing into action the law of attraction.

23. Man is so constituted that he must first create the tools, or implements by which he gains the power to think. The mind cannot comprehend an entirely new idea until a corresponding vibratory brain cell has been prepared to receive it. This explains why it is so difficult for us to receive or appreciate an entirely new idea; we have no brain cell capable of receiving it; we are therefore incredulous; we do not believe it.

24. If, therefore, you have not been familiar with the Omnipotence of the law of attraction, and the scientific method by which it can be put into operation, or if you have not been familiar with the unlimited possibilities which it opens to those who are enabled to take advantage of the resources it offers, begin now and create the necessary brain cells which will enable you to comprehend the unlimited powers which may be yours by co-operating with Natural Law. This is done by concentration or attention.

25. The intention governs the attention. Power comes through repose. It is by concentration that deep thoughts, wise speech and all forces of high potentiality are accomplished.

26. It is in the Silence that you get into touch with the omnipotent power of the subconscious mind from which all power is evolved.

27. He who desires wisdom, power or permanent success of any kind will find it only within; it is an unfoldment. The unthinking may conclude that the silence is very simple and easily attained, but it should be remembered that only in absolute silence may one come into contact with Divinity itself; may learn of the unchangeable law and open for himself the channels by which persistent practice and concentration lead to perfection.

28. Now go to the same room, take the same chair, the same position as heretofore; be sure to relax, let go, both mentally and physically; always do this; never try to do any mental work under pressure; see that there are no tense muscles or nerves, that you are entirely comfortable. Now realize your unity with omnipotence; get into touch with this power, come into a deep and vital understanding, appreciation and realization of the fact that your ability to think is your ability to act upon the Universal Mind, and bring it into manifestation, realize that it will meet any and every requirement; that you have exactly the same potential ability which any individual ever did have or ever will have, because each is but an expression or Manifestation of the One, all are parts of the whole, there is no difference in kind or quality, the only difference being one of degree.

✴

111. *How may any purpose in life be best accomplished?*
Through a scientific understanding of the spiritual nature of thought.

112. *What three steps are absolutely essential?*
The knowledge of our power, the courage to dare, the faith to do.

113. *How is the Practical Working knowledge secured?*
By an understanding of Natural laws.

114. *What is the reward of an understanding of these laws?*
A conscious realization of our ability to adjust ourselves to Divine and unchanging principle.

115. *What will indicate the degree of success with which we meet?*
The degree in which we realize that we cannot change the Infinite but must co-operate with it.

116. *What is the principle that gives thought its dynamic power?*
The Law of Attraction which rests on vibration, which in turn rests upon the law of love. Thought impregnated with love becomes invincible.

117. *Why is this law irresistible?*
Because it is a Natural law. All Natural laws are irresistible and unchangeable and act with mathematical exactitude. There is no deviation or variation.

118. *Why then does it sometimes seem to be difficult to find the solution to our problems in life?*
For the same reason that it is sometimes difficult to find the correct solution to a difficult mathematical problem. The operator is uninformed or inexperienced.

119. *Why is it impossible for the mind to grasp an entirely new idea?*
We have no corresponding vibratory brain cell capable of receiving the idea.

220. *How is wisdom secured?*
By concentration; it is unfoldment; it comes from within.

—Thought cannot conceive of anything that may not be brought to expression. He who first uttered it may be only the suggester, but the doer will appear.

—Wilson.

ADVICE

Remember—
  Fully to understand grand and beautiful thought requires, perhaps, as much
  time as to conceive it.
                                                                    –JOUBERT

If you wish to enjoy the utmost practical benefit form "The Master Key"—
  go slowly.

Transfuse into your mind the contents of one part only, each week for twenty-
  four weeks.

Realize the meaning of every phrase.

Consult "The Master Key" constantly, as your perpetual help and stimulus.

Each time you read the work you will get a better understanding of the eternal
  cosmic principles.

Tell others of "The Master Key" so that more and more people may reciprocate
  with you, as conscious adepts in harmony.

PART THIRTEEN

This Part explains why certain forms of thought often result in disaster and frequently sweep away the result of a lifetime of effort. It explains the modern method of thinking and shows how actual, tangible results are thereby secured, and how conditions must change in order to meet the requirements of a changed consciousness. It explains the process by which this change is brought about and how we may hasten it.

Physical science is responsible for the marvellous age of invention in which we are now living, but spiritual science is now setting out on a career whose possibilities no one can foretell.

Spiritual science has heretofore been the football of the uneducated, the superstitious, the mystical; but men are now interested in definite methods and demonstrated facts only.

We have come to know that thinking is a spiritual process, that vision and imagination precede action and event, that the day of the dreamer has come. The following lines by Mr. Herbert Kaufman, relating to people who first dream and then achieve, are interesting in this connection.

"They are the architects of greatness, their vision lies within their souls, they peer beyond the veils and mists of doubt and pierce the walls of unborn Time. The belted wheel, the trail of steel, the churning screw, are shuttles in the loom on which they weave their magic tapestries. Makers of Empire, they have fought for bigger things than crowns and higher seats than thrones. Your, homes are set upon a land that dreamers built to greatness. The pictures on its walls are visions from the souls of dreamers.

"They are the chosen few—the blazers of the way. Walls crumble and Empires fall, the tidal wave sweeps from the sea and tears a fortress from its rocks. The rotting nations drop from off Time's bough, and only things the dreamers make live on."

Part Thirteen tells why the dreams of the dreamer come true. It explains the law of causation by which dreamers, inventors, authors, organizers, bring about the realization of their desires. It explains the law by which the thing pictured upon our mind eventually becomes our own.

✸

1. It has been the tendency, and, as might be proved, a necessity for science to seek the explanation of every-day facts by a generalization of those others which are less frequent and form the exception. Thus does the eruption of the volcano manifest the heat that is continually at work in the interior of the earth and to which the latter owes much of her configuration.

2. Thus does the lightning reveal a subtle power constantly busy to produce changes in the inorganic world; and, as dead languages now seldom heard were once ruling among the nations, so does a giant tooth in Siberia, or a fossil in the depth of the earth, not only bear record of the evolution of past ages, but thereby explains to us the origin of the hills and valleys which we inhabit to-day.

3. In this way a generalization of facts which are rare, strange, or form the

exception, has been the magnetic needle guiding to all the discoveries of inductive science.

4. This method is founded upon reason and experience and thereby destroyed superstition, precedent and conventionality.

5. It is more than two hundred years since Bacon recommended this method of study, to which the civilized nations owe the greater part of their prosperity and the more valuable part of their knowledge; purging the mind from narrow prejudices, denominating theories, more effectually than by the keenest irony; calling the attention of men from heaven to earth more successfully by surprising experiments than by the most forcible demonstrations of their ignorance; educating the inventive faculties more powerfully by the near prospect of useful discoveries thrown open to all, than by talk of bringing to light the innate laws of our mind.

6. The method of Bacon has seized the spirit and aim of the great philosophers of Greece and carried them into effect by the new means of observation which another age offered; thus gradually revealing a wondrous field of knowledge in the infinite space of astronomy, in the microscopic egg of embryology, and the dim age of geology; disclosing an order of the pulse which the logic of Aristotle could never have unveiled, and analyzing into formerly unknown elements the material combinations which no dialectic of the scholastics could force apart.

7. It has lengthened life; it has mitigated pain; it has extinguished diseases; it has increased the fertility of the soil; it has given new securities to the mariner; it has spanned great rivers with bridges of form unknown to our fathers; it has guided the thunderbolt from heaven to earth; it has lighted up night with the splendour of day; it has extended the range of human vision; it has multiplied the power of the human muscles; it has accelerated motion; it has annihilated distance; it has facilitated intercourse, correspondence, all friendly office all dispatch of business; it has enabled men to descend into the depths of the sea, to soar into the air, to penetrate securely into the noxious recesses of the earth.

8. This then is the true nature and scope of induction. But the greater the success which men have achieved in the inductive science, the more does the whole tenor of their teachings and example impress us with the necessity of observing carefully, patiently, accurately, with all the instruments and resources at our command the individual facts before venturing upon a statement of general laws.

9. We ascertain the bearing of the spark drawn from the electric machine under every variety of circumstances, that we thus may be emboldened with Franklin to address, in the form of a kite, the question to the cloud about the nature of the lightning. We assure ourselves with the exactness of a Galileo, of the manner in which bodies fall, that with Newton we may dare to ask the moon about the force that fastens it to the earth.

10. In short, by the value we set upon truth; by our hope in a steady and universal progress; by our resolve not to permit a tyrannical prejudice to neglect or mutilate unwelcome facts, we rear the superstructure of science upon the broad

and unchangeable basis, of full attention paid to the most isolated as well as the most frequent phenomena.

11. An ever-increasing material may be collected by observation, but the accumulated facts differ in their value to assist the explanation of nature, and as we esteem most highly those useful qualities of men that are of the rarest occurrence, so does natural philosophy sift the facts and attach a pre-eminent importance to that striking class which cannot be accounted for by the usual and daily observation of life.

12. If then, we find that certain persons seem to possess unusual power, what are we to conclude? Firstly, we may say, it is not so, which is simply an acknowledgment of our lack of information because every honest investigator admits that there are many strange and heretofore unaccountable phenomena constantly occurring. Those, however, who become acquainted with the creative power of thought, will no longer consider them unaccountable.

13. Secondly, we may say that they are the result of supernatural interference; but a scientific understanding of Natural Laws will convince us that there is nothing supernatural. Every phenomenon is the result of an accurate, definite cause, and the cause is an immutable law or principle, which operates with invariable precision, whether the law is put into operation consciously or unconsciously.

14. Thirdly, we may say that we are on "forbidden ground," that there are some things that we should not know. This objection was used against every advance in human knowledge. Every individual who ever advanced a new idea, whether a Columbus, a Darwin, a Galileo, a Watt, a Fulton, a Stephenson, a Faraday, or an Emerson, was subjected to ridicule or persecution. Hence this objection should receive no serious consideration. On the contrary, we should carefully consider every fact that is brought to our attention; by doing this we will more readily ascertain the law upon which it is based.

15. It will be found that the creative power of thought will explain every possible condition or experience, whether physical, mental or spiritual.

16. Thought will bring about conditions in correspondence with the predominant mental attitude. Therefore, as fear is a powerful form of thought, if we fear disaster, disaster will be the certain result of our thinking. It is this form of thought that frequently sweeps away the result of many years of toil and effort.

17. If we think of some form of material wealth we may secure it. By concentrated thought the required conditions will be brought about, and the proper effort put forth, which will result in bringing about the circumstances necessary to realize our desires; but we often find that when we secure the things we thought we wanted, they do not have the effect we expected. That is, the satisfaction is only temporary, or possibly is the reverse of what we expected.

18. What, then, is the proper method of procedure? What are we to think in order to secure what we really desire? What you and I desire, what we all desire, what every one is seeking, is Happiness and Harmony. If we can be truly happy we

shall have everything the world can give. If we are happy ourselves we can make others happy.

19. But we cannot be happy unless we have health, strength, congenial friends, pleasant environment, sufficient supply, not only to take care of our necessities but to provide for those comforts and luxuries to which we are entitled.

20. The old orthodox way of thinking was to be "a worm," to be satisfied with our portion whatever it is; but the modern idea is to know that we are entitled to the best of everything, that the "Father and I are one" and that the "Father" is the Universal Mind, the Creator, the Original Substance from which all things proceed.

21. Now admitting that this is all true in theory, and it has been taught for two thousand years, and is the essence of every system of Philosophy or Religion, how are we to make it practical in our lives? How are we to get the actual, tangible results here and now?

22. In the first place, we must put our knowledge into practice. Nothing can be accomplished in any other way. The athlete may read books and lessons on physical training all his life, but unless he begins to give out strength by actual work he will never receive any strength; he will eventually get exactly what he gives; but he will have to give it first. It is exactly the same with us; we will get exactly what we give, but we shall have to give it first. It will then return to us many fold, and the giving is simply a mental process, because thoughts are causes and conditions are effects; therefore in giving thoughts of courage, inspiration, health or help of any kind we are setting causes in motion which will bring about their effect.

23. Thought is a spiritual activity and is therefore creative; but, make no mistake, thought will create nothing unless it is consciously, systematically, and constructively directed; and herein is the difference between idle thinking, which is simply a dissipation of effort, and constructive thinking, which means practically unlimited achievement.

24. We have found that everything we get comes to us by the Law of Attraction. A happy thought cannot exist in an unhappy consciousness; therefore the consciousness must change, and, as the consciousness changes, all conditions necessary to meet the changed consciousness must gradually change, in order to meet the requirements of the new situation.

25. In creating a Mental Image or an Ideal, we are projecting a thought into the Universal Substance from which all things are created. Universal Substance is Omnipresent, Omnipotent and Omniscient. Are we to inform the Omniscient as to the proper channel to be used to materialize our demand? Can the finite advise the Infinite? This is the cause of failure; of every failure. We recognize the Omnipresence of the Universal Substance, but we fail to appreciate the fact that this substance is not only Omnipresent, but is Omnipotent and Omniscient, and consequently will set causes in motion concerning which we may be entirely ignorant.

26. We can best conserve our interests by recognizing the Infinite Power and

Infinite Wisdom of the Universal Mind. In this way we become a channel whereby the Infinite can bring about the realization of our desire. This means that recognition brings about realization. Therefore for your next exercise make use of the principle, recognize the fact, that you are a part of the whole, and that a part must be the same in kind and quality as the whole; that the only difference there can possibly be, is in degree.

27. When this tremendous fact begins to permeate your consciousness; when you really come into a realization of the fact that you, not your body but the Ego, the "I," the spirit which thinks, is an integral part of the great whole, that it is the same in substance, in quality, in kind, that the Creator could create nothing different from Himself, you will also be able to say, "The Father and I are one" and you will come into an understanding of the beauty, the grandeur, the transcendental opportunities which have been placed at your disposal.

> Increase in me that wisdom
> Which discovers my truest interest,
> Strengthen my resolution
> To perform that which wisdom dictates.

> —Franklin.

✱

121. *What is the method by which natural philosophers obtain and apply their knowledge?*
    To observe individual facts carefully, patiently, accurately, with all the instruments and resources at their command, before venturing upon a statement of general laws.

122. *How may we be certain that this method is correct?*
    By not permitting a tyrannical prejudice to neglect or mutilate unwelcome facts.

123. *What class of acts are esteemed most highly?*
    Those which cannot be accounted for by the usual daily observations of life.

124. *Upon what is this principle founded?*
    Upon reason and experience.

125. *What does it destroy?*
    Superstition, precedent and conventionality.

126. *How have these laws been discovered?*
    By a generalization of facts which are uncommon, rare, strange and form the exception.

127. *How may we account for much of the strange and heretofore unexplainable Phenomena that are constantly taking place?*
    By the creative power of thought.

128. *Why is this so?*

Because when we learn of a fact we can be sure that it is the result of a certain definite cause and that this cause will operate with invariable precision.

129. *What is the result of this knowledge?*

It will explain the cause of every possible condition, whether physical, mental or spiritual.

130. *How will our best interest be conserved?*

By a recognition of the fact that a knowledge of the creative nature of thought puts us in touch with Infinite power.

The old thoughts never die; immortal dreams outlive their dreamers and are ours for aye; no thought once formed and uttered ever can expire.

—Mackay.

PART FOURTEEN

This Part explains the source of all Power, Wisdom and Intelligence, and how we may bring it into harmonious relations in our affairs. It shows that those who understand the principle get results in exact accordance with their understanding and their ability to make the proper application. This opens up possibilities hitherto undreamed of and by an orderly sequence of law. It explains the source of all energy and all substance and the method by which this Universal Substance is differentiated into form. It explains the nature of electrons and of cells upon which the maintenance of health and life depend; it explains how we may bring about radical changes in our life and what the result of such changes must necessarily be.

You have found from your study thus far that thought is a spiritual activity and is therefore endowed with creative power. This does not mean that some thought is creative. All thought is creative. And thought can be used in negative way, through the process of denial.

The conscious and subconscious are but two phases of action in connection with one mind. The relation of the subconscious to the conscious is quite analogous to that existing between a weather-vane and the atmosphere. Just as the least pressure of the atmosphere causes an action on the part of the weather-vane, so does the least thought entertained by the conscious mind produce within your subconscious mind action in exact proportion to the depth of feeling characterizing the thought and the intensity with which the thought is indulged.

It follows that if you deny unsatisfactory conditions, you are withdrawing the creative power of your thought from these conditions. You are cutting them away at the root. You are sapping their vitality.

Remember that the law of growth necessarily governs every manifestation in the objective, so that a denial of unsatisfactory conditions will not bring about instant change. A plant will remain visible for some time after its roots have been cut, but it will gradually fade away and eventually disappear; so the withdrawal of your thought from the contemplation of unsatisfactory conditions will gradually but surely terminate these conditions.

You will see that this is an exactly opposite course from the one that we would naturally be inclined to adopt. It will therefore have an exactly opposite effect to the one usually secured. Most persons concentrate intently upon an unsatisfactory condition, thereby giving the condition that measure of energy and vitality that is necessary in order to supply a vigorous growth.

✻

1. The Universal Energy in which all motion, light, heat, and colour have their origin, does not partake of the limitation of the many effects of which it is the cause, but it is supreme over them all. This Universal Substance is the source of all Power, Wisdom and Intelligence.

2. To recognize this Intelligence is to acquaint yourself with the knowing quality of Mind and through it to move upon the Universal Substance, and bring it into harmonious relations in your affairs.

3. This is something that the most learned physical science teacher has not attempted—a field of discovery upon which he has not yet launched; in fact, but few of the materialistic schools have ever caught the first ray of this light. It does

not seem to have dawned upon them that wisdom is just as much present everywhere as are force and substance.

4. Some will say, if these principles are true, why are we not demonstrating them? As the fundamental principle is obviously correct, why do we not get proper results? We do. We get results in exact accordance with our understanding of the law and our ability to make the proper application. We secured no results from the laws governing electricity until some one formulated the law and showed us how to apply it.

5. This puts us in an entirely new relation to our environment, opening up possibilities hitherto undreamed of, and this by an orderly sequence of law that is naturally involved in our new mental attitude.

6. Mind is creative and the Principle upon which this law is based is sound and legitimate and is inherent in the nature of things; but this creative power does not originate in the individual but in the Universal, which is the source and fountain of all energy and substance. The individual is simply the channel for the distribution of this energy. The individual is the means by which the Universal produces the various combinations that result in the formation of phenomena.

7. We know that scientists have resolved matter into an immense number of molecules; these molecules have been resolved into atoms, and the atoms into electrons. The discovery of electrons in high vacuum glass tubes containing fused terminals of hard metal, indicates conclusively that these electrons fill all space; that they exist everywhere, that they are omnipresent. They fill all material bodies and occupy the whole of what we call empty space. This, then, is the Universal Substance from which all things proceed.

8. Electrons would forever remain electrons unless directed where to go to be assembled into atoms and molecules, and this director is around Mind. A number of electrons revolving around a centre of force constitutes an atom; atoms unite in absolutely regular mathematical ratios arid form molecules, and these unite with each other to form a multitude of compounds which unite to build the Universe.

9. The lightest known atom is hydrogen and this is 1,700 times heavier than an electron. An atom of mercury is 300,000 times heavier than an electron. Electrons are pure negative electricity, and as they have the same potential velocity as all other cosmic energy, such as heat, light, electricity and thought, of about 186,000 miles a second, neither time or space require consideration. The manner in which the velocity of light was ascertained is interesting.

10. The velocity of light was obtained by the Danish astronomer Roemer in 1676, by observing the eclipses of Jupiter's moons. When the earth was nearest to Jupiter, the eclipse appeared about eight and one-half minutes too soon for the calculations, and when the earth was most remote from Jupiter, they were about eight and one-half minutes too late. Roemer concluded the reason to be that it required seventeen minutes for light from the planet to traverse the diameter of the earth's orbit, which measured the difference of the distances of the earth from Jupiter. This

calculation has since been verified, and proves that light travels about 186,000 miles a second.

11. Electrons manifest in the body as cells, and possess mind and intelligence sufficient for them to perform their offices in the human physical anatomy. Every part of the body is composed of cells, some of which operate independently; others in communities. Some are busy building tissue, while others are engaged in forming the various secretions necessary for the body. Some act as carriers of material; others are the surgeons whose work it is to repair damage; others are scavengers, carrying off waste; others are constantly ready to repel invaders or other undesirable intruders of the germ family.

12. All these cells are moving for a common purpose and each one is not only a living organism, but has sufficient intelligence to enable it to perform its necessary duties. It is also endowed with sufficient intelligence to conserve the energies and perpetuate its own life. It must, therefore, secure sufficient nourishment and it has been found that it exercises choice in the selection of such nourishment.

13. Each cell is born, reproduces itself, dies and is absorbed. The maintenance of health and life itself depends upon the constant regeneration of these cells.

14. It is therefore apparent that there is mind in every atom of the body; this mind is negative mind, and the power of the individual to think makes him positive, so that he can control this negative mind. This is the scientific explanation for metaphysical healing, and will enable anyone to understand the principle upon which this remarkable phenomenon rests.

15. This negative mind, which is contained in every cell of the body, has been called the subconscious mind, because it acts without our conscious knowledge. We have found that this sub-conscious mind is responsive to the will of the conscious mind.

16. All things have their origin in mind, and appearances are the result of thought. So that we see that Things in themselves have no origin, permanency or reality. Since they are produced by thought they can be erased by thought.

17. In mental, as in natural science, experiments are being made, and each discovery lifts man one step higher toward his possible goal. We find that every man is the reflection of the thought he has entertained during his lifetime. This is stamped on his face, his form, his character, his environment.

18. Behind every effect there is a cause, and if we follow the trail to its starting point, we shall find the creative principle out of which it grew. Proofs of this are now so complete that this truth is generally accepted.

19. The objective world is controlled by an unseen and, heretofore, unexplainable power. We have, heretofore, personalized this power and called it God. We have now, however, learned to look upon it as the permeating essence or principle of all that exists—the Infinite or Universal Mind.

20. The Universal Mind, being infinite and omnipotent, has unlimited resources at its command, and when we remember that it is also omnipresent, we

cannot escape the conclusion that we must be an expression or manifestation of that Mind.

21. A recognition and understanding of the resources of the sub-conscious mind will indicate that the only difference between the subconscious and the Universal is one of degree. They differ only as a drop of water differs from the ocean. They are the same in kind and quality, the difference is one of degree only.

22. Do you, can you, appreciate the value of this all-important fact; do you realize that a recognition of this tremendous fact places you in touch with Omnipotence? The subconscious mind being the connecting link between the Universal Mind and the conscious mind, is it not evident that the conscious mind can consciously suggest thoughts which the subconscious mind will put into action, and as the sub-conscious is one with the Universal, is it not evident that no limit can be placed upon its activities?

23. A scientific understanding of this principle will explain the wonderful results that are secured through the power of prayer. The results that are secured in this way are not brought about by any special dispensations of providence, but on the contrary, they are the result of the operation of a perfectly natural law. There is, therefore, nothing either religious or mysterious about it.

24. Yet there are many who are not ready to enter into the discipline necessary to think correctly, even though it is evident that wrong thinking has brought failure.

25. Thought is the only reality; conditions are but the outward manifestations; as the thought changes, all outward or material conditions must change in order to be in harmony with their creator, which is thought.

26. But the thought must be clear cut, steady, fixed, definite, unchangeable; you cannot take one step forward and two steps backward, neither can you spend twenty or thirty years of your life building up negative conditions as the result of negative thoughts, and then expect to see them all melt away as the result of fifteen or twenty minutes of right thinking.

27. If you enter into the discipline necessary to bring about a radical change in your life, you must do so deliberately, after giving the matter careful thought and full consideration, and then you must allow nothing to interfere with your decision.

28. This discipline, this change of thought, this mental attitude will not only bring you the material things which are necessary for your highest and best welfare, but will bring health and harmonious conditions generally.

29. If you wish harmonious conditions in your life, you must develop an harmonious mental attitude.

30. Your world without will be a reflection of your world within.

31. For your next exercise concentrate on Harmony, and when I say concentrate, I mean all that the word implies; concentrate so deeply, so earnestly, that you will be conscious of nothing but harmony. Remember, we learn by doing. Reading this book will get you nowhere. It is in the practical application that the value consists.

*Learn to keep the door shut, keep out of your mind and out of your world
every element that seeks admittance with no definite helpful end in view.*
—George Matthew Adams.

✸

131. *What is the source of all Wisdom, Power and Intelligence?*
The Universal Mind.

132. *Where do all motion, light, heat and colour have their origin?*
In the Universal Energy, which is one manifestation of the Universal Mind.

133. *Where does the creative power of thought originate?*
In the Universal Mind.

134. *What is thought?*
Mind in motion.

135. *How is the Universal differentiated in form?*
The individual is the means by which the Universal produces the various combinations that result in the formation of phenomena.

136. *How is this accomplished?*
The power of the individual to think is his ability to act upon the Universal and bring it into manifestation.

137. *What is the first form which the Universal takes so far as we know?*
Electrons, which fill all space.

138. *Where do all things have their origin?*
In mind.

139. *What is the result of a change of thought?*
A change in conditions.

140. *What is the result of a harmonious mental attitude?*
Harmonious conditions in life.

*Thought, immaterial though it may be, is the matrix that shapes the issues
of life. The mind has been active in all fields during this fruitful century, but
it is to science we must look for the thoughts that have shaped all thinking.*
—Selected.

ADVICE

Remember—
Fully to understand grand and beautiful thought requires, perhaps, as much
time as to conceive it.
                                                                    –JOUBERT

If you wish to enjoy the utmost practical benefit form "The Master Key"— go slowly.

Transfuse into your mind the contents of one part only, each week for twenty-four weeks.

Realize the meaning of every phrase.

Consult "The Master Key" constantly, as your perpetual help and stimulus.

Each time you read the work you will get a better understanding of the eternal cosmic principles.

Tell others of "The Master Key" so that more and more people may reciprocate with you, as conscious adepts in harmony.

PART FIFTEEN

This Part explains the Law of Growth, and explains why we cannot obtain if we tenaciously cling to what we have, and that difficulties, inharmonies and obstacles indicate that we are either refusing to give up what we no longer need, or refusing to accept what we require; we are holding on to worn-out and useless material, or we are allowing a deficiency to exist and are not obtaining the material necessary for our growth. It explains bow the ability to appropriate what we require for our growth is secured. It explains how vitality is important to thought, and what determines the importance of words the vessels in which thought is carried. How abundance may be secured and why we must be prepared to assume the responsibility for every thought and action. It explains the necessity of Insight, its value in examining facts and conditions at long range and in turning our attention to profitable channels instead of working with problems that contain no possibility of any kind.

Experiments with parasites found on plants indicate that even the lowest order of life is enabled to take advantage of natural law.

This experiment was made by Jaques Loeb, M.D., Ph.D., a member of the Rockefeller Institute.

"In order to obtain the material, potted rose bushes are brought into a room and placed in front of a closed window. If the plants are allowed to dry out, the aphides (parasites), previously wingless, change to winged insects. After the metamorphosis, the animals leave the plants, fly to the window and then creep upward on the glass."

It is evident that these tiny insects found that the plants on which they had been thriving were dead, and that they could therefore secure nothing more to eat and drink from this source. The only method by which they could save themselves from starvation was to grow temporary wings and fly, which they did.

Experiments such as these indicate that Omniscience as well as Omnipotence is omnipresent and that the tiniest living thing can take advantage of it in an emergency.

Part Fifteen will tell you more about the laws under which we live. It will explain that these laws operate to our advantage, that all conditions and experiences that come to us are for our benefit; that we gain strength in proportion to the effort expended, and that our happiness is best attained through a conscious co-operation with natural laws.

1. The laws under which we live are designed solely for our advantage. These laws are immutable and we cannot escape from their operation.

2. All the great eternal forces act in solemn silence, but it is in our power to place ourselves in harmony with them and thus express a life of comparative peace and happiness.

3. Difficulties, inharmonies, and obstacles, indicate that we are either refusing to give out what we no longer need, or refusing to accept what we require.

4. Growth is attained through an exchange of the old for the new, of the good for the better; it is a conditional or reciprocal action, for each of us is a complete thought entity and this completeness makes it possible for us to receive only as we give.

5. We cannot obtain what we lack if we tenaciously cling to what we have. We are able to consciously control our conditions as we come to sense the purpose of what we attract, and are able to extract from each experience only what we require for our further growth. Our ability to do this determines the degree of harmony or happiness we attain.

6. The ability to appropriate what we require for our growth, continually increases as we reach higher planes and broader visions, and the greater our ability to know what we require, the more certain we shall be to discern its presence, to attract it and to absorb it. Nothing may reach us except what is necessary for our growth.

7. All conditions and experiences that come to us do so for our benefit. Difficulties and obstacles will continue to come until we absorb their wisdom and gather from them the essentials of further growth.

8. That we reap what we sow is mathematically exact. We gain permanent strength exactly to the extent of the effort required to overcome difficulties.

9. The inexorable requirements of growth demand that we exert the greatest degree of attraction for what is perfectly in accord with us. Our highest happiness will be best attained through our understanding of, and conscious co-operation with, natural laws.

10. In order to possess vitality thought must be impregnated with love. Love is a product of the emotions. It is therefore essential that the emotions be controlled and guided by the intellect and reason.

11. It is love which imparts vitality to thought and thus enables it to germinate. The law of attraction, or the law of love, for they are one and the same, will bring to it the necessary material for its growth and maturity.

12. The first form which thought will find is language, or words; this determines the importance of words; they are the first Manifestation of thought—, the vessels in which thought is carried. They take hold of the ether and by setting it in motion reproduce the thought to others in the form of sound.

13. Thought may lead to action of any kind, but whatever the action, it is simply the thought attempting to express itself in visible form. It is evident, therefore, that if we wish desirable conditions, we can afford to entertain only desirable thoughts.

14. This leads to the inevitable conclusion that if we wish to express abundance in our lives, we can afford to think abundance only, and as words are only thoughts taking form, we must be especially careful to use nothing but constructive and harmonious language, which when finally crystallized into objective forms, will prove to our advantage.

15. We cannot escape from the pictures we incessantly photograph on the mind, and this photography of erroneous conceptions is exactly what is being done by the use of words, when we use any form of language which is not identified with our welfare.

16. We manifest more and more life as our thought becomes clarified and takes higher planes. This is obtained with greater facility as we use word pictures that are clearly defined, and relieved of the conceptions attached to them on lower planes of thought.

17. It is with words that we must express our thoughts, and if we are to make use of higher forms of truth, we may use only such material as has been carefully and intelligently selected with this purpose in view.

18. This wonderful power of clothing thoughts in the form of words is what differentiates man from the rest of the animal kingdom; by the use of the written word he has been enabled to look back over the centuries and see the stirring scenes by which he has come into his present inheritance.

19. He has been enabled to come into communion with the greatest writers and thinkers of all time, and the combined record which we possess today is therefore the expression of Universal Thought as it has been seeking to take form in the mind of Man.

20. We know that the Universal Thought has for its goal the creation of form, and we know that the individual thought is likewise for ever attempting to express itself in form, and we know that the word is a thought form and a sentence is a combination of thought forms, therefore, if we wish our ideal to be beautiful or strong, we must see that the words out of which this temple will eventually be created are exact, that they are put together carefully, because accuracy in building words and sentences is the highest form of architecture in civilization and is a passport to success.

21. Words are thoughts and therefore an invisible and invincible power which will finally objectify themselves in the form they are given.

22. Words may become mental palaces that will live for ever, or they may become shanties that the first breeze will carry away. They may delight the eye as well as the ear; they may contain all knowledge; in them we find the history of the past as well as the hope of the future; they are living messengers from which every human and superhuman activity is born.

23. The beauty of the word consists in the beauty of the thought; the power of the word consists in the power of the thought, and the power of the thought consists in its vitality. How shall we identify a vital thought? What are its distinguishing characteristics? It must have principle. How shall we identify principle?

24. There is a principle of Mathematics, but none of error; there is a principle of health, but none of disease; there is a principle of truth, but none of dishonesty; there is a principle of light, but none of darkness, and there is a principle of abundance, but none of poverty.

25. How shall we know that this is true? Because if we apply the principle of Mathematics correctly we shall be certain of our results. Where there is health there will be no disease. If we know the Truth we cannot be deceived by error. If we let in light there can be no darkness, and where there is abundance there can be no poverty.

26. These are self-evident facts, but the all important truth that a thought containing principle is vital and therefore contains life and consequently takes root, and eventually but surely and certainly displaces the negative thoughts, which by their very nature can contain no vitality, is one which seems to have been overlooked.

27. But this is a fact which win enable you to destroy every manner of discord, lack and limitation.

28. There can be no question but that he who "is wise enough to understand" will readily recognize that the creative power of thought places an invincible weapon in his hands and makes him a master of destiny.

29. In the physical world there is a law of compensation which is that "the appearance of a given amount of energy anywhere means the disappearance of the same amount somewhere else," and so we find that we can get only what we give;

if we pledge ourselves to a certain action we must be prepared to assume the responsibility for the development of that action. The sub-conscious cannot reason. It takes us at our word; we have asked for something; we are now to receive it; we have made our bed, we are now to lie on it; the die has been cast; the threads will carry out the pattern we have made.

30. For this reason Insight must be exercised so that the thought that we entertain contains no mental, moral or physical germ that we do not wish objectified in our lives.

31. Insight is a faculty of the mind whereby we are enabled to examine facts and conditions at long range, a kind of human telescope; it enables us to understand the difficulties as well as the possibilities in any undertaking.

32. Insight enables us to be prepared for the obstacles that we shall meet; we can therefore overcome them before they have any opportunity of causing difficulty.

33. Insight enables us to plan to advantage and turn our thought and attention in the right direction, instead of into channels that can yield no possible return.

34. Insight is therefore absolutely essential for the development of any great achievement; with it we may enter, explore and possess any mental field.

35. Insight is a product of the world within and is developed in the Silence, by concentration.

36. For your next exercise, concentrate on Insight; take your accustomed position and focus the thought on the fact that to have a knowledge of the creative power of thought does not mean to possess the art of thinking. Let the thought dwell on the fact that knowledge does not apply itself. That our actions are not governed by knowledge, but by custom, precedent and habit. That the only way we ran get ourselves to apply knowledge is by a determined conscious effort. Call to mind the fact that knowledge unused passes from the mind, that the value of the information is in the application of the principle; continue this line of thought until you gain sufficient insight to formulate a definite program for applying this, principle to your own particular problem.

> "Think truly, and thy thoughts
> Shall the world's famine feed;
> Speak truly, and each word of thine
> Shall be a fruitful seed;
> Live truly, and thy life shall be
> A great and noble creed."
>
> —Horatio Bonar.

✹

141. *What determines the degree of harmony which we attain?*
   Our ability to appropriate what we require for our growth from each experience.

142. *What do difficulties and obstacles indicate?*
That they are necessary for our wisdom and spiritual growth.

143. *How may these difficulties be avoided?*
By a conscious understanding of and co-operation with Natural laws.

144. *What is the principle by which thought manifests itself in form?*
The Law of Attraction.

145. *How is the necessary material secured by which the growth, development and maturity of the idea take form?*
The law of love, which is the creative principle of the Universe, imparts vitality to the thought, and the law of attraction brings the necessary substance by the law of growth.

146. *How are desirable conditions secured?*
By entertaining desirable thoughts only.

147. *How are undesirable conditions brought about?*
By thinking, discussing and visualizing conditions of lack, limitation, disease, disharmony and discord of every kind. This mental photography of erroneous conceptions is taken up by the subconscious and the law of attraction will inevitably crystallize it into objective form. That we reap what we sow is scientifically exact.

148. *How can we overcome every kind of fear, lack, limitation, poverty and discord?*
By substituting principle for error.

149. *How may we recognize principle?*
By a conscious realization of the fact that Truth invariably destroys error. We do not have to laboriously shovel the darkness out; all that is necessary is to turn on the light. The same principle applies to every form of negative thought.

150. *What is the value, of Insight?*
It enables us to understand the value of making application of the knowledge that we gain. Many seem to think that knowledge will automatically apply itself, which is by no means true.

PART SIXTEEN

This Part explains the nature of Wealth, it shows how it is created and upon what it depends. It shows why success is contingent upon an ideal higher than the mere accumulation of riches. It shows that success depends upon creative ability and explains the necessary condition for attainment. It explains why premature wealth is but the forerunner of humiliation and disaster. It explains the methods by which we may take our fate out of the hands of chance and consciously make for ourselves the conditions which we desire, it tells how we may compel success by the utilization of scientific and exact methods, and it explains that while we have the ability to create harmonious and constructive conditions we also have the ability to create inharmonious and destructive conditions, and unfortunately, through ignorance of the law, this is what many are doing.

The vibratory activities of the planetary Universe are governed by a law of periodicity. Everything that lives has periods of birth, growth, fruition and decline. These periods are governed by the Septimal Law.

The Law of Sevens governs the days of the week, the phases of the moon, the harmonies of sound, light, heat, electricity, magnetism, atomic structure. It governs the life of individuals and of nations, and it dominates the activities of the commercial world.

Life is growth, and growth is change. Each seven years period takes us into a new cycle. The first seven years is the period of infancy. The next seven, the period of childhood, representing the beginning of individual responsibility. The next seven represents the period of adolescence. The fourth period marks the attainment of full growth. The fifth period is the constructive period, when men begin to acquire property, possessions, a home and family. The next, from thirty-five to forty-two, is a period of reactions and changes, and this in turn is followed by a period of reconstruction, adjustment and recuperation, so as to be ready for a new cycle of sevens, beginning with the fiftieth year.

There are many who think that the world is just about to pass out of the sixth period; that it will soon enter into the seventh period, the period of readjustment, reconstruction and harmony; the period that is frequently referred to as the Millenium.

Those familiar with these cycles will not be disturbed when things seem to go wrong, but can apply the principle outlined in The Master Key, with the full assurance that a higher law will invariably control all other laws, and that through an understanding and conscious operation of spiritual laws we can convert every seeming difficulty into a blessing.

✻

1. Wealth is a product of labour. Capital is an effect, not a cause; a servant, not a master; a means, not an end.

2. The most commonly accepted definition of wealth is that it consists of all useful and agreeable things that possess exchange value. It is this exchange value that is the predominant characteristic of wealth.

3. When we consider the small addition made by wealth to the happiness of the possessor, we find that the true value consists not in its utility but in its exchange value.

4. This exchange value makes it a medium for securing the things of real value whereby our ideals may be realized.

5. Wealth should then never be desired as an end, but simply as a means of accomplishing an end. Success is contingent upon a higher ideal than the mere

accumulation of riches, and he who aspires to such success must formulate an ideal for which he is willing to strive.

6. With such an ideal in mind, the ways and means can and will be provided, but the mistake must not be made of substituting the means for the end. There must be a definite fixed purpose, an ideal.

7. Prentice Mulford said: "The man of success is the man possessed of the greatest spiritual understanding and every great fortune comes of superior and truly spiritual power." Unfortunately, there are those who fail to recognize this power; they forget that Andrew Carnegie's mother had to help support the family when they went to America, that Harriman's father was a poor clergyman with a salary of only $200.00 a year, that Sir Thomas Lipton started with only one shilling. These men had no other power to depend upon, but it did not fail them.

8. The power to create depends entirely upon spiritual power; there are three steps, idealization, visualization and materialization. Every captain of industry depends upon this power exclusively. In an article in *Everybody's Magazine,* Henry Flagier, the Standard Oil multi-millionaire, admitted that the secret of his success was his power to see a thing in its completeness. The following conversation with a reporter shows his power of idealization, concentration and visualization, all spiritual powers:

9. "Did you actually picture to yourself the whole thing? I mean, did you, or could you, really close your eyes and see the tracks? And the trains running? And hear the whistles blowing? Did you go as far as that?" "Yes." "How Clearly?" "Very Clearly."

10. Here we have a vision of the law; we see "cause and effect," we see that thought necessarily precedes and determines action. If we are wise, we shall come into a realization of the tremendous fact that no arbitrary condition can exist for a moment, and that human experience is the result of an orderly and harmonious sequence.

11. The successful businessman is more often than not an idealist and is ever striving for higher and higher standards. The subtle forces of thought as they crystallize in our daily moods are what constitute life.

12. Thought is the plastic material with which we build images of our growing conception of life. Use determines its existence. As in all other things our ability to recognize it and use it properly is the necessary condition for attainment.

13. Premature wealth is but the forerunner of humiliation and disaster, because we cannot permanently retain anything which we do not merit or which we have not earned.

14. The conditions with which we meet in the world without, correspond to the conditions which we find in the world within. This is brought about by the law of attraction. How then shall we determine what is to enter into the world within?

15. Whatever enters the mind through the senses or the objective mind will impress the mind and result in a mental image that will become a pattern for the

creative energies. These experiences are largely the result of environment, chance, past thinking and other forms of negative thought, and must be subjected to careful analysis before being entertained. On the other hand, we can form our own mental images, through our own interior processes of thought regardless of the thoughts of others, regardless of exterior conditions, regardless of environment of every kind, and it is by the exercise of this power that we can control our own destiny, body, mind and soul.

16. It is by the exercise of this power that we take our fate out of the hands of chance, and consciously make for ourselves the experiences which we desire, because when we consciously realize a condition, that condition will eventually manifest in our lives; it is therefore evident that in the last analysis thinking is the one great cause in life.

17. Therefore, to control thought is to control circumstances, conditions, environment and destiny.

19. How then, are we to control thought what is the process? To think is to create a thought, but the result of the thought will depend upon its form, its quality and its vitality.

19. The form will depend upon the mental image from which it emanates; this will depend upon the depth of the impression, the predominance of the idea, the clarity of the vision, the boldness of the image.

20. The quality depends upon its substance and this depends upon the material of which the mind is composed; if this material has been woven from thoughts of vigor, strength, courage, determination, the thought will possess these qualities.

21. And finally, the vitality depends upon the feeling with which the thought is impregnated. If the thought is constructive, it will possess vitality; it will have life, it will grow, develop, expand; it will be creative; it will attract to itself everything necessary for its complete development.

22. If the thought is destructive, it will have within itself the germ of its own dissolution; it will die, but in the process of dying it will bring sickness, disease, and every other form of discord.

23. This we call evil, and when we bring it upon ourselves, some of us are disposed to attribute our difficulties to a supreme being, but this supreme being is simply Mind in equilibrium.

24. It is neither good nor bad, it simply is.

25. Our ability to differentiate it into form is our ability to manifest good or evil.

26. Good and evil therefore are not entities, they are simply words which we use to indicate the result of our actions, and these actions are in turn predetermined by the character of our thought.

27. If our thought is constructive and harmonious we manifest good; if it is destructive and discordant we manifest evil.

28. If you desire to visualize a different environment, the process is simply to hold the ideal in mind, until your vision has been made real; give no thought to

persons, places or things; these have no place in the absolute; the environment you desire will contain everything necessary the right persons, and the right things will come at the right time and in the right place.

29. It is sometimes not plain how character, ability, attainment, achievement, environment and destiny can be controlled through the power of visualization, but this is an exact scientific fact.

30. You will readily see that what we think determines the quality of mind, and that the quality of mind in turn determines our ability and mental capacity, and you can readily understand that the improvement in our ability will naturally be followed by increase in attainment and a greater control of circumstances.

31. It will thus be seen that Natural laws work in a perfectly natural and harmonious manner; everything seems to just happen. If you want any evidence of this fact simply compare results of your efforts in your own life, when your actions were prompted by high ideals and when you had selfish or ulterior motives in mind. You will need no further evidence.

32. If you wish to bring about the realization of any desire, form a mental picture of success in your mind, by consciously visualizing your desire; in this way you will be compelling success, you will be externalizing it in your life by scientific methods.

33. We can only see what already exists in the objective world, but what we visualize, already exists in the spiritual world, and this visualization is a substantial token of what will one day appear in the world, if we are faithful to our ideal. The reason for this is not difficult; visualization is a form of imagination; this process of thinking forms impressions on the mind, and these impressions in turn form concepts and ideals, and they in turn are the plans from which the Master Architect will weave the future.

34. The psychologists have come to the conclusion that there is but one sense, the sense of feeling, and that all other senses are but modifications of this one sense; this being true, we know why feeling is the very fountain head of power, why the emotions so easily overcome the intellect, and why we must put feeling into our thought if we wish results. Thought and feeling are the irresistible combination.

35. Visualization must, of course, be directed by the will; we are to visualize exactly what we want; we must be careful not to let the imagination run riot. Imagination is a good servant but a poor master, and unless it is controlled, it may easily lead us into all kinds of speculations and conclusions that have no basis or foundation of fact whatever. Every kind of plausible opinion is liable to be accepted without any analytical examination and the inevitable result is mental chaos.

36. We must therefore construct only such mental images as are known to be scientifically true. Subject every idea to a searching analysis and accept nothing that is not scientifically exact. When you do this you will attempt nothing but what you know you can carry out and success will crown your efforts; this is what business men call far-sightedness; it is much the same as insight, and is one of the great

THE MASTER KEY: PART SIXTEEN   385

secrets of success in all important undertakings.

37. For your next exercise, try to bring yourself to a realization of the important fact that harmony and happiness are states of consciousness and do not depend upon the possession of things. That things are effects and come as a consequence of correct mental states. So that if we desire material possession of any kind our chief concern should be to acquire the mental attitude that will bring about the result desired. This mental attitude is brought about by a realization of our spiritual nature and our unity with the Universal Mind that is the substance of all things. This realization will bring about everything that is necessary for our complete enjoyment. This is scientific or correct thinking. When we succeed in bringing about this mental attitude it is comparatively easy to realize our desire as an already accomplished fact; when we can do this we shall have found the "Truth" which makes us "free" from every lack or limitation of any kind.

> *A man might frame and let loose a star, to roll in its orbit, and yet not have done so memorable a thing before God as he who lets a golden-orbed thought to roll through the generations of time.*
>
> —H. W. Beecher.

✸

151. *Upon what does wealth depend?*
Upon an understanding of the creative nature of thought.
152. *Upon what does its true value consist?*
Upon its exchange value.
153. *Upon what does success depend?*
Upon spiritual power.
154. *Upon what does this power depend?*
Upon use; use determines its existence.
155. *How may we take our fate out of the hands of chance?*
By consciously realizing the conditions that we desire to see manifested in our lives.
156. *What then is the great business in life?*
Thinking.
157. *Why is this so*
Because thought is spiritual and therefore creative. To consciously control thought is therefore to control circumstances, conditions, environment and destiny.
158. *What is the source of all evil?*
Destructive thinking.
159. *What is the source of all good?*
Scientific correct thinking.
160. *What is scientific thinking?*

A recognition of the creative nature of spiritual energy and our ability to control it.

"To every man there openeth a way,
And the high soul climbs the high way,
And the low soul gropes the low;
And in between on the misty flats,
The rest drift to and fro.
But to every man there openeth
A high way and a low
And every man decideth
The way his soul shall go."

ADVICE

Remember—
 Fully to understand grand and beautiful thought requires, perhaps, as much
 time as to conceive it.
 —JOUBERT

If you wish to enjoy the utmost practical benefit form "The Master Key"— go slowly.

Transfuse into your mind the contents of one part only, each week for twenty-four weeks.

Realize the meaning of every phrase.

Consult "The Master Key" constantly, as your perpetual help and stimulus.

Each time you read the work you will get a better understanding of the eternal cosmic principles.

Tell others of "The Master Key" so that more and more people may reciprocate with you, as conscious adepts in harmony.

PART SEVENTEEN

This Part tells of the Law of Vibration and why the highest principle necessarily determines the circumstances, aspects and relations of everything with which it comes in contact. It tells why and how a knowledge of these higher forces makes all physical force sink into insignificance. It explains the nature of concentration; it tells something of the practice of concentration; it tells something of the results of concentration. It tells how the mind may become a magnet, how it may irresistibly attract the conditions which it desires; it tells why it is necessary "to be" in order "to have." It tells bow to unfasten the prison bars of weakness, impotence and self-belittlement and realize the joy of overcoming obstacles. It tells how the intuitive power is set in operation and how this inevitably leads to success. It tells of the difference between real power and the symbols of power, and why the symbols turn to ashes just as we overtake them.

The kind of Deity that a man, consciously or unconsciously, worships, indicates the intellectual status of the worshipper.

Ask the Indian of God, and he will describe to you a powerful chieftain of a glorious tribe. Ask the Pagan of God, and he will tell you of a God of fire, a God of water, a God of this, that and the other.

Ask the Israelite of God, and he will tell you of the God of Moses, who conceived it expedient to rule by coercive measures; hence, the Ten Commandments. Or he will tell you of Joshua, who led the Israelites into battle, confiscated property, murdered the prisoners and laid cities waste.

The so-called heathen made "graven images" of their Gods, whom they were accustomed to worship, but among the most intelligent, at least, these images were but the visible emblems which they used to facilitate mental concentration on the qualities which they desired to externalize in their lives.

We of the twentieth century worship a God of Love in theory, but in practice we make for ourselves "graven images" of "Wealth," "Power," "Fashion," "Custom" and "Conventionality." We "fall down" before them and worship them. We concentrate on them and they are thereby externalized in our lives.

The reader who masters the contents of Part Seventeen will not mistake symbols for reality, he will be interested in causes, rather than effects. He will concentrate on the realities of life, and will then not be disappointed in the results.

✳

1. We are told that Man has "dominion over all things"; this dominion is established through Mind. Thought is the activity that controls every principle beneath it. The highest principle by reason of its superior essence and qualities necessarily determines the circumstances, aspects and relation of everything with which it comes into contact.

2. The vibrations of Mental forces are the finest and consequently the most powerful in existence. To those who perceive the nature and transcendency of mental force, all physical power sinks into insignificance.

3. We are accustomed to look upon the Universe with a lens of five senses, and from these experiences our anthropomorphic conceptions originate, but true conceptions are only secured by spiritual insight. This insight requires a quickening of the vibrations of the Mind, and is only secured when the mind is continuously concentrated in a given direction.

4. Continuous concentration means an even, unbroken flow of thought and is the result of patient, persistent, persevering and well-regulated system.

5. Great discoveries are the result of long-continued investigation. The science

of mathmatics requires years of concentrated effort to master it, and the greatest science—that of the Mind—is revealed only through concentrated effort.

6. Concentration is much misunderstood; there seems to be an idea of effort or activity associated with it, when just the contrary is necessary. The greatness of an actor lies in the fact that he forgets himself in the portrayal of his character, becoming so identified with it that the audience is swayed by the realism of the performance. This will give you a good idea of true concentration: you should be so interested in your thought, so engrossed in your subject, as to be conscious of nothing else. Such concentration leads to intuitive perception and immediate insight into the nature of the object concentrated upon.

7. All knowledge is the result of concentration of this kind; it is thus that the secrets have been wrested from Heaven and Earth; it is thus that the mind becomes a magnet and the desire to know draws the knowledge, irresistibly attracts it, makes it your own.

8. Desire is largely subconscious; conscious desire rarely realizes its object when the latter is out of immediate reach. Sub-conscious desire arouses the latent faculties of the mind, and difficult problems seem to solve themselves.

9. The subconscious mind may be aroused and brought into action in any direction and made to serve us for any purpose, by concentration. The practice of concentration requires the control of the physical, mental and psychical being; all modes of consciousness, whether physical, mental or psychical, must be under control.

10. Spiritual Truth is therefore the controlling factor; it is this that will enable you to grow out of limited attainment and reach a point where you will be able to translate modes of thought into character and consciousness.

11. Concentration does not mean mere thinking of thoughts, but the transmutation of these thoughts into practical values; the average person has no conception of the meaning of concentration. There is always the cry "to have" but never the cry "to be"; people fail to understand that they cannot have one without the other, that they must first find the "kingdom" before they can have the "things added." Momentary enthusiasm is of no value; it is only by unbounded self-confidence that the goal is reached.

12. The mind may place the ideal a little too high and fall short of the mark; it may attempt to soar on untrained wings and, instead of flying, fall to earth; but that is no reason for not making another attempt.

13. Weakness is the only barrier to mental attainment; attribute your weakness to physical limitations or mental uncertainties and try again; ease and perfection are gained by repetition.

14. The astronomer centres his mind on the stars and they give forth their secrets; the geologist centres his mind on the construction of the earth and we have geology; so with all things. Men centre their minds on the problems of life, and the result is apparent in the vast and complex social order of the day.

15. All mental discovery and attainment are the result of desire plus concentration; desire is the strongest motive to action; the more persistent the desire, the

more authoritative the revelation. Desire added to concentration will wrench any secret from nature.

16. In realizing great thoughts, in experiencing great emotions that correspond with great thoughts, the mind is in a state where it appreciates the value of higher things.

17. The intensity of one moment's earnest concentration and the intense longing to become and to attain may take you further than years of slow normal and forced effort; it will unfasten the prison bars of unbelief, weakness, impotence and self-belittlement, and you will come into a realization of the joy of overcoming.

18. The spirit of initiative and originality is developed through persistence and continuity of mental effort. Business teaches the value of concentration and encourages decision of character; it develops practical insight and quickness of conclusion. The mental element in every commercial pursuit is dominant as the controlling factor, and desire is the predominating force; all commercial relations are the externalization of desire.

19. Many of the sturdy and substantial virtues are developed in commercial employment; the mind is steadied and directed; it becomes efficient. The principal necessity is the strengthening of the mind so that it rises superior to the distractions and wayward impulses of instinctive life and thus successfully prevails in the conflict between the higher and lower self.

20. All of us are dynamos, but the dynamo of itself is nothing; the mind must work the dynamo; then it is useful and its energy can be definitely concentrated. The mind is an engine whose power is undreamed; thought is an omni-working power. It is the ruler and creator of all form and all events occurring in form. Physical energy is nothing in comparison with the omnipotence of thought, because thought enables man to harness all other natural power.

21. Vibration is the action of thought; it is vibration which reaches out and attracts the material necessary to construct and build. There is nothing mysterious concerning the power of thought; concentration simply implies that consciousness can be focalized to the point where it becomes identified with the object of its attention. As food absorbed is the essence of the body, so the mind absorbs the object of its attention, gives it life and being.

22. If you concentrate on some matter of importance, the intuitive power will be set in operation, and help will come in the nature of information which will lead to success.

23. Intuition arrives at conclusions without the aid of experience or memory. Intuition often solves problems that are beyond the grasp of the reasoning power. Intuition often comes with a suddenness that is startling; it reveals the truth for which we are searching, so directly that it seems to come from a higher power. Intuition can be cultivated and developed. In order to do this it must be recognized and appreciated; if the intuitive visitor is given a royal welcome when he comes, he will come again; the more cordial the welcome the more frequent his visits will become, but if he is ignored or neglected he will make his visits few and far apart.

24. Intuition usually comes in the Silence; great minds seek solitude frequently; it is here that all the larger problems of life are worked out. For this reason every business man who can afford it has a private office, where he will not be disturbed; if you cannot afford a private office you can at least find somewhere where you can be alone a few minutes each day, to train the thought along lines which will enable you to develop that invincible power which is necessary to achieve.

25. Remember that fundamentally the subconscious is omnipotent; there is no limit to the things that can be done when it is given the power to act. Your degree of success is determined by the nature of your desire. If the nature of your desire is in harmony with Natural Law or the Universal Mind, it will gradually emancipate the mind and give you invincible courage.

26. Every obstacle conquered, every victory gained, will give you more faith in your power, and you will have greater ability to win. Your strength is determined by your mental attitude; if this attitude is one of success, and is permanently held with an unswerving purpose, you will attract to yourself from the invisible domain the things you silently demand.

27. By keeping the thought in mind, it will gradually take tangible form. A definite purpose sets causes in motion which go out in the invisible world and find the material necessary to serve your purpose.

28. You may be pursuing the symbols of power, instead of power itself. You may be pursuing fame instead of honour, riches instead of wealth, position instead of service; in either event you will find that they turn to ashes just as you overtake them.

29. Premature wealth or position cannot be retained because it has not been earned; we get only what we give, and those who try to get without giving always find that the law of compensation is relentlessly bringing about an exact equilibrium.

30. The race has hitherto been for money and other mere symbols of power, but with an understanding of the true source of power we can afford to ignore the symbols. The man with a large bank account finds it unnecessary to load his pockets down with gold; so with the man who has found the true source of power; he is no longer interested in its shams or pretentions.

31. Thought ordinarily leads outwardly in evolutionary directions, but it can be turned within where it will take hold of the basic principles of things, the heart of things, the spirit of things. When you get to the heart of things it is comparatively easy to understand and command them.

32. This is because the Spirit of a thing is the thing itself, the vital part of it the real substance. The form is simply the outward manifestation of the spiritual activity within.

33. For your next exercise concentrate as nearly as possible in accordance with the method outlined in this Part; let there be no conscious effort or activity associated with your purpose. Relax completely, avoid any thought of anxiety as to results. Remember that power comes through repose. Let the thought dwell upon your object until it is completely identified with it, until you are conscious of nothing else.

34. If you wish to eliminate fear concentrate on courage.

35. If you wish to eliminate lack concentrate on abundance.

36. If you wish to eliminate disease concentrate on health.

37. Always concentrate on the ideal as an already existing fact; this is the Elohim, the germ cell, the life principle which goes forth, and enters in, and becomes, sets in motion those causes which guide, direct and bring about the necessary relation, which eventually manifests in form.

Thought is the property of those only who can entertain it.

—Emerson.

PART SEVENTEEN

161. *What is the true method of concentration?*

To become so identified with the object of your thought that you are conscious of nothing else.

162. *What is the result of this method of concentration?*

Invisible forces are set in motion that irresistibly bring about conditions in correspondence with your thought.

163. *What is the controlling factor in this method of thought?*

Spiritual Truth.

164. *Why is this so?*

Because the nature of our desire must be in harmony with Natural Law.

165. *What is the practical value of this method of concentration?*

Thought is transmuted into character, and character is the magnet that creates the environment of the individual.

166. *What is the controlling factor in every commercial pursuit?*

The mental element.

167. *Why is this so?*

Because Mind is the ruler and creator of all form and all events occurring in form.

168. *How does concentration operate?*

By the development of the powers of perception, wisdom, intuition, and sagacity.

169. *Why is intuition superior to reason?*

Because it does not depend upon experience or memory and frequently brings about the solution of our problem by methods concerning which we are in entire ignorance.

170. *What is the result of pursuing the symbol of the reality?*

Symbols frequently turn to ashes just as we overtake them, because the symbol is only the outward form of the spiritual activity within; therefore, unless we can possess the spiritual reality the form disappears.

The greatest events of an age are its best thoughts. It is the nature of thought to find its way into action.

—Bovee.

PART EIGHTEEN

This Part tells of a change in the thought of men, a change which is silently transpiring in our midst and which is unparalleled in the history of the world. The fetters of tradition are being melted off from humanity and truth is rising full orbed before an astonished multitude. It tells how the individual is enabled to control every form of intelligence that has not yet reached this level of self-recognition. It tells when and how the creative power originates, it tells how the Universal produces the various combinations which result in the formation of phenomena, it explains the principle of attraction by which things are brought together, which is the sole means by which existence is carried into effect. It explains the real source of wealth of the individual. It explains the method by which attention and concentration may be developed and shows why the power of attention is the distinguishing characteristic of every man of ability.

In order to grow we must obtain what is necessary for our growth. This is brought about through the law of attraction. This principle is the sole means by which the individual is differentiated from the Universal.

Think for a moment, what would a man be if he were not a husband, father or brother, if he were not interested in the social, economical, political or religious world? He would be nothing but an abstract theoretical ego. He exists, therefore, only in his relation to the whole, in his relation to other men, in his relation to society. This relation constitutes his environment; he exists, therefore, in his relation to his environment and in no other way.

Hence it is evident that the individual is simply the differentiation of the one Universal Mind, "which lighteth every man that cometh into the world," and his so-called individuality or personality consists of nothing but the manner in which he relates with the whole.

This we call his environment and it is brought about by the Law of Attraction. Part Eighteen has something more to say concerning this important law.

1. There is a change in the thought of the world. This change is silently transpiring in our midst, and is more important than any that the world has undergone since the downfall of Paganism.

2. The present revolution in the opinions of all classes of men, the highest and most cultured of men as well as those of the labouring class, stands unparalleled in the history of the world.

3. Science has of late made such vast discoveries, has revealed such an infinity of resources, has unveiled such enormous possibilities and such unsuspected forces, that scientific men more and more hesitate to affirm certain theories as established and indubitable or to deny other theories as absurd or impossible.

4. A new civilization is being born; customs, creeds, and precedent are passing; vision, faith and service are taking their place. The fetters of tradition are being melted off from humanity, and as the dross of materialism is being consumed thought is being liberated and truth is rising full orbed before an astonished multitude.

5. The whole world is on the eve of a new consciousness, a new power, and a new realization within the self.

6. Physical Science has resolved matter into molecules, molecules into atoms, atoms into energy, and it has remained for Sir Ambrose Fleming, in an address before the Royal Institution, to resolve this energy into mind. He says: "In its ultimate essence, energy may be incomprehensible by us except as an exhibition of the direct operation of that which we call Mind or Will."

7. And this mind is the indwelling and ultimate. It is imminent in matter as in spirit. It is the sustaining, energizing, all-pervading Spirit of the universe.

8. Every living thing must be sustained by its omnipotent Intelligence, and we find the difference in individual lives to be largely measured by the degree of this intelligence, which they manifest. It is greater intelligence that places the animal in a higher scale of being than the plant, the man higher than the animal, and we find that this increased intelligence is again indicated by the power of the individual to control modes of action and thus to consciously adjust himself to his environment.

9. It is this adjustment that occupies the attention of the greatest minds, and this adjustment consists in nothing else than the recognition of an order existing in the universal mind, for it is well known that this mind will obey us precisely in proportion as we first obey it.

10. It is the recognition of Natural Laws that has enabled us to annihilate time and space, to soar in the air and to make iron float, and the greater the degree of intelligence the greater will be our recognition of these Natural Laws and the greater will be the power we can possess.

11. It is the recognition of the self as an individualization of this Universal Intelligence that enables the individual to control those forms of intelligence which have not yet reached this level of self-recognition; they do not know that this Universal Intelligence permeates all things, ready to be called into action; they do not know that it is responsive to every demand, and they are therefore in bondage to the law of their own being.

12. Thought is creative and the principle on which the law is based is sound and legitimate and is inherent in the nature of things; but this creative power does not originate in the individual, but in the universal, which is the source and foundation of all energy and substance; the individual is simply the channel for the distribution of this energy.

13. The individual is simply a means by which the universal produces various combinations that result in the formation of phenomena. These depend upon the law of vibration, whereby various rates of rapidity of motion in the primary substance form new substances only in certain exact numerical ratios.

14. Thought is the invisible link by which the individual comes into communication with the Universal, the finite with the Infinite, the seen with the Unseen. Thought is the magic by which the human being is transformed into a being who thinks and knows and feels and acts.

15. As the proper apparatus has enabled the eye to discover worlds without number millions of miles away, so, with the proper understanding, man has been enabled to communicate with the Universal Mind, the source of all power.

16. The Understanding which is usually developed is about as valuable as a telephone box without wires or an exchange; in fact, it is usually nothing more than a "belief" which means nothing at all. The Indians believe something and so do the savages of the Cannibal Islands; but that proves nothing.

17. The only belief that is of any value to any one is a belief that has been put to a test and demonstrated to be a fact; it is then no longer a belief, but has become a living Faith or the Truth.

18. And this Truth has been put to the test by hundreds of thousands of people and has been found to be the Truth exactly in proportion to the usefulness of the apparatus that they used.

19. A man would not expect to locate stars hundreds of millions of miles away without a sufficiently strong telescope, and for this reason Science is continually engaged in building larger and more powerful telescopes and is continually rewarded by additional knowledge of the heavenly bodies.

20. So with understanding; men are continually making progress in the methods that they use to come into communication with the Universal Mind and its infinite possibilities.

21. The Universal Mind manifests itself in the objective, through the principle of attraction that each atom has for every other atom, in infinite degrees of intensity.

22. It is by this principle of combining and attracting that things are brought together. This principle is of universal application and is the sole means whereby the purpose of existence is carried into effect.

23. The expression of growth is met in a most beautiful manner through the instrumentality of this Universal Principle.

24. In order to grow we must obtain what is essential for our growth, but as we are at all times a complete thought entity, this completeness makes it possible for us to receive only as we give; growth is therefore conditioned on reciprocal action, and we find that on the mental plane like attracts like, that mental vibrations respond only to the extent of their vibratory harmony.

25. It is clear, therefore, that thoughts of abundance will respond only to similar thoughts; the wealth of the individual is seen to be what he inherently is. Affluence within is found to be the secret of attraction for affluence without. The ability to produce is found to be the real source of wealth of the individual. It is for this reason that he who has his heart in his work is certain to meet with unbounded success. He will give and continually give, and the more he gives the more he will receive.

26. What do the great financiers of the City and Wall Street, the captains of industry, the statesmen, the great company lawyers, the inventors, the physicians, the authors—what do each of these contribute to the sum of human happiness but the power of their thought?

27. Thought is the energy by which the law of attraction is brought into operation, which eventually manifests in abundance.

28. The Universal Mind is static Mind, or Substance in equilibrium. It is differentiated into form by our power to think. Thought is the dynamic phase of mind.

29. Power depends upon consciousness of power; unless we use it, we shall lose it, and unless we are conscious of it we cannot use it.

30. The use of this power depends upon attention; the degree of attention determines our capacity for the acquirement of knowledge, which is another name for power.

31. Attention has been held to be the distinguishing mark of genius. The cultivation of attention depends upon practice.

32. The incentive of attention is interest; the greater the interest, the greater the attention; the greater the attention, the greater the interest, action and reaction; begin by paying attention; before long you will have aroused interest; this interest will attract more attention, and this attention will produce more interest, and so on. This practice will enable you to cultivate the power of attention.

33. Now concentrate upon your power to create; seek insight, perception; try to find a logical basis for the faith that is in you. Let the thought dwell on the fact that the physical man lives and moves and has his being in the sustainer of all organic life; in air, which he must breathe to live. Then let the thought rest on the fact that the spiritual man also lives and moves and has his being in a similar but subtler energy upon which he must depend for life, and that is in the physical world no life assumes form until after a seed is sown, and no higher fruit than that of the parent stock can be produced; so in the spiritual world no effect can be produced until the seed is sown and the fruit will depend upon the nature of the seed, so that the results which you secure depend upon your perception of law in the mighty domain of causation, which knowledge is the highest evolution of human consciousness.

Thought engenders thought. Place one idea upon paper, another will follow it, and still another, until you have written a page. You cannot fathom your mind. It is a well of thought which has no bottom. The more you draw from it, the more clear and fruitful it will be. If you neglect to think yourself, and use other people's thoughts, giving them utterance only, you will never know what you are capable of.

—G. A. Sala.

✳

171. *How is the difference in individual lives measured?*
    By the degree of intelligence that they manifest.

172. *What is the law by which the individual may control other forms of intelligence?*
    A recognition of the self as an individualization of the Universal Intelligence.

173. *Where does the creative power originate?*
    In the Universal.

174. *How does the, Universal create form?*
    By means of the individual.

175. *What is the connecting link between the individual and the Universal?*
    Thought.

176. *What is the principle by which the means of existence is carried into effect?*
   The Law of Love.

177. *How is this principle brought into expression?*
   By the law of growth.

178. *Upon what condition does the law of growth depend?*
   Upon reciprocal action. The individual is complete at all times and this makes it possible to receive only as we give.

179. *What is it that we give?*
   Thought.

180. *What do we receive?*
   Thought, which is substance in equilibrium and which is constantly being differentiated in form by what we think.

The happiness of your life depends upon the quality of your thoughts. Therefore, guard accordingly; and take care that you entertain no notions unsuitable to virtue and reasonable nature.

—Marcus Antonius.

ADVICE

Remember—
   Fully to understand grand and beautiful thought requires, perhaps, as much
                                                   time as to conceive it.
                                                       –JOUBERT

If you wish to enjoy the utmost practical benefit form "The Master Key"— go slowly.

Transfuse into your mind the contents of one part only, each week for twenty-four weeks.

Realize the meaning of every phrase.

Consult "The Master Key" constantly, as your perpetual help and stimulus.

Each time you read the work you will get a better understanding of the eternal cosmic principles.

Tell others of "The Master Key" so that more and more people may reciprocate with you, as conscious adepts in harmony.

PART NINETEEN

This Part tells of the search for truth, which is another name for ultimate cause. If we can find the truth we shall have found the cause for every effect, and having found the cause we shall be in a position to control the effect. It explains that all things are finally resolvable into one thing, and that as they are thus translatable they must ever be in relation and can never be in opposition to one another. It explains that a knowledge of this primary substance is power; it explains that a knowledge of cause and effect is power, that wealth is the offspring of power, that events and conditions are significant only as they effect power, and finally that all things certain forms and degrees of power. It tells of a certain form of power that can control every other power, why it is superior and how we may make use of this superior power.

Fear is a powerful form of thought. It paralyses the nerve centres, thus affecting the circulation of the blood. This, in turn, paralyses the muscular system, so that fear affects the entire being, body, brain and nerve, physical, mental and muscular.

Of course the way to overcome fear is to become conscious of power. What is this mysterious vital force which we call power? We do not know; neither do we know what electricity is. But we do know that by conforming to the requirements of the law by which electricity is governed, it will be our obedient servant; that it will light our homes, our cities, run our machinery and serve us in many useful capacities.

And so it is with vital force. Although we do not know what it is, and possibly may never know, we do know that it is a primary force which manifests through living bodies, and that by complying with the laws and principles by which it is governed. We can open ourselves to a more abundant inflow of this vital energy, and thus express the highest possible degree of mental, moral and spiritual efficiency.

Part Nineteen, which follows, tells of a very simple way of developing this vital force. If you put into practice the information outlined in this Part you win soon develop the sense of power that has ever been the distinguishing mark of genius.

✺

1. The search for truth is no longer a haphazard adventure, but it is a systematic process, and is logical in its operation. Every kind of experience is given a voice in shaping its decision.

2. In seeking the truth we are seeking ultimate cause; we know that every human experience is an effect; then if we may ascertain the cause, and if we shall find that this cause is one that we can consciously control, the effect or the experience will be within our control also.

3. Human experience will then no longer be the football of fate; a man will not be the child, of fortune, but destiny, fate and fortune will be controlled as readily as a captain controls his vessel, or an engineer his train.

4. All things are finally resolvable into the same element and as they are thus translatable, one into the other, they must ever be in relation and may never be in opposition to one another.

5. In the physical world there are innumerable contrasts, and these may for convenience sake be designated by distinctive names. There are sizes, colours, shades or ends to all things. There is a North Pole, and a South Pole, an inside and an outside, a seen and an unseen, but these expressions merely serve to place extremes in contrast.

6. They are names given to two different parts of one quantity. The two extremes are relative; they are not separate entities, but are two parts or aspects of the whole.

7. In the mental world we find the same law; we speak of knowledge and ignorance, but ignorance is only a lack of knowledge and is therefore found to be simply a word to express the absence of knowledge; it has no principle in itself.

8. In the Moral World we again find the same law; we speak of good and evil, but Good is a reality, something tangible, while Evil is found to be simply a negative condition, the absence of Good. Evil is sometimes thought to be a very real condition, but it has no principle, no vitality, no life; we know this because it can always be destroyed by Good; just as Truth destroys Error and light destroys darkness, so Evil vanishes when Good appears; there is therefore but one principle in the Moral World.

9. We find exactly the same law obtaining in the Spiritual world; we speak of Mind and Matter as two separate entities, but dearer insight makes it evident that there is but one operative principle, and that is Mind.

10. Mind is the real and the eternal. Matter is for ever changing; we know that in the aeons of time a hundred years is but as a day. If we stand in any large city and let the eye rest or the innumerable large and magnificent buildings, the railways, the electric trams, the telephones, the electric lights and all the other conveniences of modern civilization, we may remember that not one of them was there 100 years ago, excepting perhaps several of the buildings; and if we could stand on the same spot in a hundred years from now, in all probability we should find that but few of them remained.

11. In the animal kingdom we find the same law of change. The millions and millions of animals come and go, a few years constituting their span of life. In the plant world the change is still more rapid. Many plants and nearly all grasses come and go in a single year. When we pass to the inorganic, we expect to find something more substantial, but as we gaze on the apparently solid continent, we are told that it arose from the ocean; we see the giant mountain and are told that the place where it now stands was once a lake; and as we stand in awe before the great cliffs in the Yosemite Valley we can easily trace the path of the glaciers which carried all before them.

12. We are in the presence of continual change, and we know that this change is but the evolution of the Universal Mind, the grand process whereby all things are continually being created anew, and we come to know that matter is but a form which Mind takes and is therefore simply a condition. Matter has no principle; Mind is the only principle.

13. We have then come to know that Mind is the only principle that is operative in the physical, mental, moral and spiritual world.

14. We also know that this mind is static, or mind at rest; and we know that the ability of the individual to think is his ability to act upon the universal Mind and convert it into dynamic mind, or mind in motion.

15. In order to do this fuel must be applied in the form of food, for man cannot think without eating, and so we find that even a spiritual activity such as thinking cannot be converted into sources of pleasure and profit except by making use of material means.

16. It requires energy of some kind to collect electricity and convert it into a dynamic power; it requires the rays of the sun to give the necessary energy to sustain plant life; so it also requires energy in the form of food to enable the individual to think and thereby act upon the Universal Mind.

17. You may know that thought constantly, eternally, is taking form, is for ever seeking expression, or you may not, but the fact remains that if your thought is powerful, constructive, and positive, this will be plainly evident in the state of your health, your business and your environment. If your thought is weak, critical, destructive and negative generally, it will manifest in your body as fear, worry and nervousness, in your finance as lack and limitation, and in discordant conditions in your environment.

18. All wealth is the offspring of power; possessions are of value only as they confer power. Events are significant only as they affect power; all things represent certain forms and degrees of power.

19. A knowledge of cause and effect as shown by the laws governing steam, electricity, chemical affinity and gravitation enables men to plan courageously and to execute fearlessly. These laws are called Natural Laws, because they govern the physical world, but all power is not physical power; there is also mental power, and there is moral and spiritual power.

20. What are our schools, our universities, but mental power-houses, places where mental power is being developed?

21. As there are many mighty power-houses for the application of power to ponderous machinery, whereby raw material is collected and converted into the necessities and comforts of life, so the mental power-houses collect the raw material and cultivate and develop it into a power which is infinitely superior to all the forces of Nature, marvellous though these may be.

22. What is this raw material that is being collected in these thousands of mental power-houses all over the world and developed into a power that is evidently controlling every other power? In its static form it is Mind, in its dynamic form it is Thought.

23. This power is superior because it exists on a higher plane, because it has enabled man to discover the law by which these wonderful forces of Nature could be harnessed and made to do the work of hundreds and thousands of men. It has enabled man to discover laws whereby time and space have been annihilated, and now apparently the law of gravitation is to be overcome.

24. Thought is the vital force or energy which is being developed and which has produced such startling results in the last half century as to bring about a world which would be absolutely inconceivable to a man existing only fifty or even

twenty-five years ago. If such results have been secured by organizing these mental power-houses in fifty years, what may not be expected in another fifty years?

25. The substance from which all things are created is infinite in quantity; we know that light travels at the rate of 186,000 miles per second, and we know that there are stars so remote that it takes light 2,000 years to reach us, and we know that such stars exist in all parts of the heaven; we know, too, that this light comes in waves, so that if the ether on which these waves travel was not continuous the light would fail to reach us; we can then only come to the conclusion that this substance, or ether, or raw material, is universally present.

26. How, then does it manifest in form? In electrical science a battery is formed by connecting the opposite poles of zinc and copper, which causes a current to flow from one to the other and so provides energy. This same process is repeated in respect to every polarity, and as all form simply depends upon the rate of vibration and consequent relations of atoms to each other if we wish to change the form of manifestation we must change the polarity. This is the principle of causation.

27. For your next exercise, concentrate, and when I use the word concentrate, I mean all that the word implies; become so absorbed in the object of your thought that you are conscious of nothing else, and do this a few minutes every day. You take the necessary time to eat in order that the body may be nourished, why not take the time to assimilate your mental food?

28. Let the thought rest on the fact that appearances are deceptive. The earth is not flat, neither is it stationary; the sky is not a dome, the sun does not move, the stars are not small specks of light, and matter which was once supposed to be fixed has been found to be in a state of perpetual flux.

29. Try to realize that the day is fast approaching—its dawn is now at hand—when modes of thought and action must be adjusted to rapidly increasing knowledge of the operation of eternal principles.

> *Nothing is comparable to the pleasure of an active and prevailing thought;*
> *a thought prevailing over the difficulty and obscurity of the object, and*
> *refreshing the soul with new discoveries and images of things; and thereby*
> *extending the bounds of apprehension, and as it were enlarging the territory*
> *of reason.*

—South.

✻

181. *How are extremes placed in contrast?*
     They are designated by distinctive names, such as inside and outside,
     top and bottom, light and dark, good and bad.
182. *Are these separate entities?*
     No, they are parts or aspects of one Whole.

183. *What is the one creative Principle in the physical, mental and spiritual world?*
     The Universal Mind, or the Eternal Energy from which all things proceed.

184. *How are we related to this creative Principle?*
     By our ability to think.

185. *How does this creative Principle become operative?*
     Thought is the seed that results in action, and action results in form.

186. *Upon what does form depend?*
     Upon the rate of vibration.

187. *How may the rate of vibration be changed?*
     By mental action.

188. *Upon what does mental action depend?*
     Upon polarity, action and reaction, between the individual and the Universal.

189. *Does the creative energy originate in the individual or the Universal?*
     In the Universal, but the Universal can manifest only through the individual.

190. *Why is the individual necessary?*
     Because the Universal is static, and requires energy to start it in motion. This is furnished by food that is converted into energy, which in turn enables the individual to think. When the individual stops eating he stops thinking; then he no longer acts upon the Universal; there is consequently no longer any action or reaction; the Universal is then only pure mind in static form—mind at rest.

There is no thought in my mind but it quickly tends to convert itself into a power and organizes a huge instrumentality of means.

—Emerson.

PART TWENTY

This Part tells what the true business of life is and the result. It shows that we can obtain no results as long as we remain oblivious to the only power there is, an understanding of the principles, forces, methods and combinations of mind and its relation to the Universal mind. It explains that the Universal can act only through the Individual; it shows that we are the channel for its activity, that it is within us, that we are it. We can, of course, fail to recognize it and so exclude it from our consciousness, but it will nevertheless be the basic fact of all existence. It tells of inspiration, the art of adjusting the individual mind to that of the Universal, the art of becoming a channel for the flow of Infinite Wisdom.

For many years there has been an endless discussion as to the origin of evil. Theologians have told us that God is Love, and that God is Omnipresent. If this is true, there is no place where God is not. Where, then, are Evil, Satan and Hell? Let us see:

God is Spirit.

Spirit is the Creative Principle of the Universe.

Man is made in the image and likeness of God.

Man is therefore a spiritual being.

The only activity which spirit possesses is the power to think.

Thinking is therefore a creative process.

All form is therefore the result of the thinking process.

The destruction of form must also be a result of the thinking process.

Fictitious representations of form are the result of the creative power of thought, as in Hypnotism.

Apparent representations of form are the result of the creative power of thought, as in Spiritualism.

Invention, organization and constructive work of all kinds are the result of the creative power of thought, as in concentration.

When the creative power of thought is manifested for the benefit of humanity, we call the result good.

When the creative power of thought is manifested in a destructive or evil manner, we call the result evil.

This indicates the origin of both good and evil; they are simply words which have been coined in order to indicate the nature of the result of the thinking or creative process.

Thought necessarily precedes and predetermines action; action precedes and predetermines condition.

Part Twenty will throw more light upon this important subject.

✸

1. The spirit of a thing is that thing; it is necessarily fixed, changeless and eternal. The spirit of you is—you; without the spirit you would be nothing. It becomes active through your recognition of it and its possibilities.

2. You may have all the wealth in Christendom, but unless you recognize it and make use of it, it will have no value; so with your spiritual wealth: unless you recognize it and use it, it will have no value. The one and only condition of spiritual power is use or recognition.

3. All great things come through recognition; the sceptre of power is consciousness, and thought is its messenger, and this messenger is constantly mould-

ing the realities of the invisible world into the conditions and environments of your objective world.

4. Thinking is the true business of life, power is the result. You are at all times dealing with the magical power of thought and consciousness. What results can you expect so long as you remain oblivious to the power that has been placed within your control?

5. So long as you do this you limit yourself to superficial conditions, and make of yourself a beast of burden for those who think; those who recognize their power; those who know that unless we are willing to think we shall have to work, and the less we think the more we shall have to work, and the less we shall get for our work.

6. The secret of power is a perfect understanding of the principles, forces, methods and combinations of Mind, and a perfect understanding of our relationship to the Universal Mind. It is well to remember that this principle is unchangeable; if this were not so, it would not be reliable; all principles are changeless.

7. This stability is your opportunity; you are its active attribute, the channel for its activity; the Universal can act only through the individual.

8. When you begin to perceive that the essence of the Universal is within yourself—is you—you begin to do things; you begin to feel your power; it is the fuel which fires the imagination; which lights the torch of inspiration; which gives vitality to thought; which enables you to connect with all the invisible forces of the Universe. It is this power which will enable you to plan fearlessly, to execute masterfully.

9. But perception will come only in the Silence; this seems to be the condition required for all great purposes. You are a visualizing entity. Imagination is your workshop. It is here that your ideal is to be visualized.

10. As a perfect understanding of the nature of this power is a primary condition for its manifestation, visualize the entire method over and over again, so that you may use it whenever occasion requires. Supreme wisdom is to follow the method whereby we may have the inspiration of the omnipotent Universal Mind on demand at any time.

11. We can fail to recognize this world within, and so exclude it from our consciousness, but it will still be the basic fact of all existence; and when we learn to recognize it, not only in ourselves, but in all persons, events, things and circumstances, we shall have found the "Kingdom of Heaven" which we are told is "within" us.

12. Our failures are a result of the operation of exactly the same principle; the principle is unchangeable; its operation is exact, there is no deviation; if we think lack, limitation, discord, we shall find their fruits on every hand; if we think poverty, unhappiness or disease, the thought messengers will carry the summons as readily as any other kind of thought and the result will be just as certain. If we fear a coming calamity, we shall be able to say with Job, "the thing I feared has come upon me"; if we think unkindly or ignorantly we shall thus attract to ourselves the results of our ignorance.

13. This power of thought, if understood and correctly used, is the greatest labour-saving device ever dreamed of, but if not understood or improperly used, the result will in all probability be disastrous, as we have already seen; by the help of this power you can confidently undertake things that are seemingly impossible, because this power is the secret of all inspiration, all genius.

14. To become inspired means to get out of the beaten path, out of the rut, because extraordinary results require extraordinary means. When we come into a recognition of the Unity of all things and that the source of all power is within, we tap the source of inspiration.

15. Inspiration is the art of imbibing, the art of self-realization; the art of adjusting the individual mind to that of the Universal Mind; the art of attaching the proper mechanism to the source of all power; the art of differentiating the formless into form; the art of becoming a channel for the flow of Infinite Wisdom; the art of visualizing perfection; the art of realizing the omnipresence of Omnipotence.

16. An understanding and appreciation of the fact that the infinite power is omnipresent and is therefore in the infinitely small as well as the infinitely large will enable us to absorb its essence; a further understanding of the fact that this power is spirit and therefore indivisible will enable us to appreciate its presence at all points at the same time.

17. An understanding of these facts, first intellectually and then emotionally, will enable us to drink deeply from this ocean of infinite power. An intellectual understanding will be of no assistance; the emotions must be brought into action; thought without feeling is cold. The required combination is thought and feeling.

18. Inspiration is from within. The Silence is necessary, the senses must be stilled, the muscles relaxed, repose cultivated. When you have thus come into possession of a sense of poise and power you will be ready to receive the information or inspiration or wisdom which may be necessary for the development of your purpose.

19. Do not confuse these methods with those of the clairvoyant; they have nothing in common. Inspiration is the art of receiving and makes for all that is best in life; your business in life is to understand and command these invisible forces instead of letting them command and rule you. Power implies service; inspiration implies power; to understand and apply the method of inspiration is to become a superman.

20. We can live more abundantly every time we breathe, if we consciously breathe with that intention. The IF is a very important condition in this case as the intention governs the attention, and without the attention you can secure only the results which every one else secures. That is, a supply equal to the demand.

21. In order to secure the larger supply your demand must be increased, and as you consciously increase the demand the supply will follow, you will find yourself coming into a larger and larger supply of life, energy and vitality.

22. The reason for this is not difficult to understand, but it is another of the vital mysteries of life that does not seem to be generally appreciated. If you make it your own you will find it one of the great realities of life.

23. We are told that "In Him we live and move and have our being," and we are told that "He" is a Spirit, and again that "He" is Love, so that every time we breathe, we breathe this life, love and spirit. This is Pranic Energy, or Pranic Ether; we could not exist a moment without it. It is the Cosmic Energy; it is the Life of the Solar Plexus.

24. Every time we breathe we fill our lungs with air and at the same time vitalize our body with this Pranic Ether which is Life itself, so that we have the opportunity of making a conscious connection with All Life, All Intelligence and All Substance.

25. A knowledge of your relation and oneness with this Principle that governs the Universe and the simple method whereby you can consciously identify yourself with it gives you a scientific understanding of a law whereby you may free yourself from disease, from lack or limitation of any kind; in fact, it enables you to breathe the "breath of life" into your own nostrils.

26. This "breath of life" is a super-conscious reality. It is the essence of the "I am." It is pure "Being" or Universal Substance and our conscious unity with it enables us to localize it, and thus exercise the powers of this creative energy.

27. Thought is creative vibration and the quality of the conditions created will depend upon the quality of our thought, because we cannot express powers that we do not possess. We must "be" before we can "do" and we can "do" only to the extent to which we "are," and so what we do will necessarily coincide with what we are "and what we are depends upon what we think."

28. Every time you think you start a train of causation that will create a condition in strict accordance with the quality of the thought that originated it. Thought which is in harmony with the Universal Mind will result in corresponding conditions. Thought which is destructive or discordant will produce corresponding results. You may use thought constructively or destructively, but the immutable law will not allow you to plant a thought of one kind and reap the fruit of another. You are free to use this marvellous creative power as you will, but you must take the consequences.

29. This is the danger from what is called Will Power. There are those who seem to think that by force of will they can coerce this law; that they can sow seed of one kind and by "Will Power" make it bear fruit of another, but the fundamental principle of creative power is the Universal, and therefore the idea of forcing a compliance with our wishes by the power of the individual will is an inverted conception, which may appear to succeed for a while but is eventually doomed to failure, because it antagonizes the very power which it is seeking to use.

30. It is the individual attempting to coerce the Universal, the finite in conflict with the Infinite. Our permanent well-being will be best conserved by a conscious co-operation with the continuous forward movement of the Great Whole.

31. For your next exercise, go into the Silence and concentrate on the fact that "In Him we live and move and have our being" is literally and scientifically exact! That You ARE because He IS, that if He is Omnipresent He must be in you. That if

He is all in all, you must be in Him! That He is Spirit and You are made in "His image and likeness" and that the only difference between His spirit and your spirit is one of degree, that a part must be the same in kind and quality as the whole. When you can realize this clearly you will have found the secret of the creative power of thought, you will have found the origin of both good and evil, you will have found the secret of the wonderful power of concentration, you will have found the key to the solution of every problem whether physical, financial or environmental.

Learning without thought is labour lost; thought without learning is perilous.

Thinkers are as scarce as gold; but he whose thoughts embrace all their subject, who pursues it uninterruptedly and fearless of consequences, is a diamond of enormous size.

—Lavater.

❋

191. *Upon what condition does power depend?*
    Upon recognition and use.
192. *What is recognition?*
    Consciousness.
193. *How do we become conscious of power?*
    By thinking.
194. *What then is the true business of life?*
    Correct scientific thinking.
195. *What is correct scientific thinking?*
    The ability to adjust our thought processes to the will of the Universal. In other words to co-operate with Natural laws.
196. *How is this accomplished?*
    By securing a perfect understanding of the principles, forces, methods and combinations of mind.
197. *What is this Universal Mind?*
    The basic fact of all existence.
198. *What is the cause of all lack, limitation, disease and discord?*
    It is due to the operation of exactly the same law, the law operates relentlessly and is continually bringing about conditions in correspondence with the thought which originated or created them.
199. *What is inspiration?*
    The art of realizing the omnipresence of Omniscience.
200. *Upon what does the conditions with which we meet depend?*
    Upon the quality of our thought. Because what we *do* depends upon what we *are* and what we are depends upon what we *think*.

All truly wise thoughts have been thought already thousands of times; but to make them truly ours we must think them over again honestly, till they take root in our personal experience.

—Goethe.

PART TWENTY-ONE

This Part explains how we may come into possession of power sufficient to meet every situation that may arise in life. It explains that the ability to eliminate imperfect conditions depends upon mental action. It explains that great ideas have a tendency to eliminate smaller ideas, so that it is well to hold ideas that are large enough to counteract and destroy all small or undesirable tendencies. This is one of the secrets of success, one of the accomplishments of the Master Mind. It explains that the creative energy finds no more difficulty in handling a large situation than a small one. It explains how conditions are produced in our lives by the predominant thoughts that we entertain. It explain how you may set causes in motion which will create an irresistible magnetic power which will bring the things you require to you. It explains the issue between the old regime and the new, it explains the crux of the social problem, it explains the true secret of health, wealth and power.

In paragraph seven of this Part you will find that one of the secrets of success, one of the methods of organizing victory, one of the accomplishments of the Master Mind is to think big thoughts.

In paragraph eight you will find that everything that we hold in our consciousness for any length of time becomes impressed upon our sub-consciousness and so becomes a pattern that the creative energy will weave into our life and environment. This is the secret of the wonderful power of prayer.

We know that the universe is governed by law; that for every effect there must be a cause, and that the same cause, under the same conditions, will invariably produce the same effect. Consequently, if prayer has ever been answered, it will always be answered, if the proper conditions are complied with. This must necessarily be true; otherwise the Universe would be a chaos instead of a cosmos. The answer to prayer is therefore subject to law, and this law is definite, exact and scientific, just as are the laws governing gravitation and electricity. An understanding of this law takes the foundation of Christianity out of the realm of superstition and credulity and places it upon the firm rock of scientific understanding.

But, unfortunately, there are comparatively few persons who know how to pray. They understand that there are laws governing electricity, mathematics and chemistry, but, for some inexplicable reason, it never seems to occur to them that there are also spiritual laws, and that these laws are also definite, scientific, exact, and operate with immutable precision

✸

1. The real secret of power is consciousness of power. The Universal Mind is unconditional; therefore, the more conscious we become of our unity with this mind, the less conscious we shall become of conditions and limitations, and as we become emancipated or freed from conditions we come into a realization of the unconditional. We have become free!

2. As soon as we become conscious of the inexhaustible power in the world within, we begin to draw on this power and apply and develop the greater possibilities that this discernment has realized, because whatever we become conscious of, is invariably manifested in the objective world, is brought forth into tangible expression.

3. This is because the Infinite mind, which is the source from which all things proceed, is one and indivisible, and each individual is a channel whereby this Eternal Energy is being manifested. Our ability to think is our ability to act upon this Universal substance, and what we think is what is created or produced in the objective world.

4. The result of this discovery is nothing less than marvellous, and means that mind is extraordinary in quality, limitless in quantity and contains possibilities without number. To become conscious of this power is to become a "live wire"; it has the same effect as placing an ordinary wire in contact with a wire that is charged. The Universal is the live wire. It carries power sufficient to meet every situation that may arise in the life of every individual. When the individual mind touches the Universal Mind it receives all the power it requires. This is the world within. All science recognizes the reality of this world, and all power is contingent upon our recognition of this world

5. The ability to eliminate imperfect conditions depends upon mental action, and mental action depends upon consciousness of power; therefore, the more conscious we become of our unity with the source of all power, the greater will be our power to control and master every condition.

6. Large ideas have a tendency to eliminate all smaller ideas so that it is well to hold ideas large enough to counteract and destroy all small or undesirable tendencies. This will remove innumerable petty and annoying obstacles from your path. You also become conscious of a larger world of thought, thereby increasing your mental capacity as well as placing yourself in position to accomplish something of value.

7. This is one of the secrets of success, one of the methods of organizing victory, one of the accomplishments of the Master-mind. He thinks big thoughts. The creative energies of mind find no more difficulty in handling large situations than small ones. Mind is just as much present in the Infinitely large as in the Infinitely small.

8. When we realize these facts concerning mind we understand how we may bring to ourselves any condition by creating the corresponding conditions in our consciousness, because everything which is held for any length of time in the consciousness, eventually becomes impressed upon the sub-conscious and thus becomes a pattern which the creative energy will weave into the life and environment of the individual.

9. In this way conditions are produced and we find that our lives are simply the reflection of our predominant thoughts, our mental attitude; we see then that the science of correct thinking is the one science, that it includes all other sciences.

10. From this science we learn that every thought creates an impression in the brain, that these impressions create mental tendencies, and these tendencies create character, ability and purpose, and that the combined action of character, ability and purpose determines the experiences with which we shall meet in life.

11. These experiences come to us through the law of attraction; through the action of this law we meet in the world without the experiences that correspond to our world within.

12. The predominant thought or the mental attitude is the magnet, and the law is that like attracts like, consequently the mental attitude will invariably attract such conditions as correspond to its nature.

13. This mental attitude is our personality and is composed of the thoughts which we have been creating in our own mind; therefore, if we wish a change in conditions all that is necessary is to change our thought; this will in turn change our mental attitude, which will in turn change our personality, which will in turn change the persons, things and conditions, or the experiences with which we meet in life.

14. It is, however, no easy matter to change the mental attitude, but by persistent effort it may be accomplished; the mental attitude is patterned after the mental pictures which have been photographed on the brain; if you do not like the pictures, destroy the negatives and create new pictures; this is the art of visualization.

15. As soon as you have done this you will begin to attract new things, and the new things will correspond to the new pictures. To do this: impress on the mind a perfect picture of the desire that you wish to have objectified and continue to hold the picture in mind until results are obtained.

16. If the desire is one that requires determination, ability, talent, courage, power or any other spiritual power, these are necessary essentials for your picture; build them in; they are the vital part of the picture; they are the feeling that combines with thought and creates the irresistible magnetic power that draws the things you require to you. They give your picture life, and life means growth, and as soon as it begins to grow, the result is practically assured.

17. Do not hesitate to aspire to the highest possible attainments in anything you may undertake, for the mind forces are ever ready to lend themselves to a purposeful will in the effort to crystallize its highest aspirations into acts, accomplishments and events.

18. An illustration of how these mind forces operate is suggested by the method in which all our habits are formed. We do a thing, then do it again, and again, and again, until it becomes easy and perhaps almost automatic; and the same rule applies in breaking any and all bad habits; we stop doing a thing, and then avoid it again, and again until we are entirely free from it; and if we do fail now and then, we should by no means lose hope, for the law is absolute and invincible and gives us credit for every effort and every success, even though our efforts and successes are perhaps intermittent.

19. There is no limit to what this law can do for you; dare to believe in your own ideal; remember that Nature is plastic to the ideal; think of the ideal as an already accomplished fact.

20. The real battle of life is one of ideas; it is being fought out by the few against the many; on the one side is the constructive and creative thought, on the other side the destructive and negative thought; the creative thought is dominated by an ideal, the passive thought is dominated by appearances. On both sides are men of science, men of letters and men of affairs.

21. On the creative side are men who spend their time in laboratories, or over microscopes and telescopes, side by side with the men who dominate the commer-

cial, political and scientific world; on the negative side are men who spend their time investigating law and precedent, men who mistake theology for religion, statesmen who mistake might for right, and all the millions who seem to prefer precedent to progress, who are eternally looking backward instead of forward, who see only the world without, but know nothing of the world within.

22. In the last analysis there are but these two classes; all men will have to take their place on one side or the other; they will have to go forward, or go back; there is no standing; it is this still in a world where all is motion; attempt to stand still that gives sanction and force to arbitrary and unequal codes of law.

23. That we are in a period of transition is evidenced by the unrest that is everywhere apparent. The complaint of humanity is as a roll of heaven's artillery, commencing with low and threatening notes and increasing until the sound is sent from cloud to cloud, and the lightning rends the air and earth.

24. The sentries who patrol the most advanced outposts of the Industrial, Political and Religious world are calling anxiously to each other. What of the night? The danger and insecurity of the position they occupy and attempt to hold is becoming more apparent every hour. The dawn of a new era necessarily declares that the existing order of things cannot much longer be.

25. The issue between the old regime and the new, the crux of the social problem, is entirely a question of conviction in the minds of the people as to the nature of the Universe. When they realize that the transcendent force of spirit or mind of the Cosmos is within each individual, it will be possible to frame laws that shall consider the liberties and rights of the many instead of the privileges of the few.

26. As long as the people regard the Cosmic Power as a power non-human and alien to humanity, so long will it be comparatively easy for a supposed privileged class to rule by Divine right in spite of every protest of social sentiment. The real interest of humanity is therefore to exalt, emancipate and recognize the divinity of the human spirit. To recognize that all power is from within. That no human being has any more power than any other human being, except such as may willingly be delegated to him. The old regime would have us believe that the law was superior to the law-makers; herein is the gist of the social crime of every form of privilege and personal inequality, the institutionalizing of the fatalistic doctrine of Divine election.

27. The Divine Mind is the Universal Mind; it does not act through sheer caprice or from anger, jealousy or wrath; neither can it be flattered, cajoled or moved by sympathy or petition to supply man with some need that he thinks necessary for his happiness or even his existence. The Divine Mind makes no exceptions in favor of any individual; but when the individual understands and realizes his Unity with the Universal Principle he will appear to be favored because he will have found the source of all health, all wealth and all power.

28. For your next exercise, concentrate on the Truth. Try to realize that the Truth shall make you free, that is, nothing can permanently stand in the way of your

perfect success when you learn to apply the scientifically correct thought methods and principles. Realize that you are eternalizing in your environment, your inherent soul potencies. Realize that the Silence offers an ever available and almost unlimited opportunity for awakening the highest conception of Truth. Try to comprehend that Omnipotence itself is absolute silence; all else is change, activity, limitation. Silent thought concentration is therefore the true method of reaching, awakening and then expressing the wonderful potential power of the world within.

The possibilities of thought training are infinite, its consequence eternal, and yet few take the pains to direct their thinking into channels that will do them good, but instead leave all to chance.

—Marden.

✳

201. *What is the real secret of power?*
The consciousness of power, because whatever we become conscious of, is invariably manifested in the objective world, is brought forth into tangible expression.

202. *What is the source of this power?*
The Universal Mind, from which all things proceed, and which is one and indivisible.

203. *How is this power being manifested?*
Through the individual. Each individual is a channel whereby this energy is being differentiated in form.

204. *How may we connect with this Omnipotence?*
Our ability to think is our ability to act on this Universal Energy, and what we think is what is produced or created in the objective world.

205. *What is the result of this discovery?*
The result is nothing less than marvellous; it opens unprecedented and limitless opportunity.

206. *How, then, may we eliminate imperfect conditions?*
By becoming conscious of our Unity with the source of all power.

207. *What is one of the distinctive characteristics of the Master Mind?*
He thinks big thoughts, he holds ideas large enough to counteract and destroy all petty and annoying obstacles.

208. *How do experiences come to us?*
Through the law of attraction.

209. *How is this law brought into operation?*
By our predominant mental attitude.

210. *What is the issue between the old regime and the new?*
A question of conviction as to the nature of the Universe. The old regime is trying to cling to the fatalistic doctrine of Divine election.

The new regime recognizes the divinity of the individual, the divinity of humanity.

The power to think, consecutively and deeply and clearly, is an avowed and deadly enemy to mistakes and blunders, superstitions, unscientific theories, irrational beliefs, unbridled enthusiasm, fanaticism.

—Haddock.

PART TWENTY-TWO

This Part explains the cause of our present character, our present environment, our present ability, our present physical condition, and tells how we can make our future what we wish it to be. It explains how the vast panorama of Nature is being constantly changed by simply changing the rate of vibration. It tells how the rate of vibration is being constantly changed in our bodies, usually unconsciously and often with detrimental and disastrous results. It tells how we may effect this change consciously and thus bring about only harmonious and salutary conditions. It explains that the Law of Health is based on the law of vibration, and that with a proper knowledge of the law we may externalize health conditions. It explains the operation of this law and how it is being more generally understood and appreciated, and how many physicians are now giving the matter their earnest attention.

In Part Twenty-Two you will find that thoughts are spiritual seeds, which, when planted in the sub-conscious mind, have a tendency to sprout and grow, but unfortunately the fruit is frequently not to our liking.

The various forms of inflammation, paralysis, nervousness and diseased conditions generally, are the manifestation of fear, worry, care, anxiety, jealousy, hatred and similar thought.

The life processes are carried on by two distinct methods: firstly, the taking up and making use of nutritive material necessary for constructing cells; secondly, the secretion and excretion of the waste material.

All life is based upon these constructive and destructive activities, and as food, water and air are the only requisites necessary for the construction of cells, it would seem that the problem of prolonging life indefinitely would not be a very difficult one.

However strange it may seem, it is the second or destructive activity that is, with rare exception, the cause of all disease. The waste material accumulates and saturates the tissues, which causes autointoxication. This may be partial or general. In the first case the disturbance will be local; in the second place it will affect the whole system.

The problem, then, before us in the healing of disease is to increase the inflow and distribution of vital energy throughout the system, and this can only be done by eliminating thoughts of fear, worry, care, anxiety, jealousy, hatred, and every other destructive thought, which tend to tear down and destroy the nerves and glands which control the excretion and elimination of poisonous and waste matter.

"Nourishing foods and strengthening tonics" cannot bestow life, because these are but secondary manifestations of life. The primary manifestation of life and how you may get in touch with it is explained in Part Twenty-Two.

✸

1. Knowledge is of priceless value, because by applying knowledge we can make our future what we wish it to be. When we realize that our present character, our present environment, our present ability, our present physical condition are the result of past methods of thinking, we shall begin to have some conception of the value of knowledge.

2. If the state of our health is not all that could be desired, let us examine our method of thinking; let us remember that every thought produces an impression on the mind; every impression is a seed which will sink into the sub-conscious and form a tendency; the tendency will be to attract other similar thoughts and before we know it we shall have a crop which must be harvested.

3. If these thoughts contain disease germs, the harvest will be sickness, decay, weakness and failure; the question is, what are we thinking, what are we creating, what is the harvest to be?

4. If there is any physical condition that it is necessary to change, the law governing visualization will be found effective. Make a mental image of physical perfection, hold it in the mind until it is absorbed by the consciousness. Many have eliminated chronic ailments in a few weeks by this method, and thousands have overcome and destroyed all manner of ordinary physical disturbances by this method in a few days, sometimes in a few minutes.

5. It is through the law of vibration that the mind exercises this control over the body. We know that every mental action is a vibration, and we know that all form is simply a mode of motion, a rate of vibration. Therefore, any given vibration immediately modifies every atom in the body, every life cell is affected and an entire chemical change is made in every group of life cells.

6. Everything in the Universe is what it is by virtue of its rate of vibration. Change the rate of vibration and you change the nature quality and form. The vast panorama of nature, both visible and invisible, is being constantly changed by simply changing the rate of vibration, and as thought is a vibration we can also exercise this power. We can change the vibration and thus produce any condition which we desire to manifest in our bodies.

7. We are all using this power every minute. The trouble is most of us are using it unconsciously and thus producing undesirable results. The problem is to use it intelligently and produce only desirable results. This should not be difficult, because we all have had sufficient experience to know what produces pleasant vibration in the body, and we also know the causes which produce the unpleasant and disagreeable sensations.

8. All that is necessary is to consult our own experience. When our thought has been uplifted, progressive, constructive, courageous, noble, kind or in any other way desirable, we have set in motion vibrations that brought about certain results. When our thought has been filled with envy, hatred, jealousy, criticism or any of the other thousand and one forms of discord, certain vibrations were set in motion which brought about certain other results of a different nature, and each of these rates of vibration, if kept up, crystallized in form. In the first case the result was mental, moral and physical health, and in the second case discord, disharmony and disease.

9. We can understand, then, something of the power which the mind possesses over the body.

10. The objective mind has certain effects on the body that are readily recognized. Some one says something to you which strikes you as ludicrous and you laugh, possibly until your whole body shakes, which shows that thought has control over the muscles of your body; or someone says something which excites your sympathy and your eyes fill with tears, which shows that thought controls the glands of the body; or some one says something which makes you angry and the

blood mounts to your cheek, which shows that thought controls the circulation of your blood. But as these experiences are all the results of the action of your objective mind over the body, the results are of a temporary nature; they soon pass away and leave the situation as it was before.

11. Let us see how the action of the subconscious mind over the body differs. You receive a wound; thousands of cells begin the work of healing at once; in a few days or a few weeks the work is complete. You may even break a bone. No surgeon on earth can weld the parts together. He may set the bone for you, and the subjective mind will immediately begin the process of welding the parts together, and in a short time the bone is as solid as it ever was. You may swallow poison; the subjective mind will immediately discover the danger and make violent efforts to eliminate it. You may become infected with a dangerous germ; the subjective will at once commence to build a wall around the infected area and destroy the infection by absorbing it in the white blood corpuscles that it supplies for the purpose.

12. These processes of the sub-conscious mind usually proceed without our personal knowledge or direction, and so long as we do not interfere the result is perfect, but, as these millions of repair cells are all intelligent and respond to our thought, they are often paralysed and rendered impotent by our thoughts of fear, doubt and anxiety. They are like an army of workmen, ready to start an important piece of work, but every time they get fairly started on the undertaking a strike is called or plans changed, until they finally get discouraged and give up.

13. The way to health is founded on the law of vibration, which is the basis of all science, and this law is brought into operation by the mind, the "world within." It is a matter of individual effort and practice. Our world of power is within; if we are wise we shall not waste time and effort in trying to deal with effects as we find them in the "world without," which is only an external, a reflection.

14. We shall always find the cause in the "world within"; by changing the cause, we change the effect.

15. Every cell in your body is intelligent and will respond to your direction. The cells are all creators and will create the exact pattern that you give them.

16. Therefore, when perfect images are placed before the subjective, the creative energies will build a perfect body.

17. Brain cells are constructed in the same way. The quality of the brain is governed by the state of mind, or mental attitude, so that if undesirable mental attitudes are conveyed to the subjective they will in turn be transferred to the body; we can therefore readily see that if we wish the body to manifest health, strength and vitality this must be the predominant thought.

18. We know then that every element of the human body is the result of a rate of vibration.

19. We know that mental action is a rate of vibration.

20. We know that a higher rate of vibration governs, modifies, controls, changes or destroys a lower rate of vibration.

21. We know that the rate of vibration is governed by the character of brain cells, and finally,

22. We know how to create these brain cells; therefore,

23. We know how to make any physical change in the body we desire, and having secured a working knowledge of the power of mind to this extent, we have come to know that there is practically no limitation that can be placed upon our ability to place ourselves in harmony with natural law, which is omnipotent.

24. This influence or control over the body by the mind is coming to be more and more generally understood, and many physicians are now giving the matter their earnest attention. Dr. Albert T. Shofield, who has written several important books on the subject, says: "The subject of mental therapeutics is still ignored in medical works generally. In our physiologies no reference is made to the central controlling power that rules the body for its good, and the power of the mind over the body is seldom spoken of.

25. "No doubt many physicians treat nervous diseases of functional origin wisely and well, but what we contend is that the knowledge they display was taught at no school, was learned from no book, but is intuitive and empirical.

26. "This is not as it should be. The power of mental therapeutics should be the subject of careful, special and scientific teaching in every medical school. We might pursue the subject of maltreatment, or want of treatment, further in detail and describe the disastrous results of neglected cases; but the task is an invidious one.

27. "There can be no doubt that few patients are aware how much they can do for themselves. What the patient can do for himself, the forces he can set in motion, are as yet unknown. We are inclined to believe that they are far greater than most imagine, and will undoubtedly be used more and more. Mental therapeutics may be directed by the patient himself to calming the mind in excitement, by arousing feelings of joy, hope, faith and love; by suggesting motives for exertion, by regular mental work, by diverting the thoughts from the malady."

28. For your next exercise concentrate on Tennyson's beautiful lines: "Speak to Him, thou, for He hears, and spirit with spirit can meet, Closer is He than breathing, and nearer than hands and feet." Then try to realize that when you do "Speak to Him," you are in touch with Omnipotence.

29. This realization and recognition of this Omnipresent power will quickly destroy any and every form of sickness or suffering and substitute harmony and perfection. Then remember there are those who seem to think that sickness and suffering are sent by God; if so, every physician, every surgeon and every Red Cross nurse is defying the will of God, and hospitals and sanatoriums are places of rebellion instead of houses of mercy. Of course, this quickly reasons itself into an absurdity, but there are many who still cherish the idea.

30. Then let the thought rest on the fact that until recently Theology has been trying to teach an impossible Creator, one who created beings capable of sinning and then allowed them to be eternally punished for such sins. Of course the nec-

essary outcome of such extraordinary ignorance was to create fear instead of love, and so, after two thousand years of this kind of propaganda, Theology is now busily engaged in apologizing for Christendom.

31. You will then the more readily appreciate the ideal man, the man made in the image and likeness of God, and you will the more readily appreciate the all originating Mind that forms, upholds, sustains, originates and creates all there is.

> "All are but parts of one stupendous whole,
> Whose body nature is, and God the soul."
>
>   –Pope.

Opportunity follows perception, action follows inspiration, growth follows knowledge, eminence follows progress. Always the spiritual first, then the transformation into the infinite and illimitable possibilities of achievement.

✳

211. *How may sickness be eliminated?*
By placing ourselves in harmony with Natural Law which is Omnipotent.

212. *What is the process?*
A realization that man is a spiritual being and that this spirit must necessarily be perfect.

213. *What is the result?*
A conscious recognition of this perfection, first intellectually, then emotionally, brings about a manifestation of this perfection.

214. *Why is this so?*
Because thought is spiritual and therefore creative and correlates with its object and brings it into manifestation.

215. *What Natural Law is brought into operation?*
The Law of Vibration.

216. *Why does this govern?*
Because a higher rate of vibration governs, modifies, controls, changes or destroys a lower rate of vibration.

217. *Is this system of mental therapeutics generally recognized?*
Yes, there are several million people in the world who make use of it in one form or another.

218. *What is the result of this system of thought?*
For the first time in the world's history every man's highest reasoning faculty can be satisfied by a demonstrable truth that is now fast flooding the world.

219. *Is this system applicable to other forms of supply?*
It will meet every human requirement or necessity.

220. Is this system scientific or religious?

Both. True science and true religion are twin sisters, where one goes the other necessarily follows.

Silent thought, is, after all, the mightiest agent in human affairs.

—Channing.

PART TWENTY-THREE

This Part tells of the money consciousness and the power which sets the current in motion which produces the attractive force which opens the doors to the arteries of commerce. It tells how the current is stopped or completely reversed and turned away from us. It tells how money is woven into the outer fabric of our existence. Why it engages the best thought of the best minds. How we make money. How to recognize opportunity. How to make a money magnet of yourself. How to get the necessary insight to perceive and utilize opportunities. How to recognize values. It tells how to convert an idea into an income, how to make a direct connection with the Universal Mind, how to secure practical results; in fact, it tells what the only really practical thing is.

In this Part you will find that money weaves itself into the entire fabric of our very existence; that the law of success is service; that we get what we give, and for this reason we should consider it a great privilege to be able to give.

We have found that thought is the creative activity behind every constructive enterprise. We can therefore give nothing of more practical value than our thought.

Creative thought requires attention, and the power of attention is, as we have found, the weapon of the Super-man. Attention develops concentration, and concentration develops Spiritual Power, and Spiritual Power is the mightiest force in existence.

This is the science which embraces all sciences. It is the art which, above all arts, is relevant to human life. In the mastery of this science and this art there is opportunity for unending progression. Perfection in this is not acquired in six days, or in six weeks, or in six months. It is the labour of a life. Not to go forward is to go backward.

It is inevitable that the entertainment of positive, constructive and unselfish thoughts should have a far-reaching effect for good. Compensation is the key-note of the universe. Nature is constantly seeking to strike an equilibrium. Where something is sent out, something must be received; lest there should be a vacuum formed. By observance of this rule you cannot fail to profit in such measure as amply to justify your effort along this line.

✸

1. The money consciousness is an attitude of mind; it is the open door to the arteries of commerce. It is the receptive attitude. Desire is the attractive force which sets the current in motion and fear is the great obstacle by which the current is stopped or completely reversed—turned away from us.

2. Fear is just the opposite from money consciousness; it is poverty consciousness, and as the law in unchangeable we get exactly what we give; if we fear we get what we feared. Money weaves itself into the entire fabric of our very existence; it engages the best thought of the best minds.

3. We make money by making friends, and we enlarge our circle of friends by making money for them, by helping them, by being of service to them. The first law of success then is service, and this in turn is built on integrity and justice. The man who at least is not fair in his intention is simply ignorant; he has missed the fundamental law of all exchange; he is impossible; he will lose surely and certainly; he may not know it; he may think he is winning, but he is doomed to certain defeat. He cannot cheat the Infinite. The law of compensation will demand of him an eye for an eye and a tooth for a tooth.

4. The forces of life are volatile; they are composed of our thoughts and ideals and these in turn are moulded into form; our problem is to keep an open mind, to constantly reach out for the new, to recognize opportunity, to be interested in the race rather than the goal, for the pleasure is in the pursuit rather than the possession.

5. You can make a money magnet of yourself, but to do so you must first consider how you can make money for other people. If you have the necessary insight to perceive and utilize opportunities and propitious conditions and recognize values, you can put yourself in position to take advantage of them, but your greatest success will come as you are enabled to assist others. What benefits one must benefit all.

6. A generous thought is filled with strength and vitality, a selfish thought contains the germs of dissolution; it will disintegrate and pass away. Great financiers like Morgan, Rothschild and others are simply channels for the distribution of wealth; enormous amounts come and go, but it would be as dangerous to stop the outgo as the income; both ends must remain open; and so our greatest success will come as we recognize that it is just as essential to give as to get.

7. If we recognize the Omnipotent power that is the source of all we supply we will adjust our consciousness to this supply in such a way that it will constantly attract all that is necessary to itself and we shall find that the more we give the more we get. Giving in this sense implies service. The banker gives his money, the merchant his goods, the author gives his thought, the workman gives his skill; all have something to give, but the more they can give, the more they can get, and the more they get the more they are enabled to give.

8. The financier gets much because he gives much; he thinks; he is seldom a man that lets any one else do his thinking for him; he wants to know how results are to be secured; you must show him; when you can do this he will furnish the means by which hundreds of thousands may profit, and in proportion as they are successful will he be successful. Morgan, Rockefeller, Carnegie, Rothschild and others did not get rich because they lost money for other people; on the contrary, it is because they made money for other people that they became the wealthiest men in the wealthiest countries on the globe.

9. The average person is entirely innocent of any deep thinking; he accepts the ideas of others, and repeats them, in very much the same way as a parrot; and this is readily seen when we understand the method which is used to form public opinion, and this docile attitude on the part of a large majority who seem perfectly willing to let a few persons do all their thinking for them is what enables a few men in a great many countries to usurp all the avenues of power and hold the millions in subjection. Creative thinking requires attention.

10. The power of attention is called concentration; this power is directed by the will; for this reason we must refuse to concentrate or think of anything except the tings we desire. Many are constantly concentrating upon sorrow, loss and discord of every kind; as thought is creative it necessarily follows that this concentra-

tion inevitably leads to more loss, more sorrow and more discord. How could it be otherwise? On the other hand, when we meet with success, gain, or any other desirable condition, we naturally concentrate upon the effects of these things and thereby create more, and so it follows that much leads to more.

11. How an understanding of this principle can be utilized in the business world is well told by Mr. Atkinson in "Advanced Thought." He says:

12. "Spirit, whatever else it may or may not be, must be considered as the Essence of Consciousness, the Substance of Mind, the reality underlying Thought. And as all Ideas are phases of the activity of Consciousness, Mind or Thought, it follows that in Spirit, and in it alone, is to be found the Ultimate Fact, the Real Thing, or Idea."

13. This being admitted, does it not seem reasonable to hold that a true understanding of Spirit, and its laws of manifestation, would be about the most "practical" thing that a "practical" person can hope to find? Does it not seem certain that if the "practical" men of the world could but realize this fact, they would "fall all over themselves" in getting to the place in which they might obtain such knowledge of spiritual things and laws? These men are not fools; they need only to grasp this fundamental fact in order to move in the direction of that which is the essence of all achievement.

14. Let me give you a concrete example. I know a man whom I had always considered to be quite materialistic. He had made several successes in life; and also several failures. The last time I had a talk with him he was practically "down and out" as compared with his former business condition. It looked as if he had indeed reached "the end of his rope," for he was well advanced into the stage of middle-age and new ideas came more slowly, and less frequently to him than in former years.

15. He said to me, in substance: "I know that all thinks that 'work out' in business are the result of Thought; any fool knows that. Just now, I seem to be short of thoughts and good ideas. But if this 'All-Mind' teaching is correct, there should be possible to the individual the attainment of 'direct connection' with Infinite Mind; and in Infinite Mind there must be the possibility of all kinds of good ideas which a man of my courage and experience could put to practical use in the business world, and make a big success of. It looks good to me; and I am going to look into it."

16. This was about two years ago. The other day I heard of this man again. Talking to a friend, I said: "What has become of our old friend X? Has he ever got on his feet again?" The friend looked at me in amazement. "Why," said he, "don't you know about X's great success? He is the Big Man in the '——— Company'." He named a concern which has made a phenomenal success during the last eighteen months and is now well known, by reason of its advertisements, from one end of the country to another, and also abroad. "He is the man who supplied the BIG IDEA for that concern. Why, he is about a half-million to the good and is moving

rapidly toward the million mark; all in the space of eighteen months." I had not connected this man with the enterprise mentioned; although I knew of the wonderful success of the company in question. Investigation has shown that the story is true, and that the above stated facts are not exaggerated in the slightest.

17. Now, what do you think of that? To me, it means that this man actually made the "direct connection" with Infinite Mind—Spirit—and, having found it, he set it to work for him. He "used it in his business."

18. Does this sound sacrilegious or blasphemous? I hope not; I do not mean it to be so. Take away the implication of Personality, or Magnified Human Nature, from the conception of "The Infinite," and you have left the conception of an Infinite Presence-Power, the Quintessence of which is Consciousness—in fact, at the last, Spirit. As this man, also at the last, must be considered as a manifestation of Spirit; there is nothing sacrilegious in the idea that he, being Spirit, should so harmonize himself with his Origin and Source that he would be able to manifest at least a minor degree of its Power. All of us do this, more or less, when we use our minds in the direction of Creative Thought. This man did more, he went about it in an intensely "practical" manner.

19. I have not consulted him about his method of procedure, though I intend on doing so at the first opportunity, but, he not only drew upon the Infinite Supply for the ideas which he needed (and which formed the seed of his success), but he also used the Creative Power of Thought in building up for himself an Idealistic Pattern of that which he hoped to manifest in material form, adding thereto, changing, improving its detail, from time to time—proceeding from the general outline to the finished detail. I judge this to be the facts of the case, not alone from my recollection of the conversation two years ago, but also because I have found the same thing to be true in the cases of other prominent men who have made similar manifestation of Creative Thought.

20. Those who may shrink from this idea of employing the Infinite Power to aid a man in his work in the material world, should remember that if the Infinite objected in the least to such a procedure the thing could never happen. The Infinite is quite able to take care of Itself.

21. "Spirituality" is quite "practical," very "practical," intensely "practical." It teaches that Spirit is the Real Thing, the Whole Thing, and that Matter is but plastic stuff, which Spirit is able to create, mould, manipulate, and fashion to its will. Spirituality is the most "practical" thing in the world—the only really and absolutely "practical" thing that there is!

22. Now concentrate on the fact that man is not a body with a spirit, but a spirit with a body, and that it is for this reason that his desires are incapable of any permanent satisfaction in anything not spiritual. Money is therefore of no value except to bring about the conditions which we desire, and these conditions are necessarily harmonious. Harmonious conditions necessitate sufficient supply, so that if there appears to be any lack, we should realize that the idea or soul of money is

service, and as this thought takes form, channels of supply will be opened, and you will have the satisfaction of knowing that spiritual methods are entirely practical.

✷

221. *What is the first law of success?*
Service.

222. *How may we be of the most service?*
By having an open mind. By being interested in the race rather than the goal, in the pursuit rather than possession.

223. *What is the result of a selfish thought?*
It contains the germs of dissolution.

224. *How will our greatest success be achieved?*
By a recognition of the fact that it is just as essential to give as to receive.

225. *Why do great organizers meet with great success?*
Because they do their own thinking.

226. *Why do the great majority in every country remain the docile and apparently willing tools of the few?*
Because they let the few do all their thinking for them.

227. *What is the effect of concentrating upon sorrow and loss?*
More sorrow and more loss.

228. *What is the effect of concentrating upon gain?*
More gain.

229. *Is this principle used in the business world?*
It is the only principle which is ever used, or ever could be used; there is no other principle. The fact that it may be used unconsciously does not alter or change the situation.

230. *What is the practical result of this principle?*
Success which is an effect, not a cause. If we wish to secure any effect we must ascertain the cause, or idea or thought by which the effect is created.

We have discovered that premeditated, orderly thinking for a purpose matures that purpose into fixed form, so that we may be absolutely sure of the result of our dynamic experiment.

—Francis Larimer Warner.

PART TWENTY-FOUR

This Part explains the entire theory and practice of every system of Metaphysics; it tells how to express harmony, how to express health, how to express abundance. It explains the nature of all conditions, and how they may be changed or removed. It explains how every difficulty, no matter what it is or where it is, can be removed or dissolved, and it explains the only way in which this is ever done or can be done. It also tells of a Master Key by which those who an wise enough to understand, broad enough to weigh the evidence, firm enough to follow their own judgment, and strong enough to make the sacrifice exacted, may enter and partake.

This is the final Part.

If you have practised each of the exercises a few minutes every day, as suggested, you will have found that you can get out of life exactly what you wish by first putting into life that which you wish, and you will probably agree with the adept who said: "The Master Key thought is almost overwhelming; it is so vast, so available, so definite, so reasonable and so usable."

The fruit of this knowledge is, as it were, a gift of the Gods; it is the "Truth" that makes men free, not only free from every lack and limitation, but free from sorrow, worry and care. Is it not wonderful to realize that omnipotent law is no respecter of persons; that it makes no difference what your past habit of thought may have been, the way has been prepared.

If you are inclined to be religious, the greatest religious teacher the world has ever known made the way so plain that all may follow. If your mental bias is toward physical science, the law will operate with mathematical certainty. If you are inclined to be philosophical, Plato or Emerson may be your teacher; but, in each case, you may, by The Master Key, means reach degrees of power to which it is impossible to assign any limit.

An understanding of The Master Key, I believe, is the secret for which the ancient Alchemists vainly sought, because it explains how gold in the mind may be transmuted into gold in the heart and in the hand.

✱

1. When the scientists first put the Sun in the centre of the Solar System and sent the earth spinning around it, there was immense surprise and consternation. The whole idea was self-evidently false; nothing was more certain than the movement of the Sun across the sky, and any one could see it descend behind the western hills and sink into the sea; scholars raged and scientists rejected the idea as absurd, yet the evidence has finally carried conviction in the minds of all.

2. We speak of a bell as a "sounding body," yet we know that all the bell can do is to produce vibrations in the air. When these vibrations come at the rate of sixteen a second they cause a sound to be heard in the mind. It is possible for the mind to hear vibrations at the rate of 38,000 a second. When the number increases beyond this all is silence again; so that we know that the sound is not in the bell, it is in our own mind.

3. We speak and even think of the Sun as "giving light." Yet we know it is simply giving forth energy which produces vibrations in the ether at the rate of four hundred trillion a second, causing what are termed light waves, so that we know that what we call light is simply a form of energy and that the only light there is, is

the sensation caused in the mind by the motion of the waves. When the number increases, the light changes in colour, each change in colour being caused by shorter and more rapid vibrations; so that although we speak of the rose as being red, the grass as being green, or the sky as being blue, we know that the colours exist only in our minds, and are the sensations experienced by us as the result of the vibrations of light waves when the vibrations, are reduced below four hundred trillion a second, they no longer affect us as light, but we experience the sensation of heat. It is evident, therefore, that we cannot depend upon the evidence of the senses for our information concerning the realities of things; if we did we should believe that the sun moved, that the world was flat instead of round, that the stars were bits of light instead of vast suns.

4. The whole range then of the theory and practice of any system of metaphysics consists in knowing the Truth concerning yourself and the world in which you live; in knowing that in order to express harmony, you must think harmony; in order to express health you must think health; and in order to express abundance you must think abundance; to do this you must reverse the evidence of the senses.

5. When you come to know that of disease, sickness, lack and limitation are simply the result of wrong thinking, you will have come to know "the Truth which shall make you free." You will see how mountains may be removed. If these mountains consist only of doubt, fear, distrust or other forms of discouragement, they are none the less real, and they need not only to be removed but to be "cast into the sea."

6. Your real work consists in convincing yourself of the truth of these statements. When you have succeeded in doing this you will have no difficulty in thinking the truth, and as has been shown, the truth contains a vital principle and will manifest itself.

7. Those who heal diseases by mental methods have come to know this truth, they demonstrate it in their lives and the lives of others daily. They know that life, health and abundance are Omnipresent, filling all space, and they know that those who allow disease or lack of any kind to manifest, have as yet not come into an understanding of this great law.

8. As all conditions are thought creations and therefore entirely mental, disease and lack are simply mental conditions in which the person fails to perceive the truth; as soon as the error is removed, the condition is removed.

9. The method for removing this error is to go into the Silence and know the Truth; as all mind is one mind, you can do this for yourself or anyone else. If you have learned to form mental images of the conditions desired, this will be the easiest and quickest way to secure results; if not, results can be accomplished by argument, by the process of convincing yourself absolutely of the truth of your statement.

10. Remember, and this is one of the most difficult as well as most wonderful statements to grasp. Remember that no matter what the difficulty is, no matter where it is, no matter who is affected, you have no patient but yourself; you have nothing to do but to convince yourself of the truth that you desire to see manifested.

11. This is an exact scientific statement in accordance with every system of Metaphysics in existence, and no permanent results are ever secured in any other way.

12. Every form of concentration, forming Mental Images, Argument, and Auto-Suggestion are all simply methods by which you are enabled to realize the Truth.

13. If you desire to help some one, to destroy some form of lack, limitation or error, the correct method is not to think of the person whom you wish to help; the intention to help them is entirely sufficient, as this puts you in mental touch with the person. Then drive out of your own mind any belief of lack, limitation, disease, danger, difficulty, or whatever the trouble might be. As soon as you have succeeded in doing this the result will have been accomplished, and the person will be free.

14. But remember that thought is creative and consequently every time you allow your thought to rest on any inharmonious condition, you must realize that such conditions are apparent only, they have no reality; that spirit is the only reality and it can never be less than perfect.

15. All thought is a form of energy, a rate of vibration, but a thought of the Truth is the highest rate of vibration known and consequently destroys every form of error in exactly the same way that light destroys darkness; no form of error can exist when the "Truth" appears, so that your entire mental work consists in coming into an understanding of the Truth. This will enable you to overcome every form of lack, limitation or disease of any kind.

16. We can get no understanding of the truth from the world without; the world without is relative only; Truth is absolute. We must therefore find it in the "world within."

17. To train the mind to see Truth only is to express true conditions only. Our ability to do this will be an indication of the progress we are making.

18. The absolute truth is that the "I" is perfect and complete; the real "I" is spiritual and can therefore never be less than perfect; it can never have any lack, limitation, or disease. The flash of genius does not have origin in the molecular motion of the brain; it is inspired by the ego, the spiritual "I" which is one with the Universal Mind, and it is our ability to recognize this Unity which is the cause of all inspiration, all genius. These results are far-reaching and have effect upon generations yet to come; they are the pillars of fire that mark the path that millions follow.

19. Truth is not the result of logical training or of experimentation, or even of observation it is the product of a developed consciousness. Truth within a Caesar, manifests in a Caesar's deportment, in his life and his action; his influence upon social forms and progress. Your life and your actions and your influence in the world will depend upon the degree of truth which you are enabled to perceive, for truth will not manifest in creeds, but in conduct.

20. Truth manifests in character, and the character of a man should be the interpretation of his religion, or what to him is truth, and this will in turn be evidenced in the character of his possessions. If a man complains of the drift of his fortune he is just as unjust to himself as if he should deny rational truth, though it stand patent and irrefutable.

21. Our environment and the innumerable circumstances and accidents of our lives already exist in the subconscious personality which attracts to itself the mental and physical material which is congenial to its nature. Thus is our future being determined from our present, and if there should be apparent injustice in any feature or phase of our personal life, we must look within for the cause, try to discover the mental fact that is responsible for the outward manifestation.

22. It is this truth that makes you "free," and it is the conscious knowledge of this truth which will enable you to overcome every difficulty.

23. The conditions with which you meet in the world without are invariably the result of the conditions obtaining in the world within; therefore it follows with scientific accuracy that by holding the perfect ideal in mind you can bring about ideal conditions in your environment.

24. If you see only the incomplete, the imperfect, the relative, the limited, these conditions will manifest in your life; but if you train your mind to see and realize the spiritual ego, the "I" which is for ever perfect and complete, harmonious; wholesome and healthful conditions only will be manifested.

25. As thought is creative, and the truth is the highest and most perfect thought which anyone can think, it is self-evident that to think the truth is to create that which is true and it is again evident that when truth comes into being that which is false must cease to be.

26. The Universal Mind is the totality of all Mind which is in existence. Spirit is Mind, because spirit is intelligent. The words are, therefore, synonymous.

27. The difficulty with which you have to contend is to realize that mind is not individual. It is omnipresent. It exists everywhere. In other words, there is no place where it is not. It is, therefore, Universal.

28. Men have, heretofore, generally used the word "God" to indicate this Universal, creative principle; but the word "God" does not convey the right meaning. Most people understand this word to mean something outside of themselves; while exactly the contrary is the fact. It is our very life. Without it we would be dead. We would cease to exist. The minute the spirit leaves the body, we are as nothing. Therefore, spirit is really all there is of us.

29. Now the only activity which the spirit Possesses is the power to think. Therefore, thought must be creative, because spirit is creative. This creative power is impersonal and your ability to think is your ability to control it and make use of it for the benefit of yourself and others

30. When the truth of this statement is realized, understood, and appreciated, You will have come into possession of the Master Key, but remember that only those who are wise enough to understand, broad enough to weigh the evidence, firm enough to follow their own judgment, and strong enough to make the sacrifice exacted, may enter and partake.

31. Now, try to realize that this is truly a wonderful world in which we live, that you are a wonderful being, that many are awakening to a knowledge of the

Truth, and as fast as they awake and come into a knowledge of the "things which have been prepared for them" they, too, realize that for them previously "Eye hath not seen, nor ear heard, neither hath it entered into the heart of man," the splendour which exists for those who find themselves in the Promised Land. They have crossed the river of judgment and have arrived at the point of discrimination between the true and the false, and have found that all they ever willed or dreamed, was but a faint concept of the dazzling reality.

Though an inheritance of acres may be bequeathed, an inheritance of knowledge and wisdom cannot. The wealthy man may pay others for doing his work for him, but it is impossible to get his thinking done for him by another, or to purchase any kind of self-culture.

—S. Smiles.

❋

231. *Upon what principle does the theory and practice of every system of Metaphysics in existence depend?*
Upon a knowledge of the "Truth" concerning yourself and the world in which you live.

232. *What is the "Truth" concerning yourself?*
The real "I" or ego is spiritual and can therefore never be less than perfect.

233. *What is the method of destroying any form of error?*
To absolutely convince yourself of the "Truth" concerning the condition that you wish to see manifested.

234. *Can we do this for others?*
The Universal Mind in which "we live and move and have our being" is one and indivisible; it is therefore just as possible to help others as to help ourselves.

235. *What is the Universal Mind?*
The totality of all Mind in existence.

236. *Where is the Universal Mind?*
The Universal Mind is omnipresent, it exists everywhere. There is no place where it is not. It is therefore within us. It is "The World within." It is our spirit, our life.

237. *What is the nature of the Universal Mind?*
It is spiritual and consequently creative. It seeks to express itself in form.

238. *How may we act on the Universal Mind?*
Our ability to think is our ability to act on the Universal Mind and bring it into manifestation for the benefit of ourselves or others.

239. *What is meant by thinking?*

Clear, decisive, calm, deliberate, sustained thought with a definite end in view.

240. *What will be the result?*

You will also be able to say, "It is not I that doeth the works, but the 'Father' that dwelleth within me, He doeth the works." You will come to know that the "Father" is the Universal Mind and that He does really and truly dwell within you, in other words, you will come to know that the wonderful promises made in the Bible are fact, not fiction, and can be demonstrated by anyone having sufficient understanding.

GLOSSARY
A Vocabulary of Words used in the text of "The Master Key,"
specially explained.

ABSOLUTE—That which cannot be measured, determined, limited, expressed; the fundamentally and self-existently real from which all other reality springs.

ACCRETION—Growth or accumulation by external additions.

ALTRUISM—The instinct and emotion that prompts to effort on behalf of others.

ANALYTICAL—Proceeding by analysis; the separating of anything into first principles.

ANTHROPOMORPHIC—The ascription of human attributes, feelings and conduct to the Deity; the natural result of the limitation of human thought and language.

APPERCEPTION—The mental process which associates and brings to attention all the ideas and memories associated with the central thought to which the attention is directly given.

ARCANA—An inner secret or mystery; something hidden from the mass of men; one of the great secrets that the alchemists sought to discover.

ATTENTION—The act or process of giving especial clearness to one or more particulars in the complex content of consciousness. Thus the difference between an ordinary mind and the mind of a Newton consists principally in this, that the one is capable of a more continuous attention than the other.

BELIEF—Confidence in the truth of a proposition that is felt to lack positive proof; acceptance without Proof; that which is believed; a creed.

CELL—The smallest element of an organized body that manifests independent vital activities. The tissues of the human body are an aggregate of cells and their products; they are from 1/125 to 1/5000 of an inch in diameter.

CONCENTRATE—To draw or direct to or toward a common centre.

CONCEPTION—The act of grasping two or more attributes into the unity of thought that we call a concept.

CONSCIOUSNESS—All forms of sensation, feeling, perception, planning and thought; a comprehensive term for the complement of all our cognitive energies.

COSMIC—Pertaining to the universe as a harmonious and orderly system as opposed to chaotic.

COSMOLOGICAL—Relating to the nature and laws of the cosmos as an instituted and alterable order of things, as a cosmological argument.

DEDUCTION—Reasoning from the general to the particular; deduction proceeds from a general principle, through an admitted instance to a conclusion.

DIFFERENTIATION—The process of making or becoming different, as the hypothesis that the characteristic cell growth and divergent particularization of all organisms are due to environment and local conditions as opposed to inherited differentiation by which the characteristics are inherent in the composition of the embryo.

EGO—The "I" which thinks, feels and acts; the conscious individual or the thinking self as distinguished from all objects of thought and from its own states or powers; the pure principle of personal identity.

ELECTRICITY—A material agency which, when in motion, exhibits magnetic, chemical and thermal effects.

ELOHIM—The Hebrew title of most frequent occurence in the Old Testament, expressing absolute Divine power.

EVOLUTION—The unity of action exhibited in the operations of nature; the act or process of evolving; the succession of changes by which a germ passes from a simple to a complex condition. "With each succeeding Kingdom, evolution has changed its direction upward from the physical to the psychical."—Funk.

ELECTRON—The smallest known component of matter; always associated with an unvarying unit charge of negative electricity.

FAITH—Active belief; belief which amounts to a basis for action upon the accepted premises.

GERMINATE—The first act of growth, in a seed, spore or ovum.

GLOSSARY—An explanatory vocabulary dealing with a class of words, as of those of a dialect or a science.

GOD—The embodiment or some aspect of reality or of some being regarded as the ultimate principle of the universe.

GRAVITATION—The tendency of every particle of matter in the universe toward every other particle; also the law which expresses this force which is; the accelerating tendency of bodies toward the centre of the earth is equal to the earth's attraction minus the centrifugal force arising from the rotation of the earth on its axis.

HARMONY—Completeness and perfection resulting from diversity in unity; agreement in relation; orderliness.

IDEA—A thought which is conceived to be in a measure independent of the thinker, and, in a sense, self existent, "Thought" is used to name the presentation which is the direct product of the active mind and could not exist apart from and which would not so used to name the acting mind, while "idea" is used to name the presentation of the mind which is no longer considered as acting; a presentation which might even exist apart from, and independently of, a mind or its activities. A thought is felt to be peculiar to the one thinking it, while the idea is felt to be, in a measure, self-determined or due to the nature of that with which it is associated so that all minds would form it the same; the term still feels the influence of Plato's conception of the ideas as the forms of fundamental reality.

IDEALIZE—To render ideal, to conform to some mental standard as of perfection.

INHIBIT—To restrict by prohibition; to check; to suppress.

IMAGINATION—The act or power of combining products of past experiences in new, modified or ideal forms. The creative or constructive power of the mind. The act of constructive intellect in grouping knowledge or thought into new, original or rational systems. "Science, Invention and Philosophy have little use for fancy, but the creative, penetrative power of imagination is to them the breath of life, and the condition of all advance and success."

IMMUTABLE—Not capable of change, either by increase or decrease, by development or self-evolution; unchangeable; invariable and permanent.

INSIGHT—A perception of the inner nature of a thing.

INDUCTION—The scientific method that proceeds by 1, exact operation; 2, correct interpretation; 3, rational explanation; 4, scientific construction. Reasoning from the particular to the general; induction proceeds from a number of collated instances, through some attribute common to them all, to a general principle.

INDIVIDUAL—A complete independent single being; incapable of division without loss of identity.

INEXORABLE—Not to be moved by entreaty; unyielding; unrelenting; implacable; inflexible.

INFINITE—Self-existent and all-inclusive reality; unmeasured, undetermined, unlimited; independent of expression, yet including all expressions, or actualized things; the absolute.

INSIGHT—A perception of the inner nature of a thing.

INSPIRATION—The inbreathing or imparting of an idea, emotion or mental or spiritual influence; the elevating and creative influence of genius.

INTANGIBLE—Incapable of being touched; not perceptible to the senses, having no clear foundation in fact.

INTUITION—A conclusion that was arrived at without the conscious use of reason and not directly traceable to ordinary understandings of sensory experiences; the faculty of (unconscious) mind by which we arrive at intuitions, or know things without being taught; direct, or immediate knowledge of physical or moral values.

KEY—Anything which discloses or opens something to the understanding, as a key to a subject or problem; that which opens the way to other projects or readers further progress possible.

KINETIC—Producing motion; active as opposed to latent; the kinetic theory has been found capable of explaining nearly all the phenomena of gases and is now generally accepted.

LEAVEN—Anything that by exerting a secret or silent influence gradually brings about a change in character or conditions.

LOGIC—The science or doctrine of correct thinking; the principles governing the reasoning faculties in the pursuit and exposition of truth.

LOVE—The outgoing or yearning of the soul for what is good or excellent.

MASTER—One who controls or has authority; a superior, a ruler or governor; one who gains the victory as "I am the master of my fate."

MASTER KEY—A key that controls a number of locks, the separate keys of which are not interchangeable.

MATTER—That form of being or substance that is characterized by extension, inertia, weight, etc.; or, in general, by the properties cognized by the senses.

MECHANISM—The structure or means of action of any mechanical contrivance. "A human organism with all its parts in harmonious action is a splendid mechanism."—Winchell.

METAPHYSICS—The science of the first principles of being and of knowledge; the reasoned doctrine of the essential nature and fundamental relations of all that is real.

MIND—An abstract, collective form for all forms of conscious intelligence.

NATURAL LAW—That which is normal or in accordance with the ordinary course of things; as opposed to the supernatural.

NEGATIVE—Absence or obscurity of anything affirmative or definite; emptiness; voidness; nullity. Thus, "You can never overthrow falsehood by negative, but by establishing the antagonistic truth."—Robertson.

OBJECTIVE—Having the nature of an object or being that is thought of or perceived; as opposed to that which thinks or perceives.

OMNISCIENCE—Knowledge of all things; infinite or unlimited knowledge.

OMNIPOTENT—Possessing unlimited or universal power, applicable to the Deity alone.

OMNIPRESENCE—Essentially present everywhere at the same time.

PERCEPTION—Any insight or intuitive judgment that implies unusual discernement of fact or truth.

PERSONAL—Pertaining to, or characteristic of a human being.

PHILOSOPHY—Knowledge, in a scientific system, of the ultimate principles, elements, cause and laws that underlie and explain all knowledge and existence, and their application in the explanation of these.

PHYSICS—That science or group of sciences that treats of the phenomena associated with matter in general, especially in its relation to energy and the laws governing these phenomena.

PHYSIOLOGY—The brunch of biology which treats of the vital phenomena manifested by animals and plants.

PLASTIC—Capable of being moulded into form; as the plastic mind of Truth; or the inner mind of man as having a plastic power over his material body.

POLARITY—That quality of a body by which its smallest parts have certain properties related to a line of direction through its mass, the properties at one end of the line being opposite to the properties at the other end of it, as in a magnet.

POSITIVE—Inherent in a thing, by and of itself; not related to other things, or to human judgment or feeling; absolute; inherent; not admitting of doubt final; undeniable and incontestable.

POTENTIAL—Possible, but not actual; possessing inherent qualities for development; inherent power, capability, efficiency, as opposed to actuality.

PRANA—The breath of life.

PRECEDENT—Something antecedent in matter, manner or form; which may be cited as an example, model, authority or justification.

PREDOMINANT—Superior in power, influence, effectiveness; having ascendancy or control.

PREMISE—A proposition laid down, proved, supposed or assumed that serves as a ground for an argument or conclusion.

PRINCIPLE—The ultimate essential element that enters into the composition of all being. The moving cause, power or force by which being manifests. The Universal truth expressing the law of this manifestation; that which determines the nature, character and essence of anything.

PROPHYLACTIC—Any measure efficacious in protecting from disease.

PSYCHICAL—Pertaining to the mind or soul; mental as distinguished from the physical of physiological.

PSYCHOLOGY—The science which treats of the mind, its functions, condition of activity and development, its essential nature and place in nature at large.

RADIANT—Emitting rays of light or brightness figuratively, beaming with joy, kindness and love.

RADICAL—Proceeding from the root, source or foundation. Hence, thorough-going, extreme, fundamental.

REALITY—That which is believed to exist independently of thoughts or opinions; the independently existent; the genuine; opposed to the imaginary or fanciful. That appears reality which receives a major share of the attention.

REASON—(1) The faculty of mind by which experiences are compared and inference drawn; (2) The process of arriving at conclusions by means of comparisons; (3) A proposition from which another is validly inferred.

RELAX—To make less vigorous or stringent; abate in strictness or severity; mitigate; to relieve from strain or effort; abate in attention or assiduity, as to relax the mind.

SAGACITY—The power of ready, far-reaching and accurate inference from slight facts; or readiness to see the result of any action; especially upon human actions or conduct.

SAMENESS—The least degree of diversity.

SCIENCE—Knowledge gained and verified by exact observations and correct thinking, methodically formulated and arranged in a rational system.

SERVICE—The act of helping another or promoting his interests in any way.

SOLAR PLEXUS—The largest sympathetic plexus in the body found behind the stomach in front of the aorta and the crura of the diaphragm. It is composed of branches of the pneumogastric and great splanchnic nerves; the most important ganglia connected with its cords are the right and left similunar. A number of smaller plexus are derived from it.

SPIRIT—The Invisible and incorporeal principle in man; the principle of self-consciousness, self-activity and of rational power in general; that which signifies a likeness in man to the Divine Being.

SUB-CONSCIOUS—That which pertains to the real nature or essence of a person or thing; proceeding from or taking place within the subject, as opposed to the objective. Thus sensation is subconscious, while perception is an objective experience.

SUBJECTIVE—Such processes as seem to have psychical characteristics, but are not attended by consciousness.

SYLLABUS—A concise statement of a subject; an epitome, abstract statement or summary.

SYLLOGISM—A logical formula or analysis of a formal argument, consisting of three propositions, the first two of which are called the premises and the third the conclusion.

SYSTEM—The orderly combination or arrangement into a whole; especially such combinations according to some rational principle or organic idea giving it unity and completeness.

TELEPATHY—(Greek, tele, at a distance, pathos, to experience.) The communication of thoughts between minds without any material medium, ordinary expression or the use of the senses.

THEOLOGY—The science that treats of the being of God, the attributes of God, the doctrine of the Trinity and creation and providence.

THERAPEUTIC—The art and science of curing disease.

TRANSCENDENTAL—Rising above the ordinary notions of men; transcending all ordinary specified bounds or powers; surpassing the limits of individual experiences, but forming the universal and necessary conditions of experiences in general.

TRUTH—A statement or belief which represents or conforms to the reality; a law or principle established by correct reasoning.

UNIVERSAL—Relating to the entire universe; all-embracing; unlimited; regarded or existing as a whole; entire.

UNIVERSAL MIND—The life principle of every atom in existence.

VIBRATION—A rapid motion back and forth; a vibration is completely determined by its amplitude, frequency and period; thus the lowest vibrations appreciated in a musical note are sixteen per second and those which produce the highest tone 41,000 per second.

VISUALIZE—To give pictorial vividness to a mental representation; to construct a visual image in the mind.

VOLATILE—Not lasting or permanent; fleeting; transient; changeable; evaporating.

WILL—The mental power to choose; the power to mould the expressions of the mind; the realization of desires; volition.

QUESTIONS AND ANSWERS
Some questions asked by Correspondents,
with the answers given by
Mr. Charles F. Haanel
Author and Exponent
of
THE MASTER KEY

1. *In referring to the sub-conscious and conscious minds, or the objective and sub-jective, which is the technically correct expression, "We have two minds which, although related, are distinct," or, "We have one mind with two distinct functions?"*

The correct expression is, "We have one mind with two distinct functions." There are not two minds.

2. *Are the Devil in religion, the Negative in Science, and the Bad in Philosophy merely imaginary manifestations of thought energy, or shall we class them as wrong yet real manifestations? If all that we have and are, all of our Powers come from one eternal source, to what must we attribute these imaginary entities?*

These are not imaginary entities. They are simply perversions. If you use electricity for light, you call it good. If you grasp a wire that has not been properly insulated and it kills you, it is not for that reason bad or evil. You were simply careless or ignorant of the laws governing electricity. For the same reason, the one Infinite Power, which is the source of all Power, manifests in your life either as good or as evil, as you make use of it constructively or destructively.

3. *Is not the Master Key Idea of "God" Pantheistic?*

This depends entirely upon your idea of Pantheism. Pantheism is a loose term and may be interpreted in various ways, for instance, pantheism conceives the Universe to be one eternal, involuntary evolution of an Infinite Being, as contrasted with Atheism, which is a positive denial of the Divine Immanence, and Agnosticism, which is a dogmatic doubt of the existence of God.

4. *Is this right? Truth is absolute, but conception of truth varies with the individual consciousness. Therefore, no one can say when the ultimate truth has been reached, because no one can say when the individual consciousness has been developed to the point where development is impossible.*

Yes, truth is absolute, but the conception of truth varies with the individual consciousness. On the other hand, truth is not a matter of belief. It is a matter of demonstration. It is not a question of authority, but a question of perception.

5. Since the real "I" is spiritual and therefore perfect, and since it "controls and directs both the body and mind," how is it that we see such imperfect results?

We see no imperfect results. We see nothing but perfection. Perfection means that the Law operates with immutable precision. Spiritual law always operates perfectly. If the individual thinks constructively, results are constructive, harmonious. If he thinks destructively, he reaps exactly what he sows. The Law works perfectly. We see no imperfect results whatever. We may freely choose what we think, but the result of our thought is governed by an immutable law.

6. "What is Life?"

Life is that quality or principle of the Universal Energy that manifests in so-called organic objects as growth and voluntary activity, and which is usually co-existent in some degree, with some manifestation of that same Universal Energy as the quality or principle termed intelligence. You must understand that there is only one Supreme Principle, evading all comprehension of its essential nature. It is the Absolute. Man can think only in terms of the relative. Therefore, he sometimes defines it as the Universal Intelligence, the Universal Substance, as Ether, Life, Mind, Spirit, Energy, Truth, Love, etc. His particular definition at any moment is governed by the particular relationship of the phenomena of Being in which he thinks of this Principle at that moment.

7. How is the law governing success or prosperity placed in operation?

The human brain is the finest and most vibrant mechanism in existence. Every time you think you send a message into the formless energy from which and by which all things are created. This starts a train of causation that relates with the things that correspond with the image of your thought. If your thought is sufficiently refined and concentrated you will be placed in harmony with the object of your thought quickly; if not, more time will be required. Most persons are busily engaged in concentrating upon lack, limitation, loss and disharmony of every kind, and they are therefore attracting these conditions, a few are busily engaged in concentrating upon success, prosperity and harmonious conditions generally, and find that their environment reflects the quality of their thought.

8. How is prayer answered?

The Universal Mind, the omnipotent Power, the Supreme Being, does not change the modus operandi of the Universe, in order to comply with our requests, nor does it make exception, but it does act through well-known laws, and these laws can be placed into operation, consciously or unconsciously, by accident or design. It is the operation of this marvellous law of attraction which has caused men in all ages and in all times to believe that there must be a personal Being who responded to their petitions and manipulated events in order to meet their demands.

9. You correctly state that, "Possession depends on use." How can this fact be best explained to show that this is the only way in which to acquire a "reservoir of power, possession, etc.," to draw on in time of emergency, etc.?

By illustration: A man desires to strengthen his arm. He wishes it to become powerful. He does not conserve what strength he has in the arm by binding it to his side. If he did this, he would soon lose what strength he already had. On the contrary, he begins to use it, he begins to exercise it, and he finds that the more he uses it, the more strength is secured. The more he gives of his strength, the more he gets. The same rule applies in regard to mental and spiritual strength.

10. "Unless we are willing to think we shall have to work, and the less we think the more we shall work, and the less we shall get for our work." Is it possible to conceive of a world in which there are no "hewers of wood"?

Thought has taken much drudgery out of work, but much so-called "scientific management" and "efficiency and engineering systems" look upon millions of human beings as mere machines capable of making so many motions less or more per hour.

To labour is to serve and all service is honourable. But a "hewer of wood" contemplates blind service instead of intelligent service. Labour is the creative instinct in manifestation. Owing to the changes that have taken place in the industrial world, the creative instinct no longer finds expression. A man cannot build his own house, he cannot even make his own garden, he can by no means direct his own labour; he is, therefore, deprived of the greatest joy which can come to man, the joy of achieving, of creating, of accomplishing, and so this great power is perverted and turned into destructive channels. He can construct nothing for himself, so he begins to destroy the works of his more fortunate fellows. Labour is, however, finding that the Universe is not a chaos but a cosmos, that it is governed by immutable laws, that every condition is the result of a cause and that the same cause invariably produces the same effect. It is finding that these causes are mental, that thought predetermines action. It is finding that constructive thought brings about constructive conditions, and destructive thought brings about destructive conditions.

11. You say that "Life is an unfoldment, not accretion; what comes to us in the world without is what we already possess its the world within." Do you not take into consideration knowledge a person acquires from books, experiences, etc.?

You can derive absolutely no benefit from books, experiences, environment or anything else until you have created brain cells capable of receiving the thought. Your world within is an exact correspondence of your world without. Suppose for the moment that you are unfamiliar with the Hebrew language. A book might be given to you with the most beautiful thoughts written in the most wonderful language, but it would mean nothing to you until you had made yourself acquainted with the Hebrew language, and so with everything else. No thought, no idea, no experience has any value for us until we are capable of receiving it. For this reason the same thought would make absolutely no impression upon one man, while it would be received with amazement and delight by another. The first man has formed no brain cells capable of receiving it. The second man is ready for it. He understands the beauties contained in the idea.

12. Is it correct to say that true religion and true science are "twins" and that the death of one means the death of the other? Why?

True science and true religion are certainly twins. There can be no death for either, because what is true cannot die. "The essential characteristic of truth is steadfast fidelity to order and Law. The mind takes offence at every phenomenon of both inner and outer experience which appears to contradict that steadiness and constancy which it regards as the very essence of truth." You will see that this applies to both science and religion. What is true in science must be true in religion. There cannot be a scientific truth and a religious truth, all truth is one and indivisible.

13. How do Materialism and Spiritualism find harmony in the Master Key System?

The Master Key System teaches that there is but one Principle—One Power. That everything which exists is a materialization of this One Power. The power itself is Spiritual, but the manifestation of the Power is material. One is subjective and the other objective. Two phases of one being. We find this everywhere in Nature, Man is a spiritual being, but he also has a material body. Spirit must manifest upon the objective plane in an objective manner. The Spiritual in this sense has nothing whatever to do with what are usually considered spiritualistic phenomena.

14. What explanation is to be given of the fact that although a great majority of the people not only throughout Europe but in the United States are sick of war and want only peace and a return to prosperous normal conditions, that the return of the desired normal prosperous conditions is such a slow hard process?

There is, of course, as you say, no desire on the part of anyone for more war, just as there is no desire for poverty, crime or for any other destructive condition, but there is, on the other hand, a conscious and a sub-conscious desire for the things which bring about war, destruction, poverty and crime, and this lust of power or separation is the old question of "who is to be the greatest in the kingdom?"

The law is not a respecter of persons. This is true concerning nations as well as individuals. Nations as well as individuals will eventually learn that force can always be met with equal if not superior force, and for this reason can never be the determining factor of any situation.

Objective harmony can come only as a result of subjective harmony, and subjective harmony can come only as a result of vision, understanding and perception.

15. In the "Acme of Achievement" aimed at by The Master Key, how is it possible to ignore Theology?

A few centuries ago it was thought that we must choose between the Bible and Galileo. Fifty years ago it was thought that we must choose between the Bible and Darwin, but as Dean Inge, of St. Paul's Cathedral, says: "Every educated man knows that the main facts of organic evolution are firmly established, and that they are quite different from the legends borrowed by the ancient Hebrews from the Babylonians. We are not required to do violence to our reason by rejecting the assured results of modern research. Traditional Christianity must be simplified and spiritualized. It is at present encumbered by bad science and caricatured by bad economics and the more convinced we are of this, the less disposed we shall be to stake the existence of our faith on superstitions which are the religion of the irreligious and the science of the unscientific."

16. *What is the meaning of the statement, "Only five per cent. have the vision to annex the strategic position, to see and feel a thing before it happens?"*

Ninety-five per cent. of the people are busy attempting to change effects. Something happens which they do not like and they try to change the situation. They soon find that they are simply changing one form of distress for another. The other five per cent. are busily engaged with causes. They know that in order to make any permanent change it is the cause that they must seek. They soon find that the cause is within their control. It is the five per cent. who do the thinking, and the ninety-five per cent. who merely accept the thought of others. It is those only who think who can see and feel a thing before it happens.

17. *What, more, explicitly, is to be understood by the term "polarity" as applied to the mental process?*

Polarity is the tendency or inclination of a thought or feeling in a particular direction. When we think along certain lines continuously the thought becomes polarized, we can see other and different points of view with difficulty or not at all.

18. *What is Truth?*

Truth is the imperative condition of all well-being. To be sure, to know the truth and to stand confidently on it is a satisfaction beside which no other is comparable. Truth is the underlying verity, the condition precedent to every business or social relation. Truth is the only solid ground in a world of conflict and doubt and danger.

Every act not in harmony with Truth, whether through ignorance or design, cuts the ground from under our feet, leads to discord, inevitable loss and confusion, for while the humblest mind can accurately foretell the result of every correct action, the greatest, most profound and penetrating mind loses its way hopelessly and can form no conception of the results due to a departure from correct principles.

19. *How are Germs created?*

Creation consists in the art of combining forces that have an affinity for each other, in the proper proportion. Thus oxygen and hydrogen combined in the proper proportions produce water. Oxygen and hydrogen are both invisible gases, but water is visible.

Germs, however, have life; they must therefore be the product of something that has life or intelligence. Spirit is the only Creative Principle in the Universe, and

Thought is the only activity which spirit possesses. Therefore, germs must be the result of a mental process.

A thought goes forth from the thinker, it meets other thoughts for which it has an affinity, they coalesce and form a nucleus for other similar thoughts: this nucleus sends out calls into the formless energy, wherein all thoughts and all things are held in solution, and soon the thought is closed in a form in accordance with the character given to it by the thinker.

A million men in the agony of death and torture on the battlefield send out thoughts of hatred and distress; soon another million men die from the effect of a germ called "influenza." None but the experienced metaphysician knows when and how the deadly germ came into existence.

As there are an infinite variety of thoughts, so there are an infinite variety of germs, constructive as well as destructive, but neither the constructive nor the destructive germ will germinate and flourish until it finds congenial soil in which to take root.

20. What has given rise to the idea of Reincarnation?

The germ plasma in each generation always contains the sum of all that has passed before it. The nucleus of every cell contains the chromosomes and these reproduce the species of nature and condition according to definite law. Each chromosome, microscopically small as it is, contains the elements of every other cell in a matured body, plus characteristics of species, plus characteristics of form and appearance, plus family resemblance, plus nature, plus mind, plus matured tendencies, plus everything that makes personality and individuality. We are then physically exactly what our forefathers were, plus environment and education. It is this persistency of the identity of the individual chromosome from generation to generation which has given rise to the idea of reincarnation.

21. What is Black Magic?

The idea that there is a phenomenon called Black Magic is attributable to credulity, superstition and a lack of understanding of the laws governing in the mental world. All thoughts and all things are held in solution in the Universal Mind. The individual may open his mental gates and thereby become receptive to thoughts of any kind or description. If he thinks that there are magicians, witches or wizards who are desirous of injuring him, he is thereby opening the door for the entrance of such thoughts, and he will be able to say with job, "The things I feared have come upon me." If, on the contrary, he thinks that there are those who are desirous of helping him, he thereby opens the door for such help, and he will find that "as thy faith is, so be it unto thee" is as true to-day as it was two thousand years ago.

22. I do not seem to grasp fully the application of the law of vibration to the thought world. How, for instance, are we to change the rate of vibration here? In what direction shall it be changed to produce best results?

Every thought changes the rate of vibration. As you are enabled to think greater, deeper, higher and more forceful thoughts, the brain cells are refined, they become more powerful, and they are enabled to receive finer vibrations.

This is not only true in the mental and spiritual world, but in the physical world. As the ear becomes trained in music, it is enabled to receive finer vibrations, until the trained musician can hear harmonies of sound of which the ordinary person is entirely unaware.

23. *Amid the seeming chaos of present day conditions is it not easy to discern the coming of that dawn which all the great ones of earth have foretold, the second coming of the Millenium?*

One of the characteristic signs of a general awakening is the optimism shining through the mist of doubt and unrest, this optimism is taking the form of illumination, and as the illumination becomes general, fear, anger, doubt, selfishness and greed pass away. We are not looking for the Christ child, but the Christ consciousness. We are anticipating a more general realization of the Truth which is to make men free. That there may be one man or one woman who shall first realize this Truth in the new era is barely possible, but the preponderance of evidence points to a more general awakening to the Light of Illumination.

24. *You speak about the originating mind that forms, upholds, sustains and creates all there is. Does this explain the source from which comes man's ability to think lack, to think war and crime, etc.?*

Yes, this includes man's ability to think lack, war and crime. If he can think constructive thought he can also think destructive thought; but as soon as man learns that thinking is a creative process, that we are creators, not creatures, he will discontinue the process of thinking destruction for himself and his fellows.

25. *You are, without doubt, correct in stating that Carlyle's attitude of hatred of the bad was not conducive toward his own best development; on the other hand, what should be the attitude toward the giant evils of the day, such as war, corruption, murder, vice, theft and the like? Is it not often true that a tearing down, a clearing away of the brushwood, so to speak, must precede constructive work?*

No, it is not true. The tearing down process is not at all necessary. We do not need to laboriously shovel the darkness out of a room before letting in the light; on the contrary, all that is necessary is to turn on the light and the darkness vanishes; likewise, if but one-tenth of one per cent. of the money and effort were spent in constructive work that is now being spent in destructive work, the giant evils of the day to which you refer would disappear as if by magic.

The unit of the Nation is the individual. The Government represents only the average intelligence of the units comprising the Nation. Therefore, our work is with the unit. When the thought of the individual has been changed the collective thought will take care of itself, but we try to reverse the process. We try to change governments instead of individuals, which cannot be done. But with a little intelligent organized effort the present destructive thought could be readily changed into constructive thought.

Temples have their sacred images, and we see what influence they have always had over a great part of mankind; but in truth, the ideas and images in men's minds are the invisible powers that constantly govern them; and to these they all pay universally a ready submission.

—Jonathan Edwards

OTHER ULYSSES PRESS BOOKS

1001 Little Health Miracles
Esme Floyd, $12.95
A treasure trove of friendly health tips that offer shortcuts to feeling good, looking great and living healthy.

1325 Buddhist Ways to Be Happy
Barbara Ann Kipfer, $13.95
Looks at everyday situations and provides the Buddha's and other Buddhist teachers' guidance for navigating them in a cheerful, positive way.

Adrenaline Junkies & Serotonin Seekers
Matt Church, $12.95
Shows how to naturally balance your brain chemistry to maximize energy, stamina, mental sharpness and emotional well-being.

Creativity Workout: 62 Exercises to Unlock Your Most Creative Ideas
Edward de Bono, $12.95
A collection of puzzles that train the mind in creative thinking.

The Happy Introvert: A Wild and Crazy Guide to Celebrating Your True Self
Elizabeth Wagele, $14.95
This fun, wacky handbook explores the richness introverts experience in their inner worlds and offers tips for enjoying life in an extroverted society.

The Law of Attraction for Love: The Secret to Finding Your Soul Mate
Debbie Frank, $12.95
Shows readers how to unleash the power behind the secret to finding the loves of their lives.

Mapping the Memory: Understanding Your Brain to Improve Your Memory
Rita Carter, $14.95
Helps readers reach a higher level of understanding about memory and how they can improve the working of their own brain function in this area.

Secrets of the People Whisperer: A Horse Whisperer's Techniques for Enhancing Communication and Building Relationships
Perry Wood, $12.95
The author shows how the same techniques for developing trust and understanding with a horse can work equally well in one's personal, business, family and romantic relationships.

Stop Living Your Job, Start Living Your Life: 85 Simple Strategies to Achieve Work/Life Balance
Andrea Molloy, $12.95
A successful personal life coach shows how to identify priorities, make meaningful decisions and take specific actions.

To order these books call 800-377-2542 or 510-601-8301, fax 510-601-8307, e-mail ulysses@ulyssespress.com, or write to Ulysses Press, P.O. Box 3440, Berkeley, CA 94703. All retail orders are shipped free of charge. California residents must include sales tax. Allow two to three weeks for delivery.